FIFTH EDITION

# ETHNIC-SENSITIVE
# SOCIAL WORK PRACTICE

## Wynetta Devore
*Syracuse University*

## Elfriede G. Schlesinger
*Rutgers University*

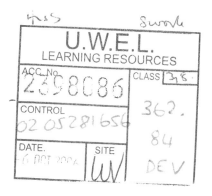

**Allyn and Bacon**
Boston • London • Toronto • Sydney • Tokyo • Singapore

*Series Editor, Social Work and Family Therapy:* Judy Fifer
*Editor-in-Chief, Social Sciences:* Karen Hanson
*Series Editorial Assistant:* Jennifer Muroff
*Marketing Manager:* Susan E. Ogar
*Editorial-Production Service:* Ruttle, Shaw & Wetherill, Inc.
*Cover Administrator:* Jenny Hart
*Manufacturing Buyer:* Dave Repetto

### Library of Congress Cataloging-in-Publication Data

Devore, Wynetta.
   Ethnic-sensitive social work practice / Wynetta Devore, Elfriede
G. Schlesinger. — 5th ed.
     p.  cm.
   ISBN 0-205-28165-6
   1. Social work with minorities.  2.  Social work with minorities—
United States.  I. Schlesinger, Elfriede G.  II. Title.
HV3176.D46   1998
361.3–dc21                         98-6774
                                           CIP

Printed in the United States of America

10  9  8  7  6                09  08  07  06

*We hope that in some small way the perspectives presented in this book will contribute to the lives of those who follow us. In this spirit we dedicate this book to our children and grandchildren, Julia Newman Bryant, David Lovell Bryant, David Seth Schlesinger, Adrienne Lee Aldermeshian, Laura Jennifer Aldermeshian, Peter Harout Aldermeshian, and Maya Sophia Schlesinger.*

# CONTENTS

# PREFACE

It has been seventeen years since we sent the manuscript of the first edition of *Ethnic-Sensitive Social Work Practice* to the publisher. We were both excited and wary, wondering how readers would react to our effort to integrate understanding of the impact of ethnicity, social class, and minority status with the principles and strategies of social work practice. We were aware that our work was among the first to attempt to effect the union between the two areas of discourse. We suggested then that "unlike psychological theories that were used to explain the functioning of individuals and groups—and used as guidelines for intervention—ethnic and class data tended to serve merely as background for identifying information. Few attempts were made to delineate how understanding of class and ethnic factors could contribute to the assessment and intervention process" [from the preface, *Ethnic-Sensitive Social Work Practice* (1st ed.), 1981. St. Louis: C. V. Mosby].

The positive response to the first and subsequent editions suggested that the profession of social work wanted, needed, and used the knowledge and strategies that were then and remain the substance of our work. This assessment is supported by the call for this fifth edition.

As we have developed each new edition, we have sought to take account of developments within our profession and within our country, and even matters of international scope.

By the time we began to work on the second edition it was becoming increasingly evident that changes in immigration legislation had made it possible for large numbers of new immigrants—especially from Asia and Latin countries—to come to the United States. We sought to incorporate understanding of their rich cultures and traditions as well as of service needs into our work. Increased interest in the issues confronting people of diverse origin had led to systematic analysis of their situation. Therefore, in the second edition we were able to present a more thorough and well-rounded treatment of the diverse perspectives on the role of ethnicity and social class.

As we worked on the third edition, the magnitude of the expanding profile of the population of the United States was becoming evident. Emerging data suggested that this profile consisted of an increasing number of persons of color who had arrived as immigrants. Also included in this group were the other, more familiar groups from Western and Eastern Europe who had arrived in large numbers in prior waves of immigration. Sufficient information about the extent of these changes was available to introduce a new chapter, "We, the People of the United States," which focused on the history and current situation of immigration to the United States. We considered the situation of the newcomers as we tried to understand their lives by drawing on prevailing theories of ethnicity and social class and minority status. These matters remain a focus of the fifth edition.

We have considerably expanded our use of case material. Each of the chapters in Part II, "Strategies for Ethnic Sensitive Practice," begins with one or two "lead cases." These cases are referred to throughout the chapter to illustrate the concepts and strategies being considered. In addition, case vignettes of varying length and complexity continue to be introduced, in keeping with the pattern established in earlier editions.

We have introduced some new chapters and have reduced the scope and length of materials included in prior editions. As always, we have tried to introduce current materials relevant to the topic at hand. In Chapter 2, "The Ethnic Reality," we introduce work that suggests new ways of looking at the adaptation of immigrants, from varying Asian and other countries, as well as work focused on people of color long resident in the United States. In this chapter, we have also expanded considerably our discussion of the concepts of ethnicity, race, and minorities. We suggest some revised terminology—specifically introducing the term *oppressed ethnic groups.*

Chapter 5, "Approaches to Social Work Practice and the Ethnic Reality," has been updated to take into account a series of developments in social work practice theory. We add a discussion of the strength perspectives and the empowerment perspective. These developments point to a greater convergence and unity of approaches than had been the case in past years.

Other changes reflect an effort to take into account the developments in social work education and in ethnic-sensitive practice. In 1992 the Council on Social Work Education developed a new Curriculum Policy statement mandating that all accredited programs of social work education, at both the baccalaureate and masters levels, must instruct students in generalist practice. Chapter 7 adds this perspective in response to this mandate. We should note that our stance on the importance of simultaneous attention to individual and systemic concerns—a notion we emphasized in all prior editions—has long been in keeping with the generalist perspective. We suggest that the generalist and the structural perspectives are congruent and important approaches to contemporary ethnic-sensitive practice.

We have made repeated reference to the increasing diversity of this country. Many people continue to come, looking to improve their chances for equality, equity, and safety. People come as families or as members of families whose relatives have been left behind. To help social workers all over the country, who find themselves working with people from diverse parts of the globe, we include a chapter on "Ethnic-Sensitive Practice with Immigrants." The new limits on immigrant eligibility for public assistance are also considered.

The chapters that have been retained are updated to take into account recent literature and emerging issues. For example, Chapter 12, formerly focused on young families receiving AFDC, has been retitled to reflect the termination of that program. The new legislation is reviewed, and such limited data as are available on client response are included. Chapter 13, "Social Work in Health Care," has been updated to reflect developments in managed care.

We recognize that increasing attention has been directed to the language used to refer to different groups, especially people of color. It is important that we let our readers know the terms we use. They are African American, Afro-Caribbean, American Indian, Asian Indian, Pilippino, Chicano, or Latino.

In introducing this fifth edition of *Ethnic-Sensitive Social Work Practice,* we believe that it is important to make some general comments about the role of ethnicity in social life. We focus on the subject because, in our professional as well as personal experiences, we have found that many elements of our being are bound up with ethnic traditions, with identity, and with the cohesion derived from membership in ethnic groups. Throughout our work we point to the fact that ethnicity is a source of comfort and cohesion as well as stress and strife. As we go to press for the fifth time, we are increasingly aware that in many sections of the world, as well as in the United States, tensions between groups often spill over into conflict. These conflicts have many sources, including oppression of people in different segments of the globe. It is our view that as social workers heighten their understanding of oppression, as well as of the positive impact of ethnic group membership on daily living, they can play an important role in reducing tensions and conflict at home as well as elsewhere in the world.

Many people helped us in our work. Especially important in this edition was the contribution of those people who shared case material with us. We thank them without identifying their institutional affiliation, as a way of preserving the anonymity of the clients whose situations are presented. They include Janice Cranch, Rebekah Clark, Vincent Corso, Mary Ruffolo, Amelia Castillo, Geneva Hayden, Victoria Tilbe, Teresa Gilman, Yuhwa Eva Lu, Sally Komar, Sally Goldman, Vivian Fu Wells, and Dee Livingston. There are others, too numerous to mention, whose discussions in various professional contexts—in our classes and at various professional meetings—contributed to our understanding of practice issues and strategies. We wish to thank the reviewers who provided valuable feedback for this revision: Gina Miranda, University of Wisconsin, Whitewater; Joan M. Jones, University of Wisconsin, Milwaukee; and Margaret J. Austin, University of North Alabama. We also thank reviewers of the fourth edition: L. René Bergeron, University of New Hampshire; Walter J. Pierce, Barry University; and Rose S. Rogers-Harris, Loyola University and reviewers of the previous editions, whose help was invaluable.

Others, too, made major contributions. Graduate assistant James Calahan at the School of Social Work at Syracuse University provided invaluable assistance. Julie Akyol, formerly of the School of Social Work at Rutgers, spent many hours above and beyond the call of duty in typing sections of the manuscript.

*W. D.*
*E. G. S.*

# ETHNIC-SENSITIVE
# SOCIAL WORK PRACTICE

# CONCEPTUAL FORMULATIONS AND PERSPECTIVES ON ETHNIC-SENSITIVE PRACTICE

Part I presents perspectives on ethnic-sensitive practice.

Chapter 1 reviews United States immigration policy from colonial times to the present. It includes a discussion of why and how people come to the United States and a review of the immigrants' experience.

Chapter 2 introduces the concept of the ethnic reality, which suggests that as ethnicity and social class intersect, distinct and identifiable dispositions are generated. This chapter places particular emphasis on how external and internal forces serve to sustain the role of social class and ethnicity in various groups.

Chapter 3 considers ethnicity and the life course.

Chapter 6 presents the assumptions and principles for ethnic-sensitive practice. These principles are built on certain assumptions about human behavior, the ethnic reality, the layers of understanding, and social work as a problem-solving endeavor.

Chapter 4 outlines the layers of understanding—the values, knowledge, skills, and self-awareness—basic to social work practice and incorporates the ethnic reality as part of these layers of understanding.

Chapter 5 examines the various approaches to social work practice. Recent developments in practice theory are reviewed and assessed to determine the extent to which ethnic and class factors have been incorporated into the basic assumptions of social work practice.

# 1

# WE, THE PEOPLE OF THE UNITED STATES...

A major aspect of the ethnic experience in the United States revolves around the means and circumstances by which people have become a part of the U.S. mosaic. Their struggles and the degree to which they were welcomed or unwanted and considered important or depreciated need to be understood. This chapter presents a discussion of why people left their homes to come to the United States, a review of the experiences of newcomers, and the development of U.S. immigration policy from colonial times to the present.

The experience in the United States has transformed immigrants, their children, and their grandchildren. In that process of transformation, they have exerted a significant influence on the nature and shape of the U.S. experience (Glazer, 1981). This book examines that experience as it relates to individuals, families, groups, and communities in their daily lives. Our goal is to help social workers to recognize the continuing influence of ethnicity at many levels of practice, ranging from direct work with individuals, families, and groups (micro practice) to planning, administration, evaluation, and community organization (macro practice), to the development of social policy.

The ethnic experience is a source of cohesion, identity, and strength; at the same time, it is a source of strain, discord, and strife. Some of that strain is related to the struggle to adapt to the possibilities as well as to the stressful expectations of the new society. During the struggle, immigrants derive comfort by drawing on familiar customs, language, and culture. This dichotomy generates tension as well as release for individuals, families, and communities as they encounter the vagaries at each stage of individual and family life.

What happens to an ethnic group's culture and tradition as its members become a part of U.S. society has continued to be a matter for debate. As early as 1789, Jedidiah Morse, a geographer, anticipated a time when the language, manners, customs, and political and religious sentiments of the inhabitants of the United States would be assimilated, with nominal distinctions lost in the "general and honorable name of Americans" (McKee, 1985, p. 261). Israel Zangwill's play *The Melting Pot*, published in 1925, continued the ideal of the United States as "God's crucible, the great Melting Pot where all races of Europe are melting and reforming."

By 1963, Glazer and Moynihan had concluded that the notion of "an unprecedented mixture of ethnic and religious groups in America had outlived its usefulness and credibility" (p. v). The melting pot has not materialized. Sowell (1981) suggested that the diverse immigrant groups have not vanished into the melting pot but rather have taken on new forms as the country has changed. Alba (1985) advances this same theme as he writes about the "twilight of ethnicity."

In its new form, ethnicity may weaken in relation to language, culture, or heritage; however, it still seems to be of significance in shaping behavior, response, and attitude, even though the original culture may fade or disappear. This does not change attachment to ethnic interests as a new ethnic class group is formed, nor does it eliminate emotional attachments to group members in distant lands (Glazer, 1981).

Vecoli (1985) highlighted the "rediscovery of ethnicity," the heightened ethnic consciousness of the 1960s and 1970s, and the "new" immigration trends of the 1980s. Like Glazer, he concluded that, "for good or ill, ethnicity has proven itself not to be a transitory phenomenon, but an enduring dimension of American society" (p. 17).

However, as we approach the year 2000 discussion related to the need to return to the melting pot surfaces. Arthur Schlesinger, Jr. (1990) suggests that it would be best if we, as a nation, looked to Hector St. John de Crevecoeur's answer to the question, "What then is the American, this new man?" In the 1700s de Crevecoeur's response was that this man left behind him "all his ancient prejudices and manners" and in their stead "embraced, the new government rank that he holds. Here individuals of all nations are melted into a new race of man." This definition is earlier than Zangwill's drama, which presented the initial image of the Great Melting Pot. We would suggest that de Crevecoeur's "man" refers to white Anglo-Saxon Protestant males and that Zangwill's perspective was indeed meant to include only the (white) races of Europe. It would appear that in this suggestion Schlesinger asks that we limit our considerations as to who may be part of "We, the people."

Ronald Takaki (1994) provides a review of the work of scholars who have contributed to this discussion. In addition to Schlesinger (1990) are Bloom (1987) and E. D. Hirsch (1987) who question the value of the many ethnic groups that contribute to our ethnic mosaic. Bloom suggests that perhaps universities would be wise to return to the study of the Great Books, rather than expecting students to learn about cultures other than their own. Takaki comments that those who seek for pluralism focus on culture while giving little attention to racial and ethnic inequality. Americans of color have been asking, "How should America and Americans be defined? Whose history is it?"

The "new" immigration trends of the 1980s have generated the Immigration Act of 1990, which increased immigration and revised grounds for exclusion. The legislation of 1996 restricts alien eligibility for public assistance and seeks to deter illegal immigration (Vialet, Krouse, Wasen, & Eig, 1996). Despite academic discussion and federal legislation, we remain a country of many people from many places.

## *THE EXPERIENCE OF NEWCOMERS*

The experience of newcomers to the United States has always been uneven, with some new arrivals finding a more cordial welcome than others. Native Americans were treated as a conquered people and frequently encountered violence at the hands of European settlers. African Americans were brought in as slaves and were later outcasts when large numbers of them migrated from the rural South to the urban North. Restrictive immigration policy prohibited the entry of large numbers of Jews fleeing from the oncoming Holocaust in the 1930s, but in the 1960s refugees from Communist Cuba were welcomed.

A review of United States immigration policy reflects this variability in our national behavior. With few exceptions the policy reflects a "like us" perspective; that is, it is preferential to Anglo-Saxons and other whites of Western European heritage.

Individuals and families continually leave the homes, villages, cities, and countries of their birth to cross national and ethnic boundaries. Many will never return. The movement is prompted by forces that endure, as people look for economic opportunities not available at home, to escape a variety of ethnic or religious persecutions, civil strifes, or natural disasters. Some migrants and immigrants are subjected to slavery, others to famine and starvation, military conscription, or impending war. Some are criminals attempting to avoid the reach of the law; others pursue superior employment opportunities (Lieberson & Waters, 1988).

Distinct among the present immigrant population are persons identified as refugees or migrants. Refugees are generally recognized as having escaped from persecution or civil strife. Indochinese groups such as the Vietnamese, Khmer, Lao, and Hmong are current examples of such refugees (Owan, 1985).

Migrants may be alien workers, generally unskilled, who cross international borders for employment. The most noted example in the United States is illegal or undocumented workers crossing the United States–Mexican border seeking agricultural employment. Migrants may hold legal status as they come to join family members.

As we will see, the time of arrival and concentration is distinct for each group, depending on conditions at home and in the United States at the time of their departure. Historians and geographers who examine immigration history have suggested that there have been several waves of immigration, beginning with the British in the colonial period. These original 17th-century settlers set the tone for what was to become the U.S. culture. Prominent among other settlers were the Welsh, Teutons, and Scotch Irish. Africans arrived in 1619 as indentured servants. Other groups present were the Germans in significant numbers, Spanish, Dutch, French, Swedish, Flemish, Italians, and Jews (Dinnerstein & Reimers, 1975; McKee, 1985).

Although the British had come seeking economic and religious opportunity, they made no pretense of being tolerant of anyone who differed from them in any significant way. New arrivals generated suspicion, as they have throughout the history of the United States. One of the earliest examples of xenophobia is seen in the British wariness of the Irish and Germans. The fear and distrust continues as communities express hostility toward the arrival of the Vietnamese and Laotian refugees. Although the United States claims to welcome the stranger–immigrant, history presents continual evidence of scorn and abuse of immigrant groups (Dinnerstein & Reimers, 1975).

Immigration policy has continually left the door open to special groups while restricting or prohibiting admission to others. Early legislation focused on character and morality, prohibiting prostitutes, criminals, the mentally ill, the disabled, and those likely "public charges." The Chinese Exclusion Act of 1882 responded to racist attitudes of the population and barred Chinese laborers from entering the country. This first legislation to identify a specific ethnic group for exclusion was not repealed until 1943 (McKee, 1985). The most recent revisions of immigration policy became law in 1996 when President Clinton introduced welfare reform legislation (P. L.104–193) that would restrict eligibility for means-tested public assistance and attempt to limit illegal entry across international borders

## *1821 TO 1930*

Between the years 1821 and 1930, immigration occurred on an unprecedented scale. New groups arrived from Northern and Western Europe—Germany, Ireland, England, Scotland, Wales, Norway, Sweden, Denmark, The Netherlands, Switzerland, Belgium, and France. Few persons came from Asia; those who did were predominantly Chinese. They were followed by immigrants from Southern and Eastern Europe—Italy, Austria, Hungary, and Russia—as well as from Canada, China, the West Indies, Asiatic Turkey, and Japan (Dinnerstein & Reimers, 1975; McKee, 1985).

A series of legislative acts sought to curtail entry into the United States. The Immigration Acts of 1891 and 1903 restricted entry to certain classes of persons and called for the deportation of those who entered illegally. The Act of 1906 required knowledge of English before naturalization. The first limitations on immigration can be found in the Act of 1924. The "national origins quota system" was established. Only 2 percent of the number of persons of a given nationality residing in the United States could be admitted in any one year (*Congressional Digest*, 1996).

Individuals and families who arrived as these policies were evolving encountered experiences that were significantly different from those who arrived earlier. Those immigrants often spoke the same language and, had similar religious beliefs and practices. Persons who arrived later from the European continent, like many immigrants of the 1990s, differed in language, economic position, social organization, prestige, education, urban, rural and industrial background, and social structures. The task for each new group of arrivals is to learn the ways of the United States. Successful completion of these arduous tasks led to a new social form of ethnicity.

## *1931 TO 1960*

The National Origins Act of 1924 became effective in 1929. The 2 percent limitation was based on the 1920 census with the total number of immigrants limited to 150,000 persons each year. This method favored Western European populations and, like the Chinese Exclusion Act, it was related to ethnic group membership, but in this case the result was inclusion rather than exclusion (*Congressional Digest*, 1996).

The Immigration and Nationality Act of 1952 (McCarran-Walter Act) was passed over the veto of President Truman, who declared that the idea behind the legislation was that "Americans with English or Irish names were better people and better citizens than Americans with Italian or Greek or Polish names." As a member of Congress, John F. Kennedy, of Irish ancestry, commented that the Emma Lazarus poem might be amended to read, "Give me your tired, your poor...as long as they come from Northern Europe, are not too tired, too poor or slightly ill, never stole a loaf of bread, never joined any questionable organization, and can document their activities for the past two years" (Novotny, 1971, p. 225).

After the passage of the Immigration and Nationality Act, the 1920 census remained the base for quota determination; however, Japan was added to the list with a quota of 115 people (Schaefer, 1988). The initial act permitted 6,524 Polish immigrants, 2,712 Russians, and 5,802 Italians. Smaller countries such as Syria, Albania, and Turkey received lower allotments, whereas England, Germany, Ireland, and the Scandinavian countries received a more substantial quota. These were never filled and could not be reallocated to other countries. By the time of the legislation, the demand for entry had been fulfilled.

There were, however, no restrictions on immigration from countries in the Western Hemisphere, allowing Canadians, Mexicans, and South Americans to enter freely (Dinnerstein & Reimers, 1975; Feagin, 1984; Novotny, 1971). This particular omission in the legislation accounted for the influx of persons from Canada, Newfoundland, Latin America, Mexico, and the West Indies during the next wave of immigration.

The restricting quality of the 1924 National Origins Act limited immigration in the 1930s. In addition, there were the devastating effects of the Great Depression. No significant pull was exerted by U.S. economic conditions to encourage immigration. The provision in the law that excluded persons "likely to become a public charge" was invoked with the encouragement of President Herbert Hoover. Americans were out of work, and strangers could not be accommodated. The focus of immigration shifted from the East Coast to the West Coast; those entering were from the Western Hemisphere and were without European roots. Immigration trends in relationship to ethnic group members were beginning to change significantly.

As early as the 1920s, Mexican workers had been recruited as laborers for developing agriculture and industry in Texas, Arizona, and California. Lacking significant skills, they could be hired at lower wages than could those required by U.S.-born laborers. This was the experience of other "foreigners" as well, including Greeks, Italians, Japanese, and Koreans. However, Mexicans dominated the work force (Dinnerstein, Nichols, & Reimers, 1979).

Early immigration legislation that excluded and limited the entry of Chinese and Japanese citizens enabled Pilippinos[1] to move into the labor void on the West

---

[1] "Pilippino" is preferred by the Pilippino community, since their language has no "f" sound.

Coast. Laborers were needed by the sugar planters in Hawaii and by the farmers in California. The commonwealth status of the Pilippinos permitted men to be recruited by the armed forces, especially the Navy, where they served as mess attendants and personal attendants to high-ranking naval staff. Pilippinos held similar domestic service positions as bellboys, houseboys, cooks, waiters, and kitchen workers in hotels and restaurants on the West Coast.

In the 1930s political events in Europe, particularly Germany, pushed many to attempt escape from the onslaught of Adolph Hitler and fascism. Jews particularly sought refuge in other countries. Despite national outrage in response to mass extermination and concentration camps, the U.S. government made no alterations in the immigration laws and permitted few allowances for victims of the atrocities. Fear of competition for scarce employment and fear of spies and the Fifth Column, along with a strong anti-Semitic sentiment, held the existing quotas in place. In 1939, measures to admit 20,000 German refugee children beyond the quota limitations were rebuffed by several patriotic societies, who feared that they may be German-Jewish children. One year later there was no opposition from similar societies when 15,000 children from Great Britain arrived on mercy ships (Novotny, 1971).

Although some patriotic groups resisted the entry of Jews, other service groups were supportive as they assisted those who did arrive in finding employment, housing, and community. Among the new arrivals were a number of intellectuals and scientists. These professionals were educated, understood and spoke English, and had a variety of professional contacts ready to use the skills that they brought with them (Dinnerstein & Reimers, 1975).

As Mexican and Pilippino immigrants were recruited on the West Coast, developing industry on the East Coast was in need of laborers, immigration quotas having cut off the European labor supply. The supply was found in the South among the African American population. The pull of possible employment, along with the push of farm mechanization, the boll weevil, Jim Crow laws, the Ku Klux Klan, segregation and discrimination, led large numbers of southern African Americans to northern and midwestern cities (such as Chicago, Detroit, and Indianapolis) during the Great Migration of 1915 to 1925.

As the Chinese, Japanese, and Pilippinos had done on the West Coast, the male rural workers found menial employment as porters, truck drivers, or cooks. Women found work as maids, restaurant workers, or dressmakers. Few African American professionals, doctors, teachers, or clergy served the African American community (Feagin, 1984).

The migration accelerated again during World War II as workers moved West for employment in the defense industries located there. The pressing need for laborers, together with executive orders issued by President Roosevelt, caused organized labor to make concessions in its discriminatory practices, which had excluded minorities. It is estimated that 250,000 African Americans migrated to West Coast cities during this era (Rozwenc & Bender, 1978).

In each migration movement, the reasons for movement have been the same as for those who came from other countries: a search for greater opportunities in employment, a reuniting of families, and an escape from persecution. Subsequent legislation did much to change long-standing policies and practices.

## *1961 TO 1980*

The Immigration and Nationality Act Amendments of 1965 changed the character of immigration significantly, adding much to ethnic diversity in the United States. The original national origins quotas were repealed. Severe restrictions on Asians were lifted, and India, Thailand, and Pakistan became new sources of immigrants.

The act satisfied in several ways those who wished to reform immigration policy. National quotas were replaced by ceilings of 20,000 per country for the Eastern Hemisphere and 120,000 for the Western Hemisphere, with no limitations or preferences. Ethnicity was no longer an essential factor in immigration. Emphasis was placed on family reunification and on admitting those who had occupational skills needed in the United States (Dinnerstein, Nichols, & Reimers, 1979; McKee, 1985).

The legislation had the effect of selecting persons who represented the "educated elite of their native countries" (Williams, 1988). The immigration visa-allocation preference system was established. First and second priority was given to children and spouses of citizens and permanent residents. Third priority was given to members of the professions with exceptional ability, along with their spouses and children. This group included many Asian Indian physicians. The lowest priority was given to skilled and unskilled workers.

Between 1971 and 1980 75 percent of new immigrants came from Latin America and Asia. Although Europeans had the opportunity to immigrate freely, they chose to remain at home. The Irish, English, Germans, Poles, Italians, and other Europeans no longer came to the United States in significant numbers. European prosperity negated the need to leave for greater opportunity (Glazer, 1988; Schaefer, 1988).

At the same time, however, many Chinese moved to established Chinatowns in San Francisco and New York. Substantial numbers of Pilippinos went to Honolulu and the Mission district of San Francisco; Koreans settled in Los Angeles on the West Coast and as far east as New York City. A considerable number of Vietnamese with refugee status settled in California.

Haitians, Dominicans, and Colombians were pushed by poverty and political upheaval to San Francisco in the West and New York City in the East. Caribbean communities of English-speaking persons from Trinidad, Barbados, and Jamaica established in Brooklyn began to include French-speaking Haitians. Other Jamaicans settled in Hartford, having gone to Connecticut to harvest vegetables and apples. Colombians were attracted to the Jackson Heights section of Queens. Central Americans lived on Long Island. In these communities immigrants found the comfort and support they needed to become established in the new country.

The ethnic mosaic of New York City, Los Angeles, San Francisco, and many other urban centers was becoming increasingly diverse. The "like us" perspective, which supported much of the early immigration policy, was beginning to lose its force.

The first federal immigration law of 1882 excluded "any convict, lunatic, idiot or any other person unable to take care of himself or herself without becoming a public charge" (Bennett, 1963, p. 17). Morality and self-sufficiency were primary concerns. Ethnic restrictions based on race began with the Chinese Exclusion Act of 1882. Through the 1907 Gentleman's Agreement with Japan, another response to racism, the Japanese agreed to restrict exit visas for laborers; however, Japanese already in the country were not expected to leave.

Although illegal entry existed, legislation did not address it with any overarching policy. Congress and the nation at large seemed ambivalent about illegal immigration. On one hand, there were those who were concerned about illegal immigrants as lawbreakers. Families and ethnic communities supported their presence, and employers found illegal immigrants a cheap source of labor and hoped that the government would ignore the issue. Intermittent policy addressing special populations and instituting sanctions against employers did little to reduce the incidence of illegal immigration (Miller, 1985). By the 1970s the number of illegal immigrants had increased. The growing concern about their numbers led to a movement to review and reform immigration policy.

## THE 1980s

In March 1981, the Hesburgh Commission, appointed by Congress to produce legislative recommendations related to illegal immigration, presented its report, which focused on employee sanctions and a legalization program. Father Hesburgh, the chair of the commission, explained that "to keep the front door open, we must close the back door; to maintain legal immigration it is important to reduce illegal immigration" (Miller, 1985, p. 55).

The congressional response to the commission's recommendations came in 1982 from Senator Alan K. Simpson and Romano L. Mazzoli, a member of Congress. Their initial reform package emphasized a balance between ending the flow of new illegal immigrants and generosity to those already here. An essential element was the call for sanctions against employers who knowingly hired illegal immigrants.

Opposition came from the Hispanic Congressional Caucus and others who saw the Hispanic population as being at particular risk if the proposed legislation passed. Critics pointed out that potential employers would refuse to hire people who looked or sounded foreign, even if they were legal residents. The bill failed when a House–Senate committee failed to reach a compromise. A second attempt in 1983 failed in the midst of more than considerable political turmoil. Finally, on November 6, 1986, President Reagan signed into law this immigration policy (Miller, 1985).

Congressman Peter W. Rodino, who had been active in the presentation of the bill, described the legislation:

*This landmark legislation effects major changes in U.S. immigration policy by providing for the legalization of undocumented aliens in the United States and by establishing a system of employer sanctions to ensure that undocumented persons are prevented from gaining employment in the United States....Congress recognized that the status quo—under which millions of persons, because of their undocumented status, are forced to live in a shadow society and under which addi-*

*tional undocumented millions travel annually to the United States in search of jobs—is simply intolerable. (Rodino, 1986, p. iii)*

The Immigration Reform and Control Act of 1986 (Public Law 99–603) was the first to address illegal immigration with controls. Liberal amnesty was granted to individuals who had established themselves as residents. Temporary-resident status would be granted to those who had resided in the United States continually after January 1, 1982. In eighteen months these individuals could become permanent residents, provided they had a minimal understanding of English and knowledge of the history and government of the United States, a requirement established for all immigrants seeking citizenship. No limitation was placed on the number of persons who could become legal residents. To maximize participation, the bill called for a period of public information and education focusing on many Hispanic communities.

Sanctions were imposed on employers who knowingly hired illegal immigrants. Potential employers would be required to establish the citizenship status of applicants before hiring. Those found in violation could be fined up to $10,000 per illegal immigrant employed.

Unifying families continued to be an important legislative focus. Previous legislation had established this pattern. A significant flaw in the 1986 legislation was that it did not specify the status of family members who did not meet the requirements for amnesty. The problem was evident in those families in which one spouse was in the United States before the cutoff date, and the other spouse and children entered after January 1, 1982. Families who sensed that they were in jeopardy seldom applied for amnesty (Molesky, 1987). Often they returned to the shadows that Rodino (1986) mentioned as he identified the goals of the legislation.

Studies that examined the implementation of the policy have shown that critics of the legislation were correct in their warnings. The report of a New York State task force concluded that "a widespread pattern of discrimination existed" (Howe, 1990, p. 1). A California study found that the law discouraged employers from hiring Hispanic Americans, Asian Americans, and legal aliens. The fears of the Hispanic Caucus were not unfounded.

Unlike the 1939 response to children who "may" have been of German-Jewish heritage, the Refugee Resettlement Act of 1980 provided procedures for the admission and resettlement of refugees who were of special humanitarian concern to the United States (*Congressional Digest*, 1996).

It is quite evident that U.S. immigration policy continues to evolve, as long as individuals and families are willing and able to leave the familiarity of their homes to search for a new life in the United States.

## THE 1990s

During the 1990s immigration continued to be an issue for national legislative bodies. In 1996 two major pieces of immigration legislation were passed by the 104th

Congress and signed into law by President Clinton. The Personal Responsibility Act of 1996 (P. L. 104–193) curtails benefit for legal aliens and denies most benefits for illegal aliens. The second act, the Illegal Immigration Reform and Immigrant Responsibility Act of 1996 (P. L. 104-208), aimed to control illegal aliens and restricted benefits for aliens. These acts continue to respond to the discomfort felt by many citizens who question the admission of too many people from other countries and are particularly concerned by the influx of illegal aliens. This population was estimated to be about 4.6 million in 1996 (Vialet, 1996).

However, the Congressional Research Service (Vialet, 1996) reports that immigrants admitted for permanent residence declined between 1994 and 1995. Some of this change may reflect the decrease in employment-based visas and the end of temporary programs. The largest number of those who were admitted could claim family relationship as spouses, children of immigrants, or as adult children or siblings of U.S. citizens. This increase in the number of immigrants may be viewed as a response to the 1965 amendments to the Immigration and Nationality Act of 1952, which provided for the "reunification of families."

The year 1965 has been marked as the year in which the "new immigration" began. About 50 percent of this new population came from Mexico, the Philippines, Vietnam, the Dominican Republic, Korea, mainland China, India, the Soviet Union, Jamaica, and Iran. Their entry has increased the diversity of the immigrant population and thereby the entire nation (Fix & Passel, 1994).

Citizens of the Soviet Union noted here may be identified as refugees. These admissions are governed by criteria that differ from other immigrants. To attain refugee status requires a finding of persecution or well-founded fear of persecution in situations of "special humanitarian concern" to the United States. Admissions numbers are allocated by the president after consultation with the Congress. The 1997 admissions ceiling was set at 78,000, with the majority allotted for European countries, particularly the former Soviet Union. The East Asian allocation is at 10,000, the lowest in thirty years (Vialet, 1996).

The immigration legislation of 1996 may give some comfort for those who, in a 1993 *Time* magazine poll, favored changing immigration law to reduce the number of legal immigrants and the tracking down of illegal aliens. Others suggested a constitutional amendment that would deny citizenship to children unless their parents were born in the United States (Nelan, 1993). In either instance, the "fear of the stranger" is evident.

Fear and apprehension continue to be evident. Advocates for reform continually make claims that illegal aliens, undocumented persons, take jobs away from American workers. A review for the Congressional Research Service conducted by Levine (1995) reveals that various studies related to the impact of immigration on native-born workers present conflicting results. It is clear that the impact of immigration is felt by one segment of the labor force, those workers who have few skills to offer in the workplace.

In 1994 California Proposition 187, the "Save our State Initiative," was aimed at eliminating "illegal" immigration by denying state services such as health care and education. An analysis of the election results, passing the proposition, indicated that ethnic group membership and religious affiliation influenced the results. White ethnic groups voted in favor of the measure while the majority of Latinos, African Americans, and Asian Americans were against the measure. Even though Cardinal Mahoney of Los Angeles opposed the measure, more than 50 percent of white Roman Catholics throughout voted for the measure (Armbruster, Geron, & Bonacich, 1995). Repeal efforts failed, and Proposition 187 became public policy in 1997. We suggest that the debate will continue and new legislation will continue to be introduced and passed.

Roberts (1994) contends that whereas there is concern about the impact of immigration on the labor market, in the long run there is a net gain as immigrants contribute energy, enterprise, and investment in the communities in which they settle and to the nation as a whole.

## BECOMING A U.S. CITIZEN

Each group of new immigrants faces similar tensions. Initially there is the decision to immigrate based on one's experiences at home. To immigrate means to consciously give up family, friends, community, church, employment, and the other comforts of primary group associations. Language, familiar social customs, cultural heritage, and a familiar social hierarchy are lost. Although economic, political, or religious persecution or personal goals may become the push toward the United States, there are many tasks that must be accomplished after relocation. Housing and employment must be found, new language skills must be acquired, and new social customs must be learned as individuals search for a place in the new environment.

There is evidence that community composition often changed as established residents fled from the newcomers. In the 1800s the Irish and Germans retreated from the Lower East Side of New York City to Brooklyn, fearing the coming of Russian Jews and Italians (Rozwenc & Bender, 1978). In the 1980s, there were tensions between longtime Texas residents and Asian immigrants who wished to participate in the local shrimp industry. Newcomers were seen as unwarranted competition in the labor market (Ford Foundation, 1983).

The experience of immigrants has not changed significantly throughout the history of United States immigration. From the earliest European settlers to the more recent Asian immigrants, the ultimate goal for most is to become U.S. citizens, yet there has been a history of resistance by those who have been called "genuine Americans" (Fairchild, 1926, p. 44).

Early Scotch-Irish newcomers were feared in Pennsylvania. Officials there complained that if they continued to come they would soon make themselves the proprietors of the state. Limits were placed on their numbers and movement in South Carolina and Maryland. Germans aroused suspicion as well. Colonists feared that they and other newcomers would overturn the established customs. The developing tradition of Anglo-Saxon Protestant values insisted on diligence in work, individual achievement, and wealth. The English legal customs and language, as well as other aspects of their culture, were the foundation of the colonial experience, upon which was built the model of what the United States was to be (Dinnerstein & Reimers, 1975).

As each successive group arrives, the expectation is that they will take on the aspects of the dominant culture. To accomplish this, immigrants must engage in a developmental process that may challenge ethnic and individual identity and result in a new U.S. ethnicity.

Schneller's (1981) work with Soviet-Jewish immigrants who had been in this country a minimum of one year and a maximum of three suggested that in order for an immigrant to invest emotionally in a new country the loss of the original country must be resolved and a grieving process must take place. Once the ties to home are relinquished, adaptation is more easily achieved. The "push" for these Soviet-Jewish immigrants was their experience of anti-Semitism in the Soviet Union and the desire to improve their children's educational prospects.

Schneller (1981) described the variations in the Soviet-Jewish experience. Some felt shock: "America was like Mars—another planet." Others were excited, relishing the differences. Still others reported physical symptoms such as tension headaches, dizziness and lightheadedness, stomach pains, forgetfulness, and sleep disturbances, all related to the grieving process.

Immigrant status had placed these responsible adults in dependent and vulnerable positions. No longer did they feel able to function at their usual level of competence. The old country often remained very attractive, and old social networks were missed, even though many had prepared to leave Russia over a period of time.

Language difficulties interfered with the sense of security, autonomy, and self-esteem. Identity was threatened by the inability to communicate effectively with others. Feelings of brokenness, of being crippled by language and self-hate, and of isolation and detachment were expressed. The resulting distance placed the immigrant on the periphery of the society; full participation remained elusive (Schneller, 1981).

Polish immigration began early in the twentieth century, long before the Russians. The young men who arrived had been farm laborers, unskilled workers, and servants. Over the years they settled in urban centers in the East and Midwest, particularly Connecticut, New York, New Jersey, Illinois, and Michigan. As their communities developed, residents have had time to become Polish Americans, holding on to their own customs and traditions and, at the same time, becoming a part of the larger American society (Lopata, 1976).

Mostwin (1989) determined that immigrants experience an identity transformation. Psychological values that are inherited from ethnic group membership, along with values provided by the new environment, contribute to the change process, which can be observed through a series of crises: transformation, redefinition, synthesis, and destruction. The result of this process may well be a step in the formation of the new social form suggested by Glazer and Moynihan (1963).

Mostwin's (1989) work with Polish immigrant communities has shown that they could hold on to the old values of patriotism, hard work, family, religion, tradition, and honesty inherited from their ethnic experience. These, combined with values such as independence, the work ethic, achievement, tolerance, pragmatism, and materialism, acquired during the years in the United States enable this community to become Polish Americans, similar to but not exactly like those who arrived first.

As might be expected, each group has had similar yet different experiences as they adapted to life in the United States. Although Soviet Jews or immigrants from Poland may struggle with language, persons from the English-speaking West Indies have less difficulty with this aspect.

Challenging the assumption that the migration experience presents a series of crises, Maingot (1985) provided evidence of a more successful transition drawn from the experiences of African Caribbeans. These immigrants arrived from a society much like the one they entered, providing some cultural uniformity. The United States and the West Indies have both been British at some point in their history, and the language is similar, as are legal and religious institutions.

Although race placed them in a marginal position along with African Americans, this group expected to be successful in the United States, realizing that real material opportunities were available. Immigration policy was such that those who entered had technical and professional skills. Often they were unable to use these skills and found employment in common laboring positions. Maingot (1985) suggested that this inconsistency of status between skill and achievement produced stress for the West Indian immigrant rather than the suggested crisis orientation suggested by Mostwin (1989) or the grief process posed by Schneller (1981).

Southeast Asians—Vietnamese, Khmer, Laotians, and Hmong—arrived as refugees. Their process of becoming American is thwarted as a result of experiences of social disruption caused by war and dislocation, which may include difficulties encountered in escaping and leaving family behind, life in refugee camps, and resettlement, which requires adjustment to the United States.

Successful resettlement of refugees requires a process similar to that experienced by other immigrant groups. There is the stress that comes with culture shock and conflict, along with fear, anger, and loneliness. New roles must be assumed by men, women, and children, particularly the young and the elderly, who lack the basic skills of language, knowledge, and employment (Bliatout et al., 1985; Kinzie, 1985).

Unlike other immigrant groups who may number the generations over many years in this country, several Southeast Asian generations arrived at the same time. Grandparents, children, and grandchildren arrived together, compounding the difficulty of the process of becoming American. As the young strive to become American, older family members seek to hold on to life as they knew it. Although this is not an uncommon intergenerational experience, it gains in magnitude where there are no earlier generations to assist in the acculturation process. The elderly are dependent on the young, who are learning the language and customs and acquiring vocational skills.

Children and adolescents are more active than adults in the exercise of becoming American as they enter the educational system. One of the roles assigned to schooling in the United States is the preparation of children for citizenship and participation in society. All children are expected to learn how to be American in school.

Goldstein's (1988) work with Hmong high school girls provides some insights into their experience. These young women expected high school to be a place where they could become integrated into U.S. society, taking on an American identity. They would accomplish this by learning communicative style, particularly colloquial English, making friends with Americans, and acquiring the American look of their peers.

The schooling experience introduced change into the ethnic community as children learned about U.S. perceptions of the meaning of ethnicity and the nature of U.S. society. The initial stage of becoming a U.S. ethnic group was in process. A new U.S. ethnic group that merges old and new dispositions will evolve over time.

More recent emigrés from the Soviet Union left under a policy of "glasnost and perestroika" (openness and restructuring). Their experiences are similar to those who arrived earlier. Drachman and Halberstadt (1992) noted that some emigrés were ill-prepared for the array of choices in several aspects of life in the United States. Conversely, rights that were assumed in the former Soviet Union, such as housing, employment, and dental and medical care, are no longer available. Views on mental health differ. The expectation is that problems such as depression may be immediately treated via medication rather than via the Western "talking" intervention.

## INTERMARRIAGE AND THE NEW ETHNICITY

Stanley Lieberson (1985) has used the term *unhyphenated white* to identify a growing group of Americans who lack any clear-cut identification with or knowledge of specific European origins. They recognize that they are not the same as some existing ethnic groups. It is assumed that they are of older Northern European origins, although newer European arrivals may be included as well. In the 1980 census, members of this group identified themselves as "American." The number increased in the 1990 census. Indeed, Lieberson suggests that unhyphenated white may well be a new ethnic group that receives little attention as we fail to recognize that ethnic groups are not static, that they change through the years, and that the degree of identification with an ethnic group may fluctuate over time with the influence of prevailing social conditions. As the level of intermarriage continues, a segment of the white population will have a mixture of origins.

In 1994 Haut and Goldstein questioned, as did Lieberson (1985), the reliability of census responses as individuals in the United States redefine their ethnicity. Their work shows that two groups, the Irish and the Germans, have increased in number. This is due to an "alleged shallowness in the ethnic attachments reported to the Census" (p. 79). They also have shown that religious similarities and diversity of the German and Irish unite. This forms an intermarriage pattern that encourages German and Irish ethnic identification.

As the level of intermarriage continues, we move closer to what *Time* magazine (1993) has called the "Rebirth of a Nation." Reporters Annapu, Monroe, Sachs, and Taylor (1993) wrote of the huddled masses having given way to the muddled masses (p. 64). They referred to the strain placed on families as children outmarry and have children. Macintosh computer software enabled *Time* to pinpoint key facial features of 14 people of various racial and ethnic backgrounds. The result presented a composite of what we may look like as a nation in the future (pp. 66–67).

Stephen and Stephen (1989) addressed concerns about overall ethnic identity as Japanese Americans and Hispanics, suggesting that ethnic boundaries may be eroding through intermarriage. The 1980 census, marriage license applications, and personal interviews provided the data for Sung's (1990) examination of Chinese-American intermarriage. She concluded that the phenomenon is growing, with physical, familial, and personal ramifications. Kalmijn (1993) showed an increase in black/white intermarriage since the Supreme Court lifted the ban on intermarriage in 1967. This analysis noted that intermarriage for black men has increased. The unions tend to be between higher-status black men and lower-status white women. Indications are that the salience of race remains closely linked to class status.

Judd (1990) addressed intermarriage in the Jewish community in a case study that called attention to the Denver Jewish community. She applauded the community for its vigor and innovative response to intermarried couples. Schmer (1990) called Gentile–Jewish intermarriage "star-crossed" in her report exploring the instances of interfaith marriages in the New York City area. She explained that the probable reason for increased intermarriage is greater religious and ethnic tolerance. The literature continues to explore this reality in the Jewish American experience (Kosmin, 1990; Price, 1990).

In examining Catholicism and intermarriage, Sandler (1993) concluded that Catholics born in the 1950s are more likely to intermarry. He cautioned that lack of changes in interfaith marriage rates over time have not considered the rates of divorce and remarriage. Adding to the discussion, Schmer (1990) commented that interdenominational marriage among Protestants is high. Haut and Goldstein (1994) concurred, indicating that rates of intermarriage are high for groups of the same faith. Few Protestants (18 percent) marry out of their denominations. Intermarriage among ethnic groups and religious groups continues to redefine ethnicity in the United States. This is clear from offerings in the popular culture and the social science literature as well.

Alba's (1985) study of the Italian American experience concluded that Italians were on the verge of the twilight of ethnicity. Vosburgh and Juliani (1990) proposed that the situation may be more complex as Irish and Italian family patterns in intermarriage are examined. The inherent complexity of intermarriage patterns for each ethnic group becomes apparent. We are less likely, in the present, to deal with these relationships with an eye toward pathology. The intricacies of this evolving occurrence must be acknowledged if we are to respond to a new ethnicity in an ethnic-sensitive fashion.

As our examination of instances of intermarriage continues, it is incumbent on us to consider the impact of these marriages on the children of these alliances. Bowles (1993) expresses concern for children whose parents are African American and white. In the search for identity some children have identified themselves as black, others identify as whites and still others claim a biracial identity. Brown (1990) contributes to the discussion as he observes that, despite our view of the United States as a melting pot, rigid divisions related to social class, and racial and ethnic groups remain. In our stratified society issues of identity are difficult for oppressed ethnic groups, such as African Americans, Hispanics, and Native Americans. When an individual has racial and cultural roots in a white group and in an oppressed ethnic group, Brown suggests that they become socially marginal. They are not full members of either group. This dual identity implies a dual ethnic and cultural focus. The consequences of this duality may be seen in the nature of personal achievement or failure, in addition to social attitudes and aspirations.

A later qualitative investigation (Kerwin, Ponterotto, Jackson, & Harris, 1993) questions Brown's (1990) observation of marginality. Rather, these researchers determined that, at least for the children in their study, there was no great sense of viewing themselves as marginal in the two cultures. The sense of being in the "middle" was expressed, but this did not imply feelings of marginality. Their parents were secure in their own racial identities and they were not alienated from their extended families, although religion was an issue for some grandparents who were Catholic and Jewish. These researchers and Brown remind us that ethnicity may indeed be in its "twilight" for many groups in addition to the Italians as Alba (1985) observes.

The children of intermarriages are real children, they are the citizens of the "Reborn Nation" suggested by Annapu, Monroe, Sachs, and Taylor (1993). Indeed, we, the people, look quite different that we did in the 1800s. It is expected that in the twenty-first century the "Browning of America" will continue and oppressed ethnic groups will hold a numerical majority in the census count. Schlesinger (1990) would prefer the goal to be a joining together, of individuals from all nations. It is our hope that through this joining together, a new American ethnicity will evolve.

## SUMMARY

This chapter has presented a view of the process that individuals undergo as they become Americans. The process continues to be influenced by an ever-evolving immigration policy. As individuals become American, familiar customs, language, traditions, and rituals merge with those found here. We have considered the increasing incidence of intermarriage among persons from different ethnic and religious groups. In each instance of immigration and intermarriage there is an emerging new ethnicity that we must serve with ethnic sensitivity.

## REFERENCES

Alba, R. D. (1985). The twilight of ethnicity among Americans of European ancestry: The case of Italians. In R. Alba (Ed.), *Ethnicity and race in the U.S.A.: Toward the twenty-first century* (pp. 134–158). London: Routledge & Kegan Paul.

Armbruster, R., Geron, K., & Bonacich, E. (1995). The assault on California's Latino immigrants: The politics of proposition 187. *Interna-*

*tional Journal of Urban and Regional Research, 19*, 655–663.

Bennett, M. T. (1963). *American immigration policies: A history.* Washington, DC: Public Affairs Press.

Bliatout, B. T., Ben, R., Do, V. T., Keopraseuth, K. O., Bliatout, H. Y., & Lee, D. T. (1985). Mental health and prevention activities targeted to southeastern Asian refugees. In T. C.

Owan (Ed.), *Southeastern Asian mental health: Treatment, prevention, services, training and research* (DHHS Publication No. ADM 85-1399, pp. 183–207). Washington, DC: U.S. Government Printing Office.

Bloom, A. D. (1987). *The closing of the American mind.* New York: Simon & Schuster.

Bowles, D. D. (1993 Winter). Bi-racial identity: Children born to African American and white couples. *Clinical Social Work, 21,* 417–428.

Brown, P. M. (1990 August). Biracial identity and social marginality. *Child and Adolescent Social Work, 7,* 319–337.

Dinnerstein, L., Nichols, R. L., & Reimers, D. M. (1979). *Natives and strangers: Ethnic groups and the building of America.* New York: Oxford University Press.

Dinnerstein, L., & Reimers, D. M. (1975). *Ethnic Americans: A history of immigration and assimilation.* New York: Dodd, Mead.

Drachman, D., & Halberstadt, A. (1992). Stage of migration framework as applied to recent Soviet emigrés. *Journal of Multicultural Social Work, 2*(1), 63–78.

Evolution of policy: A century of immigration legislation (1996 May). *Congressional Digest, 75,* 130.

Feagin, J. R. (1984). *Racial and ethnic relations* (2nd ed.). Englewood Cliffs, NJ: Prentice-Hall.

Fix, M., & Passel, J. S. (1994). *Immigration and immigrants: Setting the record straight.* Washington, DC: The Urban Institute.

Ford Foundation (1983). *Refugees and migrants: Problems and program responses.* New York: Ford Foundation.

Glazer, N. (1981). Beyond the melting pot: Twenty years after. *Journal of American Ethnic History, 1*(1), 43–55.

Glazer, N. (1988). *The new immigration: A challenge to American society.* San Diego, CA: San Diego State University Press.

Glazer, N., & Moynihan, D. P. (1963). *Beyond the melting pot: The Negroes, Puerto Ricans, Jews, Italians and Irish of New York City.* Cambridge, MA: M.I.T. Press.

Goldstein, B. L. (1988). In search of survival: The education and integration of Hmong refugee girls. *Journal of Ethnic Studies, 16*(2), 1–27.

Haut, M., & Goldstein, J. R. (1994). How 4.5 million Irish immigrants became 40 million Irish Americans: Demographic and subjective aspects of the ethnic composition of white Americans. *American Sociological Review, 59,* 64–82.

Hirsch, E. D. (1987). *Cultural literacy: What every American needs to know.* Boston: Houghton Mifflin.

Judd, E. P. (1990). Intermarriage and the maintenance of religio-ethnic identity. A case study: the Denver Jewish community. *Journal of Comparative Family Studies, 21,* 251–267.

Kalmijn, M. (1993). Trends in Black/White intermarriage. *Social Forces, 72,* 119–146.

Kinzie, J. D. (1985). Overview of clinical issues in the treatment for Southeast Asian refugee children. In T. C. Owan, (Ed.), *Southeast Asian mental health: Treatment, prevention, services, training and research* (DHHS Publication No. ADM 85-1399, pp. 113–135). Washington, DC: U.S. Government Printing Office.

Kosmin, B. A. (1990). The demographic imperatives of outreach. *Journal of Jewish Communal Service, 66*(208–211).

Levine, L. (1995, March 30). Immigration: The effects on native-born workers. Washington, DC: Congressional Research Service.

Lieberson, S. (1985). Unhyphenated white in the United States. In R. Alba (Ed.), *Ethnicity and race in the U.S.A.: Toward the twenty-first century* (pp. 159–180). London: Routledge & Kegan Paul.

Lieberson, S., & Waters, M. C. (1988). *From many strands: Ethnic and racial groups in contemporary America.* New York: Russell Sage Foundation.

Maingot, A. (1985). The stress factors in migration: A dissenting view. *Migration Today, 13*(5), 26–29.

McKee, J. O. (1985). Humanity on the move. In J. O. McKee (Ed.), *Ethnicity in contemporary America: A geographical appraisal* (pp. 1–30). Dubuque, IA: Kendall Hunt.

Miller, H. N. (1985). The right thing to do: A history of Simpson-Mazzoli. In N. Glazer (Ed.), *Clamor at the gates: The new American immigration* (pp. 49–72). San Francisco: Institute for Contemporary Studies.

Novotny, A. (1971). *Strangers at the door: Ellis Island, Castle Garden and the great migration to America.* New York: Bantam.

Owan, T. C. (1985). Southeast Asian mental health: Transition from treatment services to prevention—A new direction. In T. C. Owan (Ed.), *Southeast Asian mental health: Treatment, prevention, services, training and research* (DHHS Publication No. ADM 85-1399, pp. 141–167). Washington, DC: U.S. Government Printing Office.

Price, R. D. (1990). Outreach to the intermarried: Understanding the risks and setting priorities. *Journal of Jewish Communal Service 66*, 224–229.

Reimers, D. M. (1985). *Still the golden door: The third world comes to America*. New York: Columbia University Press.

Rodino, P. W. (1986). The "Immigration and Reform Act of 1986" (P. L. 99-603): A Summary and Explanation. Committee on the Judiciary, House of Representatives, 99th Congress. Washington, DC: U.S. Government Printing Office.

Rozwenc, E., & Bender, T. (1978). *The making of American society* (Vol. 2, 2nd ed.). New York: Alfred A. Knopf.

Sandler, W. (1993). Catholicism and intermarriage in the United States. *Journal of Marriage and the Family, 55*, 1037–1041.

Schaefer, R. T. (1988). *Racial and ethnic groups* (3rd ed.). Glenview, IL: Scott, Foresman.

Schlesinger, A., Jr. (1990). The return to the melting pot. In R. Takaki (Ed.), *From different shores: Perspectives on race and ethnicity in America* (pp. 293–295). New York: Oxford University Press.

Schlesinger, A. M. (1992). *The disuniting of America*. New York: Norton.

Schneller, D. P. (1981). The immigrant's challenge: Mourning the loss of homeland and adapting to the new world. *Smith College Studies in Social Work, 51*(2), 97–125.

Stephen, C. W., & Stephen, W. G. (1989). After intermarriage: Ethnic identity among mixed-heritage Japanese-Americans and Hispanics. *Journal of Marriage and the Family, 51*, 507–519.

Sowell, T. (1981). *Ethnic America: A history*. New York: Basic Books.

Sung, B. L. (1990). Chinese American intermarriage. *Journal of Comparative Family Studies, 21*, 337–352.

Takaki, R. (1994). At the end of the century: The "Culture Wars" in the U.S. In R. Takaki (Ed.), *From different shores: Perspectives on race and ethnicity in America* (pp. 296–299).

Vecoli, R. J. (1985). Return to the melting pot: Ethnicity in the United States in the eighties. *Journal of American Ethnic History, 5*(l), 7–20.

Vialet, J. (1996, December 3). Immigration fundamentals. The Library of Congress: Congressional Research Service.

Vialet, J. (1996, December 31). Immigration: Legal immigration—Facts and issues. The Library of Congress: Congressional Research Service.

Williams, R. B. (1988). *Religions of immigrants from India and Pakistan: New threads in the American tapestry*. Cambridge, MA: Cambridge University Press.

# 2

# THE ETHNIC REALITY

*In this chapter, major perspectives on the role played by ethnicity in life in the United States are reviewed. These include the concept of ethclass, assimilationism, the melting pot, ethnic conflict, ethnic stratification, and ethnic pluralism. Also reviewed are racism, ethnocentrism, and discrimination.*

*Major attention is also focused on the meaning of social class and the stratification system found in the United States. The nature of work done by members of the different social classes is reviewed. A major theme is the persistence of ethnicity as a feature of social life.*

*We close with a discussion of the ethnic reality and suggest how the intersect of ethnicity and social class generates the distinct and identifiable dispositions to life that need to be understood by social workers.*

The United States is a dynamic, diverse, multiethnic society. Just how diverse and ever changing it is was shown in Chapter 1. Membership in ethnic and social class groups that constitute this nation has far-reaching effects on the various problems of living with which social work aims to help. There are many perspectives on how ethnic group membership, social class, and membership in oppressed groups affect individual and group life. We will examine and assess a number of these perspectives. Our basic aim is to cull those insights that can serve as the basis for developing practice principles based on sensitive understanding of the values and dispositions related to ethnic group membership and position in the social class system.

The means by which diverse people of different culture, background religion, color, national origin, and socioeconomic status accommodate one another have long been of interest to social scientists and the public. A number of schools of thought have been developed to explain these processes. Some emphasize the importance of social class, and some focus on group culture as a major factor shaping people's lives. Others emphasize conflict among groups, and yet another school of thought focuses on accommodation and pluralism.

The recent growth in immigration by people from the Far East, Latin America, and Africa—people whose native cultures are substantially different from what some consider the "core" or "mainstream" in the United States—has raised a series of new issues. Long-standing assumptions about acculturation and assimilation are being challenged. We will review some of these new concepts.

Analysis of the discussion of the role of ethnicity in social life has drawn on a number of conceptual formulations. A recent review of the social work literature (Schlesinger & Devore, 1995) shows that analysts have drawn on concepts of culture, power, minority status, ethnicity as a group boundary phenomenon, and social stratification theory.

The perspective presented in this book draws extensively on theories of social stratification and on the meaning of ethnicity in social life. Social class refers to the horizontal stratification of a population related to economic life and to differences based on income, wealth, occupation, status, community, power, group identification, and level of consumption. Social class position thus plays a major role in the degree of access to what some term as life chances—economic wherewithal, health status, education, power, and prestige—as does ethnicity.

## ETHNIC STRATIFICATION

Another dimension of stratification is important to the present consideration. The concept of ethnic stratification refers to the ranking of people based on their ethnic group membership as well as their economic position. Marger (1994) has suggested that ethnic stratification is a "system of structural inequality" in which there is a hierarchal arrangement of ethnic groups. One group establishes itself as dominant. This group has the most power to shape ethnic relations. "Other subordinate, ethnic groups exert less power corresponding to their place in the hierarchy, extending down to the lowest ranking groups which may wield little or no power." Group rank is determined mainly on the basis of distance from the dominant group in culture and physical appearance (p. 44).

Figure 2.1 depicts our perspective on the relationship between social class and ethnic group membership. Table 2.1 on page 24 depicts the concept of ethnic stratification that derives from our view of the ethnic reality and suggests that both class and ethnic stratification systems are found in the United States. Whereas Figure 2.1 points to the intersection between class and ethnicity for the whole society, Table 2.1 shows the class structure for each of the major ethnic subgroups.

## MAJOR PERSPECTIVES ON THE ROLE OF ETHNICITY IN AMERICAN LIFE

Until the beginnings of industrialization and modernization, there was little reason to think about the role of ethnicity in social life. People lived in relatively stable communities where identity was based largely on gender and age. In less complex

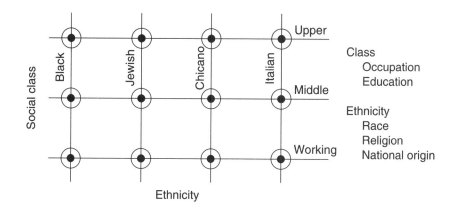

**FIGURE 2.1     The Ethnic Reality: Ethclass in Action.**     The "social space" created by the intersect of social class and ethnicity has been called ethclass. The disposition and behaviors that flow from this are termed the ethnic reality or ethclass in action. Ethnicity and the associated sense of "peoplehood" are represented by the vertical axis and stress the fact that ethnicity is a component of social life at all social class levels. Social class is represented by the horizontal axes. The circles represent the ethnic reality and suggest that as social class intersects with ethnicity a unique configuration is formed.

societies, where the work to be done was less diversified, work tasks were assigned primarily on the basis of age and gender. National, regional, and even occupational distinctions were less pronounced, and communication between different groups was nonexistent. Questions about identity and belonging were not likely to be asked, for people simply were men or women or children, old or young, and belonged to highly circumscribed undifferentiated social groups.

Much of this stability began to break down in the course of development of large agricultural societies and subsequent massive industrialization and urbanization. Population increases and the development of nation states gave rise to diverse bases of identity. The question, "Who am I?" now is likely to evoke multiple responses as people think of themselves as members of the world community, their country, their region of birth, their occupational groups, their social class group, and their ethnic groups. In the course of life, these may shift as people move geographically and as they experience mobility up or down the social class ladder. Many people have ethnic group memberships by virtue of having parents of different ethnic origins or by the choices they make about marriage and other meaningful relationships. Indeed, given these complex and multiple bases of identification, many analysts have predicted that as societies divided into the multiple groups already mentioned, ethnicity would fade as a basis of identity. Ethnicity was thought to be identified with

**TABLE 2.1    Ethnic Ranking and Class
Stratification in the United States**

English Origin People
    Upper class
    Middle class
    Lower class

Other White European People and Some Latino People
    Upper class
    Middle class
    Lower class

Jewish People
    Upper class
    Middle class
    Lower class

Asian People
    Upper class
    Middle class
    Lower class

African American People
    Upper class
    Middle class
    Lower class

Native American People
    Middle class
    Lower class

Puerto Rican People and Mexican Americans
    Upper class
    Middle class
    Lower class

consciousness of kind and with a solidarity that was a feature of preindustrial, small, peasant communities. It was expected that the "bonds of blood and place" would be replaced by the impersonal relationships associated with large cities and the highly bureaucratized, large workplace (Glazer & Moynihan, 1963; Hraba, 1979).

A look at the world around us suggests that the demise of ethnicity has not taken place. Rather, it seems that the ethnic basis of identity remains quite powerful. Indeed, a review of the world's trouble spots—where conflict and wars appear to have become an ongoing part of life—suggests that conflict between ethnic groups, each of which clings desperately to its sense of identity, or territory, or power, becomes more pronounced than ever. As shall be noted frequently in this book, ethnicity continues to serve as a basis of cohesion and strength at the same time that it is a source of stress and strife. All around us is ample evidence of the positive and negative impact of ethnicity. Gordon's assertion, made in 1964, holds true more than 30 years later:

> *...the sense of ethnicity has proved to be hardy as though with a wily cunning of its own, as though there were some essential element in man's nature that demanded it—something that compelled him to merge his lonely individual identity in some ancestral group of the nation—the sense of ethnic belonging has survived...in various forms and with various names, but it has not perished,... (p. 25)*

Clearly, it is important that we understand this issue and aim to identify the positive, humanizing aspect. Past analysis of the ethnic and immigrant experience focused on the extent to which newcomers retained or abandoned their customary ways of life as they encountered the American mainstream culture. Recent analysis suggests that the notion that there was a clear choice between "Americanization" or retention of "ethnic attachment" is not congruent with the reality of the ethnic experience of recent newly arrived groups. For example, studies of Korean immigrants point to "additive modes of adaptation," whereby there is strong retention of ethnic ties as well as considerable evidence of adaptation to U.S. society (Kim & Hurh, 1993). Similar patterns have been documented in other groups. We will consider related matters throughout the discussion in this chapter.

## DEFINITION OF TERMS: DEFINITIONAL ISSUES

At first thought it might seem as though defining the terms under discussion is a routine matter, a task to be carried out just to be sure that readers and authors ascribe the same meaning to commonly used terms. Nothing could be further from the truth. Discussions of ethnicity, of social class, of culture, of "race," of "minority group status" are fraught with disagreement and tension. Differences of opinion range on the very existence of such groups as ethnic groups. As shall soon become evident, there are increasing numbers of analysts, the present authors among them, who seriously challenge the notion that there are races, and that the concept as used in many contexts is not only lacking in any scientific basis, but is also pejorative and divisive. The meanings of such terms as *social class* have long been sources of much debate; most recently, the term *underclass* has come into use at the same time as it is seriously challenged.

A similar situation pertains in respect to the names by which different groups prefer to be called. The change in preferred terminology to designate one group of people—for example, from Negro, to Black, to African American—is a case in point. Although the term *African American* is not preferred by all the members of this group, there appears, nevertheless, to be considerable consensus around its use.

In the discussion that follows we present some commonly used terms and, where appropriate, consider the variations in meaning as advanced by different people. We indicate our preference, which derives both from our immersion in this work and what has been written on the subject.

## Culture

*Culture* is a commonly used concept that is difficult to define. It revolves around the fact that human groups differ in the way they structure their behavior, in their world view, in their perspectives on the rhythms and patterns of life, and in their concept of the essential nature of the human condition.

Lum (1995) analyzed the concept of culture and how that concept can aid us in understanding behavior that arises out of ethnic group memberships and out of the interaction between different groups.

Lum identified various dimensions of culture, including what are termed "etic" and "emic" dimensions of cultural values. "Etic" refers to principles valid in all cultures. "Emic" refers to the elements meaningful in any one culture. Taking his departure from the point of cultural interaction, he identified five perspectives on culture that apply in culturally pluralistic societies. The transcultural perspective focuses on the transition from one culture to another; this concept bears on understanding by dominant groups of ethnic and minority cultures. The cross-cultural perspective concerns the synthesis and interaction of two distinct cultures. The paracultural perspective examines the relationships between recent immigrants and multigenerational U.S.-born descendants. The metacultural perspective addresses commonalities between people of color. The pancultural perspective focuses on universal cultural characteristics. These perspectives all bear on our effort to understand relations between different groups.

## Ethnic Groups and Ethnicity as Concepts

There are a number of definitions of *ethnic group*. There appears to be general agreement that ethnic groups are one of the important subgroups in contemporary society. Members are drawn together by a common history as well as by shared experiences in the present. Ethnic groups usually share a common culture, a common religion, similar physical features, a common language, or some combination of these (Marger, 1996). Gordon has suggested that the ethnic group, "above all serves as a psychological referent in creating a 'sense of peoplehood'" (Gordon, cited in Marger, 1996, p. 13). An important notion is introduced by Blauner (1992) who suggests that members of ethnic groups "feel an affinity for each other," that there is "a comfort zone that leads to congregating together " even when not forced to do so by external factors of oppression or exclusion. Gordon's formulation, developed in 1988 is still useful:

*...a population entity which considers itself to have a common historical ancestry and identity—a sense of peoplehood, of constituting a "people"—and is so regarded by others. It may be co-extensive with a particular nation, or it may be a sub-population within a nation. It may be based on a common religion, a common language, a common national background, or a common racial ancestry or frequency, or some combination of several of these factors. (p. 129)*

Some common themes run through these definitions. They include consciousness of kind, a sense of being like the others in the group, and a sense of identity based on a shared social history. The "self-definition in terms of the past makes an ethnic group different from most other kinds of social groups and constitutes the sine qua non of its existence" (Alba, 1985, p. 17).

Analysts continue to debate the meaning of *ethnicity,* its essential features, the ways in which ethnic groups are alike or differ from other groups such as those joined by religion, or nationality, or skin color. Others (e.g., Alba 1985) suggest that ethnic groups, especially those who are members of white ethnic groups (e.g., Italians), are becoming less and less important as a basis of identity. Others believe the nature of ethnic identity is transformed but retained (Kivisto, 1995; Jenkins, 1997). In our view, ethnic groups remain important, viable groups that give meaning to the lives of their members.

Jenkins (1997) presents what he terms *the basic anthropological model of ethnicity.* This model is highly congruent with the social work perspective on ethnicity that is the focus of this book. The following features of ethnicity are identified.

1. Ethnicity is cultural differentiation.
2. Ethnicity focuses on culture as shared meaning as well as being rooted in individual lives.
3. Ethnicity is as fluid or stable as the culture of which it is a part.
4. Ethnicity is both an individual and a collective phenomenon that is externalized in social interaction and personal at the level of self-identification.

The anthropological view of ethnicity and ethnic group membership as having consequences for individuals as well as the groups of which they are a part is thoroughly congruent with social work perspectives.

## WHAT DO MEMBERS OF ETHNIC GROUPS PREFER TO BE CALLED?

Discussion about how to refer to various ethnic groups has become more and more controversial. There are several issues. One revolves around the name used to refer to various groups. Another revolves around whether some groups are properly referred to as ethnic groups, minority groups, racial groups, cultural groups, or others.

The answer is seldom based solely on scholarly opinion but may be rooted in political considerations, in practical issues, or in a group's distress about having names assigned by the larger society that, in the view of many members of the group, are not accurate, are pejorative, or are simply rejected because they were externally imposed.

Guidelines for describing people in ways that are not pejorative and that are sensitive to the wishes of the members of the group under discussion have been issued by the publishers of this book, by the press of the National Association of Social Workers, and by others. We adhere to these guidelines where possible. However, we do not agree with all of the recommendations made by any of these groups.

Our practice is guided by the notion that when one is writing about a specific group, though that group may be a member of a subgroup (e.g., Puerto Rican members of the Latino group, Chinese members of the larger group of Asians), we use the name of the group. When the specific group is not known, or when making assertions that can reasonably be ascribed to the larger group, such terms as Latino, American Indian, or Asian will be used.

## "Race"

The reader may have already noted that quotation marks are used for the heading in this section. We have done this to alert the reader to our view that "race" is *not* a legitimate scientific concept that accurately describes or facilitates useful analysis of apparent differences between individuals and the groups of which they are members such as skin color or hair texture. We share Manger's view (1996) that

> *the term is one of the most misunderstood, misused, and often dangerous concepts of the modern world. It is not applied dispassionately by lay people or, even to a great extent, by social scientists.*

Rather it arouses emotions such as hate, fear, anger, loyalty, pride, and prejudice. It has also been used to justify some of the most appalling injustices and mistreatment of humans by other humans(pp. 18, 19). *The Encyclopedia of Social Work* (1995) does not have an entry under the term *race,* though groups ranging from African Americans to "White Ethnic Groups" are listed as racial and ethnic groups.

The reader then may ask how come we give the term sufficient credence to use it as a section heading, whether or not we enclose it in quotation marks as a way of alerting the reader to our wariness about this term. We do so because, unfortunately, the term is in constant common use and used extensively by well-meaning analysts and advocates, as well as those who use the term in pejorative and negative ways. In its most benign sense, the term describes physical differences, such as skin color and hair color and texture, and is not intended to hurt, or to disparage, or to deprive people of resources and important aspects of daily living. On the other hand, in its most destructive sense, the term ascribes great significance to these physical differences and suggests that race accounts for differences in intelligence as well as other important attributes. Often, when the term is invoked, it is used in this negative sense. It is for this reason that many of us who pay special attention to these matters in our work, and in our own lives reject the use of this term. Gordon suggests that the term refers to "differential" concentrations of gene frequencies responsible for traits that are confined to physical manifestations such as skin color or hair form (Gordon, 1964, p. 27). Jaynes and Williams (1989) propose that the distinguishing features, "though biologically trivial," have been used as markers for ascribing great differences in power and privilege. Despite its negative connotations and limited utility, the term *race* is used extensively. The U.S. Census Bureau and the Office of Management and Budget have created four official racial categories in order that data vital to affirmative action and other programs may be collected. The categories are American Indian or Alaska Native, Asian and Pacific Islander, black, and white. "Hispanic" is defined as an ethnic category, separate from race (Sandor, 1994).

The dissatisfaction with this emotionally laden and unsatisfactory term is illustrated by some responses to the Census questions (Sandor, 1994). For example, some Hispanic people have difficulty identifying themselves separately in ethnic and racial terms. Some members of the same family are dark skinned and dark eyed, whereas others are pale skinned and light eyed. The distinctions as set up by the Census Bureau do not conform to their sense of themselves.

The categorization scheme does not take account of "mixed-race" children. Their numbers have increased, as has the number of persons who refuse to place themselves in "boxes." All this suggests continuing difficulty with the term *race*. Some suggest eliminating the question from the Census form. Others point out that this would make it difficult to obtain the needed data for the very reason they are being collected: to enforce a variety of antidiscriminatory legislation.

From a conceptual point of view, we consider the term *ethnic group* to be a more meaningful and less pejorative means of categorizing people. Mixed ethnic categories could readily be developed.

Marger's comments (1971) on this perspective bear noting. He believes that the term *race* has been abandoned entirely by many social scientists. In his view using the term *ethnic* to subsume the groups commonly found in the United States seems "reasonable." The definition of an ethnic group includes common physical characteristics, as well as "consistent and significant cultural traits that set them off from other groups" (p. 26). Alba's view is also useful. Marger, citing Alba, suggests that "A racial group is...an ethnic group whose members are believed, by others if not also by themselves, to be physiologically distinctive" (Alba, cited by Marger, 1997, p. 26).

In this book we avoid, as much as possible, the term *race,* and instead use the term *ethnic group* as a way of categorizing the various subgroups that are a part of this country.

# USE OF THE TERMS "WHITES" AND "BLACKS"

## "Whites"

In the preceding discussion of "race," we contend that classifications of people on the basis of presumed "racial" characteristics is neither analytically nor scientifically sound, and yet it has become commonplace, even in many official government documents, to use the term *whites* as if there were an ethnic group or a national or cultural group called *white*. There is no such group. There are, in this country, many European people who tend to be described as white. They usually are members of groups that have names such as Italian Americans, Jewish Americans, Irish Americans, Germans, English people, and others. The tendency to use the term *white* as a catchall phrase for these and other people is inaccurate and groups together people of various histories, cultures, and needs. There are, of course, people who prefer not to be identified as hyphenated Americans (e.g., Irish-American) but simply prefer to view themselves as "American."

Lee (1993) analyzes the practices of the U.S. Census between 1890 and 1990 in regard to the racial classifications used. She traces the history of this practice and suggests that it is rooted in "prevailing ideologies of race" (p. 80) and finds that "a two-category system based on perceived skin color, whites and others can be traced through years of changing census classification schemes. In the period under study, the people who were considered white have differed enormously. There are many examples. Asian Indians used to be considered white but are now considered Asian Indians. Mexicans used to be considered a separate race, then for a period were considered white, and now are considered Hispanic. Lee further contends that the changing census classifications and the bureau's absorption with race has "transformed diverse ethnic groups into pan-ethnic races" (p. 84). "In short, the social construction of a panethnic racial group called White served to minimize ethnic differences among the numerous European ethnic groups while fostering a common racial identity. It also hardened the division between White and Others" (p. 85). Some members of some European ethnic groups probably appreciated being classified as "white" and enjoying thereby, a degree of acceptance they had not been given in earlier periods of their settlement in the United States. This designation separated them from people of color, so long maligned.

Lee's analysis suggests that political considerations, rather than clear social scientific analysis, contributed to the creation of a white ethnic group. While creating a "white" group for census purposes, the real differences between the many European American subgroups have not been eliminated. In our view, to consider "whites" as an undifferentiated, relatively monolithic group of people—a notion implicit in any analysis when whites are compared to other groups such as African Americans, Asian Indians, or Latino people—obscures major differences within the group with largely European origins.

We avoid the use of the term *white*, except when the work and analysis of others we cite makes it impossible for us not to do so.

## *"Blacks"*

Logically, the term *Black* has the same flaws as the term *whites*—subsuming into one group, on the basis of skin color—people who have such distinct histories and cultures as African Americans, people of color from the Caribbean, immigrants from Africa, and others. Use of the term has a different history, in that for a period of time, in the past twenty years or so, the term was preferred by many people now commonly called African Americans. The term was selected by leaders of this group as preferred to *Negro,* a term imposed by what is often referred to as the "white power structure."

In recent years, there is a tendency, albeit not universal, to minimize the use of the term "Black" and to refer to people by the groups to which they truly belong (e.g., Bermudians, Jamaicans, African Americans).

In this respect, too, we will follow the preferred practice of using ethnic group names as above. When information is available using the term *Black* to refer to any group, we will capitalize the term, thus giving the people under discussion the status of an ethnic group.

## *Oppressed Ethnic Groups[1]*

As best as we know, there is no multiethnic society in the world in which all ethnic groups in that society have equal status. Ethnic stratification is almost universally found in societies where people of different groups have come together, by whatever means, and for whatever reasons. Sadly, then, there are clearly established and well-recognized patterns of dominance and hierarchy everywhere.

In the United States, as in many parts of the world, many of the people with the least power, who experience the most unequal treatment, are people of color—members of various ethnic groups, chief among which are African Americans, American Indians, Mexican Americans, Puerto Ricans, many people from various countries in the Caribbean, and a number of Asian groups including Chinese Americans, Japanese Americans, Vietnamese Americans, some Asian Indians, and others.

For many years social scientists, as well as advocates for many of the groups referred to above, referred to these groups as minority groups. Minority groups were defined as the underprivileged in a system of ethnic stratification and people of low standing—people who receive unequal treatment and who, therefore, come to regard themselves as objects of discrimination. As is often the case, a number of people who belong to the groups identified as minorities raised objections to its use. Some simply found the term offensive, and preferred that the names of the specific groups under discussion at any point in time be used. Others had different reasons.

As we have worked on different issues of this book, we have given considerable thought to this issue of language. We are firmly committed to the importance

---

[1]We consciously substitute this term for the term "minority groups," a term found distasteful by many people—especially people of color—who are considered oppressed.

of using language that is sensitive to the hurts and sensibilities of the persons most affected by the groups' status. At the same time, there are very few times where a significant majority of any group's members are in full agreement about what constitutes appropriate language. Given this we must use our good judgment, as well as our knowledge of the various schools of thought found in political, as well as academic, circles.

The title of this section—Oppressed Ethnic Groups—reflects our current thinking on the matter. It is in keeping with our position that all groups, whether oppressed or not, whether members of the majority or a subordinate group, are ethnic groups in the way that term is traditionally defined. The heading also recognizes the special, oppressive nature of the conditions under which many people live in this country at the present time in history. It is true that almost without exception, the people so affected are "people of color." That term is useful, but selects only one of the bases of identification around which ethnic groups form and are sustained. We reject the term "racial and ethnic groups" as a substitute for the term "minority" as recommended by the *NASW Press* (undated) precisely because it focuses, willy-nilly, on the distinction based on some presumed racial characteristic, negating the richness of factors that contribute to ethnic identity, despite and in the face of severe oppression.

## People of Color

Contending that the term *minority group* has come to be used to refer to groups (such as women, gays, and lesbians) other than those ethnic groups that are especially oppressed, Hopps (1982) and others have suggested that the term *people of color* be used to refer to people who face a pervasive kind of oppression and discrimination because of racial stereotypes associated with and indelibly marked by the color of their skin. Although many forms of exclusion and discrimination exist in this country, none is so deeply rooted, persistent and intractable as that based on color (p. 3). We will use both terms interchangeably in this book. We agree that the term *minority group* loses force when applied to groups other than ethnic groups that face special and destructive kinds of deprivation. Nevertheless, in the context in which it will be used in this book, the term has an honorable history in that it is traditionally identified with groups that are oppressed because of their ethnic group membership.

## "Middleman" Minority Groups

A number of writers have identified yet another group, minorities in the middle (Zenner, 1991) or middleman minorities (Marger, 1994). These groups are said to occupy a status between the dominant groups and the upper stratum of the ethnic hierarchy and the most subordinate groups at the bottom. They tend to play intermediate occupational roles such as traders, shopkeepers, moneylenders, and independent professionals. They are vulnerable to scapegoating and hostility, both from those at the top and bottom of the prestige hierarchy.

Some examples in the United States are Jewish people and Asian people. Whether people are designated as a member of the minority or the dominant group varies. Customarily, Jewish people have been part of the minority. However, by comparison with many African Americans, whose economic status and prestige rank lower, they are perceived to be part of the majority.

## ASSIMILATIONISM AND THE MELTING POT

*Assimilationism* is not a theory or a scientific concept. Rather, the term encompasses several viewpoints about what some people believe should happen to newly arriving ethnic groups as they become part of U.S. society. The term has its roots in two somewhat opposing views about newcomers. These viewpoints were developed primarily in response to the earlier migration of Europeans. One is based on idealistic beliefs that immigrants freed of the shackles of the old social order in their country of origin would merge into a new "race of man." The second is based on fear and distrust of the large numbers of poor, hungry people who fled famine and persecution in Europe. The first group had a vision of the United States as "a pristine world, where a new society could develop freed of the social shackles, the political and religious despotism of the Old World" (Alba, 1985). S. Hector St. John (cited in Alba, 1985) expands on this vision.

> *What is the American, this new man? . . . He is an American who leaving behind him all his ancient prejudices and manners, receives new ones from the new mode of life he has embraced, the new government he obeys, and the new rank he holds. Here, individuals of all nations are melted into a new race of men, whose labors and posterity will one day cause great changes in the world.*

It is evident that the well-known view that the United States is a melting pot, introduced in Chapter 1, has its origins in this kind of thinking. This vision was idealistic, but unrealistic. More important was the burden imposed on many people who neither wanted to nor could shed their old ways like so much old clothing ready to be discarded. The old ways spelled comfort and provided guidelines for behavior and contact with like people.

A more destructive view of how immigrants should behave came out of the Americanization movement, which Gordon (1964) referred to as an "onslaught on the immigrant's culture, social organization and self-regard" (p. 136). This movement demanded that the immigrant "divest himself at once of the culture of his homeland, that he cease to speak its language, that he regard with the same suspicion and hostility as his attackers his familiar and psychologically satisfying ethnic institutions and organizations" (p. 136). So destructive was the impact of this "onslaught" that efforts to counteract the negative effects became a major focus of activity of the settlement house movement, spearheaded by Jane Addams and her colleagues at Hull House. Displays of craft and skills and dress from many lands were developed in an effort to demonstrate to immigrants the legitimacy, importance, and beauty of their ethnic language and other elements of their groups' culture (Gordon, 1964).

In recent years, others have come to question the emphasis on assimilation that was prevalent at Hull House. There is little doubt that even in its most idealistic and egalitarian sense, the notion of the melting pot was hard on new families. Old ways spell comfort and provide guidelines for behavior. When people migrate, they do so for many reasons, whether it be economic distress, political or religious persecution, or hope for a better life. Taking this step does not necessarily involve rejecting the customs, traditions, and approaches to problem solving learned in the land of origin.

Earlier we mentioned that this movement barely took account of the situation of people of color—African Americans, Native Americans, and the few people from the Orient present during much of the 18th and 19th centuries. That this kind of omission or neglect was possible is testimony to the fact that denial of the essential humanity of people of color was long an element of thought and policy in this country. It is a legacy that has still not been completely overturned.

The view of the United States as a melting pot dies hard. It is a term still used in the current literature as a way of thinking about the degree to which newcomers have become immersed in the country. Few still cling to the notion that an entirely new type of person, one who abandons all elements of the old, is created in this country.

Instead, there is considerable variety in how people from different lands adapt. For example, Kibria (1997) identifies a process of "ethnogenesis" that involves recognition of the shared personal experiences and orientations of persons from Asia. She suggests that this pattern of strong identification with their Asian origin group is related to the experience of growing up Asian in the United States. This involves the cultural values stressed, such as the importance of family. The sense of being "outsiders," of being excluded by the mainstream culture, is also a common experience. The author wonders whether ethnogenesis may replace classic assimilation as a modal pattern for newer immigrant groups.

As people struggle with the vicissitudes of daily life, they retain elements of their old beings and identities; at the same time, they acquire new modes of thinking and adapting in response to their particular experience. Some of that experience includes conflict with the core society.

## *ETHNIC CONFLICT THEORY*

As we have already seen, division into ethnic groups is a major feature of contemporary society. Competition and conflict are thought to characterize the relationships between multiple groups. This is thought to be the case between ethnic groups. Some definitions will help to clarify the important issues.

*Ethnic competition* refers to "the mutually opposed efforts of ethnic groups to secure the same scarce objectives" (Hraba, 1979, p. 92). This concept implies that resources and access to certain jobs, education, or housing are scarce and that groups will engage in a variety of strategies designed to get advantage over others in acquiring these resources.

*Ethnic conflict* "is a form of group relationship…involving struggle over the rewards or resources of a society or over social values, in which conflicting parties attempt to neutralize or injure each other" (Hraba, 1979, p. 92, citing Newman).

*Ethnic stratification* refers to the horizontal stratification of ethnic groups in which powerful ethnic groups limit the access of subordinate groups to wealth, power, and prestige.

*Ethnocentrism* refers to the view of one group that the appearance and way of life of its members is superior to those of others (Hraba, 1979).

*Racism* is a central feature of these relationships. The term has a number of meanings, including "patterns of belief and related action that overtly embrace the notion of genetic or biological difference between human groups. [The term is also used] to designate feelings of cultural superiority" (Jaynes & Williams, 1989, p. 566). Some people limit use of the term to refer to situations in which members of the privileged groups injure or do other kinds of damage to disadvantaged groups.

Feagin & Vera (1995) define white racism as "the socially organized set of attitudes, ideas, and practices that deny African Americans and other people of color the dignity, opportunities, freedoms, and rewards that this nation offers white Americans" (p. 7). Institutionalized racism refers to the view that racist acts and practices are institutionalized and "embedded in and shaped by social contexts" (Feagin & Vera, p. 7) Though some of the actions that fall in this category are illegal, such as blatant discrimination in education, employment, and housing, some may be too subtle and embedded in the social structure for the present legal system to deal with them.

Some other concepts to be elaborated upon later in this chapter must be briefly introduced here. The most important of these is the concept of social stratification, which is the result of competition for wealth and power. Power is used to control resources.[2]

There are major differences of opinion about the nature and source of ethnic conflict. Some, especially Marxists, believe that the struggle for economic advantage is the prime motivation that triggers and sustains ethnic conflict. They believe that racism is a device brought into play in order to facilitate the exploitation of others. Some contend that sentiments such as racism and anti-Semitism have their own dynamics and are sustained by hate, misunderstanding, and mistrust.

As social workers go about their daily work, it is important that they be aware of the context in which people live and of the strains and pressures that impinge as they seek to work, raise families, and resolve the problems of living that relate to illness, marital strife, care of the elderly, and problems in child rearing.

---

[2]A discussion of the dynamics of power is beyond the purview of this book. It is nevertheless useful to note that power is ultimately based on control through coercion. The power of a group is based on its numbers and its control of other power resources. The recent history of the intergroup struggles that have taken place in the United States shows that power does indeed play a part. A review of the civil rights struggle of the 1960s reminds us that the coercive power of the state and federal governments were used to defend the racist status quo in the attacks on civil rights workers by police and other officials. Similarly, the power of the federal government was used to effect positive change when federal marshals stood at the gates of several major southern universities to allow the admission of African American students.

## ETHNIC PLURALISM

Common sense suggests that just as there is conflict between ethnic and racial groups, there is accommodation and assimilation. *Ethnic pluralists* focus on this component of the ethnic experience. They suggest that distinct ethnic groups, identity, and ethnically based ways of life do not disappear as various groups struggle to adapt to life in this country. As was suggested in Chapter 1, their sense of themselves shifts as their ethnicity evolves into new forms, responding to the experiences of life in a different society and historical era. Pluralists ask how diverse groups manage to reduce intergroup conflict sufficiently so as to carry out the tasks of daily living. Gordon (1964) posed the question this way: "What happens when peoples meet?" (p. 60). The processes and results of ethnic "meetings" have been termed *assimilation* or *acculturation*. Clearly, no single process or experience is involved. People meet and come together under all sorts of circumstances. At one level are the contacts that take place in the workplace. At another is the level of interaction in which differences in values and culture and religion are likely to be manifest and important, such as in church and school. Also to be considered are the kinds of interactions that lead to friendship, marriage, and other intimate relationships.

A model for describing and explaining the processes of assimilation was presented by Gordon (1964). He identified seven dimensions of the assimilation process: (1) cultural, (2) structural, (3) marital, (4) identificational, (5) attitude receptional (absence of prejudice), (6) behavioral receptional (absence of discrimination), and (7) civic (absence of value and power conflict). In cultural or behavioral assimilation, the major themes or behaviors of the dominant society, especially its language, have been adopted. This enables people to enter the workplace, to interact with others in commercial transactions, and, for children, to go to school. In structural assimilation, there are extensive primary group relationships between different groups of immigrants, including intermarriage. Gordon hypothesized that after a group's arrival, the first type of assimilation to take place is cultural assimilation. Structural assimilation often does not take place. This can continue indefinitely.

A more current view is offered by Marger (1997) who presents the view that assimilation takes place when people interact freely and become more alike. This perspective, though appealing, makes it more difficult to determine the process of assimilation or to what extent.

The assimilation experiences of different groups vary widely. Marger (1997) suggested that there is a relationship between how people enter the society and their assimilation experience. In the United States, ethnic groups of European origins who entered voluntarily assimilated at a fairly rapid pace, the rate being somewhat controlled by their members. By contrast, those groups who became members involuntarily—African Americans, Native Americans, and the Mexicans who were conquered—have fewer options and are more likely to resent the "new social order." Other factors are also operative.

This brief review of key perspectives on ethnicity in U.S. life suggests that earlier assimilationist and melting pot theories were not, and are not, consistent with the bulk of daily experience. Rather, the sense of identification with ethnic groups remains strong, even for those people who intermarry or who in other ways have achieved a fairly high degree of structural assimilation.

People of color and many of the newer immigrant groups have not yet had an opportunity equal to that of people of European origins to experience substantial degrees of assimilation. Most people want equality of opportunity. At the same time, many people want to maintain ties and identity with their ethnic groups. This is suggested by our review of pertinent materials and by our experience as social work practitioners, as social work educators, and as citizens. The additive model whereby people retain strong ethnic ties while becoming immersed in society's major institutions corresponds to the experience of many people.

## THE SENSE OF ETHNICITY

We have seen that ethnic groups and ethnic group membership are persistent and ongoing facts of social life. Nevertheless, a number of analysts have suggested that ethnic identity is losing its hold on people, especially those of European origins. Alba (1985) referred to the "twilight of ethnicity" and presented evidence to show that people of European descent are less likely to adhere to a variety of ethnicity-based behaviors and rituals more than used to be the case.

Accounts of extensive intermarriage in the Jewish community are presented as evidence of the erosion of Jewish ethnic identity. Nevertheless, Alba found that as many as 40 to 50 percent of people adhere to ethnically based rituals and beliefs. Cohen (1988) suggested that the high rate of intermarriage may be viewed as re-transformation rather than decline (Alba, 1993).

For newer groups—those from Asia, Latin America, and Africa—there is no question that their ethnic identities and cultures, coupled with the oppression and discrimination experienced by many, remain a major element of life. In order to assess the forces that contribute to the persistence of ethnicity, we looked at a variety of materials. They included systematic sociological analyses, novels, and television dramas, as well as personal documents and personal accounts that reflected on unique and emotionally meaningful experiences. Some common themes emerged from our explorations. These themes involved the comfort, joy, and importance of belonging. Closely related are those themes that addressed the pull and tug to belong under circumstances of stress and conflict. Whatever other sentiments or viewpoints were expressed, there was a sense of certainty about the importance of long-standing identities. When we asked people, sometimes half jokingly, "Do you want to be assimilated?" the replies were similar to that of a well-educated Jewish woman who said, "Do you mean giving up my Jewishness and becoming just like everybody else? If that's what you mean, I don't want it. I'm part of this country, and I pay my taxes and I want my children to go to school, but I want to remain different in many important ways" (E. Jacob, personal communication). An older Hungarian woman commented, "You know, when I came to this country I was so happy to be here that I wanted to be a complete American, to do everything the American way. Then I found out that I could not stop being Hungarian. I could not give up the Hungarian ways" (M. Heczag, personal communication).

The tension between old ethnic and community-based friendships and new, prestigious, mainstream-based ways of life was illustrated in the fictional situation that confronted Victor, a handsome Chicano lawyer and a member of an illustrious law firm in Los Angeles. A childhood friend, convicted of murder, was about to be executed. The prisoner and his family asked Victor's help in trying to reverse the planned execution. Victor was torn and resentful at being called upon to act out of loyalty to old friendships and associations he no longer maintained. The prisoner recalled their times together, and Victor agreed to plead the young man's case. He lost the appeal but agreed to the young man's wish that he witness the execution. The camera presented a vivid and devastating portrayal of the execution. Victor then joined the family at their home in an evening of mourning. The vicissitudes of life once more intervened to solidify a sense of ethnicity (Wallace & Kelly, 1990).

Another theme that emerged from our exploration was the sense of protection from the outside world. The world "out there" often reacts to people in racist and other bigoted ways, and the ethnic group can give solace and put the ethnic slur into perspective. The group does so either via humor or by providing a comfortable setting within which to ventilate anger. Much of that comfort is provided as the group draws on its rituals and strengths. For those who experience the particular effects of discrimination—those ethnic groups that are also minority groups—the process of conveying ethnic identity serves as a means of protection from the larger world, which all too often demeans, sometimes by vociferous intent and often out of ignorance. African Americans, especially young men, tell of feeling tension building up as they walk the streets outside their own African American communities. Too often, their mere presence evokes fear in passersby, fear that the young African American men will commit crimes.

Muslim women who want to wear the traditional head scarf as they go about life in urban America may be threatened with job loss or otherwise made to feel ill at ease. Orthodox Jewish men who cannot work on Saturdays are often unwelcome in jobs outside of their community. And so, often unable to walk the streets in comfort, they turn to the family and the neighborhood for affirmation of their essential humanity. Sometimes they ask for advice about whether the negative sense would be diminished if they always "dressed up, always looked respectable."

Ethnicity surfaces when world events crowd in around us. Jewish Americans watch with hope or dismay as the Israeli/Arab peace process waxes and wanes. Armenian Americans recall the massacre of millions of their people by taking to the streets of large U.S. cities to protest political actions that would present a faulty interpretation of the massacre of 1915. When the Chinese government attacked rebelling students and working people in Tiananmen Square in Beijing in 1989, many Chinese Americans, well established, with roots in American life, took to the streets, perhaps publicly identifying with their Chinese heritage for the first time, as the dramatic events stirred their sense of identity and kinship with those so far away. They do so again when the president of that country is welcomed to the United States.

Kivisto (1995) reviewed considerable work focused on determining whether ethnicity is declining. He suggested that Alba's notion of the twilight of ethnicity may be correct. Nevertheless, new forms of ethnicity may be emerging. For example, Greeley (1974) found that in the process of socialization, new ethnicity-related patterns emerge. Kivisto referred to symbolic ethnicity. He suggested that third-generation white European ethnics use ethnic-related symbols and rituals. On a census question most people, when free to choose, identify with their ethnic groups. "They pick and choose features of the ethnic tradition to valorize, while ignoring or abandoning others, such as tradition that is sexist" (p. 288).

In considering the sense of ethnicity, we have tried to convey the diffuse but persistent character of this element of human functioning. It is as if for some a sense of ethnicity is there to be used or not, as seems appropriate and necessary by individuals and collectivities, as individual or group need arises.

## THE DEVELOPMENT AND MAINTENANCE OF ETHNIC IDENTITY

Throughout this chapter we suggest that members of ethnic groups share a consciousness of kind that derives from a common history, a common language, and other common experiences. We also point out that in the course of their history, groups develop approaches to problems of living that serve their members and that must be understood in the process of solving the problems of daily living. We now focus on the processes that foster the development and maintenance of ethnic identity.

### Language

The extent to which groups share and use a common language varies enormously. For example, among recent immigrant groups, such as the Vietnamese, Chinese, Koreans, Russian Jews, some Puerto Ricans, and people from Colombia and other Latin American countries, the native language remains the major form of communication within the family. Children, usually more quick to learn English than their elders, become both teachers to and translators for the adults in the family. Bilingual education, now public policy in many places, allows children to maintain the necessary pace of studies while they learn English. In many groups, a self-conscious and deliberate bilingualism is sustained as members seek to preserve their own culture but at the same time do not question the need to master English. Language is most important. It may be Spanish, Polish, Hungarian, Yiddish, Vietnamese, Chinese, or a soulful sound "metered without the intention of the speaker to invoke it" (Brown, 1972), as in the language of soul. A common language provides a psychic bond, a uniqueness that signifies membership in a particular ethnic group, as well as a base for the coordination of activities both social and political. At times it is necessary to cope with the oppression of the mainstream society, which may forbid the use of the native tongue in the public arena. Ethnicity can be heard or felt when young African Americans "play the dozens" or "get their programs together." It is the deliberation of the Spanish *a poco a poco*, the joy of the Italian *aldia*, or the audacity conveyed by the Yiddish term *chutzpah*. Each of these words and many others retain their ethnic uniqueness in that they are not readily translated.

## Rituals and Celebrations

Rituals involve religious practices and the rites and celebrations surrounding life cycle events: births, deaths, and marriages. They are an integral part of holiday celebrations. Western, Asian, and Eastern religious rituals are built into the core of daily living. The ethnic church, temple, mosque, or synagogue are places where those with similar histories and problems gather to affirm their identities and beliefs. On Yom Kippur, the holiest of all days for Jews, even the most secular Jews go to synagogue to atone for their sins (Cohen, 1988). Catholic people all over attend mass and go to confession when troubles external to the church perplex them. Asian Indians—a new designation for recent immigrants from India and Pakistan—actively see to it that priests serving the various Indian and Pakistani religious groupings are available to conduct funerals and other religious rites. These newcomers, many young, relatively affluent professional people, believe it to be most important to maintain religious rituals and teachings as a way of assuring that their children retain an ethnic identity (Williams, 1988). People from Arab lands—Iran, Jordan, Syria, and other Middle Eastern countries—celebrate their holy days in similar ways, building mosques in which they can face East. The excitement of celebrations catches people up in the throes of ethnic existence. The preparations for a wedding, the rituals surrounding birth, and the traditions involved in a funeral remind us of our heritage.

Those who live in families in which members of two ethnic groups are joined in marriage may experience either strain or "double joy," depending on how they handle the situation. Some families in which one member is of Jewish background and the other a Christian background may struggle and develop tensions, not knowing whether to celebrate Christmas or ignore it, whether to send the children to church or to synagogue or to ignore the whole thing. Some joyfully do it all (Cohen, 1988; Schumer, 1990). Christmas, Hanukkah, and the glorious celebration of freedom that is Passover are occasions for family gatherings that attest to the capacity of peoples to transcend the daily tensions that characterize so much of life.

## Ethnic Schools and Parochial Schools

Enrollment in ethnic schools and parochial schools is a self-conscious way of trying to preserve children's adherence to language, rituals, and traditions. There is the Jewish Hebrew school, where young people gather frequently to prepare for the adolescent ritual of bar or bas mitzvah. These schools not only teach the required ritual, they also provide a focal point where like-minded youngsters meet and further their sense of identification with the group. Eastern European people have schools that children attend to learn rituals and the native language, and Asian Indians use their homes as centers for religion gatherings.

## *Primary Groups*

In primary groups, relationships are most often personal, intimate, and all encompassing. Ideally, these are the types of groups in which people can be themselves, such as family and friends, in which their foibles are understood and they are intrinsically loved and wanted. The major types of activities performed in primary groups highlight their importance in transmitting the sense of ethnicity. It is these groups that convey values and a sense of belonging, warmth, and cohesion. What is important and striking about the activities confined to or mainly carried out within primary groups is that they involve the core of the personality and important emotional relationships. How do primary groups such as the family and the peer group convey and sustain this sense of "ancestral and future-oriented identification" with the group? It takes the form of subtle reminders conveyed by the way children are consoled or admonished, by the transmitted clues for appropriate behavior in puberty, and by the way in which these are reinforced by the larger society.

The pull exerted by family and community and kin as they seek to keep the young within the fold is well known to most youngsters. The almost universal request made by parents of adolescent girls—that their dates pick them up at home—reflects a need to protect and a concern for safety and decorum. Often, it also includes the implicit question, "Is he one of us?" And if he is not, how far removed is he? As interethnic group marriage among white people increases, the fearful question in these groups becomes, "Is he of another color?" Some people of color share this fear. This developmental stage is often preceded by small and subtle actions of parents, ranging from looking for the "right" schools, which may really mean looking for neighbors of one's own kind, to joining the temple or church "for the children" and sending the children to religious school.

The family actively acts to carry out the customs of the groups. Women social work students of Asian Indian descent have told us how their families attempt to abide by the custom of arranging marriages for them. Men thought to be suitable husbands are brought home. Young women are not allowed to date. Some of these young people are in major turmoil about these expectations and restrictions, not unlike their immigrant predecessors in the early part of the century.

A three-generational study of Jewish, Italian, and Slavic American women in the Pittsburgh area found that ethnic group–related differences are transmitted in a number of ways (Krause, 1978). Many Italian American families continue to exert a strong pull on grown offspring to remain within the confines of the family. Many believe that daughters should not leave the family home except in a wedding gown or a casket (Johnson, 1985, pp. 185–186). Home is considered good and is the place where one is safe and protected. Much effort goes into bringing the young back home.

Roger and Cooney (1984) studied the persistence of ethnic identity in two generations of Puerto Ricans who had come to the mainland. Distinguishing them by such factors as age, gender, and age at arrival, the researchers measured adherence to ethnically related values and noted an expected tendency for these to diminish in the younger generation. Nevertheless, all groups were similar in perceiving themselves to have values that derive essentially from being Puerto Rican.

An enduring aspect of Puerto Rican American life is the strong sense of community felt by members of this group. Studies (e.g., Padilla, 1993) have shown that as Puerto Ricans aspire for a better life in suburban America, reaching for community and using community supports are an integral part.

The degree to which deeply ingrained ethnic dispositions persist into the third and fourth generations of immigrant families is of interest and remains to be seen. As some groups increase their levels of education and move up in the occupational structure (a situation that is true, for example, for many Italian Americans), it is not unlikely that some of the sense of group identity will diminish. This is a matter for future study. For the near future it seems unlikely that ethnic identity will be obliterated. Most Italian Americans alive in the 1970s had some memory or close connection to the immigrant experience; at least half had at least one immigrant parent (Alba, 1985).

The importance of group identity and of marrying one's own kind is transmitted and conveyed in some extreme responses to transgression. If guidelines are clear and parents vehement, there is often pain and turmoil; not infrequently, a total rupture in the family relationships ensues. Some Orthodox Jews may go so far as to "sit Shiva" for a child who has married outside the group. We have personal knowledge of instances in which families have been torn asunder as some members maintain contact with the child who has "out-married," whereas others consider the transgression too serious to condone. Despite the increasing rate at which young Jewish people marry out, even the most liberal and assimilated Jewish families remain highly sensitive to the issue, which may continue to signify betrayal of the family and the community (Herz & Rosen, 1982). The new families approach ethnic and religious socialization in a number of different ways. Some decide to adopt the faith of one of the members, going through religious conversion. Some will consciously expose their children to the rituals and customs of both groups.

The family, usually kind and protective but sometimes destructive, guides the young into the "right" schools, into playing with the "right" kinds of children, and into marriages with the "right" people, these often being "our own kind." "Man's most primal needs and emotions declare themselves first within the family. Man learns his greatest fears, loves, hatreds, and hopes within this social unit" (Greeley, 1974, p. 174).

Another set of factors that influences the maintenance of ethnic identity is the group's experience with migration and with settling into this country.

## THE MIGRATION EXPERIENCE

Bean and Tienda (1987) suggested that "one becomes ethnic by virtue of leaving the homeland, and by virtue of one's social status vis-a-vis the dominant majority in the receiving society. Frequently, a common sense of nationality emerges only after immigration" (p. 8). Using this perspective, they suggested that ethnicity is organized and develops around physical and cultural differences. Boundaries between the group and the rest of the society are determined in part by the degree of ethnic and racial antagonism. The sense of ethnicity seems to intensify in the face of hostility. As suggested in Chapter 1, a new social form is developed.

Bean and Tienda conclude that a number of factors contribute to ethnic identity, including (1) the immigration law in effect when the main thrust of migration for a particular group took place, (2) the need for labor in the United States at the time of the group's arrival, (3) the nature of the economy, and (4) the urban spatial and residential structure. In their view it is these kinds of factors more than cultural dispositions that shape the group's eventual adaptation and the development of ethnic group solidarity. They used this framework to compare the migration experience of three groups of Latinos—Mexicans, Cubans, and Puerto Ricans. The Mexicans entered seasonal industries in declining economic sectors. Puerto Ricans, like Mexicans, were poor and uneducated. Neither group was welcomed. Cubans, by contrast, were educated people fleeing a repressive government. The first wave received a hero's welcome. These groups now differ substantially. Puerto Ricans and Mexicans remain among the poorest and least well educated of a number of people who have come to this country from various parts of the world.

Lyman (1986), studying the communities formed by the Chinese, found that by establishing Chinatowns in most of the cities where they settled, the Chinese were creatively adapting the customs that they had brought with them. The Japanese drew on customs acquired at home that counted on their personal characters and individual struggle; thus there are few "little Tokyos." The type of immigrant associations formed by the Chinese in Chinatowns were less important to the Japanese, who measure their group identity in accord with geo-generational distance from their country of origin. There are the Issei, the original immigrant generation; the Nisei, or American-born children of Issei; the Sansei, or American-born grandchildren of the Issei; the Gosei, or American-born great-grandchildren of the Issei; and the Kibei, who are Nisei educated in their formative years in Japan and then returned to the United States. This lets all know where they stand in relationship to their country of origin as well as to the United States. The experience of some other peoples also sheds light on how a group's experience and customs interact with the circumstances found in the larger society to generate a unique set of experiences for each group. Sandefur and Tienda (1988) reviewed the experience of American Indians. There are about 700 tribal entities whose people identify themselves as Native Americans or American Indians. They nevertheless share a long history of discrimination, persecution, and blatant destruction of their people. Westward expansion nearly demolished their way of life. Treated with violence and disrespect, many have nevertheless preserved their cultural traditions through reliance on the family. Although there are many different groups, they share some elements of a common culture. These include an emphasis on harmony with nature, sharing, and cooperation, as contrasted with accumulation and competition, and a respect for age. Their orientation to life is focused on the present. Many of these characteristics are in conflict with the dominant culture.

As many American Indian nations are reclaiming rights to land as well as some governmental powers lost earlier, they have developed major business enterprises. At the same time, they strive to adhere to long-standing, long-valued traditions.

The experience of American Indians casts a somewhat different light on the process of identity formation. Here is a group that was persecuted and attacked, many of whose members continue to experience extreme poverty. Conflict remains between some of their basic cultural tenets and those found in the mainstream of the United States.

This section has focused on the ethnic component of ethclass, examining how it is experienced and what factors contribute to its persistence. The discussion has considered the inequality associated with membership in those ethnic groups that are especially subject to racism and discrimination. It is now time to consider another important concept, one that is intrinsically related to stratification and inequality, that of social class.

## SOCIAL STRATIFICATION, SOCIAL CLASS, AND INEQUALITY

Social analysts differ considerably about the concept of *social class*. Some question whether there really are social classes in U.S. society (Wrong, 1959). Others suggest that social class plays a major role in defining the conditions of people's lives but that these conditions are also intricately connected with ethnic group membership and minority group status (Gordon, 1964, 1988). As has been suggested in earlier sections of this chapter, that is the view taken here.

### Social Inequality

Social class is about inequality. It refers to the fact that some people have more income, find themselves in more highly valued and rewarded occupations, and have more prestige than others. This in turn affects well-being in such respects as health and illness, the ability to exert power and influence to achieve desired ends, the sense of self-respect, and the degree of dignity conferred by others. Differences related to wealth, occupation, and education are generally referred to as social class differences.

### Social Class

The term *social class* usually designates the existence of different social strata. Gordon has suggested that social class refers to the horizontal stratification of a population, related to economic life and to differences based on wealth, income, occupation, status, community power, group identification, level of consumption, and family background. We have suggested (Table 2.1) that each of the major ethnic groups is in turn divided into social class groups. We also have suggested an ethnic ranking system.

## *Indicators of Social Class*

There have been long-standing efforts to delineate the social class system that exists in the United States.

Sociologists have long tried to learn more about what constitutes a social class and the factors that determine whether people remain in or move out of the social class groups in which they find themselves at any one point in time. Warner (1949) made what is now viewed to be a classic analysis of the U.S. class structure and developed the following classification scheme: (1) the upper upper class, composed of old, wealthy families; (2) the lower upper class, whose wealth is newly acquired; (3) the upper middle class, which consists of successful professional and business people; (4) the lower middle class, generally made up of white-collar workers; (5) the upper lower class, those who are thought of as blue-collar workers; and (6) the lower lower class, which includes but is not limited to the unemployed and recipients of public assistance. This classification scheme not only divided people into classes, but in so doing explained the reasons for placing them into particular niches. For example, those in the upper upper class have wealth that has been accumulating in their families for some time. By contrast, people at the lowest level tend not to accumulate wealth of any kind. This scheme makes no reference to the role of education in deterring position in the class structure. Technological changes have increased the need for highly skilled people, especially at the upper levels of society. Education has come to be increasingly important in determining where people are situated in the social class system. Subsequent classification systems (e.g., Hollingshead & Redlich, 1958) used area of residence, the kind of work people do, and how much education they have as criteria for social class designation. A more current classification scheme uses criteria similar to those considered by Hollingshead and Redlich and was presented by Gilbert and Kahl (1987). They suggested that the class structure arises out of the economic system, and they identify three basic sources of income of U.S. families: capitalist property, labor force participation, and government transfers. The second accounts for most of the income available to U.S. households. How much people earn depends in large measure on occupation. Occupation, in turn, depends increasingly on education. Also important are the places where people work: the large, bureaucratized organizations so prevalent in our society, such as the factories, the large corporations, and various segments of government. Combining the factors of source of income, occupation, and educational credentials, Gilbert and Kahl generated what is considered an "ideal type" class structure as follows:

1. A capitalist class of people who derive their income largely from return on assets and who wield extensive power over the nation's economic decisions.
2. An upper middle class of people with university training who are professionals and managers; some of these rise in the bureaucracies and become part of the capitalist class.
3. A middle class of people who tend to follow orders from people in the upper middle class; they have good skills, earn good incomes, feel secure in their situations, and have some hope of moving up out of their present positions.

4. A working class of people who have less skills than do members of the middle class; their work tends to be highly routinized; they are supervised and do manual and clerical work; their income tends to be stable; because they lack educational credentials, their prospect of advancing upward in the hierarchy is limited.
5. A working poor class consisting of people who work in low-skill jobs. They tend to be laborers and service workers; income is limited and below mainstream living standards; the unsteady character of their employment puts them at risk of dropping into the class below them.
6. An underclass consisting of people with limited participation in the labor market. They lack skills, are poorly educated, and have spotty employment records.

In summary, they suggest a model of the class structure based on a series of qualitative economic distinctions. From top to bottom they are: ownership of income-producing assets, possession of sophisticated educational credentials, a combination of independence and freedom from routinization at work, entrapment in the marginal sector of the labor market, and limited labor force participation (p. 347). This classification system readily reveals that social class is a powerful determinant of life's chances.

## *Social Class Distribution: Income, Poverty, Education*

As is to be expected, the population is not distributed evenly into the six social class groups just described. There are more people at the bottom and very few at the top. Gilbert and Kahl (1987) suggested that the capitalist class includes about 1 percent of the population, the upper middle class about 14 percent, the middle and working class 65 percent, and the working poor and the underclass about 2 percent. Important for our consideration is the relationship between indicators of poverty and social class. O'Hare (1988) pointed out that in 1986 the poverty population was 32.4 million. Included in this group are more than 10 million of the working poor people who are either working or looking for work who don't earn enough to rise above the government's poverty index. How applicable these types of indicators are to members of minority groups has been questioned. As early as 1899, DuBois suggested that African Americans should be divided according to two different schemes—one based on family income and the other on "moral considerations"—suggesting that in a scheme based on income alone, many African Americans would fall way down the economic ladder. In his major work on African American families, Billingsley (1968) suggests that social class indicators overestimate the number of lower-class African Americans. Jaynes and Williams (1989) provided related data. Information available for 1985 shows that 40 percent of whites and 26 percent of African Americans over age 25 have attended one or more years of college. Source of income, as we have seen, is also an important indicator. African Americans and whites differ in a number of major areas. One percent of African Americans but 7 percent of whites have some income from stocks and mutual funds, and 21 percent of whites and and 6 percent of African Americans have interest-bearing checking accounts. A less direct indicator that seems to support Billingsley's earlier contentions is that comparing the earnings of African Americans to whites. Although African Americans have made substantial gains relative to whites since before World War II, substantial differences remain. The lowest earners (comparing women and men, African American and white) are African American women.

Some information is also available on other groups. Looking at economic information for eight ethnic groups in California, Jiobu (1988) used a number of categories of employment and ranked a number of ethnic groups by income. With a few exceptions, the rankings were as follows, from high to low: white, Japanese, Chinese, Korean, African American, Pilippino, Mexican, and Vietnamese. People of color, with the exception of the Japanese clearly (at least for the state of California), were the most seriously disadvantaged. For these groups education has not had the expected effect on income. Clearly there is a strong ethnic effect on earnings; this further supports the view presented here and elsewhere that people of color continue to be seriously disadvantaged economically.

The following recent data support this contention. The first focuses on median household income, reported by the U.S. Census Bureau for 1996, distinguishing between various ethnic groups. (U.S. Census, 1997.)

### Median Household Income (1996)

1. All "Races"                    $35,492
2. Whites                         37,161
3. Blacks                         23,482
4. Hispanic Origin                24,906
5. Asian or Pacific Islanders     43,276

These data show marked contrasts between whites and Asians and Pacific Islanders on the one hand, and other people of color on the other. The data on Asians and Pacific Islanders bury some data on some of the Asian groups. Less current data (Jiobu, 1988), referred to above, shows Vietnamese people as having incomes below those of Mexicans, with Pilipinos also ranking low.

These data are also in marked contrast to those showing incomes for the upper segments. In 1996 the lower limit in annual income for the group of whites falling in the top 5 percent income bracket was $122,647 per annum, for Blacks $85,000, and for Hispanics $86,000.

Also important are poverty levels for the same time period.

## Poverty Data for 1996

1. 13.7 percent of the total population was reported as living below the poverty level.
2. A little over 12 percent of the group at below the poverty level live in families.
3. Almost 20 percent of these are related children under age 18.

**4.** 11.2 percent of whites were living below poverty level.
**5.** 28.4 percent of Blacks were in the groups living below poverty level.
**6.** 29.4 percent of the people of Hispanic origin were living below poverty level.
**7.** 14 percent of Asians and Pacific Islanders were living below poverty level.

The data on disparities in well-being, as these are reflected by income, are startling and distressing and remain an ongoing concern for the ethnic-sensitive social worker. There are some more positive signs.

The close connection between education and social class suggests that any increases in educational level, especially in post secondary education, portend well for even the most oppressed group. Recent data released by the U.S. Census (U.S. Census, 1997) show that in contrast to 1965 when only 27 percent of Blacks had completed high school, by 1993 over 70 percent of Blacks had done so, comparing with 81.5 percent of whites. Among Hispanics the rate had risen to somewhat over 53 percent. The college graduate rate for the three groups as of 1993 was 22.6 percent for whites, 12.2 percent for Blacks, and 9 percent for the Hispanic origin groups.

Educational attainment for the Asians and Pacific Islander groups is high, with nearly nine out of 10 members of this group having at least a high school diploma. The rates vary substantially within groups. The Hmong people, among the most recent arrivals, show a rate of eleven percent as compared to 88 percent for the Japanese people who have been here a long time. In 1994 at least 40 percent of this group had a bachelors degree.

## Class and Rank

All that we have just said makes it clear that the highest rankings in U.S. society are assigned to those who perform the tasks most highly valued by U.S. society. These include those people who manage and own major business enterprises, those who play leadership roles in government and education, those who interpret the law, and those who heal the sick. Members of minority groups who perform these valued tasks are considered to be in the upper strata of the society. However, they earn less doing the same work, and they encounter racism as a daily part of their experience.

Those people who perform menial tasks or who are not employed at all and those who take rather than give direction are held in low esteem. These rankings are a reflection of basic U.S. tenets—an emphasis on worldliness, on mastery of nature, and on activism. These basic themes or ways of structuring and ascribing meaning to behaviors are translated into standards of adequacy and worthiness and are the basis for gratification and security.

Much of what is subsumed under the term *social class* is about work and money and the values placed on that work by the larger society. These evaluations are internalized and permeate our lives. The condition of work, its security and autonomy, and the range and type of experiences to which that work exposes us seep into the very core and substance of our being, affecting the way we feel both about work and about what we can or cannot buy with the money we earn. If we earn sufficient money to make meaningful choices about the things we buy, this affects our tastes and preferences in furnishings, music, and clothes. It affects our outlook on the larger world, particularly our perceptions of life's opportunities and constraints. In the view of many, our perceptions of opportunities and constraints derive from class position, which affects family life, attitude toward sex, and extent of involvement in the world of politics and voluntary organizations. Our perceptions affect our views of the education our children receive, our marriages, and the other intimate relationships in which we are involved, as well as the importance we attach to what is happening in the world beyond our daily existence.

## LIFE IN THE VARIOUS SOCIAL CLASSES

### The Working Class

In the previous classification scheme, two categories of the working class were identified. There are those who, like the "blue-collar aristocrats" (LeMasters, 1975), are unionized and well paid. They include construction workers, truck drivers, carpenters, electricians, and others whose work involves considerable decision making. For this group of workers, supervision is loose. For the plumber, a day's work is planned in the morning, and there is no further contact with the central office unless there is trouble. A good carpenter would view close supervision as a reflection on his or her competence. Despite high pay and autonomy, these workers are particularly subject to layoff and to the vagaries of the marketplace. Sick leave and disability provision in union contracts do not allay the fear of layoffs or the worry that benefits will be exhausted. Retrenchment in the automobile industry, occasioned by economic uncertainty, recent economic recessions, and competition from abroad, has shown that these fears are not groundless.

Although automobile workers are well paid and unionized, their work tends to be routinized and repetitive and allows for limited self-direction. Unions have lost ground over the past decade. In this group Gilbert and Kahl (1982) also include salespeople, those people in higher paid service jobs.

Changes are beginning to take place in the life of the assembly worker. Baker and Armstrong (1996) discuss the introduction of computerization and other technologies that require considerable skill and technical knowhow. These call for additional education. There is also less dehumanization and more control over day-to-day work.

> *"Today, life on the line requires more brain than brawn—so laborers are heading for the classroom." (p. 59)*

Milkman reports the same phenomena in her analysis of several sites. However, she is less sanguine about the potential for dehumanizing effects. Her studies of at least one plant suggest that the hoped for autonomy is far from being realized. She also detected some (though by no means universal) tendency for the better jobs to go to whites rather than minority workers.

Over the years there has been much effort to learn something about the relationship between the work people do and their outlook on other spheres of life. Some years ago (Blumberg, 1972) it was suggested that the conditions of working-class workaday life produce responses that prepare people to cope with adversity. Work and limited income restrict the opportunities for participation in spheres outside work and family life. Such an outlook was thought to be consonant with the ethnic-based dispositions of many of the Eastern European "blue-collar ethnics" who occupy this segment of the social class structure. Close involvement with the family, neighbors, the church, and the immediately surrounding community was said to characterize many people of Italian, Polish, and Slavic heritage. Gans's classic study (1962) of working-class life showed a pervasive skepticism and mistrust that extends to doctors, hospitals, and other caretakers. Lack of skill and limited education make working-class people aware that their chances of moving up out of their social class position is limited. More recent analysis has sought to cast some new light on this contention.

Steinitz and Solomon (1986) studied three groups of working-class youth from different communities who shared one major feature. They were the "promising" adolescents who hoped to go and then went on to college. They found that the fears of working-class youth of leaving their accustomed place are well-founded. When they do step out, they continue to see themselves as being worlds apart from the upper-class and upper middle-class students. Behavior intended to increase their upward mobility makes them more vulnerable. "Their experience of lowered status and social rejection during high school, their own rejection of the values of wealthier peers, their parents' relatively low status in their community and inability to understand their children's lives—such realities underlie the belief of these adolescents that the future is uncertain and that there are few moorings to which they can anchor their ambitions" (Steinitz & Solomon, 1986, p. 230).

It has been suggested that working-class people often feel uncomfortable and resentful when they interact with the middle class. Ehrenreich (1989) cited the comments of one steelworker: "As far as I'm concerned I got no use for the intellectual, the so-called expert, who sits around all day dreaming up new ways to control my life" (p. 138).

This distrust of people with considerable education extends to social workers. Their style, their language, and their interpretations of the problems people experience often seem incongruous and unreal to working class people. Ehrenreich suggests that working-class people feel demeaned, talked down to by social workers, and that this generates frustration and hostility.

*God, I hate that woman. She makes me feel so stupid. Seems like everything that I do is wrong—the way I am with my kids, with my husband, even my sex life. She knows it all. Personally, I think her ideas are a little screwed up.*

Much of the analysis reported here is based on studies of "whites" of European background. Considerably more analysis is needed to learn how skilled workers from other groups view these matters.

## The Middle Class

Two segments of the middle class have been identified, the upper, most shaped by formal education (Gilbert & Kahl, 1987), and those below them who are comfortable but tend to follow orders from those in the upper group. Ehrenreich (1989) characterized the upper middle class as the "professional managerial class." The upper middle class consists mainly of professional people—doctors, lawyers, and college professors, as well as journalists, consultants, and factory owners. The lower middle class is a much more diffuse grouping and includes people such as skilled office workers and salespeople, as well as, in the view of some, teachers. In his classic description and analysis of the role of work in society, Turkel (1974) suggested that most middle-class people enjoy the work they do and have a sense of autonomy and control. For the most part, they are positively evaluated by others. They use other middle-class occupations as guidelines as they assess the prestige and value of their work. Money is a concern, and the lower down on the middle-class ladder people go, the more disappointed they are about the discrepancy between their expectations and what they actually do or earn.

As one tries to capture the relationship between the lives of middle-class people, the work they do, and their perceptions of life, a paradox emerges. On the one hand, it is this group that is generally viewed as the "mainstream" of the United States. Middle-class people typify the U.S. virtues of hard work, diligence, thrift, and independence. These characteristics were believed to be essential for those who wanted to climb the prestige ladder. With the decline of small business and the growth of large, bureaucratic organizations, some of the old middle-class ethic has begun to diminish, in reality if not in rhetoric. With few exceptions it is the life of the middle class that is portrayed in daily soap operas, in the movies, and in the mass circulation magazines. The cars, home furnishings, clothing, and jobs portrayed are for the most part those encompassed by the middle-class vision.

These days, that vision portrayed on television includes extensive reliance on technology, as in the ever-present computers, fax machines, copiers, and cell phones to be sold. Importantly, the people shown being engaged in middle-class work are African American, Asian, and Hispanic, as well as white. Many among them are women. The selection of television anchorpersons is clearly reflective of some effort to represent the diverse populations of a region. It is not uncommon to see African American women, Asian women, and Chicano or Puerto Rican women and men occupying important, visible news positions.

As a group, people in the middle class are eager to get ahead themselves, and above all, they value education for their children. Although the African American middle class may differ in some key features from other less demeaned elements of the society, this element of middle-class life is most important to African Americans.

Middle-class people move readily for jobs, are active in voluntary organizations, and rely heavily on the advice of experts for advice on how to rear their children and on how to eat and exercise properly for the purpose of achieving and maintaining good health.

Almost by definition, the true work or paid employment of this class does not involve physical exertion. In fact, exemption from manual labor is the most ancient privilege of the "mental worker," from village scribe to Madison Avenue copy-writer. He or she does not bend, lift, scrub, shovel, haul, or engage in other poten-tially damaging exertions for a living (p. 233).

Although highly valued and appreciated, middle-class people are far from feeling secure. As economic changes began to have a negative effect on all people living in the United States, many of those who would have thought they had a secure place in the middle class began to experience some fear about their status. Not only lower level white-collar employees, but schoolteachers and even higher status professionals and their families "found themselves scrambling to remain in place" (Ehrenreich, 1989, p. 200). Recent corporate downsizing has shaken many middle-class people.

The middle-class clearly occupies a favored place in U.S. society. People are autonomous in their work and are, by and large, highly regarded by others. Yet the nature of their work pits them against equally large segments of the population: the working class, over whose lives they exert considerable control.

People of color who achieve middle-class status usually work very hard to get there. In achieving these positions, they frequently experience a tug and pull between their new status and the position of their people who remain on the lower rungs of the class system.

## The Underclass

The term *underclass* was long used to refer to those people in the society who do menial work and whose work is not highly regarded by almost everyone else. They were the garbage collectors and domestic workers and street cleaners. They were the people who did essential but dirty work for little pay, but who were not appre-ciated by the rest of the society.

The term *underclass* is now used in a number of ways and describes several overlapping phenomena. Gilbert and Kahl's (1987) description is in keeping with their view that class position is determined by a person's relationship to the labor market and the economy. They suggest that members of the underclass participate minimally in the labor force and find it difficult to find regular work because of their limited skills and education. Many are supported by government programs such as welfare. Income from illegal activities is not uncommon. Low self-esteem and long-term deprivation are characteristic. Others (e.g., Katz, 1989) have suggested that many of the members of this group who cannot sustain themselves contribute to the growing numbers of homeless people. Many analysts (e.g., Gilbert & Kahl, 1982, 1987; Glasgow, 1980; Katz 1989; Wilson, 1987) agree that a disproportionately large number of underclass people are also members of oppressed ethnic groups. Recently (Friend, 1994) similar phenomena were being reported in what is being termed the white underclass. By the beginning of the 1980s and even earlier, the term *underclass* came to be used in ways that deflected attention from people's rela-tionship to the economy and the labor market. Increasingly, there was a focus on the racial and behavioral characteristics of certain segments of poor people. Social scientists as well as the media took this stance. In 1977 one prominent popular magazine (*Time*) identified a group "behind [the ghetto's] crumbling walls...socially alien" whose "values and behavior differ sharply from those of other Americans" (cited in Katz, 1989, p. 196). Emphasis was on the high level of delinquency, addiction, and family disruption and on the large number of welfare mothers.

Katz (1989) has suggested that these descriptions were imprecise, pejorative, and controversial. Drawing on his studies of young African American men who had participated in the Watts riots, Glasgow (1980) used the term to mean "a permanently entrapped population of poor persons, unused and unwanted, accumulated in various parts of the country" (p. 3). Like other analysts, Glasgow pointed to the high number of minority people in this group. They are the "static poor, trapped in their situation by a variety of forces, primarily constricted opportunities" and "limited alternatives provide socialization patterns" (Glasgow, cited in Katz, 1989, p. 199).

In 1987, William Julius Wilson, a prominent African American sociologist, published *The Truly Disadvantaged*. Wilson advanced a number of reasons for the emergence of the underclass phenomenon. The themes advanced have sparked considerable debate and controversy.

In making the case for the existence of an urban underclass, Wilson drew on the history of migration, the civil rights movement, and the changing economy. During the first half of the twentieth century, the rate of poverty in urban ghettos was high. It was not until the mid 1970s, however, that the rate of unemployment, teen pregnancy, out-of-wedlock births, welfare dependency, and serious crime reached catastrophic proportions. In his view, an underclass had emerged consisting of

> ...*individuals who lack training and skills and either experience long term unemployment or are not members of the labor force, individuals who are engaged in street crime and other forms of aberrant behavior and families that experience long term spells of poverty and/or welfare dependency. (pp. 7–8)*

Wilson described a series of changes that have taken place in the ghetto neighborhoods to explain the phenomenon. Those people that remain in the inner city are different from their predecessors. Because of the exodus of many working- and middle-class people from the ghetto, present residents interact mainly with one another. They are increasingly isolated from mainstream patterns and norms of behavior. The rate of unemployment is high, as is the number of families headed by women, the rate of out-of-wedlock pregnancy, and the crime rate.

Wilson turns to both recent and past history to explain the situation, citing the civil rights movement, which opened up educational and other opportunities for substantial numbers of African Americans. Those who were not able to use the new opportunities were left behind in the ghettos. The departure of substantial numbers of working- and middle-class people has removed an important social buffer as well as role models who had stressed the importance of education and of visible, steady employment. Now it is less likely that children will interact regularly with people who are employed or with families that have a steady breadwinner. Consequently, they are less likely to develop the job-related skills needed to enter the world of work.

The major features of Wilson's thesis as presented here have been critiqued by many. Among these is a group of analysts whose work was published in a special issue of the *Journal of Sociology and Social Welfare* (December 1989). One member of this group, Billingsley (1989), challenged Wilson's definition of the underclass. He suggested that there is no unique constellation of factors that characterizes this group and distinguishes it from others.

Marks (1989) questioned Wilson's view that in the past the members of the African American middle class served as significant role models, contending that their numbers in the past were too small to have a meaningful effect. Most recently (De Parle, 1990), Wilson himself questioned the appropriateness of using the term *underclass*. Although not abandoning his analysis, he nevertheless believes that the term may be pejorative and take on racist connotations.

Moore and Pinderhughes (1993) edited a volume of studies that sought to determine the applicability of Wilson's thesis, based primarily on analysis of the African American community in what he termed deindustrialized Chicago to various urban Latino communities. They conclude that economic restructuring has contributed to the growing poverty in the Latino communities. However, with the exception of the Puerto Rican communities in New York and Chicago, they do not find the picture to be quite as grim as that described by Wilson. In many communities there are strong ethnic business enclaves, ethnic networks, and a strong sense of community that transcends class lines.

Zelly (1995) challenged the notion that the underclass as described by Wilson, the popular media, and others is truly a class. Referring to the basic dimensions of social class as consisting of education, occupation, and income, he contended that the recent discussion departed from traditional sociological analytic modes; instead he saw the discussion as pejorative, a reaction by those who feel threat to their privileged status. He suggested that the term has no legitimate place in the vocabulary of social stratification. He cited Marion Wright Edelman (1987) of the Children's Defense Fund as follows:

> *References to the "underclass" will add nothing to our understanding of poverty, but will erode public confidence in our ability to do something about it and may reinforce the misguided belief that poverty is the product solely or primarily of individual pathology, ignoring the institutional forces in . . .*

We have presented material on ethnic group membership, on ethnicity, and on the mechanisms thought to sustain ethnic group identification. We also have considered the nature of the U.S. social class system.

## THE ETHNIC REALITY

At the beginning of this chapter, we suggested that the intersect of ethnic group membership and social class, what Gordon termed *ethclass*, generates identifiable dispositions and behaviors. We characterize these dispositions and the behaviors that flow from them as the ethnic reality or ethclass in action. In the preceding sections we suggested some ways in which ethnicity and class are experienced and transmitted and have demonstrated that each has a somewhat distinct and separate effect on the lives we lead. We now consider how the two elements of experience join to generate a unique configuration.

Throughout the preceding discussion, repeated reference has been made to the special oppression experienced by people of color. Racism appears to be endemic in U.S. society. Some groups especially are the objects of persistent discrimination, which translates into low status. Not all people of color are equally oppressed in respect to education and position in the occupational structure and income.

And so it seems that, for the most part, to be a member of an oppressed ethnic group—one of the people of color—means that one will likely encounter racism. For the members of some groups—whatever the historical reasons—the likelihood of being especially disadvantaged and demeaned is especially high.

In preparing to work on this fifth edition, we gave a lot of thought to these matters. We wondered whether our conceptual formulation that focuses on the intersect of ethnicity and social class was sufficient to help us and others to take account of the factor of race and color that so permeates life in the United States. For example, writing in 1989, Jaynes and Williams, in their major work on African Americans (they use the term *Black Americans*), rejected the view that African Americans constitute an ethnic group analogous to ethnic groups of European origin or that similar analytic tools are useful in analyzing the experience of whites and Blacks. They suggested that the "uniqueness of race as an 'irreducible' category has emerged from the...debates" (p. 565). And yet their definition of what they term the category *Black* is not dissimilar to our view of the ethnic reality. Citing the work of others, they suggested that the category *Black* be treated "as a social reality that combines class, ethnicity, cultural heritage, political interests, and self-definition" (p. 565).

Earlier in this chapter we cited recent work that suggests that the term *race* is truly unacceptable, because of its unscientific and pejorative character. By contrast, the term *ethnic group* seems to hold up, as do social class concepts when income data and data on power are analyzed.

We have introduced an ethnic ranking system suggesting (from a conceptual perspective) that ethnic groups can be ranked according to their prestige and dominance. We suggest that people of color occupy the lower ranked positions. We suggest that within each ethnic group, people can be found located in the three major class groups.

We suggest that our view of the ethnic reality, as presented here and in our earlier work (Devore & Schlesinger; 1981, 1987, 1991, & 1995) is sufficient to capture the diverse features that are associated with membership in a variety of racial and ethnic groups. The ethnic rank is part of the ethnic reality.

It is our view that the ethnic reality generates identifiable dispositions and behaviors. These dispositions arise out of (1) a group's cultural values as embodied in its history, rituals, and religion; (2) a group's migration experience or other processes through which the encounter with mainstream culture took place; and (3) the way a group organizes its family systems.

Each ethnic group has a unique history with respect to oppression and discrimination, and each has different emphases and values attached to academic pursuits, to family, to the respective roles of men and women, to the way the elderly are to be cared for, and to the ways in which religious teachings are translated into dictums for daily living.

Social class factors join with factors arising out of ethnic history to give shape to how people will respond to the psychosocial problems they encounter in the course of living.

All groups experience events external to them that affect the way they live, feel, and think. These include the history of slavery for African Americans, the Holocaust and continuing anti-semitism for Jewish people, and the 1915 slaughter of Armenians for that group (Phillips, 1989).

One such event is the women's movement and a closely related phenomenon, the entry of large numbers of women, including mothers of young children, into the labor force. Most cultures have long-standing guidelines for the respective roles of men and women. The importance of male leadership of the family and the man's role as economic provider have long been fairly universal themes found in many groups. How these themes are played out varies from culture to culture. Many Mexican Americans, Puerto Ricans, and Italian Americans, to name a few, find it particularly difficult to make this transition. And the lower the educational level, the more difficult it is for both men and women to depart from conceptions of their traditional roles. However, it is these very people whose economic circumstances are such that both partners of a marital pair must go to work. The literature on ethnicity and family life is replete with examples of how pained both men and women can feel when the men cannot provide for the family in the expected ways. Economic necessity propels many women into the work force. This wrenching experience adds further to the confusion and challenge accompanying the efforts to adapt to a new land. Many recent immigrants from Southeast Asia find this to be the case (Conference, "Enhancing Asian Family Life," New York, April 25, 1986).

Among the other external events that impinge on people with particular force are those kinds of economic changes that are thought to have contributed to the development of the underclass discussed in the preceding section. These changes make it increasingly difficult for young, unskilled African American men to find work. This in turn affects their sense of themselves and their relationships with their women. Unable to fulfill economic roles, many do not form stable family units. And so, too many young African American people who live in the inner-city urban ghettos do not marry. At the same time, their extended family systems, drawing on a long-standing focus on family and community, fill the gap left by the difficulties in forming stable, traditional unions. For those so affected, these factors form a major component of the ethnic reality as they experience it.

The traditions transmitted by the family, the special inflection of language, and the foods we eat let us know we are among our own, whether "our own" are those in the middle class or in the lower strata. For many middle-class people, to be with one's own also means to be with, or to think about, or to worry about people who have not made it. Others worry little and are simply pleased with their success.

There is little doubt that both types of responses are part of the experience of minority people who have made it into the middle class. This is an important part of their ethnic reality. And as they encounter problems in living, helping professionals must remember that the tensions and discomforts related to the ethnic reality are part of the context and substance within which problem solving takes place.

For all those members of oppressed ethnic groups, no matter where they are located in the class structure, the ethnic reality may translate into continuing and persistent discrimination in jobs and housing, poor schooling, and negative reception by the workplace. These factors impact with considerable force on the poor.

Some groups have habits and customs that have served them well in their own groups but that are called into question in the encounter with the mainstream culture. Earlier reference was made to the discordance between some basic tenets of American Indian culture and the competitive, time-oriented U.S. society. American Indians give priority to family, to community, and to helping a stranger who comes along unexpectedly. But when this orientation to life means that people repeatedly come to work late or not at all because they have stopped to help a friend along the way, their jobs are placed in jeopardy. All too often, those very aspects of heritage that have sustained and that are part of a proud tradition do not serve their members well in segments of the society that do not value that heritage. The difference between Asian and other people's view of the family and the individual's role in it are profound. Lum (1992) and others (Ho, 1987) pointed to the importance of the family and the collective. These differences emerge in daily life in the workplace, as well as in encounters with helping professionals.

Members of different ethnic groups with a history of poverty and discrimination move into segments of the middle class at varying rates. When the numbers of a particular group who make this jump are relatively small, those in the new-found position keenly feel the lack of opportunity to interact with others like themselves. For example, the number of university professors who are members of minority groups is small. Consequently, the opportunity to share common experiences is limited and detrimental to the faculty members' morale. Equally important is the potential impact these small numbers have on up-and-coming young minority students who need role models to help them stay in school and to set their sights high. This too is part of the ethnic component of the minority experience.

Although many third- and fourth-generation Italian Americans are rapidly "making it" occupationally and educationally, our informal contacts suggest that tensions between the old and new are still present. Stone (1978) reported on the conflict between ethnic traditions and class- and occupation-related orientations. Career goals have the effect of pulling away from the family toward the world of occupations. But the family seeks to keep the young within its fold, without change. There is a constant tension between the two. The ethnic reality for some Italian Americans manifests itself in the struggle to straddle two worlds.

Not all groups experience these same strains. For many Jewish people, the gap between life in the working class and the move to the middle class was less problematic. "It's very funny. . . . If you were Jewish and working class, people said, 'Oh well, Jews are into books.' But if you're Italian and working class then it's 'how did it happen?'" (Stone, 1978).

Another element of the ethnic reality relates to a group's migration experience. In trying to understand ingrained habits of thought and feeling and action, it is important to remember how a group and its individual members have fared and what feelings about past experience they bring to the present. The encounter with mainstream culture has taken many forms. Some, like American Indians and many Chicanos, view themselves as a conquered people. Others, including the early Anglo-Saxon settlers, fled religious oppression. The nature of their arrival is etched into the core of U.S. history. These experiences, recent for some and an element of the distant past for others, often have bearing on how their members perceive and organize life and how they are perceived by others. Howe (1975) suggested that the earlier generations of Jewish migrants, fleeing oppression and economic hardship, thought it necessary to propel sons and daughters into the outer world, or more precisely, to propel them into the outer world as social beings while trying to keep them spiritually within the Jewish orbit. The sons and daughters of street peddlers, and of "girls" who had worked in the sweatshops of the Lower East Side, were encouraged to become educated. Jews' traditional respect for learning and the particular urban skills in which they had been schooled—a function of anti-Semitism in Eastern Europe, where they were not permitted to work the land (Zborowski & Herzog, 1952)—converged to speed their entry into middle-class America. Fear of physical hurt and anxiety over the sheer pointlessness of play among people so long persecuted seeps into the psyche. Together, these matters become part of the ethnic reality as Jews encounter the vicissitudes of daily living.

After the Japanese attack on Pearl Harbor in December 1941, 110,000 Japanese Americans were removed from their homes and detained in relocation centers. The relocation experience exposed many to work for the first time because discrimination and other factors had prevented many from entering the workplace. The adaptation of the group of Japanese Americans who suffered this racist disruption of their lives has been remarkable. It has been suggested that the relocation experience actually speeded the process of absorption into the mainstream by turning over the leadership in the camps to the second generation at a much faster pace than is usually the case (conjecture based on S. Oniki, personal communication). This experience of relocation and a cultural disposition that places high value on skill, personal character, and living up to the ideal (Lyman, 1986) has contributed to the marked socioeconomic success of a people so recently subjugated.

As we have seen, the sense of ethclass as it has been defined is readily articulated. The nature of work and ethnic heritage do indeed result in persistent and discernible differences in the lives of people of the same social class level who have different ethnic backgrounds.

We have suggested that those who do not speak the mainstream language are tied to their own ethnic groups in ways that provide succor, but at the same time they encounter society with myriad handicaps. This is their ethnic reality. Similar barriers are faced by those with strong commitments to powerful and meaningful cultural values that are not understood or appreciated and that indeed are maligned by the larger society. Among these are many underclass Puerto Ricans. The barriers to full economic and social participation in society experienced by many Puerto Rican people can be understood by reference to the employment situation they encountered on arrival. Proximity to Puerto Rico and inexpensive air fares to Puerto Rico also played a part. Many Puerto Rican people came to New York City at a time when the garment industry in New York was beginning to go into decline. Opportunities that had been anticipated were not as available as many had hoped, thus contributing to unemployment and other economic problems. Because it was so easy to get on a plane and return to Puerto Rico, many Puerto Ricans did not have full commitment to life here. Many Mexican Americans find themselves in a somewhat similar situation.

Encounters with racism are part of the ethnic reality of many people. Pilippinos, Laotians, Chinese, Cambodians, and Koreans all experience racism at some level. Ethnic competition also triggers hostility between groups.

Some of the related tensions are also major tragedies of current life. Black–Jewish disputes in Crown Heights in Brooklyn, New York, and those involving African Americans and Koreans will take a long time to heal. But efforts are under way. The same is true of tensions between some European origin ethnic groups and African Americans, as told by Rieder (1985) as he describes the backlash against liberalism by various white ethnic groups as they tried to hold on to hard-won gains that seemed threatened by the advances of people of color.

There are others whose position within the mainstream is much more firmly established. They are "behaviorally assimilated" in that they speak English, are solidly ensconced in the workplace, and have a greater range of experience with and exposure to the large society's values and goals. However, the work they do is viewed as marginal by much of society, and as they struggle with the reality of that work—its hazards and insecurities—they are viewed as lesser beings. They are the members of the lower working class, whose jobs are relatively poorly paid and insecure. Among them are people of almost all ethnic groups.

Then there are those who have made it—the Hispanic, African American, and Asian academicians and businesspeople, the Pakistani doctors, and the Armenian intellectuals. Their work entails autonomy, economic security, and prestige.

This mosaic of experiences—oppression and renewal, ethnic cohesion and strife—these all constitute the ethnic reality.

As individual members of diverse groups send their children to school, become ill, encounter marital difficulties, and simply live their lives, they bring with them a unique ethnic and class tradition, as well as a personal history within that tradition. As they confront "helpers" or "caretakers," they expect, whether or not they articulate that expectation, that these aspects of their being, what we have called the ethnic reality, will be understood despite the fact that many may be unaware that some of their strengths and tensions are related to this aspect of their lives. Those charged with the responsibility of educating and helping have an obligation to be sensitive to the ethnic reality. An examination of these phenomena has increasingly become part of social work practice.

## SUMMARY

This chapter has reviewed a number of perspectives on the role of ethnicity in American life, including assimilationism and the melting pot concepts, ethnic conflict theory, ethnic pluralism, and ethnic stratification. The authors' view on the relationship between social class and ethnic group membership was presented, and an ethnic ranking system was introduced. Both are thought to exert profound influence on lifestyle and life chances. The point at which they intersect has been termed *ethclass*. We characterize this intersect and the basic dispositions to life related to the convergence of ethnicity and social class as the ethnic reality. The ethnic reality affects dispositions to life such as perspectives on child rearing, sexuality, and the roles customarily associated with gender.

## REFERENCES

Adams, B. N. (1975). *The family: A sociological interpretation*. Chicago: Rand McNally.

Alba, R. D. (1985). *Italian-Americans: Into the twilight of ethnicity*. Englewood Cliffs, NJ: Prentice-Hall, Inc.

Asamooah, Y., Garcia, D., Hendricks, C. O., & Walker, S. (1991). What we call ourselves. *Journal of Multicultural Social Work, 1*(1), 7–22.

Baker, S., & Armstrong, L. (1996). The factory worker in 1995. *Business Week* (September 30), 59–68.

Bean, F. D., & Tienda, M. (1987). The structuring of Hispanic ethnicity: Theoretical and historical considerations. In F. D. Bean & M. Tienda (Eds.), *The Hispanic Population of the United States*. New York: Russell Sage Foundation.

Billingsley, A. (1968). *Black families in white America*. Englewood Cliffs, NJ: Prentice-Hall.

Billingsley, A. (1989). The Sociology of knowledge of William J. Wilson: Placing the truly disadvantaged in its socio-historical context. *Journal of Sociology and Social Welfare, 16*(4), 7–40.

Blauner, R. (1992). Talking past each other: Black and white language of race. *American Prospect 10* (Summer), 55–64.

Blumberg, P. (1972). *The impact of social class: Selected readings*. New York: Thomas Y. Crowell.

Brown, C. (1972). The language of soul. In T. Kochmman (Ed.), *Rappin and stylin' out*. Chicago: University of Chicago Press.

Cohen, S. M. (1988). *American assimilation or Jewish revival?* Indianapolis: Indiana University Press.

De Parle, J. (1990, August 26). What to call the poorest poor? *The New York Times*, p. 4.

Devore, W., & Schlesinger, E. G. (1981). *Ethnic-sensitive social work practice*. St. Louis: C. V. Mosby.

Devore, W., & Schlesinger, E. G. (1987). Ethnic-sensitive practice. In A. Minahan (Ed.), *Encyclopedia of social work* (18th ed., vol.1, pp. 512–516). Silver Spring, MD: National Association of Social Workers.

Devore, W. W., & Schlesinger, E. G. (1987). *Ethnic-sensitive social work practice*. (2nd ed.). Columbus, OH: Merrill.

Devore, W. W., & Schlesinger, E. G. (1991). *Ethnic-sensitive social work practice*. New York: Merrill.

Devore, W., & Schlesinger, E. (1995). *Ethnic-sensitive social work practice*. (5th ed.). Needham Heights, MA: Allyn & Bacon.

Duberman, L. (1976). *Social inequality: Class and caste in America*. New York: J. B. Lippincott.

DuBois, W. E. B. (1899). *The Philadelphia Negro*. Philadelphia: University of Pennsylvania.

Ehrenreich, B. (1989). *Fear of falling; the inner life of the middle class*. New York: Pantheon.

Eitzen, S. D. (1985). *In conflict and order: understanding society* (3rd ed.). Boston: Allyn & Bacon.

"Enhancing Asian family life" Conference, New York, April 1986.

Feagin, J., and Vera, N. (1995). *White racism*. New York: Rontledge.

Friend, T. (1994). The white trashing of America. *New York, 27*(33), 22–31.

Gans, H. (1962). *The urban villagers: Group and class in the life of Italian-Americans*. New York: The Free Press.

Gilbert, D., & Kahl, J. A. (1987). *The American class structure*. Homewood, IL.

Gilbert, D., & Kahl, J. (1987). *The American class structure* (3rd ed.). Belmont, CA: Wadsworth.

Glasgow, D. G. (1980). *The Black underclass: Poverty, unemployment and entrapment of ghetto youth*. New York: Random House.

Glazer, N., & Moynihan, P. (1963). *Beyond the melting pot*. Cambridge, MA: Harvard University Press.

Gordon, M. (1964). *Assimilation in American life*. New York: Oxford University Press.

Gordon, M. M. (1973). *Human nature, class and ethnicity*. New York: Oxford University Press.

Gordon, M. M. (1988). *The scope of sociology*. New York: Oxford University Press.

Greeley, A. M. (1974). *Ethnicity in the United States*. New York: John Wiley & Sons.

Herman, S. (1977). *Jewish identity*. Beverly Hills, CA: Sage.

Herz, F. M., & Rosen, E. J. (1982). Jewish families. In McGoldrick, M. Pearce, J., & Giordano, J. (Eds.), *Ethnicity and family therapy* (pp. 364–393). New York: Guilford.

Hill, R. B. (1986). The black middle class: past, present and future. In Williams, J. D. (Ed.), *The state of Black America* (pp. 43–46). National Urban League.

Ho, M. K. (1987). Family therapy with ethnic minorities. Newbury Park, CA: Sage.

Hodges, H. M. Jr. (1964). *Social stratification*. Cambridge, MA: Schenkman.

Hollingshead, A. B., & Redlich, F. C. (1958). *Social class and mental illness*. New York: John Wiley & Sons.

Hopps, J. G. (1982). Oppression based on color. *Social work, 27*(1), 3–5.

Hopps, J. G. Minorities: people of color 1983–84. *Supplement to the Encyclopedia of Social Work*

(17th Ed.). Silver Spring, MD: National Association of Social Workers.

Howe, I. (1976). *Faith of our fathers*. New York: Harcourt Brace Jovanovich.

Hraba, J. (1979). *American ethnicity*. Itasca, IL: F. E. Peacock.

Hurh, W. M., & Kim, K. C. (1984). Adhesive sociocultural adaptation of Korean immigrants in the U.S.: An alternative strategy of minority adaptation. *International Migration Review, 18*(2), 188–216.

Jaynes, G. D., & Williams, R. M. Jr. (1989). *A common destiny: blacks and American society*. Washington D.C.: National Academy Press.

Jenkins, S. B. (1969). The impact of black identity crisis on community psychiatry. *Journal of the National Medical Association*, September.

Jenkins, R. (1997). *Rethinking ethnicity*. London: Sage Publications.

Jiobu, R. M. (1988). *Ethnicity and assimilation*. Albany, NY: State University of New York Press.

Johnson, C. L. (1985). *Growing up and growing old in Italian American families*. New Brunswick, NJ: Rutgers University Press.

Johnson, R. S. (1997). *The new black power. Fortune*, August 4, p. 46.

Katz, M. B. (1989). *The undeserving poor; from the war on poverty to the war on welfare*. New York: Pantheon Books.

Kibria, N. (1997). The construction of 'Asian-American': Reflections on intermarriage and ethnic identity among second generation Chinese and Korean Americans. *Ethnic and Racial Studies 20*(3), July. 523–544.

Kivisto, P. (1995). *Americans all*. Belmont, CA: Wadsworth.

Krause, C. A. (1978). *Grandmothers, mothers and daughters: an oral history study of ethnicity, mental health and continuity of three generations of Jewish, Italian and Slavic-American women*. New York: The Institute on Pluralism and Group Identity of the American Jewish Committee.

Lee, J. (1996). The empowerment approach to social work practice. In Turner, F. (Ed.), *Social work treatment*, (4th ed.). New York: The Free Press.

Lee, S. M. (1993). *Racial classifications in the U.S. Census: 1890–1990. Ethnic and racial studies, 16* (1). January, 74–94.

LeMasters. E. E. (1975). *Blue collar aristocrats—lifestyles at a working class tavern.* Madison, WI: University of Wisconsin Press.

Lieberson, S., & Waters, M. C. *From many strands: Ethnic and racial groups in contemporary America.* New York: Russell Sage Foundation.

Longres, J. (1982). Minority groups: an interest group perspective. *Social work, 27*(1), 7–14.

Lum, D. (1986). *Social work practice and people of color: a process-stage approach.* Monterey, CA: Brooks/Cole.

Lum, D. (1992). *Social work practice and people of color* (2nd ed.). Monterey, CA: Brooks/Cole.

Lum, D. (1995). Cultural values and minority people of color. *Journal of Sociology and Social Welfare. XXII* (1) March. 59–74.

Lyman, M. (1986). *Chinatown and little Tokyo: conflict and community among Chinese, and Japanese immigrants in America.* New York: Associated Faculty Press.

Marger, M. N. (1997). *Race and ethnic relations* (4th ed.) Belmont, CA: Wadsworth.

Marks, C. (1989). Occasional labourers and chronic want: A review of Wiliam J. Wilson's *The Truly Disadvantaged. Journal of Sociology and Social Welfare, 16*(4), 57–68.

Milkman, R. (1997). *Farewell to the factory.* Berkeley, California: University of California Press.

Min, J. H. (1990, May 19). Opinion piece. *The New York Times,* p. 23.

Mohr, N. (1974). *Nilda.* New York: Bantam Books.

Moore, S., & Pinderhughes, R. (1993). *In the barrios: Latinos and the underclass debate.* Introduction. New York: Russel Sage Foundation. XI–XXXIX.

Mostwin, D. (1973). In search of ethnic identity. *Social Casework.* May.

Norton, D. G. (1978). *The dual perspective.* New York: Council on Social Work Education.

O'Hare, W. (1988). The working poor. *Population Today, 16*(2).

Padilla, F. M. (1993). The quest for community: Puerto Ricans in Chicago. In J. Moore, and R. Pinderhughes (Eds.), *In the Barrios: Latinos and the underclass debate.* New York: Russell Sage.

Phillips, J. (1989). *Symbol, Myth and Rhetoric: The politics of culture in an Armenian-American population.* New York: AMS Press.

Rieder, J. (1985). *Canarsie: The Jews and Italians of Brooklyn against liberalism.* Cambridge, MA: Harvard University Press.

Roger, L. H., & Cooney, R. S. (1984). *Puerto Rican families in New York City: Intergenerational processes.* Maplewood, NJ: Waterfront Press.

Saleeby, D. (1997). *The strengths perspective in social work practice,* 2nd Ed. New York: Longman.

Sandefur, G. D., & Tienda, M. (1988). *Divided opportunities: Minorities, poverty and social policy.* New York: Plenum.

Sandor, G. (1994). *The other Americans.* American Demographics. (pp. 36–42).

Schlesinger, E. G., & Devore, W. Ethnic-sensitive social work practice; the state of the art. (1995). *Journal of Sociology and Social Welfare, XXII*(1), 29–58.

Schumer, F. (1990). Star-crossed. *New York, 25*(13), 30–39.

Sennett, R., & Cobb, J. (1972). *The hidden injuries of class.* New York: Alfred E. Knopf.

Shibutani, T., & Kwan, K. M. (1965). *Ethnic stratification.* New York: MacMillan.

Silberman, C. E. (1986). *A certain people; American Jews and their lives today.* New York: Summit Books.

Sotomayor, M. (1971). Mexican-American interaction with social systems. *Social Casework, 52*(5), 316–322.

Steinitz, V. A., & Solomon, E. R. (1986). *Starting out: Class and community in the lives of working class youth.* Philadelphia: Temple University Press.

Stone, E. (1978). It's still hard to grow up Italian. *The New York Times Magazine.* December 17, 1978.

Turkel, S. (1974). *Working people talk about what they do all day and how they feel about what they do.* New York: Pantheon Books.

Tricarico, D. (1984). The new Italian-American ethnicity. *The Journal of Ethnic Studies, 12*(3), 5–93.

Wallace, R., & Kelly, D. (Executive Producers). (1990). The last gasp. *L.A. Law* [Television Program]. NBC.

Warner, W. (1949). *Social class in America.* New York: Harper Books.

Williams, R. B. (1988). *Religions of immigrants from India and Pakistan: New threads in the American tapestry*. Cambridge, MA: Cambridge University Press.

Wilson, J. (1987). *The truly disadvantaged: the inner city, the underclass and public policy*. Chicago: The University of Chicago Press.

Wrong, D. (1959). The functional theory of stratification: Some neglected considerations. *American Sociological Review, 24*, 772–782.

Yinger, M. J. (1985). Assimilation in the United States: The Mexican Americans. In W. Connor, (Ed.). *Mexican-Americans in comparative perspective*. Washington D.C.: The Urban Institute Press.

Zborowski, M., & Herzog, E. (1952). *Life is with people: The culture of the shtetl*. New York: Schocken Books.

Zelly, E. W. Jr. (1995). Is the "underclass" truly a class? *Journal of Sociology and Social Welfare, XXII*(1) March. 75–86.

Zenner, W. P. (1991). *Minorities in the middle: A cross cultural analysis*. Albany, NY: State University of New York Press.

# 3

# ETHNICITY AND THE LIFE COURSE

*This chapter examines the universal movement of individuals through the life course from entry to old age. The manner of the movement and the response to the stress and strain as well as the joy it invokes are influenced by ethnic group membership as well as social class position. Ethnic groups have time-honored rituals related to birth, the movement into adolescence, and death that serve to reinforce ethnic identity and social status.*

*We will discuss the work of several theorists in relation to their notions of the nature of the movement through time.*

## THE LIFE COURSE CONCEPT

The ethnic-sensitive response to individual movement through time is directly related to the ethnic reality. This consideration suggests that movement will not be as universal as we may have thought. Germain (1990) asked for a reconsideration of the stage model of individual development and suggested the term *life course*. This "refers to the unique paths of development people take in varied environments, as well as their varied life experiences from birth to old age" (pp. 138–139). In addition, the life course concept assumes that individual developmental processes take place in the context of families and other groups and considers the meaning of race, ethnicity, social class, and gender socialization. Sexual orientation and disability are considered as well.

Elder (1978), an early proponent of the life course perspective, refers to the documentation of change within families dating from the turn of the twentieth century. The earliest research in family life cycle experiences was a 1901 study in York, England. Most life course offerings have been developed since 1955; Germain may be included in that number. Elder and Germain pay particular attention to cohort experiences, life span development, life history, and the temporal structure of life events. Elder claims that "life course refers to the pathways through the age-differentiated life span, to the social patterns in the timing, duration, spacing, and order of events" (p. 21).

An African American male born in 1900 experienced segregation, perhaps the Ku Klux Klan, World Wars I and II, the Civil Rights Movement, integration of public schools, and desegregation of the armed forces, and gained the right to vote. An Italian American male born at the same time may have experienced segregation but it was not "the law," he was not segregated in the armed forces, he and his parents could vote, and the civil rights movement may well have called attention to the joy of ethnic group membership.

An individual's life history is embedded in *historical* time. Social workers hear life histories in the assessment process. The query, "tell me about it" invites the life story. Autobiographies of the famous and not-so-famous recount various ethnic experiences. *Breaking the Surface* (Louganis & Marcus, 1996) is an account of the experiences of Greg Louganis, an Olympic gold medal swimmer. Greg was adopted by the Louganis family when he was nine months old. His birth father was Samoan, his mother Northern European, blond and blue-eyed. The adoption agency had difficulty in placing him because of his dark coloring. This complexion brought the taunts of school children who labeled him, "sissy" "nigger," and "retard." They saw his dark skin, heard his stutter, and could not understand his interest in acrobatics. Much later his sexual orientation began to have an impact on his life and lifestyle. HIV/AIDS has become a part of his story as an adult. Ethnicity, sexual orientation, and disability converge in the telling of this life history.

The life histories of Katie Cannon, Charles Ogletree, Toni Scheisler, Tony Earls, Cheryle Wills, and Orlando Bragwell may be found in Sara Lawrence-Lightfoot's work, *I've Known Rivers: Lives of Loss and Liberation* (1994). The six stories present portraits of middle-class African American men and women, a clergy person, a lawyer, academics, and a filmmaker. The book jacket explains that this is a "very all-American tale; the universal story of people growing up and out of their communities of origin toward some uncharted future."

Historical events such as the Great Depression, World War I and II, the Vietnam War, majority community responses to the Civil Rights Movement or the American Indian Movement (AIM)—all part of our collective history—at the same time they are part of the *social time* of many individuals and families.

*Social time* calls attention to the timing of collective life issues in a family group or community (Germain & Gitterman, 1996). Familiar, expected events in life course experiences no longer pertain. We would hope for some assurance of the timing of life events. This surety no longer remains. Children attend preschool and Head Start. Our children do not readily leave home to marry or work; three generations often live in one household with no plans to change the arrangement. Childbearing is postponed as couples, husband and wife, are employed in various occupations. Some will choose not to have children. Still other young people will chose not to marry at all. And, if parents do work, grandparents, traditional caregivers, are employed or busy with their own activities. Adults are found in undergraduate programs, continuing education, or on the way to Elder Hostel events.

Communities may establish their own *social time* through special events: the Westcott Street Fair, the Kwanzaa Celebration, or the Latino Festival. There are community myths about Indian Nations that lived on certain plots of land, or there are stories about early civic events.

A consideration of the expansion of gender crossover acknowledges changes in family roles that have been assigned by gender. Families have been able to establish patterns of child care and household management quite different from their childhood family experiences. Careers in law or medicine are possible for women, or they may choose to drive buses or fly airplanes. Male nurses are as competent and nurturing as female nurses.

Social workers need to understand these changes and the effort it will take for many individuals and families to make the necessary adaptations. Some individuals will find success and others will falter (Germain & Gitterman, 1996). Client experiences in *historical time, individual time* and *social time* will be influenced by gender, age, position in the family, changing family constellations, and the ethnic reality.

## VARIOUS CONCEPTIONS ABOUT THE LIFE CYCLE

The universal movement through life's stages has captured the imagination and attention of many scholars, the most noteworthy being Freud (1916–1917), whose interest was in psychosexual development; Erikson (1950), who explored psychosocial development; Piaget (1965), who examined cognitive development; and Kohlberg (1979), whose interest was in moral development.

Although their emphases varied, all sought to identify those aspects of the life cycle that represent crucial points of change, the kind of life experiences during each stage that promote health and well-being, and the social or psychological factors that impede growth and learning. All touch on the part played by family and society. Most have pointed out that a comfortable progression from one stage to the next takes place when the psychological, physiological, and social tasks or events associated with the preceding stage have been completed in a satisfactory manner. Unlike the more inclusive life course perspective, scant attention has been paid to the experiences of women, the impact of ethnicity or social class, or the historical context.

Logan (1981) accepted the theoretical notion of ego development in all human beings through their life experiences. She also called attention to "the lack of systematic recognition of the effect of race on life experience and its impact on personality development" (p. 47). Her significant contribution is a developmental framework for African American children and youth, and she called for social workers to be aware of the "overwhelming tendency on the part of scholars to minimize the importance of ethnicity and socioeconomic factors in the study of any minority group, especially Black Americans" (p. 51).

The work of Gilligan (1982) presented a major criticism to Kohlberg's (1979) theory of moral development, which was based on work with male subjects. She presented a female perspective on the development of morality, with emphasis on feeling and concern for others that is significantly different from Kohlberg's male moral-judgment view.

Norton (1983) challenged strict adherence to Piaget's (1965) theory of cognitive development, particularly in relation to concepts of "irreversibility" and African American children. Her work suggested that these poor urban children may well be at risk in school systems that do not recognize the validity of the language they bring to the educational experience. Their language models have been as effective as the models of white suburban children. However, the "internal consistency" of the language is different from standard English—the language of the classroom— and less valuable. To recognize the cultural difference is to open the boundaries set by Piaget's cognitive theory.

Anthropologists have called attention to the diverse rituals and meanings associated with movement from one stage to the next. The extent to which these derive from ingrained beliefs concerning the nature of the universe and person-to-person and person-to-God relationships has often been noted (Van Gennep, 1960).

The characterizations presented here begin with a recognition that as individuals move through the life course aspects of their lives, their experience will be determined by physical growth and change related to chronological age, ethnic group membership, and gender.

Much activity is guided by and responsive to the physical changes accompanying childhood, adolescence, adulthood, and old age. For example, it is not possible for children to engage in activities beyond the range of those congruent with their physical and cognitive development. It is because of their physically based helplessness that children everywhere require protection. They are unable to obtain their own food and such protective shelter and clothing as the elements require. Similarly, menarche and menopause set the boundaries for the childbearing period, and aging inevitably signals some decline in physical faculties. Within these broad limits there is, of course, enormous variability.

In our American society, adulthood is a complex stage lasting for several years. The long-idealized nuclear family, the glorification of youth, and the high value placed on autonomy all serve to give a different stamp to the varying periods of adulthood. The early period of childbearing and rearing may be one of excitement and challenge. As children become adolescents and adults, there are shifting role expectations. Activity once cherished—such as protecting and nurturing—may be seen as interference. For these and other reasons, we divide adulthood into several periods. The first of these is emerging adulthood, a time for mate selection and perhaps marriage, as well as for decisions concerning occupation, which will ultimately determine one's social class. This is followed by adulthood, the middle stage, which requires skills in relationships with mates, skills in the nurturing of children to provide them with a sense of ethnic pride and identity, and, most particularly, skills in developing and maintaining a standard of living satisfactory to oneself and one's family. At the final stage, later adulthood, one is confronted by the physiological changes that signal aging. Children once requiring nurture begin to claim their freedom. Aging parents require more commitment, and, upon their death, there is the struggle to grapple with the loss.

Erikson, Freud, and others postulated that each stage of life involves the mastery of a series of psychosexual, psychological, and social tasks. According to

Erikson, if a sense of trust is not developed in infancy, the ability to relate positively to peers, teachers, and others is impaired. The child denied autonomy may in later years lack the sense of adventure that adds much to the fullness of adulthood.

Our perspective incorporates race, ethnicity, and gender as aspects of life course development suggested by Germain (1990, 1994). At the same time, we consider the tasks suggested by life cycle theorists, placing emphasis on how they may be interpreted and defined by various ethnic groups. Focusing on transitional points of the life course as they are bounded by physical growth and change, we identify universal positions in the life course and the accompanying tasks:

I. Entry
  Tasks: Surviving
      Establishing trust

II. Childhood
  Tasks: Developing physical skills
      Acquiring language
      Acquiring cognitive skills
      Acquiring moral judgment
      Acquiring awareness of self
      Acquiring awareness of sex-role arrangement
      Moving out of home into peer group, into school

III. Adolescence
  Tasks: Coping with physical aspects of puberty
      Coping with psychological aspects of puberty
      Coping with sexual awareness/feelings
      Developing relationships with peers of both sexes
      Seeking to achieve increasing independence
      Developing skills required for independent living

IV. Emerging adulthood
  Tasks: Deciding about relationships, getting married
      Deciding on an occupation or career
      Developing sexual behavior
      Developing standards of moral-ethical behavior
      Locating and identifying with a congenial social group
      Developing competence in the political-economic area

V. Adulthood
  Tasks: Relating to peers of the same sex
      Relating to peers of the opposite sex
      Relating to a spouse or companion
      Establishing an occupation or career
      Establishing a home

Bearing and nurturing children
Developing and maintaining a standard of living
Transmitting a sense of peoplehood and the ethnic reality

VI. Later adulthood
    Tasks:  Adapting to physiological changes
            Adapting to the emancipation of children
            Maintaining relationships with aging parents
            Coping with loss of aging parents

VII. Old age
     Tasks:  Combating failing health
             Coping with diminishing work role
             Viewing past with satisfaction
             Passing on wisdom—the ethnic reality

Different people's perceptions and how they move within these stages is subject to enormous variability. Whether children are viewed as small replicas of adults or as emerging human beings, are coddled and pampered or treated matter-of-factly, is often a matter of cultural and class perception. The view of adolescence as the period of preparation for the tasks of adulthood as opposed to one that sees this period as the beginning of adulthood is a matter of historical and group perspective.

The discussion that follows considers movement through the life course in greater detail, placing particular emphasis on the ethnic reality.

## ENTRY

Birth is the initial trauma in the life course. It is the culmination of a process that has been ongoing for about nine months. As male sperm joins with female egg, a child is conceived. The news of pregnancy may be met with alarm, joy, surprise, or fear, anger, or distress. Family and other caretakers must recognize the impact prenatal influences will have on childhood and beyond.

As the fetus develops, preparing for entry, its growth is linked directly to the physical, social, and psychological health and well-being of the adults in the environment. Social class affects the ability of parents or others to provide for the mother's health and nutrition. The impact of illegal drug usage and smoking is significant despite social class. Addicted mothers bear addicted children, mothers who abuse alcohol and smoke excessively discover that these behaviors may be precursors to fetal alcohol syndrome. Mothers infected with the HIV virus that causes AIDS may infect their newborn.

Of particular interest here is that increasingly HIV/AIDS mothers are members of oppressed ethnic groups, notably African American and Hispanic women. Despite the risks listed here the neonate will breathe normally and cry as they complete the birth process.

Having accomplished birth, the infant must rely on those in its surroundings to supply the basic survival needs, which are experienced as the discomforts of thirst and hunger. These discomforts are vague, diffuse, and relieved by others. The process of becoming "hooked on being human" (Prof. Bredemeier, lecture, Rutgers University, 1964) has begun, for the centrality of other beings is conveyed by the fact that relief from discomfort comes only through them. At the same time, the manner in which infants are touched, fondled, and fed says much to them about the emotions of adults: is the infant wanted or merely tolerated? Was the arrival a joy, a disaster, or an event to be neither celebrated nor negated?

The successful experiencing of trust will depend on the manner in which early needs are met by individuals and the group into which the child has been cast. If adults have insufficient food and lack the emotional support needed to cope with the dependent new being, comfort and warmth may be difficult to obtain.

Social class position determines the ability of a parent to supply the concrete needs for nurturance. A prosperous Polish merchant whose shop provides specialty food items in an affluent suburb has ample ability to provide for his infant son. His income is more than sufficient to enable the child to develop in the environment by virtue of the abundance of goods available through his father's middle-class status. The Polish clerk who checks out and bags the groceries in a large supermarket chain is faceless to the many harried shoppers. His job provides a meager income that must be stretched to provide his infant son with the bare necessities. Yet each child has the potential of receiving nurture that comes from the soothing sounds of caretakers, the stroking of skin, or the embrace that dispels discomfort (Winch, 1971).

When the media blare news of the abandonment or killing of a newborn, the inability of the involved individuals to nurture, to welcome, and to guide is highlighted. The fact that such events are newsworthy points to the fact that most groups and individuals celebrate new life and expect new parents to preserve it.

At the celebration of baptism, the Chicano child becomes a member of the church. At the same time, *compadres* of the parents present themselves as caretakers, assuming responsibility with the parents for continuity in the faith as well as in the group. The giving of gifts celebrates entry, and rituals symbolize its importance. Hispanic and European female infants are "marked" by the ceremony of ear piercing. This act identifies them as female, one of the group, and in need of protection. The "marking" of a Jewish male infant through circumcision is a sign of union, a permanent mark that incorporates him into the social group. At the time of celebration, parents are informed of the community expectations for their son. The parents in turn publicly reaffirm their commitment to meet these expectations. There are the themes of joy and pride on the birth of the child (Eilberg, 1984). The gifts given on each of these occasions follow ethnic tradition. They spell acceptance and ethnic continuity.

The preparation for birth and manner of entry into the group derives in large measure from the ethnic reality. The manner of birth relates to a group's beliefs about the nature of the social order, their economic security, and the esteem in which they hold their children. Early on, then, the child's life course—the sources of strength, weakness, and struggle—are evident in the nature of the preparation for and management of the event of birth.

The activities of women during pregnancy are often designed to protect the child from real or perceived danger while in the womb, in the belief that adverse behavior may mark the fetus in some way. In some instances these beliefs and the surrounding rituals are powerful, serve a psychologically reassuring function, and in no way put mother or unborn child at risk. For example, some African American women avoid eating strawberries while pregnant, fearing that the child may be born with a strawberry-shaped birthmark on the abdomen. Other women are careful about certain aspects of posture, believing that if they fold their arms around their abdomen or cross their legs they may cause the umbilical cord to wrap around the baby's neck and cause it to choke.

Other ingrained beliefs and fears may lead to actions that put mother and baby at risk. There are Navajo women who believe that both mother and child are vulnerable to the influences of witchcraft and who therefore keep the news of the pregnancy even from the husband until it is observable (Brownlee, 1978). Wariness of witchcraft may keep the mother from seeking prenatal care, thus risking preventable problems. The African American woman who rubs her stomach with dirty dishwater to ensure an easy delivery or others who insert cobwebs and soot mixed with sugar into the vaginal tract to prevent hemorrhage are placing themselves and their unborn children at risk.

There are genetic factors linked to ethnic group membership over which parents have little control. Tay-Sachs disease and sickle-cell anemia plague some Jewish and African American families. Although found most often in African American families, sickle-cell disease also occurs in other groups, including southern Italians and Sicilians, northern Greeks, and central and southern Asian Indians. The disease is a severe blood disorder in which red blood cells become abnormal in shape, or "sickled," and cannot carry oxygen normally. The disease is usually debilitating and often fatal in early childhood (Schild & Black, 1984).

The Jewish infant affected with Tay-Sachs disease appears normal at birth. At about 6 months of age there begins a progressive mental and physical decline that leads to death in early childhood. Carriers of both diseases, the parents, are usually healthy, showing no signs of the disease, yet their children are at risk due to their ethnic heritage.

For children the major task at entry is to learn to survive in an alien world. The trust that comes from warmth and comfort may be difficult to attain for those who are in oppressed ethnic groups at lower income levels. Social class and ethnicity in these instances deny parents access to the various resources that would guarantee the child a joyful entry.

## CHILDHOOD

At forty-two Joseph Bruchac (1993) recalls his childhood. Although he was raised by a beloved Abenaki grandfather, he can claim Slavic and French ancestry as well.

He could claim other names that identified him more clearly as an Abenaki, he could be known as "Quiet Bear" or *Gah*-neh-go-he-yo, which means "the Good Mind." Raised by older relatives, he was different; in school he wrote poetry and talked about animals as though they were people. Although his grandfather jokingly called him "mongrel," others who made the remark were not joking.

The fourth-grade children whose school experiences are recorded by Greene and Ryan (1967) live in Harlem and East Harlem, New York City. Ricardo, Jesus, Marshall, and Pablo are among the students in Room 33B. As the teacher arrives they are playing handball with Richardo's book. There is yelling and screaming. When there is some calm, the day begins with the salute to the flag, and a review of the days of the week and the months of the year. When the attendance roll is taken, it can be noted that attendance is not perfect, but this is ordinary. Notes from home reveal the quality of life for these children. "You quit make my kid cry, sign, M. Peraro." Other notes give more information about life. "Pedro was out with asthma. The heat was off for three days, we had to go to my sister's house" (p. 11). By the time these African American and Puerto Rican children are five, they have developed a withdrawal smile: eyes down, lips pouting, cheek turned or nestled against the shoulder. Sometimes it is fear or shyness, for the most part it has been learned from older children.

These experiences of childhood are unlike the idealized world of television's Beaver Cleaver or even Bart Simpson. The struggle with the burden of membership in oppressed ethnic groups is debilitating at this early age. As this chapter continues, attention will be paid to other experiences in childhood as children attempt to accomplish the tasks assigned to them within the context of family. These tasks serve to *socialize* the children as they become members of the family, the group, the neighborhood, and the larger society. Parents, primarily mothers, are assigned the role of culture bearers and respond to this assignment in various ways that will influence development at this early stage of the life course.

## The Vagaries of Childhood

### Gender
Children have much to accomplish during this period of development. Sex-specific experiences and assignments begin early. The clarity and experiences vary among ethnic groups. Many Orthodox Jewish girls learn early that they have a particular position in the religious community. Pogrebin (1991) recalls a sign in a New York City community advertising a Talmud course: TALMUD FOR EVERYONE—MEN ONLY. This stands as a reminder of childhood experiences during which she wondered about women being excluded from certain rituals. Under Jewish law, children are obligated to say Kaddish for deceased parents. Sons are obligated, and daughters are not prohibited, but they have been effectively prohibited. The position of women in this religious community is learned during childhood.

### Discipline
An integral part of the socialization of children is to prepare them to act in responsible ways in the family, at school, and in the community. If the established rules

are violated, then discipline is necessary. A study of the discipline styles of African American families adds to our understanding of the experience of childhood for these children. Denby and Alford (1996) discovered that through discipline, sometimes including spanking, parents wished to teach their children responsibility and accountability, to be able to distinguish between right and wrong, and to curb inappropriate behavior before it escalated. They also wished to help their children to learn to be respectful, to abide by rules, and to recognize the consequences when rules are broken.

Other messages were related to the matter of race and racism, a reality that cannot be avoided. They wanted their children to understand that as African American children they must work extra hard because discrimination remains prevalent. Parents recognized the need for children to be armed with survival techniques as they related to race (Denby & Alford, 1996).

### Parents: Mothers and Fathers

The Italian American woman holds an exalted position as mother, and within this role she is to devote herself exclusively to the children. The roles of nurturer and caretaker are ethnic group expectations; it is from this activity that she receives her satisfaction. This devotion and commitment presents rewards of life-long loyalty and devotion. However, this ethnic directive for an exclusive maternal relationship, begun during childhood, presents a barrier at the time of separation.

The elevation of Italian American mothers gives reason to consider the father's relationship with his children and the influence he may have on their development. Johnson (1985) contends that while the mother's role seemed to have a timeless quality, major changes evolve that involve the role of fathers and the dilution of his authority. While he may exercise final judgment in family matters, a father is less likely to instill the fear described in early accounts of Italian families. Children may expect that their fathers will be provider and protector and to have a greater role in child bearing and other activities in the family. This is unlike the experience of his father or grandfather. A father in Johnson's study presented his philosophy on child-drearing, "I tell my children, don't think of 'I' or 'me,' think of 'we' and 'us.'"

Andrew Billingsley's (1993) examination of the enduring legacy of the African American family reveals that by the year 2000 there will be about 3.2 million children. Most of these children will have working mothers. Special effort must be made for adult supervision after school. In the past the extended family, particularly grandmothers, were available, but in the present grandmothers are in the workforce as well.

### Social Class—Poverty

Our presentation of the vagaries of childhood must include those children who by virtue of social class may be found in poverty. They do not have the ability to even approach many of the tasks of childhood enumerated earlier. DuBray (1992) maintains that the homelessness of American Indian adults may be related to early childhood placement in non-Indian homes. These placement decisions have contributed to feelings of alienation, identity problems, mental breakdowns, and alcoholism.

Social service staff members at Cardinal McCloskey Services in New York City explain that the "War on the Poor" has a significant impact on the lives of children and their families (Moore, Watkins, Greaux, & McMurray, 1997). The consequences of this institutional behavior are highlighted by the following vignettes:

> *A Nicaraguan family includes an alcoholic father, a recovering mother, a 40 pound, 10 year old with an eating disorder and an unsupervised five year old. The father collects discarded things on the street to sell. The two bedroom apartment is filthy.*

> *An 18 year old mother of four. The children were placed after the four year old gashed his stomach with a broken TV picture tube which required 10 stitches. The other three children had marks all over their bodies.*

The children who receive services at the Cardinal McCloskey Services suffer from sexual abuse and domestic violence often related to the abuse of drugs and/or alcohol. Parents present themselves as angry, hostile, fearful, and hopeless. These childhood experiences transcend ethnicity; social class is the ethnic reality component that is operational in their lives, not the idealized view of childhood that may be found in textbooks or on television and movie screens.

These poor children, like all children, have much to do and much to learn. Their socialization is a process that occurs within the vagaries of their lives. The positive and negative events experienced in childhood, the skills learned, and the attitudes internalized will be modified as they move through the life course. Children who have been loved, taught, and given a chance to test life without being subjected to family or structurally induced trauma are more likely to be successful and well-integrated human beings, ready for transition to a crucial and perhaps intrinsically dramatic stage—adolescence.

## ADOLESCENCE

The move to adolescence or puberty is both physiologically and socially determined. Although it cannot readily be said that childhood has ended, there are events that are indicative of impending manhood and womanhood. The onset of menstrual flow, development of pubic hair, and breast growth in girls are in large measure public and visible, as are the growth of facial hair and the voice change in boys.

The ethnic response to these psychological and anatomical facts is diverse. In some families and communities these events mark the assumption of the rights and obligations of adulthood. In others, they appear to be treated as unwelcome events for they portend the emergence of physiological sexual capacity and sexual arousal in a social milieu never quite prepared to deal with these realities. Whatever the case, adolescence is a time of continued growth and preparation for the responsibilities of adult life. Social puberty is a concern in our consideration of the ethnic reality, for children move from asexual childhood into a more sexual world in which girls and boys become young women and men.

As the Puerto Rican female child learns the female role by imitating her mother, she receives much affirmation from the entire family. Gradually she takes on more female responsibility in caring for young siblings—the babies—but there is no talk of sex. She gains knowledge from friends with a similarly meager experience and from overheard conversations of adults.

This practice is not limited to the Puerto Rican experience. Talk of sex is taboo among Irish and Italian people as well (Biddle, 1976; Krause, 1978a). Daughters know little of sexual functioning. The limited information that is given is at best mysterious. The education of children in matters related to sex and sexuality is an issue that transcends the ethnic reality and in many communities becomes a source of much tension.

Adolescent women who are mothers must care for their own babies. Many African American teenage women have engaged in sexual behavior that places them at risk: early sexual behavior often with multiple partners without the effective use of birth control; drug abuse; and lack of information on birth control and devices (Ladner & Gourdine, 1992). The tasks of adulthood needed for childbearing and nurturing must be accomplished before the necessary skills have been acquired. More appropriate tasks require coping with physical and psychological aspects of puberty along with developing sexual awareness and developing relationships with peers of both sexes.

Adolescent members of other oppressed ethnic groups have concerns unique to their ethnic reality. Korean adolescents, children of immigrant parents, report that their parents attempt to impose traditional values emphasizing conformity and docility. They sense that their parents do not wish them to express opinions that differ from their own and that they may be critical of behaviors including dating and grooming. In their struggle to adapt to Western ways, adolescents question the Korean values of patriarchy and filial piety as they conflict with values of individualism and self-assertion. Thus, a generation gap begins to develop (Rhee, 1996).

Prothrow-Stith (1991) has defined adolescence as "The Dangerous Passage," a long tunnel connecting two positions in the life course. A child enters the tunnel, an adult emerges at the other end. The processes of adolescence occur inside the tunnel. Four tasks must be accomplished to be healthy, functioning adults as they exit. Each child will have his or her own special trip during which these tasks may be accomplished: (1) separating from the family, (2) forging a healthy sexual identity, (3) preparing for the future, and (4) forging a moral value system.

The ethnic reality influences the manner in which each task is accomplished. There is evidence that separation may be extremely difficult because their parents do not expect that adolescents would want to leave the warmth and protection of the family and the mother (Messina, 1994). As noted earlier, Korean adolescents struggle with the traditional values of their parents and the values they encounter in the larger society. Their parents believe that it is their responsibility and right to make decisions related to the present as well as the future (Rhee, 1996).

No matter what the adolescence experience may be, Prothrow-Stith (1991) reminds us that adolescence is a normal phase of life, not a pathology.

## EMERGING ADULTHOOD

Adolescence sets the stage for young adulthood, a time in the life course during which individuals are expected to direct energies toward the larger society. The potential for intimacy, emotional commitment, and giving to others increases. Decisions need to be made. Questions are posed; some are answered, others are not. Marriage? Career? Education? Each requires an answer. We have indicated that tasks for these young people include deciding about relationships in a congenial social group and sexual behavior within the context of moral-ethical behavior. The ethnic reality's influence in this decision-making process will be tested as children approach young adulthood.

Young African Americans move into this life course position much like their peers in other ethnic groups, full of promise. Those who are prepared will search for success in community colleges, four-year colleges or universities, schools or programs that are preparation for certain technical careers, or interesting entry-level jobs (Billingsley, 1992).

However, many emerging adults have difficulty making the transition from adolescence. Although the majority of young African American males (75 percent) are not in the criminal justice system, the remainder find themselves in the system serving long jail terms, among the underemployed, or unemployed. Discovering that they cannot maintain themselves, they return to live with their parents. Unmarried mothers seek protection in the homes of mothers and grandmothers (Billingsley, 1992).

### The Search for a Mate

Although freedom to select one's own marriage partner is the U.S. ideal, parents continue to influence the decision. They select homes in particular neighborhoods and provide recreational activities that will ensure association with children in families who are "like us." The validity of these residential choices will become evident as young adults begin to locate compatible companions with similar ethnic traditions and experiences. Within this social group one may find a special person who will become a life-long partner.

Clearly the family hope is for a marriage that will provide continuity in traditions and rituals. Although young Korean-Americans are more tolerant of out-group marriage than their parents, they still feel that other Koreans are preferable as spouses (Pyong Gap Min, 1988). Greek families who have been in the United States for at least three generations have relinquished the earlier emphasis on ethnoreligious concerns, and social class considerations become important. Still, those young people who maintain their ethnic identification tend to date and marry within their own ethclass (Kourvetaris, 1988).

Bodine (1972) has observed that within the Pueblo nation the Taos and Santo Domingo have made overt attempts to control the marriages with outsiders and residents on the reservation. The degree of "Indianness" is not to be questioned; rather, the concern is for the examination of strict endogamy in the search for clues to the acculturation of a pueblo and the success of attempts to resist outside pressures.

African American families hold marriage as an ancient tradition. It is valued because it offers expressive and instrumental benefits. Young men and women desire to be married because these benefits are believed to improve their overall life satisfaction (Blackman, 1995).

There is increasing evidence that emerging adults who have been able to come in contact with other ethnic groups at school, at work, or in social situations are likely *not* to marry people who are "like us." A majority of African American women college students reveal that they do not feel pressure from family or friends in relation to the ethnicity of men they date or marry. Only 20 percent of the women in this particular study indicate that they sense pressure to marry within their own group (Porter & Bronzaft, 1995).

The increase in mixed marriages is examined in the popular culture in various ways. James McBride (1997) in the search for his mother's story discovered her Orthodox Jewish heritage. With this she married two African American men and bore twelve children who identify themselves as African American.

In *Beyond the Whiteness of Whiteness: Memoir of a White Mother of Black Sons,* Jane Lazarre (1996) tells the story of her marriage to Douglas White, an African American man. Both were young adults when they met during a strike of public assistance workers against the New York City Welfare Department. Through this protest, both began to develop skills and competence in the political–economic area, a significant task for the emerging adult.

### Emerging Men and Woman

Ethnic dispositions relating to the role of woman as caretaker are questioned as women reevaluate that role. This reevaluation, however, may place them at risk of diluting and losing many of the characteristics that made them "female" and initially attractive to their ethnic male counterparts. Murillo (1978) cited the example of a Chicano male graduate student greatly concerned about his decision to marry a young Chicana woman. He wished her to maintain the old ways, which required her to be devoted to her husband and children, serve their needs, support her husband's actions and decisions, and take care of the home. She opposed this and conflict arose. As emerging adults, both were in the process of preparing for a career, but for the woman, a Chicana, this is a relatively new adventure, the more familiar career being that of wife and mother.

For young Jewish women there is less of a problem. The plan to work continues a tradition established long ago by grandmothers and mothers whose diverse occupations were important to the survival of the family. Jewish tradition more easily accepts employment of women. In the present, however, the emerging Jewish woman has choice. The Jewish value of education is traditional but in the past was more reserved for men. Women now attend college in equal numbers with men but may experience conflict as they make the choice. "As a young Jewish woman I am achievement oriented, committed to individual achievement, accomplishment and career— but, I am equally committed to marriage. What then of my children? If I am to be a responsible mother then I must remain at home with my young children" (Krause, 1978a). Such is the ethnic dilemma shared by Italians and Slavic young women.

A young married Navajo woman expects to hold to the traditions of the past. Her husband is the formal head of the household, but she has as much, or perhaps even more, influence in the family management due to a reverence for matrilineal descent. This tradition provides her with support from the extended family, with her brothers assuming responsibility in the teaching and discipline of their nieces and nephews. Women and men, sisters and brothers participate in the retention of the ethnic reality (DuBray, 1992).

We are reminded continually that young African American males find themselves continually at risk in relation to their peers in other ethnic groups (Gibbs, 1988; Billingsley, 1993; Davis & Beverly, 1991). Gibbs has characterized them as "endangered, embittered, and embattled." Billingsley speaks of murder and young African American men who are the victims, while Prothrow-Stith and Spivak (1992) look for solutions through a community-based prevention project.

Indeed there is statistical evidence and rationales for these experiences. Too often they are revealed on the six and eleven o'clock news. Seldom is there news of the humiliation felt when young men are stopped by the police for being in the "wrong" neighborhood, at the "wrong" time of day or night; when waiters in upscale restaurants give minimal service; and when sales clerks still question the validity of credit cards. Billingsley's (1993) explorations have discovered that young African American men have more positive feelings about themselves than do African American women and feel good about themselves more often as well.

This sense of well-being has led many young men and women into the managerial ranks of major American cooperations. Davis and Watson (1985) have described the experience as, "swimming in the mainstream." The exercise is not a particularly refreshing one; rather there had been, and continues to be, an atmosphere in which race, an important variable in the experience, is not addressed. Within this tenuous environment these emerging adults have learned to make accommodations to the work in the same manner as their white colleagues. The position requires a commitment and necessitates adapting one's personal behavioral style to fit the demands of the system. It is important that the media and societal view of African American young men expands to incorporate the stories of this cohort of young adults. African American men are so much more than persons in trouble with the law, entertainers, sports figures, or politicians.

Competence is essential if young men and women are to enter the political arena. Although Wilma Mankiller was forty years old when she became the first woman principal chief of the Cherokees, the election was a culmination of political activism that had begun earlier when her family was moved from Adair County, Oklahoma, to San Francisco, California, as part of the Bureau of Indian Affairs (BIA) relocation program (Mankiller & Wallis, 1994). Mary Crow Dog (1990), a Lakota woman, became involved in a political movement that changed her personal life as she and other American Indians challenged the federal policy relating to Indian nations. The American Indian Movement (AIM) occupied the offices of the Washington, DC, offices of the BIA. *Lakota Woman* is Crow Dog's story of coming of age politically. Competence was essential if Mankiller and Crow Dog, along with other American Indians, were to make a significant change in federal policy as it intruded on the lives of Native people.

All young adults do not become as committed to social change as did these young women; others remain at the margins looking on. The successful young men and women will be able to move confidently into adulthood ready for the tasks of *generativity.*

## ADULTHOOD

*Generativity,* an aspect of adulthood suggested by Erikson, is primarily concerned with establishing and guiding the next generation; it is a time of productivity and creativity (Erikson, 1950). Generativity is the longest stage in the life cycle, during which individuals assume responsibility for the care of others, primarily through the role of parent, but also in varying career, job, and political experiences.

Children move from entry to adolescence and emerge into adulthood under the supervision of adults. Imparting a sense of ethnicity is a task that is accomplished, for the most part, unconsciously. But in this process children receive a sense of belonging to a special group that has special food, a language of its own, exciting holidays, and celebrations with family and friends; usually there is devotion to a particular religion. For Napierkowski (1976), recollections of an ethnic childhood include a father aware of discrimination against Polish Americans who remained proud of their Polish American identity and openly contemptuous of the "cowardice" of Poles who anglicized their last names. As an adult, Napierkowski has the Polish heritage transmitted by his father. He feels a conscious need to help his children to grow up to be Polish Americans. This means that he is their protector when their names are garbled, when they are called "Polack," or when they are victims of an insensitive Polish joke, an experience that brings a tightness to his chest. To be the bearer of ethnicity is not always a pleasant task. The Polish experience is paralleled by that of Italians, who recoil from the term "dago" or "wop"; Puerto Ricans from "spick"; Asians from "chink" or "jap"; and African Americans from the viciousness of "nigger." As one assumes the role of adult protector and feels increasing pride in this achievement, one realizes that the ethnic heritage held so dearly may be viewed by others as a joke.

Other adult Polish Americans speak of a childhood in which aspects of Polish heritage were set aside in order to become American; for example, the Polish language was not spoken and English was used daily. To speak Polish would call attention to the fact of Polish descent, which might serve as a barrier to upward mobility (Wrobel, 1973). The purpose of this conscious denial of ethnicity is to protect children from the experiences of discrimination. Adults, each in his or her own way, function as protectors of the young from the hidden injuries of ethnicity.

Color, the banner of ethnicity for African Americans, identifies them immediately. Parents become the bearers of ethnicity. Hair that is so often described as "kinky" and "bad" can become a crown of pride and glory. The joy of black hair is in this description: like a bunched-up cloud or dense-packed candy floss with the smell of milky coconut easing through the delicate braids (Roy, 1992). Parental failure to affirm is described in Toni Morrison's novel, *The Bluest Eye* (1972). Pecola wishes for "blue eyes, prettier than the sky, prettier than Alice and Jerry storybook eyes." Such a wish cannot be fulfilled. Unprotected by her parents, she becomes unable to cope with life. Most African American parents understand and do protect their young, knowing that they will not acquire blue eyes. But they know that with blue eyes their children would not suffer from the effects of racism that calls their skin color and hair texture into question.

In addition to protection, there are the tasks of nurture of the young through the provision of basic needs of food, clothing, and shelter. These are provided through the income received from activity in the workplace. The job or jobs and the level of income they produce will determine the social class of the family.

Middle-aged, middle-class African Americans have spent time in adolescence and emerging adulthood investing in an education that has moved them to this level. Both men and women have made this investment despite institutional racism. As adults they marry and together gain a social status that gives them the ability to provide their children with opportunities they missed in childhood. These may include music lessons, recreational activities, and perhaps private schools.

The vigor with which these parents have taken on the tasks of generativity has presented them with a dilemma. They have discovered that with integrated neighborhoods and schools, they must strive hard to guide their children into a strong ethnic awareness. While they provide the better life, they must help their children to "establish a Black identity and pride while they are learning white mainstream cultural values" (Morgan, 1985, p. 32).

Work for many adults is an absorbing experience. Middle-class African Americans manifest the Puritan orientation toward work and success; this striving leaves many with little time for recreation and other community experiences. The regard for work is shared by Slavic Americans, who live to work and who believe that if one cannot work, one is useless. "Work is the capacity for good, not to work lets in bad. Work is God's work, laziness is the devil's work" (Stein, 1976, p. 123). Slavic Americans have labored at almost any employment to be found, but primarily in blue-collar occupations. When both husband and wife work, this joint effort yields a comfortable existence. Efforts to move into the professional ranks may be viewed as more problematical.

It is important to note that ethnicity may discourage certain types of employment. Although employment is not ruled out, the Italian American woman rarely works as a domestic. Such employment in the home of others is seen as a usurpation of her loyalty to the family. Thus, such employment has been left to Irish, German, African American, Hispanic, English, Scandinavian, and French women (Gambino, 1974). The primary responsibility for Italian women is to maintain a home, nurture the children, keep a home that is immaculately clean (a symbol of a sound family), and be attuned to the needs of her husband. Italian women married to Italian men in the present are less likely to work than are women in other ethnic groups. The differences, however, are not significant, suggesting a change in adult role assignments. Socioeconomic status and the ethnic reality will influence the decision to enter the work force, with working-class women more likely to work when their children are older (Johnson, 1985).

The consequence of failure to respond wholeheartedly to the role of nurturer can be seen in the story of one of our Italian undergraduate students. An exceptional student in her thirties, she was proud of her Italian heritage and during her senior year was deeply involved in preparations for her teenage daughter's wedding. However, one year after graduation she appeared at a college function fifteen pounds lighter, with a new hairstyle and a special radiance. In that year she had found employment and separated from her husband. She explained that part of her difficulty had been the energy that it took for her to be the good Italian wife and mother. She added the role of student quite successfully but lost favor in the community. Her children, like many others, disapprove of her new lifestyle and her rejection of their father. But it is her feeling that part of their discomfort is due to her rejection of the Italian way of life that she, as bearer of the ethnicity, had taught them. As culture-bearer she played the woman's role of nurturer, supportive wife, and mother. The comments of family and others implied that she was expected to continue to assume the assigned domestic responsibilities rather than enter higher education, a pursuit left to men. Status was lost when she shifted her interest, resisting the responsibility that is the focus of Italian American life, the family. Her conclusions show considerable insight into aspects of ethnic disposition and move her well along into an understanding of herself (Sirely & Valerio, 1982).

This Italian woman chose to be a single parent, a position of risk. But for many African American women the choice has not been a conscious one. Many assume this head-of-family status by virtue of being widowed or separated from their husband involuntarily, often by the husband's incarceration. Emasculation of the African American male by institutional racism has made him less available instrumentally and expressively to his family. The low-income African American woman, unlike the middle-class woman described earlier, is aware that the woman may become the primary support for her children. This is a role she does not cherish, but she wishes for a more viable family unit (Painter, 1977). Generativity, caring for the next generation, is acted out alone, but not without difficulty. Greater energy is needed to accomplish the universal tasks.

Admittedly, many adults are not sufficiently prepared for marriage and parenthood. Individuals take on these roles without adequate credentials. Subtle messages with clues as to the best behavior have been given but are not always appreciated or even understood.

*Machismo,* in American popular culture, has become a term most often associated with a rugged, aggressive male. Although derived from the Spanish word *macho* meaning male animal or iron tools related to husbandry, it has come to depict rugged, aggressive male behavior, particularly of Latino males. Mayo (1997) offers a view of machismo that has been overlooked as we examine the ethnic reality. We seldom affirm the nurturing, caring, and protective roles of fathers, thereby limiting our appreciation for the ability of these adults to be successful in the adult task of nurturing children.

In a similar light, African American males are continually assumed to be unreliable, shifty, lazy, and criminal. The popular culture, particularly television, has begun to present alternative views of the African American male and his position in the family. Bill Cosby has been a professional father, a physician. Now a more mature Cosby presents himself in retirement. In each family situation comedy he is a respected husband and father; first a physician, then a working class retiree. In neither instance may he be called or thought of as "boy," a racist description of an African American male no matter what his age may be.

Jewish men, like Hispanic men, are expected to protect their women. Adults are expected to marry. Marriage is *mitzvah* (duty); besides procreation it provides companionship and fulfillment. The biblical directives "Be fruitful and multiply" and "It is not good for man to be alone; I will make him a helpmate" legitimize the expectation, but the vow of the groom makes public his intention: "Be my wife in accordance with the law of Moses and Israel. I will work for you, I will honor you, support and maintain you as it becomes Jewish husbands who work for their wives, honoring and supporting them faithfully" (Birnbaum, 1975).

The traditional marriage contract is seen by some as an act of acquisition by the man. The woman's role is a passive and dependent one. The ceremony contains unilateral action on the part of the groom, with the bride's role limited to her silently indicating her consent. In order to circumvent such inequities, many couples write their own contracts, which eliminate some of the problems for women under Jewish marriage law (Schneider, 1984).

Biblical directive again provides clues for appropriate behavior for the Jewish housewife. On each Sabbath eve, the religious Jewish man is expected to remind his wife of these expectations: "She is trusted by her husband, obeyed by her servants, admired by the community, kind to the poor and needy; she cares well for her household and is not idle. And in return her children rise up and call her blessed and her husband praises her" (Proverbs 31:10–31). This passage also gives affirmation to the Jewish tradition of work for adult women; indeed, the work allows for creativity, a characteristic of this adult phase. The directive includes selecting a field and planting a vineyard, making linen garments and selling them to a merchant, taking produce to the market for sale, and making her own clothes. Schneider (1984) added that nothing is said about doing the laundry, raising the children, or participating in any volunteer organizations except in being kind to the poor.

Jewish women have a varied history in the United States in relation to work. One of their significant contributions of generativity was in the organization of the International Ladies Garment Workers Union after the tragic 1911 Triangle shirtwaist fire, in which many working Jewish women lost their lives.

Each ethnic group benefits if there is a tradition that gives support to behavior that is experienced and observed in the present. The ancient Asian tradition of filial piety provides a framework for parent–child relations in Chinese and Japanese families. The directive is for reciprocal obligations from parent to child and child to parent in day-to-day family interactions as well as in major family decisions (Kitano, 1974).

In Jewish and Asian families, men traditionally hold positions as protectors and heads of household. On many occasions African American men seeking the role of protector are denied the role and their manhood. More often the media and literature present them in relation to the things they cannot do in the position of husband and father; they say little about what African American men may be really like, alluding only to toughness and ignoring tenderness (Hannerz, 1969).

## Child Rearing

The intricate day-to-day tasks of child care require much concentration, for the outcome will influence the future. Given the privilege of motherhood, the Slavic American mother's ethnic behavior may deny her children early autonomy by binding them to her, letting them know that they have no mind of their own, no will of their own, no separate existence apart from her. They are expected to be strong, resist adversity, and fight worry, and they begin to understand the importance of work by picking up after their play (Stein, 1976).

A contrasting practice permits the American Indian child more freedom. An Indian child may have available innumerable family members who assume responsibility for care. Parents do not see themselves as figures of authority but as guides or role models. This style, however, has placed American Indian children in jeopardy, for the mainstream interpretation has been that these children are running wild without the care of their parents. Permissiveness, allowing for individual development, is a different but effective way of discipline accepted by the American Indian community. Unfortunately, the American Indian children are in greater jeopardy for, once removed from their families, their experiences prevent the learning of skills necessary in later stages of development.

The Indian Child Welfare Acts of 1978 and 1980 addressed concerns related to the disproportionately large number of American Indian children who were removed from their families, the frequency with which they were placed in non-Indian settings, and a failure by public agencies to consider legitimate cultural differences when working with Indian families. The act reaffirmed tribal jurisdiction over child welfare matters for children living on the reservation, reestablished tribal authority to accept or reject jurisdiction over children living off the reservation, and specified that public agencies are to give preference to members of the child's extended family or tribe and other Indian families in making substitute care and adoptive placements (Plantz, Hubbell, Barrett, & Dobrec, 1989). Progress has been made in implementation of the Indian Child Welfare Act. Indian children's rights to their cultural heritage are being protected better than in the past. The role of Indian parents and tribes in protecting those rights has been strengthened.

In many localities public agencies have attempted to comply with the Act. Some states have passed Indian child welfare legislation and negotiated state–tribal agreements and service contracts. Federal efforts have been limited. Permanency planning in Bureau of Indian Affairs (BIA) agencies is not practiced as well as it is in tribal social services. Children in BIA care remain longer and are less likely to be discharged to family settings. Tribal-based services have been found to have performed well in following standards of good casework practice and achieving family-based permanency for children in out-of-home care (Plantz, Hubbell, Barrett, & Dobrec, 1989). This attention gives greater assurance of child-rearing practices that will give a greater sense of ethnic identity, one that will support continued growth and development.

## *Friends*

For the adult, peer friendships round out one's existence and provide confidants and associates for recreation. The initial source for these friendships is the extended family, followed by members of the same ethnic group, which often means those with the same religious affiliation.

The hierarchy of friendship for the Italian begins with those who are *sangu du me sangu* (blood of my blood); next there are *compari* and *comare* (godparents), who are intimate friends. Few Italians limit their friendships to other Italians. Increasing intermarriage makes this difficult. Respondents in Johnson's (1985) examination of Italian American families found the creation of "Little Italies" distasteful. Childhood experiences in insular communities had limited their exposure to other American values. As a result, 60 percent of those interviewed reported a mixed friendship group. This group and other Italians have close friendships with family, neighborhood friends, and friends from childhood, as well as persons who in earlier times were viewed as *strameri* (strangers) (Gambino, 1974).

*Compadrazo* and *compadres* are terms that identify those Mexican American adults who hold the same status as *compari* or *comare* to Italian Americans. They are godparents and most cherished friends, reliable in times of stress imposed by various insensitive institutions. In times of joy they are available for the celebration, for they are family. Although the Mexican American man has freedom of movement in the larger society, the woman is expected to remain close to the home, and so her friendship group contains her daughters, even after they have gained maturity, and other female relatives, such as cousins and nieces. There is comfort here and the women often become confidantes (Murillo, 1978). In the Polish experience, friends outside of the immediate family may be found in the neighborhood, but they still are not as close as family (Wrobel, 1973).

As adults attempt to find the friendship of others like them, they form ethnic communities, ethnic islands; sometimes these are labeled ghetto or barrio in the negative sense of the word. These may be communities of rejected people who, despite the barrenness of their existence, find a sense of belonging and cohesion that is characteristic of ethnic communities. It is here that adults attempt to maintain their homes; it is here that they find friends and a church. Howell (1973) and LeMasters (1975) suggest that in such a Polish neighborhood a homeowner may work in a local factory while his wife remains at home to care for the children. On Wednesday evenings he bowls in an all-male league, but on most evenings he stops by the local tavern to drink with the other men. On Tuesday his wife occasionally plays bingo, and on Sunday she goes to church (he goes only on special occasions). Their neighbors are their best friends, but they maintain relatively close relationships with their parents, siblings, and extended family and are wary of outsiders. This pattern is found again and again within the ethnic groups we are concerned with. African Americans have long maintained kinship networks that have provided emotional as well as financial resources. Stack (1975), in her study of kinship networks, has established their presence for low-income families, whereas Willie (1974) and Mc-Adoo (1979, 1981) have done the same for middle-income families.

Early Italian communities, often called "Little Italies," served as a place of refuge with family and friends. Immigration patterns were such that the bulk of a community may have arrived in the United States together, reestablishing the home community and the friendships that it maintained. In time, friendships extended into the larger society as jobs became available outside the neighborhood and politics drew Italian Americans into the public arena. Mutual benefit societies and Italian language newspapers presented the possibility of developing friendship outside the family and immediate community (Monti, 1994).

Outside the immediate family circle, the adult task of relating to peers is achieved in the ethnic neighborhood: Chinatown, Little Italy, or American Indian communities in cities or on the reservation. In these spaces families feel at home. The elderly provide the sounds of the language of home; the odors of food associated with ritual and celebration provide comfort. It is here that adults assume the care of two cohorts of the family, the elderly and the young. In this middle ground adults attempt to carry out assigned tasks as they move along their own life course.

## LATER ADULTHOOD

To recognize that one is in later adulthood is to realize that time is in constant motion, and with this movement there are physiological and emotional changes. The climacteric tells women very clearly that their childbearing years are ended. What then will be the life for women whose ethnic assignment was to bear children and care for them? Time has moved them into adulthood and independence, but in many instances the ethnic dispositions permit and encourage a closeness that can be observed by determining the geographical distance. It is not uncommon to find that Italian, Polish, and African American emancipated children and their families remain in the neighborhood. Those who move, perhaps from the city to the suburbs, are seen as far away (Gans, 1962). The telephone is a resource that provides the possibility, daily or weekly, for communication.

The expectation for care of aging parents manifests itself in various ways. To the middle-aged Italian, responsibility for aging parents is an unwritten law, a tie that cannot be broken. The motives for caring range from duty and repayment to love (Johnson, 1985). The tradition of filial piety in Chinese families directs that children, youth, and adults respect and care for aging parents (Yu, 1984).

The work of Chatters and Taylor (1993) has determined that among African American families adult children are frequent providers of assistance to their parents. These findings are consistent with earlier reports that intergenerational support is a characteristic of African American families. This support of the elderly is critical to their sense of well-being.

The sense of generation and ethnicity both remain strong. Most older Americans expect some measure of regard from the younger generation. The passage of time, technology, and lifestyle changes have all contributed to the need for older family members to adapt to a world that, although it holds them in regard, does not respond in the old ways.

## OLD AGE

Old age is a position in the life course to be held with pride. Individuals have lived through historical and social changes. Length of life may be related to health practices and the availability of quality health care. Jews have higher rates of heart problems than do other ethnic groups. Gelfand (1982) related this to social class, the stress of employment, or high-cholesterol diet. The oldest African Americans (over eighty-five years) are more likely to be poor, have four or more chronic conditions, and very serious health problems (Gibson & Jackson, 1992).

As old age approaches, work performed with ease in earlier years becomes a burden. Limitations are obvious. There are those who, recognizing this, would not accept employment if it were appropriate and available. The lack of work may be humiliating for others. Slavic Americans perceive work as good. When many men reach retirement age, changes in behavior may be noted. Rather than admit to aging, which implies incapacity, inactivity, weakness, and dependency, they may attempt to work even more vigorously. This invariably fails. Retirement follows and with it, for many, comes depression, apathy, despair, and assumed uselessness. Time used in the past at labor is used in wandering aimlessly around the home and neighborhood. Once a respected figure, he now becomes dependent, perpetually in motion; his wife and children respond by becoming bossy (Stein, 1976).

Stein posed the possibility that in some instances long-hidden conflicts surface in regard to the retired male's loss of authority, power, and respect, even though there is evidence of almost universal respect for and deference to the aging.

Historical time influences the experiences of elderly persons who immigrated to the United States in the mid-nineteenth century. Among these were single and married Chinese men with a dream of wealth that could be shared when they returned home. A variety of immigration acts, wars, and the fall of China changed the direction of their life courses and they remained in the United States, particularly in Chinese ethnic enclaves, such as Chinatowns. Many older residents of these communities are the single men who arrived in the early 1900s (Kim, 1990).

Kim noted that this first generation continues to live with problems associated with speaking English poorly or not speaking English at all. Many elderly in San Francisco's Chinatown are in poor health, evident by physical limitations and visits to doctors and herbalists. Mental and emotional problems are evident as well.

Elderly American Indians rarely seek help from mental health systems in urban or rural reservation communities. Complaints to professionals are related to physical ailments or ailments that are not immediately identified as psychiatric. The result is that psychiatric problems may be the most difficult diagnostic issue for Indian elderly (Neligh & Scully, 1990).

Evidence of integrity may be gleaned from elderly Indian men, who comment, "Our challenge is great to our people, but so is the dedication of man (and woman) to seek good medicine" (p. 184) and "Indian medicine is a guide to health, rather than a treatment. The choice of being well instead of being ill is not taken away from an Indian person" (Garrett, 1990, p. 180). The practice of Indian medicine promotes a way of life that encourages a focus on wellness and internal harmony of the physical, mental, spiritual, and personal with the balance of family and the environment. These practices have sustained many elderly Indian men and women.

Grandparents often assume strong leadership roles in the extended family that may include aunts, uncles, or cousins. Tradition in the Lakota tribes of South Dakota calls for grandparents to rear the eldest grandchild from infancy. Children benefit from this act of integrity; they are usually responsible adults, with great respect for elders in the community (DuBray, 1992).

Kinship ties among all generations would seem to be a resource, particularly if all are in the same household. Because of the reality of institutional racism, elderly African Americans may reside with children, grandchildren, or great grandchildren without emotional support. The arrangement is necessary, but economic difficulties make for a stressful situation.

Religion plays an important part in the lives of many African Americans. Studies of religious involvement based on the National Survey of Black Americans show that in comparison with younger people elderly African Americans have a higher probability of having a religious affiliation, of attending religious services as an adult, and of being a church member. In addition, they read religious materials, watch/listen to religious broadcasts, pray and request prayer from others. Accumulating evidence suggests that religion is important in maintaining positive mental health by reducing stress and enhancing self-esteem. The church provides personal and emotional support as well as spiritual guidance (Taylor, 1993).

The element of religion distinguishes Jews from other ethnic groups defined by national origin and/or language; consequently Jews may be considered to be a religioethnic group. Within this designation one will find Orthodox Jews, Conservative Jews, and Reform Jews. Orthodox Jews adhere to traditional values, and conservatives hold to traditional values but are more flexible than Orthodoxes in the demands placed on members. Elderly Jews are more often members of Orthodox synagogues. These preferences influence the value systems and interaction patterns of individual Jews (Kart, 1987).

The myth that ethnic communities "take care of their own" clouds the reality of experience in Lebanese American families. Some families follow an ideal traditional pattern, which claims that aging members should be cared for in the context of the extended family. Like the elderly in other ethnic groups, Lebanese Americans strive to remain on their own and care for themselves as long as they can. They would rather that children visit (Shenk, 1990).

In other instances support is expected but is not forthcoming. The elderly expect to hold a viable role in the extended family. Shenk presented the case of Mrs. Khoury, a widow whose expectations for assistance and support are not met. Her son and daughter-in-law provide her with meals, take her shopping, and keep her house in good repair. They do the best they can within the limits of their life-style and job responsibilities. The problem is their inability to meet aging Mrs. Khoury's high expectations. A number of families may be confronted with this problem as attitudes and values of the young Lebanese Americans change and expectations of the elderly remain the same.

Continuity is a fundamental necessity for human life, collectively and individually. The elderly offer continuity in the social, cultural, historical, and spiritual aspects of our lives (Myerhoff, 1978). Knowledge about ethnic dispositions related to death increases. We understand more when urban Native Americans return to the reservation as old age approaches. Many who have lived in cities wish to be buried on the reservation, a desire that is indicative of a sacredness of the land (DuBray, 1992).

Elderly African Americans accept death and are not fearful, sensing that they have completed the seasons of their life. Death may be a reason for celebration; festivity and music become an integral part of the grieving process (Brown, 1990). There are no studies that provide us with the Puerto Rican view of death, but literature, songs, poetry, and art reflect views of death. Attitudes, values, and interpretation of death are present in communities where expressions such as *Que sera, sera* (whatever will be, will be) or *A todos se nos llega la hora* (our time is set) reflect a value of fatalism. Fatalism means the universe and individuals are controlled by exterior forces (Campos, 1990).

Death does not always wait for the end of the life course, but if one is able to survive, the reality is that death usually occurs at the end of the life course. Death may be experienced with integrity or despair, with an acceptance of decline that recognizes the affirmation of the past, or with submission to the forces that seem designed to make life unbearable.

## SUMMARY

In the life course concept, individuals move through life in various ways that are influenced by race, gender, ethnicity, or social class—the ethnicity reality. The concept helps us to understand that life experiences happen within the context of historical, individual, and social time. Tasks assigned to various positions in the life course respond to the ethnic dispositions of each group. This knowledge is essential for ethnic-sensitive practice.

## REFERENCES

Biddle, E. H. (1976). The American Catholic family. In C. H. Mindel & R. W. Habenstein (Eds.), *Ethnic families in America: Patterns and variations* (pp. 89–123). New York: Elsevier Scientific.

Billingsley, A. (1992). *Climbing Jacob's ladder The enduring legacy of African-American families.* New York: Simon & Schuster.

Birnbaum, P. (1975). *A book of Jewish concepts* (rev. ed.). New York: Hebrew Publishing.

Blackman, L. (1995). Marriage enrichment: A potential strategy for promoting marital satisfaction and stability among African Americans. *Black Caucus Journal of NABSW.2* (2), 21–27.

Bodine, J. J. (1972). Acculturation processes and population acculturation. In A. Ortiz (Ed.), *New perspectives on the Pueblos.* Albuquerque: University of New Mexico Press.

Brown, J. A. (1990). Social work practice with the terminally ill in the Black community. In J. K. Parry (Ed.), *Social work practice with the terminally ill: A transcultural perspective.* Springfield, IL: Charles C. Thomas.

Brownlee, A. T. (1978). *Community, culture and care: A cross-cultural guide for health workers.* St. Louis: C. V. Mosby.

Bruchac, J. (1993). Notes of a translator's son. In Riley, P., *Growing up Native American: An anthology.* New York: William Morrow and Company.

Chatters, L. M., & Taylor, R. J. (1993).

Crow Dog, M., & Erdoes, R. (1990). *Lakota woman.* New York: HarperCollins Publishers.

Davis, E., & Beverly, C. (1991). Youth violence: An action research project. *Journal of Multicultural Social Work 1* (3), 33–44.

Davis, G., & Watson, G. (1985). *Black life in corporate America: Swimming in the mainstream.* Garden City: Anchor Press.

Denby, R., & Alford, K. (1996). Understanding African American discipline styles: Suggestions for effective social work intervention. *Journal of Multicultural Social Work 4*(3), 81–98.

DuBray, W. H. (1992). *Human services and American Indians.* Minneapolis/St. Paul: West Publishing Company.

Eilberg, A. (1984). Views of human development in Jewish rituals: A comparison with Ericksonian theory. *Smith College Studies in Social Work, 55*(1), 1–23.

Elder, G. H. (1978) Family history and the life course. In T. K. Hareven (Ed.), *Transitions of the family and the life course in historical perspective* (pp. 17–64). New York: Academic.

Erikson, E. (1950). *Childhood and society* (2nd ed.). New York: W. W. Norton.

Freud, S. (1916–1917). *The standard edition of the complete psychological works of Sigmund Freud.* London: Hogarth.

Gambino, R. (1974). *Blood of my blood: The dilemma of the Italian Americans.* Garden City, NY: Anchor Books, Doubleday.

Gans, H. (1962). *The urban villagers: Group and class in the life of Italian-Americans.* New York: The Free Press.

Garrett, J. T. (1990). Indian health: Values, beliefs, and practices. In M. S. Harper (Ed.), *Minority aging: Essential curricula content for selected health and allied health professions* (pp. 179–191). Health Resources and Services Administration, Department of Health and Human Services. Washington, DC: U. S. Government Printing Office.

Gelfand, D. E. (1982). *Aging: The ethnic factor.* Boston: Little, Brown & Company.

Germain, C. B. (1990). Life forces and the anatomy of practice. *Smith College Studies in Social Work, 60,* 138–152.

Germain, C. B. (1994). Emerging conceptions of family development over the life course. *Families in Society, 75*(5), 259–267.

Germain, C. B., & Gitterman, A. (1996). *The life model of social work practice: Advances in theory & practice* (2nd ed.) New York: Columbia University Press.

Gibbs, J. T. (1988). Young black males in America: Endangered, embittered, and embattled. In J. T. Gibbs (Ed.), *Young, black, and male in America: An endangered species.* Dover, MA: Auburn House.

Gibson, R. C., & Jackson, J. S. (1992). The Black oldest old: Health functioning, and informal support. In R. M. Suzman, D. P. Willis, & K. G. Manton (Eds.), *The oldest old* (p. 321–340). New York: Oxford University Press.

Gilligan, C. (1982). *In a different voice: Psychological theory and women's development.* Cambridge, MA: Harvard University Press.

Green, M. F., & Ryan, O. (1967). *The school children growing up in the slums.* New York: A Signet Book.

Hannerz, U. (1969). *Soulside: Inquiries into ghetto culture and community.* New York: Columbia University Press.

Howell, J. T. (1973). *Hard living on Clay Street: Portraits of blue collar families.* Garden City, NY: Anchor Books.

Jackson, J. S., Chatters, L. M., & Taylor, R. J. (1993). Status and functioning of future cohorts of African-American elderly: Conclusions and speculations. In J. S. Jackson, L. M. Chatters, &

R. J. Taylor (Eds.), *Aging in Black America.* Newbury Park: Sage Publications.

Johnson, C. L. (1985). *Growing up and growing old in Italian American families.* New Brunswick, NJ: Rutgers University Press.

Kart, C. S. (1987). Age and religious commitment in the American-Jewish community. In Gelfand, D. E., & Barresi, C. M. (Eds.), *Ethnic dimensions of aging.* New York: Springer.

Kim, P. K. H. (1990). Asian-American families and the elderly. In M. S. Harper (Ed.), *Minority aging: Essential curricula content for selected health and allied health professions* (pp. 349–363). Health Resources and Services Administration, Department of Health and Human Services. DHHS Publication No. (P-DV-90-4). Washington, DC: U. S. Government Printing Office.

Kitano, H. II. L. (1974a). *Japanese Americans* (2nd ed.). Englewood Cliffs, NJ: Prentice-Hall.

Kohlberg, L. (1979). Revisions in the theory and practice of moral development. *New Directions for Child Development, 2,* 83–87.

Kourvetaris, G. A. (1988). The Greek American family. In C. H. Mindel, R. W., Habenstein, & R. Wright. *Ethnic families in America: Patterns and variations.* New York: Elsevier.

Krause, C. A. (1978a). *Grandmothers, mothers, and daughters, An oral history study of ethnicity, mental health and continuity of three generations of Jewish, Italian and Slavic-American women.* New York: The Institute of Pluralism and Group Identity of the American Jewish Committee.

Krause, C. A. (1978b, June). Grandmothers, mothers and daughters; especially those who are Jewish. Paper presented at the Meeting on the Role of Women, American Jewish Committee.

Ladner, J. A., & Gourdine, R. M. (1992). Adolescent pregnancy in the African American community. In R. L. Braithwaite & S. E. Taylor, (Eds.), *Health issues in the Black community* (pp. 206–221). San Francisco: Jossey-Bass.

Lawrence-Lightfoot, S. (1994) *I've known rivers: Lives of loss and liberation.* Reading, Mass: Addison-Wesley Publishing.

Lazarre, J. (1996). *Beyond the whiteness of whiteness: Memoir of a white mother of Black sons.* Durham: Duke University Press.

LeMasters, E. E. (1975). *Blue collar aristocrats: Life styles at a working class tavern.* Madison. WI: University of Wisconsin Press.

Logan, S. L. (1981). Race, identity, and Black children: A developmental perspective. *Social Case work, 62*(1), 47–56.

Louganis, G., with Marcus, E. (1996). *Breaking the surface.* New York: Penguin Books.

Mankiller, W., & Wallis, M. (1994). *Mankiller: A chief and her people.* New York: St. Martin's Press.

Mayo, Y. (1997). Machismo, fatherhood and the Latino family: Understanding the concept. *Journal of Multicultural Social Work 5* (1/2), 49–61.

McAdoo, H. P. (1979, May). Black kinship. *Psychology Today,* pp. 67, 79–110.

McAdoo, H. P. (1981). Patterns of upward mobility in Black families. In H. P. McAdoo (Ed.), *Black families.* Beverly Hills, CA: Sage.

McBride, J. (1997). *The color of water: A black man's tribute to his white mother.* New York: Riverhead Books.

Messina, E. G. (1994). Life span development and Italian-American women. In J. Krase & J. N. DeSena (Eds.), *Italian Americans in a multicultural society.* Stony Brook, NY: Forum Italicum.

Meyerhoff, B. (1978). *Number our days.* New York: A Touchstone Book, Simon & Schuster.

Monti, D. J. (1994). The working and reworking of Italian ethnicity in the United States. In J. Krase & J. N. DeSena (Eds.), *Italian Americans in a multicultural society.* Stony Brook, NY: Forum Italicum.

Moore, J. G., Watkins, L., Greaux, M., & McMurray, B. (1997). The war against the poor and repercussions for an agency's child welfare service. In *Crises in health and social services.* *"IMPACT" 97* Human Services Council of New York.

Morgan, T. (1985, October 27). The world ahead. *The New York Times Magazine,* pp. 32, 34, 35, 90, 92, 96–99.

Morrison, T. (1972). *The bluest eye.* New York: Pocket Books, Holt, Rinehart & Winston.

Murillo, N. (1978). The Mexican American family. In R. A. Martinez (Ed.), *Hispanic culture and health care: Fact, fiction, folklore* (pp. 3–18). St. Louis: C. V. Mosby.

Myerhoff, B. J. (1978). A symbol perfected in death: Continuity and ritual and the life and death of an elderly Jew. In B. J. Myerhoff & A. Simic (Eds.), *Life career–aging: Cultural variations on growing old* (pp. 163–206). Beverly Hills, CA: Sage.

Napierkowski, T. (1976). Stepchild of America: Growing up Polish. In M. Novac (Ed.), *Growing up Slavic in America.* Bayville, NY: EMPAC.

Neligh, G., & Scully, J. (1990). Differential diagnosis of major mental disorders among American Indian elderly. In M. S. Harper (Ed.), *Minority aging: Essential curricula content for selected health and allied health professionals* (p. 165–177). Health Resources and Services Administration, Department of Health and Human Services. DHHS Publication No. HRS (P-DV-90-4). Washington, DC: U. S. Government Printing Office.

Norton, D. (1983). Black family patterns: The development of self and cognitive development of Black children. In G. J. Powell (Ed.), *The psychosocial development of minority group children* (pp. 151–167). New York: Brunner/Mazel.

Painter, D. H. (1977). Black women and the family. In J. R. Chapman & M. Gates (Eds.), *Women into wives: The legal and economic impact of marriage.* Beverly Hills, CA: Sage.

Piaget, J. (1965). *The moral judgment of the child.* New York: The Free Press.

Plantz, M. C., Hubbell, R., Barrett, B. J., & Dobrec, A. (1989). Indian child welfare: A status report. *Children Today, 18*(1), 24–28.

Pogrebin, L. C. (1991). *Deborah, Golda, and me: Being female and Jewish in America.* New York: Crown Publishers.

Porter, M. M., & Bronzaft, A. L. (1995). Do the future plans of educated Black women include Black mates? *Journal of Negro Education 64* (2) 162–170.

Prothrow–Stith, D. (1991). Adolescence: The dangerous passage. In Human Behavior Faculty of Boston University School of Social Work (Eds.), *Readings in human behavior and the social environment.* New York: American Heritage–Custom Publishing Group.

Prothrow–Stith, D., & Spivak, S. (1992). Homicide and violence: Contemporary health problems for America's Black community. In R. L. Braithwaite, & S. E. Taylor (Eds.), *Health issues in the Black community.* San Francisco: Jossey-Bass.

Pyong Gap Min. (1988). The Korean American family. In C. H. Mindel, R. W. Habenstein, & R. Wright (Eds.), *Ethnic families in America: Patterns and variations* (3rd ed.) New York: Elsevier.

Roy, L. (1992). If you know black hair. In M. Busby (Ed.) *Daughters of Africa: An international anthology of words and writings by women of African descent from ancient Egyptian to the present.* New York: Pantheon Books.

Rhee, S. (1996). Effective social work practice with Korean immigrant families. *Journal of Multicultural Social Work 4*(1), 49–61.

Schild, S., & Black, R. B. (1984). *Social work and genetics: A guide for practice.* New York: Haworth.

Schneider, S. W. (1984). *Jewish and female: Choices and changes in our lives.* New York: Simon & Schuster.

Shenk, D. (1990). Aging in a changing ethnic context: The Lebanese-American family. *Ethnic Groups, 8,* 147–161.

Sirely, A. R., & Valerio, A. M. (1982). Italian-American women: Women in transition. *Ethnic Groups, 4,* 177–189.

Stack, C. B. (1975). *All our kin: Strategies for survival in a Black community.* New York: Harper Colophon Books, Harper & Row.

Stein, H. F. (1976). A dialectical model of health and illness: Attitudes and behavior among Slovac-Americans. *International Journal of Mental Health, 5*(2), 117–137.

Taylor, R. J. (1993). Religion and religious observances. In J. S. Jackson, L. M. Chatters, & R. J. Taylor (Eds.), *Aging in Black America* (p. 101–123). Newbury Park, CA: Sage Publications.

Van Gennep, A. (1960). *The rites of passage.* London: Routledge & Kegan Paul.

Willie, C. V. (1974). The Black family and social class. *American Journal of Orthopsychiatry, 44*(1), 50–60.

Winch, R. F. (1971). *The modern family* (3rd ed.). New York: Holt, Rinehart & Winston.

Wrobel, P. (1973). Becoming a Polish American: A personal point of view. In J. A. Ryan (Ed.), *White ethnic: Their life in working class America.* Englewood Cliffs, NJ: Prentice-Hall.

Yu, L. C. (1984). Acculturation and stress within Chinese American families. *Journal of Comparative Family Studies, 15*(1), 77–94.

# 4

# THE LAYERS OF UNDERSTANDING

*This chapter presents examples of social work practice that illustrate how knowledge, values, and skills converge, forming the layers of understanding. These layers include (1) an awareness and positive response to social work values, (2) basic knowledge of human behavior, (3) knowledge and skill related to social welfare policy and services, (4) insight into one's own ethnicity and its influence on one's perspective, (5) an understanding of the impact of the ethnic reality on daily life, (6) a knowledge of the various routes to the social worker, and (7) the adaptation of strategies and procedures for ethnic-sensitive practice.*

## BLENDING KNOWLEDGE, VALUES, AND SKILLS

Social work practice has been called a creative blending of knowledge, values, and skills (Johnson, 1995). The three provide a foundation for ethnic-sensitive practice. Much of social work knowledge is drawn from disciplines in the social sciences: sociology, psychology, and anthropology. Political science and economics make contributions, as do the natural sciences.

The values of the social work profession have been codified in the Code of Ethics, which serve to guide practice behavior with colleagues and clients, responsibility to employers and the profession. Skills and procedures used for intervention must be grounded in these values and others that grow from them. We present cases to illustrate how the creative blending of knowledge, values, and skills supports ethnic-sensitive practice.

### A Mother's Struggle

*Brenda Baker, a 35-year-old African American single mother, lives with her 10-year-old-son Tom in a welfare hotel. The walls are stained and dirty, giving scant evidence of earlier grandeur. The Bakers have two rooms but only a hot plate for cooking; meal preparation is limited.*

*Brenda and Tom moved to the hotel 2 years ago. Brenda has a BA degree and worked full-time until she experienced an emotional crisis and lost her job and home. Even though she can work, jobs are scarce and her health is a barrier.*

*Tom is frightened by other tenants in the hotel, the noise, and the drug use. He dislikes school, where teachers seem to avoid the "hotel kids." Brenda's mother, sisters, and brother live in another part of the city, but there is little contact. Tom's father, an underemployed alcoholic, has no contact. Brenda enrolled Tom in an after-school program at a nearby YMCA. She hoped that he would be able to play there and find a caring environment. The group worker, concerned about Tom, suggested that Brenda see a social worker in the family division of the YMCA.*

Miss Baker followed the suggestion from the group worker and made an appointment at the YMCA Family Division. When she met the social worker, she brought her particular perspective on Tom's problem and her own. Her view is influenced by her personality, life course position, family of origin, views about work and education, and response to illness as well as economic stress. She has had little experience with social services except as a recipient of public assistance. This has shaped her expectations for the client role. The social worker brings a professional perspective, recognizing Miss Baker's hope for insights into Tom's trouble in the hotel and at school. Knowledge of community resources will go a long way toward helping mother and son find a home that will give them a sense of comfort and well-being. The professional perspective consists of seven components, which we term the layers of understanding.

1. Social work values
2. A basic knowledge of human behavior
3. Knowledge of and skill in using social welfare policies and services
4. Self-awareness, including awareness of one's own ethnicity and an understanding of how it may influence professional practice
5. The impact of the ethnic reality upon the daily life of clients
6. An understanding that the route taken to the social worker has considerable impact on the manner in which social services will be perceived and delivered
7. Adaptation and modification of skills and techniques in response to the ethnic-reality

These components continue to be considered basic to professional social work practice. They are in congruence with the Code of Ethics and statements of social work purpose. We discuss them here in order to highlight their basic thrust and suggest additional dimensions required for ethnic-sensitive practice. The situation of Brenda and Tom Baker illustrates how and why these layers must be incorporated into ethnic-sensitive practice.

## LAYER 1—SOCIAL WORK VALUES

The foundation values of social work practice continue to be scrutinized (Reid & Popple, 1991). Although there is stability in the core values, they are not static and must be responsive to emerging social, political and economic developments. For example, the impact of acquired immune deficiency syndrome (AIDS) forces us to confront our values. This disease challenges our notions of confidentiality, of public versus individual rights, and considerations of the common good. Expanded computer technology threatens the whole area of confidentiality and requires that we recommit ourselves to people's well-being and to the identification of new strategies that enable us to act on these commitments.

Social work values have been the subject of considerable discussion (see Reamer, 1995). Although analysts differ in their emphasis, there is a common base. Reamer (1995) points to the following: value of individual worth and dignity, respect for people, valuing people's capacity for change, provision of opportunity, meeting common human needs, commitment to social change and social justice, and equal opportunity. Also stressed have been respect for diversity and equal opportunity. Levy's formulation (1973) is particularly relevant to the conceptions embodied in ethnic-sensitive social work practice.

His basic formulation focuses on (1) values as preferred conceptions of people, (2) values as preferred outcomes for people, and (3) values as preferred instrumentalities for dealing with people.

The first focuses on orientations about the relationships between people and their environments, the second on the quality of life and beliefs about social provision and policy designed to enhance the quality of life, and the third on views about how people ought to be treated.

The first guides to us viewing Brenda Baker as a person of intrinsic value with the capacity to grow and develop the skills necessary for coping with her present family situation as well as with problems that will present themselves in the future.

These values recognize that individuals such as Miss Baker have a responsibility not only to themselves but to the larger society as well. At present, her participation in the larger community is marginal, due to the stress related to unemployment and inadequate housing, yet her potential remains. The special importance of this value lies in the recognition of the particular uniqueness of each individual. We will see how the ethnic reality and other characteristics make Miss Baker "special" in her own right.

The second set of values involves the familiar areas of self-realization, self-actualization, and equality of opportunity. Miss Baker's social worker and other members of the profession must continually affirm individual and group struggles for growth and development. It is our contention that the ethnic reality sometimes enhances the struggle. At other times societal biases present impediments.

The final category focuses on the importance of treating people in a way that maximizes the opportunity for self-direction. Stereotyping and prejudgment of Brenda Baker as an irresponsible single parent limits her possibility for self-direction. Irresponsible persons need guidance to take charge of their lives. As the social worker incorporates this value, Miss Baker can be assured of practice that encourages her participation in the helping process.

The newly revised *Code of Ethics* (1996) identifies the acquisition of "cultural competence" as an ethical standard (Standard 1.05, p. 9, 1996).

# LAYER 2—BASIC KNOWLEDGE OF HUMAN BEHAVIOR

Understanding of what is termed "human behavior and the social environment" has long been considered essential knowledge for social work practice. Most recently the Council on Social Work Education has identified a number of areas that must be covered in the curricula of all undergraduate and graduate programs of social work education.[1] These include theories and knowledge related to human biopsychosocial development, knowledge of the range of social systems, and understanding of the interaction among biological, social, psychological, and cultural systems.

Also noted are those areas of inquiry and knowledge that identify the factors that facilitate or hamper human achievement, maximum health, and other aspects of well-being.

Many theories and concepts are thought to aid in explaining human behavior, the kinds of problems that are brought to social workers and that are thought to explain human change processes.

A number of these theoretical formulations are, in our view, especially useful for those who seek to bring an ethnic-sensitive perspective to their work.

## *Individual and Family Life Course Considerations*

An awareness of the significance of varying behaviors that occur from birth to old age enhances the possibilities for success. At the same time it is essential to be alert to the tasks assigned to families as they move from joining together to the launching of children and moving on to new adult roles. Attention must be focused on the fact that Miss Baker is approaching middle age, with apprehensions that accompany movement to that stage of life. Her family life course position is difficult. Single parents with young children assume all parenting roles. For many this is a formidable task. Tom must fulfill the physical, cognitive, and moral judgment tasks of childhood. This is not easy, and he has difficulty in the school setting. Brenda has assumed the tasks related to Tom's adolescence given the absence of his father. Instrumental tasks have been difficult; the hotel is not the home she had hoped to provide. When she was employed she was able to provide a suitable home. Illness changed her life chances and her ability to fulfill instrumental tasks. However, expressive responsibilities can be more easily accomplished, and her concern for Tom leads her to seek out social workers in the Family Division of the local YMCA. Professionals there may be expected to respond to the purpose of social work as they help Miss Baker to develop greater competence and to increase her problem-solving skills and coping abilities while they seek resources that will enable this small family find more suitable housing (National Association of Social Workers, 1981).

---

[1]Curriculum policy for master's degree and baccalaureate degree programs in social work education, adopted by the board of Directors, Council on Social Work Education, 1994.

## Social Role Theory

Knowledge of the concept of social role adds greater vitality to our understanding of the Baker family (Germain, 1991). In most families, members are assigned to roles related to age, gender, and other positions in the family. Particular behaviors are assigned to each of these roles, and when different roles are not complementary, problems can be anticipated. Individuals are often expected to fulfill roles for which they have few skills or are assigned more roles than they desire to manage. This appears to be the case with Brenda and Tom Baker. Data collection will no doubt reveal problems related to family life course position that call for Miss Baker to be mother/nurturer. She has no one to help her with these roles, although her family is not far away geographically. The role of protector is forced upon her given the danger of the hotel environment. The burden of these roles and the inability to carry them out successfully led Miss Baker to take the advice given by Tom's group worker.

## Social Systems Theory

The incorporation of social systems theory into the practice of social work has provided a means by which we can gain a clearer perspective of the reciprocal influences among individuals, families, groups, and the environment. Garbarino and Abramowitz (1992a) have provided an ecological systems map that gives a picture of the connections between individuals and families, the church, the school, peer groups, and the systems that they represent. The worker with this ecological systems view is aware of the physical environment as well as the impact of social, economic, and political forces. Understanding the concept of the family as a social system gives greater insight into Miss Baker's family (Garbarino & Abramowitz, 1992b). It must be understood that the family changes as it moves through time. Its members are seen as less interdependent, with the behavior of each affecting the behavior of others. Tom's distress causes his mother to be uncomfortable as well.

As a boundary-maintaining unit, the family supported itself financially until it had to turn to public assistance; the boundary was opened to allow for this transaction, which placed them in the hotel. Attempted transactions with employers have not been successful. Each transaction required new behaviors, which have been acquired and used appropriately. The stressful situation continues as Miss Baker attempts to perform the tasks needed to maintain a balance in her family system.

## Sociological Theory

Sociological theory consists of a broad and diverse body of theories focused on the study of social behavior. Many of the theories and concepts commonly used by social workers stem from sociology. These include theories about the nature and functioning of society, studies of the family, studies of "deviant behavior," studies of culture and ethnicity, studies of health and illness behavior, and many others. The basic theoretical conceptions on which this book is based, as spelled out in

Chapter 2, derive from classic sociological conceptions about social class, ethnicity, and the effects on people when those different ethnic and class backgrounds meet, as in the case of immigration or in neighborhoods or in the workplace and family.

## Psychological Theories

Social work has long relied on a number of theories thought to explain psychological functioning, human development, and the processes that lead to some of the problems in living with which social workers aim to help people. The list is long and can only be touched on here.

### Psychodynamic Theories

Early in its history as a profession many social workers thought that psychoanalytic theories—those concepts also known as Freudian theory—would be extremely useful in social work's quest to try to understand people. This body of theory includes Freud's well-known conception of the psychosexual stages of development, the view that all human beings are governed by an id, unknown and uncontrollable impulses; the ego, that aspect of human functioning that is in basic contact with the world; and the superego, akin to conscience.

    This body of theory has come under considerable criticism and its usefulness has been challenged by many sources. Vocal among the critics are advocates of the poor, feminists, people who are strongly committed to the view that theories of practice must be empirically supported, and others. Nevertheless, some of the basic conceptions associated with psychodynamic perspectives have seeped into the very core of professional functioning. In Chapter 5 we briefly turn to the area of nonconscious aspects of human behavior and the importance of understanding how culture seeps into aspects of functioning usually not within people's awareness.

    It is important that social workers become knowledgeable about this body of theory so that they can use it when useful and develop their own perspective on this body of thought.[2]

### Egopsychology

Longres (1995) reviews key components of ego psychology. Ego psychology derives from classical psychoanalytic formulations as developed by Freud. The classical Freudian formulation emphasized the conflict between the id and the ego, and psychosexual development as involving an intrinsic conflict between the individual and society. Another area deals with the conflict-free aspect of the ego and is focused on adaptation and coping.

    The concept of "ego defenses" as "intrapsychic processes operating unconsciously, which are employed to seek relief from anxiety" (Longres citing Polansky,

---

[2]For a more extended and most useful discussion of this subject especially as developmental theory, see John Longres, *Human Behavior in the Social Environment*, 1995. Itasca, IL: F. E. Peacock Publishers, pp. 413–420.

p. 422) has been employed by the ego psychologists. They are said to be ever present and to be used by everyone. Included are the commonly used concepts of regression (returning to an earlier state of feeling or behavior to avoid present anxiety; this takes place out of conscious awareness) and projection (attributing uncomfortable or unacceptable thoughts or feelings to others). Also included are the concepts of displacement—displacing unacceptable feelings about one person onto another—such as displacing negative feelings toward a member of the family on someone close but outside the family such as a valued teacher, and sublimation (transforming negative thoughts or actions into those with a more positive connotation; examples are taking part in physically violent sports instead of battering a wife or other partner).

Many of the concepts associated with coping are identified with ego psychology. These include various components of coping and developing competence to interact effectively with the environment. Important in this connection, especially in our focus on ethnic-sensitive practice, is the view that competence is not merely a set of personal attributes but a result of transactions between people and their environments. The nature of the environment and the extent to which it supports competence is critical.

There are, of course, many other theories of human behavior, especially those that have relevance to a life span perspective, including Piaget's theory of cognitive development, object relations theories, and learning theories. Longres (1995) also identifies theories explicitly focused on women and other oppressed groups.

In introducing this section on psychological theories, we have already made reference to the considerable criticism leveled at some of these, especially at psychodynamic concepts. Yet, it is not unreasonable to suggest that each of these can be of value as social workers seek to aid persons like Brenda Baker, whose situation we presented earlier.

It does not seem unreasonable to consider the possibility that Brenda Baker has many negative feelings about her past and present situation that are out of her awareness. How useful it would be to assess her situation in classical psychoanalytic terms is questionable. It does seem that much of her difficulty stems from illness, from a stratification system in a society that tolerates homelessness and the type of racism to which she, no doubt, has been subjected. However, the concepts of ego psychology—with their emphasis on the transactional components of coping—can be extremely helpful in work with Brenda Baker focused on identifying her sense of vulnerability, those areas in which she has managed to retain some strength, and to focus on these in psychological as well as environmentally focused interventive efforts.

## *Domain Specific Theories*

To this point we have identified many, though by no means all, of the major theories that have been used by social workers as a way of understanding the situation of their clients and the social and environmental systems in which their clients function.

There is another level, or type of theory, with which social workers need familiarity. These are the theories that are specific to the domain or substance of the problem under consideration. For example, in later chapters in this book we focus on issues of immigration, of the family, and on health care. Each of these areas, as well as others embedded within them, entails theories to help to explain and guide our assessment and intervention. Much thinking about how people respond to illness is infused by a concept termed *health and illness* behavior that helps us to identify some of the ways people cope with illness, and importantly, how people of different ethnic and class groups vary in their reaction to illness, loss, and pain. Indeed, each of the specialized practice areas dealt with in the closing chapters of this book, as well as many that are not covered, have developed a rich body of knowledge about the response of members of diverse groups.

## *LAYER 3 — KNOWLEDGE AND SKILL IN AGENCY POLICY AND SERVICES INFLUENCE PROFESSIONAL PRACTICE*

Miss Baker's meeting with the social worker was preceded by her request for services. This was handled by a receptionist, who gave her a date for an appointment. It was at this initial meeting that intake occurred, enabling the Division to assist her. The Family Division of the YMCA provides services for participants in YMCA programs and their families. Their particular concern is with family problems that inhibit the growth of children and adults who come initially for recreation and educational programs. They offer no financial assistance. Miss Baker used to receive that kind of help from the Assistance for Families with Dependent Children (AFDC) program. Having determined that services could be provided, the Division assigned Miss Baker a worker so that the services could begin. The organizational aspects of the YMCA and their Family Division have already begun to influence Miss Baker's experience. The worker, too, is influenced by structure, goals, and functions. Recognizing this, a worker must become aware of the ways in which the organization may constrain as well as facilitate effective practice. The worker may deem a visit to the hotel essential, whereas Division policy may discourage visits into welfare hotels. In order to provide needed services, the worker must recognize and use those organizational resources that facilitate practice. These may include funds that enable Miss Baker to extend her search for employment beyond walking distance. She will surely need to do this now, since the new welfare law insists recipients look for work.

Unwittingly, Miss Baker has entered a complex social service bureaucracy. It is made up of a variety of units, subunits, and individuals whose tasks are assigned in relation to their position in the Division hierarchy. Johnson (1995) described the distinctive qualities of a social service agency as having the goal of caring for people rather than producing a product. In the caring process, goals are set for changes in knowledge, beliefs, attitudes, and skills. However, it is difficult to measure the outcome of the helping process or the work of the Division.

The major component of the Division is the core of professional persons who function with a degree of autonomy and commitment to the client. This may at times conflict with the classic, efficient functioning of organizations. Miss Baker may expect a professional social worker to assist in ways that will bring about significant changes in her life. The social worker hopes to find supports within the system to aid the process. Tom's group worker may be expected to contribute some of the support that will be needed.

The Division provides a supervisor who will assist in decision making regarding services to Miss Baker. A consultant may be available to advise in areas where the social worker and supervisor need greater insights and support. The structure of the YMCA demands a professional director and a lay board. The Family Division is but one of the components in the YMCA structure. Its work will reflect decisions of the board concerning its mission, structure, and budget. Miss Baker may be unaware of the structure and its influence, but the worker must be aware of the structure as well as the organization's interdependence with other community agencies. Miss Baker already has a relationship with the public welfare agency. During the course of the helping process, contact with the public school may be a reasonable expectation, as is contact with other agencies that might supply additional services for mother and son.

Knowledge of policy and services available in the YMCA and the Family Division helps the social worker to carry out professional responsibility in ways that enhance Miss Baker and Tom's chances to restore equilibrium in their lives.

## LAYER 4—SELF-AWARENESS, INCLUDING INSIGHT INTO THE IMPACT OF ONE'S OWN ETHNICITY

The 1958 working definition of social work practice proposed that workers have knowledge of themselves, "which enables them to be aware of and to take responsibility for their own emotions and attitudes as they affect professional function." Time has not changed the need for such awareness.

Self-awareness is essential because the disciplined and aware self remains one of the profession's major tools that must be developed into a fine instrument. The beginning of the honing process is the heightening of self-awareness, the ability to look at and recognize oneself—not always nice, and sometimes judgmental, prejudiced, and noncaring. Self-awareness is the ability to recognize when the judgmental, noncaring self interferes with the ability to reach out, to explore, and to help others mobilize their coping capacities. Self-awareness involves the capacity to recognize that foibles and strengths may trigger our tendencies for empathy or destructiveness. And it refers to the ability to make use of this type of understanding to attempt to hold in check those narcissistic or destructive impulses that impede service delivery.

Although self-awareness is considered essential for practice, educators acknowledge difficulty in "teaching" it. Hamilton (1954) identified self-awareness in social work practice as attendant learning; when pursued as an object in itself it becomes more elusive. It must be "caught." How, then, does one catch it?

In an attempt to teach self-awareness, Schulman (1991) presented procedures for self-understanding. An exercise entitled "Getting at the Who of You" poses three questions:

1. Who am I?
2. Who do others think I am?
3. Who would I like to be?

The exercise that follows has been designed to enable students to begin to consider these questions. The actual process involves a lifetime, and the answers change continually during a professional career. Answering these questions taps students' ability to recognize with some accuracy their perceptions of themselves, the perceptions of others about them, and their dreams of what they might be.

The initial question, "Who am I?" must move from a superficial one, which would identify the various roles assumed, to a level at which it is expanded to "Who am I in relation to my feeling about myself and others?" This subjective question has the ability to bring hidden feelings to the surface. Answering these questions is part of catching self-awareness. It grows from within and has been described as a process midway between knowing and feeling. One may be aware of something without being able to describe it (Grossbard, 1954).

Crucial to this process is social workers' awareness of their own ethnicity and the ability to recognize how it affects their practice. "Who am I in the ethnic sense?" may be added to the original question, followed by, "What does that mean to me?" and "How does it shape my perceptions of persons who are my clients?"

The childhood experience of a social worker and the aspects of her experiences growing up in an ethnic setting points out how such experiences will influence practitioners who have begun to answer the "Who am I?" questions:

### Childhood Experience of a Social Worker

*I am the youngest of two daughters born to middle-class, first-generation Jewish parents. I was born and raised in an apartment house in Brooklyn, New York, where I remained until I was married at 20 years of age. The neighborhood in which I lived consisted predominantly of Jewish and Italian families. Traditions were followed, and young children growing up fulfilled their parents' expectations. This was a very protected environment in one sense in that, until high school, I did not have contact with people other than those of Jewish or Italian ancestry. However, Brooklyn was then a relatively safe place to live, and, at an early age, I traveled by bus or train to pursue different interests.*

*Reflecting back, I think of both my parents as dominant figures in my growing up. My father, a laborer, believed in the old work ethic, working long hours each day. However, when he came home life centered around him. My mother and father raised my sister and me on love, understanding, and consideration for others, allowing me flexibility to discover my own self.*

*My parents were simple people. Religious ritual played a minimal part in their life. They did not even go to synagogue on the High Holy Days, although my mother fasted on Yom Kippur, the Day of Atonement, and fussed because my sister, father, friends, and I insisted on eating.*

*But the family was most concerned about their fellow Jews in Europe, and the fate of Israel was eagerly followed on radio and television.*

*There was no question that I identified as a Jew. When I dated non-Jewish boys, my mother could not help but show her concern on her face.*

*Thinking back on this, I realize that, without much verbalization, my parents conveyed a strong sense of family, derived strength—and some pain—from their identity as Jews. I realize now that when I see Jewish clients who are in marital distress, or where parents treat children with lack of consideration, my "gut reaction" is negative and judgmental.*

*Without ever having been told so in so many words, I realize that I grew up with the sense that that's not how Jews are supposed to be. And somehow, in realizing that "my own people" don't always shape up to ideals, I also begin to realize who I am in relation to other kinds of people. For I recognize that just as I approached "my own" from a dim, somewhat unarticulated perception of what "they were supposed to be," I was viewing others in the same vein.*

*"Textbook learning" about African American people, or Chicanos, or Chinese people was not sufficient to overcome the effects of media or other experiences. I began to both "think and feel through" my reactions.*

When workers begin to "think and feel through" the impact of their own ethnicity on their perception of themselves and others, more is involved than the particular ethnic identity. What emerges is a total perception of "appropriate" family life roles.

## Dual Ethnic Background

Earlier discussion addressed the increase in intermarriage between racial and ethnic groups. Persons who may share the same religious backgrounds but different ethnic histories, as well as those with a totally different religious heritage, marry and establish new families. The social worker who has a partner of another ethnic background or is the child of such a marriage has more ethnic influences to consider. The answer to "Who am I in the ethnic sense?" becomes more complex. The following account by a social worker is illustrative:

### Dual Ethnicity in a Social Worker

*My father is Irish Catholic and my mother German Lutheran. I identified with the Irish ethos to some degree because, first, my father was the dominant member of the family; secondly, my religion was Catholic (our parish church was staffed by Irish clergy). There was little contact with my mother's family because disapproval of her marriage kept them at a distance. External social pressures tended to force identification with paternal ethnicity, as my name was Irish. Though of course I realized I shared an Irish heritage, I don't remember ever having a feeling of a shared future with the Irish as a group.*

*I in turn married a man whose background was overwhelmingly Italian, in spite of a French great-grandmother. My children have no ethnic identification that I can perceive. St. Patrick's Day is just another day; Columbus Day is a school holiday.*

When social workers of dual heritage begin to think and feel through the impact of ethnicity on their perceptions of themselves, they may return to an earlier question: "Who am I?" The pervasive influence of an Irish Catholic heritage did not in this particular instance carry with it the sense of peoplehood with a shared future. In the background there is the lost German Lutheran heritage, the loss imposed by the rejection of a daughter who would not marry within the ethnic tradition.

Workers who have little sense of ethnic identification must realize that for many others ethnicity is a force that shapes movement through the individual and family life cycle and determines appropriate marriage partners, language, certain dietary selections, and the various subtleties of daily life.

Miss Baker's social worker must consider the "Who am I?" questions as work proceeds, asking, "Who am I in the ethnic sense, and does that influence my practice in any significant way?"

A heightened self-awareness and a greater awareness of ethnicity as it influences the personal and professional life form this fourth layer of understanding.

## LAYER 5—THE IMPACT OF THE ETHNIC REALITY

It must be recognized that ethnicity is but one of the many pieces of identifying information necessary for assessment in any approach to practice. We know Miss Baker's age, gender, marital status, and employment status and that Tom, age 10, is her only child. His response to hotel living and school are the immediate problems. This additional ethnic data enables the worker to establish the Baker's eth-class and the dispositions that may surround that juncture.

Miss Baker's lack of employment and her present status as a recipient of public financial aid place her family firmly in a lower income position. Her ethclass—low-income African American—has no power. Its occupants work at unskilled, low-paid employment, are underemployed, or receive public assistance. They are often the victims of institutional racism and discrimination.

It is a difficult position for Miss Baker. She earned her BA degree and was employed in business. She was able to provide a middle-class life for herself and her son. Despite evidence that African American families value kinship and will provide support (Staples & Johnson, 1993; Williams & Wright, 1992), Miss Baker seems to be abandoned by her family.

African American families' investment in higher education speaks to their strength and understanding of education as a tool of empowerment (Williams & Wright, 1992). Brenda Baker understood this and still holds her degree as a tool that may be used in the future to change her ethclass position.

Still she is powerless at the moment. She is unable to provide a safe environment for herself and her son. Young Tom is oppressed, as are many other African American children, male and female. Miss Baker and other parents must protect their male children from the potential insults of racism heaped on young African American males. They must provide them with as many viable coping techniques as possible to help them develop maturity and creativity that will strengthen them and enable them to work their way through environmental situations with dexterity (Ladner, 1972).

In this ethclass environment, children must be responsible for their own protection. African American children at the middle- and upper-class levels can expect greater protection from their parents. This is not the case with Miss Baker. Her strengths are used up by tasks that help her to survive in a welfare hotel. The social worker must assess institutional resources in relation to their responses to Miss Baker and Tom and must be aware that children's responses to their ethnic reality involve the development of sophisticated coping mechanisms not always understood by the larger society.

Tom, in his own way, struggles with the role of protector. His mother is at risk in the hotel. He must leave her every day to attend school where he is not welcomed. The only place where comfort may be found is at the YMCA.

The impact of the ethnic reality on the daily life of clients is evident at all positions in the individual and family life course and in any environment in which they may find themselves.

## LAYER 6—AN UNDERSTANDING THAT THE ROUTE TO THE SOCIAL WORKER HAS AN IMPACT ON HOW SOCIAL SERVICES ARE PERCEIVED AND DELIVERED

Social work theoreticians continue to stress the need to focus on problems as perceived and defined by clients. This is in response to some aspects of past practice, in which worker rather than client definitions were given major attention in problem solving. In the view of many theoreticians, psychodynamically oriented workers are particularly prone to emphasize "nonconscious" factors and to minimize those concerns consciously articulated by clients. Miss Baker asks for help with Tom, who is fearful in the hotel and having problems in school. An assessment may suggest that she is looking to young Tom for support that would have come from his father or a husband, or that the problem may come from an inability to adapt to changing situations. In either instance, this is not the problem for which Miss Baker is seeking help. Problem definition reflects the current aspects in Miss Baker's life situation that sustain the problem. We know of her life as a single parent, the loss of employment, the need to apply for public assistance, and the move into a welfare hotel.

Another area of concern in past practice is a certain degree of paternalism. The assumption is made that the worker's definition of the problem is more legitimate, more valid than the client's. In this sense, problems are sometimes attributed to clients that they neither experience nor articulate.

Consider the following possibility. When Miss Baker turned to the public assistance agency, she wanted financial assistance to support her through unemployment and illness. In the assessment phase the worker assumes that the problem is Miss Baker's lack of parenting skills as a single mother with a developing 10-year-old. This can be "corrected," however, by participation in a counseling group for mature single mothers.

This is not an uncommon assumption. Indeed, Mullen, Chazin, and Feldstein (1970) carried out a major investigation to test whether intensive professional services would decrease rates of disorganization presumed to be associated with entering the welfare system. Reid and Epstein (1972) have grappled with these and related issues by making the distinction between attributed and acknowledged problems.

In their view, Miss Baker should receive counseling only if she feels the need for it or if Tom is in trouble. If the latter is the case, social control, not an intervention function, would be exercised.

This is an important distinction that highlights the need at this layer of understanding to work with people on issues they define as important. Nevertheless, the continuing discussions about the distinction between real and presenting problems and the debate about the difference between attributed and acknowledged problems does not fully address the reality. People get to service agencies through various routes. Their problems, for the most part, are very real. Whether they perceive the social worker as a potential source of help in the terms defined by social work practice is another issue. Much service is rendered in contexts that have a coercive or nonvoluntary component. This is illustrated by a continuum of routes to the social worker that range from totally coercive to totally voluntary requests for service (Table 4.1).

As Table 4.1 shows, whether involvement with social work services is voluntary or coercive is in large measure related to the context in which service is rendered or to what is often termed the social work field of practice. This does not

**TABLE 4.1 Routes to the Social Worker**

| Routes to the Social Worker | Clients | Fields of Practice |
|---|---|---|
| Totally coercive | Clients assigned by the courts to probation, parole, or protective services | Child welfare Corrections |
| Highly coercive | Welfare clients expected to enter job training or counseling in order to maintain eligibility; person assigned to drug rehabilitation center or Job Corps as an alternative to jail | Public welfare Corrections |
| Somewhat coercive | Patient involvement with hospital social worker for discharge planning; student in interview with school social worker to maintain child's presence in school; client in alcohol treatment program suggested by employer | Health services Schools |
| Somewhat voluntary | Husband entering marriage counseling at wife's request | Mental health Family services |
| Highly voluntary | Family enters into treatment at the suggestion of the clergy | Mental health Family services |
| Totally voluntary | Individual presenting self for family counseling; individual in psychotherapy | Family services Private practice |

negate the fact that there are voluntary and coercive elements in all fields of practice. Elderly patients in nursing homes may request help from social workers; by the same token, many people, such as Miss Baker, seek family counseling under stress.

In addition to the components of practice depicted in the table, there are others, including outreach, social work–initiated community development activities, and certain preventive efforts to combat problems identified by professionals rather than articulated by clients.

There are clear-cut differences in the initial approach to the client–worker encounter related to the variations along the coercive–voluntary continuum. These differences relate to whether intervention is mandated by legal authority; encouraged or required by the workplace or by the needs of various social institutions such as hospitals, nursing homes, schools, and the family; or prompted by individual discomfort. Additional work has further illuminated these distinctions and related practice strategies. Epstein (1980) referred to "mandated target problems" as those that originate "with a legal or social authority, whether or not the client is in agreement. . . . Mandated to act in a certain manner [implies] that there is an obligation placed on the client and the agency to change a situation by retraining or curbing identified actions" (p. 112). Legislation, actual or threatened court orders, professional opinion, or public opinion as to negative behavior are the source of mandated behavior changes.

Epstein's (1980) view is related to our conception that those who we would term "somewhat" coerced or "somewhat" voluntary are unlikely to work on problems as they are identified by typical referral sources. For these reasons, the problems as perceived by clients such as Miss Baker should be the central focus of the intervention process. If a totally coercive or legal mandate is at issue, as is the case with a person on parole or an abusing parent, work on the mandated problem should be accompanied by efforts to work simultaneously on issues identified by the client.

Professional perspective on the origin or solutions of problems affects the initial client–worker encounter. A structural perspective would focus on environmental rather than individual change (Wood & Middleman, 1989). Activities designed to change environments are not easily classified as coercive or voluntary. They often involve the assumption of professional responsibility for populations at risk.

The route to the social worker takes many forms. Whatever the route, working with problems in terms identified by clients is an essential layer of understanding and a dictum of ethnic-sensitive practice. The initial worker–client encounter, wherever it falls on the continuum, must focus on efforts to help clients formulate the problem in terms manageable to them.

These perspectives point to the range of possibilities for expanding the scope of client-directed self-direction, even under the most adverse authoritative conditions. For Miss Baker and other voluntary clients, the potential for using the momentum generated by the process of seeking help is considerable. This is suggested by a body of evidence that has linked the act of help seeking to accelerated problem-solving capacities (Reid & Epstein, 1972).

It is clear that many people become involved with social welfare delivery systems, whether or not they acknowledge a problem. Given this, we propose the following formulation:

1. Initial problem definition and formulation is in large measure related to the route to the social worker.
2. Regardless of the route, the social worker's responsibility is to cast the problem in terms of professional values and the client's understanding of the problem.

Social workers are obliged to be aware of the origins of problems and the evident interface between private troubles and public issues. They must be aware of the route to the social worker as well as the function in various arenas.

The following family experience focuses on individuals in the adult years of their lives. Poor health causes Mrs. Meyer to be placed in a nursing home. The placement is highly coercive in that she resents the decision made by her children and her physician. The route to the social worker would be highly coercive as well; such placements often generate trauma, despite the protection and care that are available. Problems generated may be related to Mrs. Meyer's poor health and family relationships, which are compounded by her ethnic reality and life course position.

### A Mother's Distress

*Bella Meyer spent her adult life working with her husband, David, in their small variety store and caring for their two children, Rose and Mark. The children left home as emerging adults to establish their own households and families. David, her husband, died when they were both age 60. Soon after, Bella's health failed and she became a resident of Ashbrook Manor, a nonsectarian nursing home. Mrs. Meyer is Jewish.*

*After a year in the home, she is unhappy. A hearing impairment causes her great despair. She is unpleasant to the other residents and prefers to be alone. The nurses on her unit have almost turned against her because of her attitude.*

*Her daughter, Rose Niemann, is employed as a clerk-typist in a local insurance company. She visits her mother regularly but stays only a few minutes because she is on her lunch hour. Mark, a shoe salesman, seldom visits. Both of the children make contributions to their mother's care.*

*Rose's and Mark's children visit their grandmother only on holidays.*

The impact of the ethnic reality on Mrs. Meyer's life may be overlooked in a nonsectarian setting that has no commitment to her Jewishness. The primary purpose of the nursing home is to provide care for aging persons with failing health. In this setting she is denied the traditional aspects of Jewish family life.

The food, although healthful, lacks what Mrs. Meyer calls *tahm* (character). Food has been an important part of her life. She had previously been able to express love and sociability to her family and friends by preparing and serving food. Here, like all patients, she is cut off from daily family life and the tasks of a caregiver. For a Jewish woman this may well be devastating.

Reverence for the Jewish aging can be seen in an extensive network of charities and residential and nursing settings. This adheres to historical concepts that expect that children will have a caring regard and respect for the elderly, including their parents (Linden, 1967). Mark and Rose, Mrs. Meyer's children, do care and have not totally abandoned her, but they are involved in small, nuclear family units that cannot readily lend themselves to the incorporation of a frail, disgruntled, elderly grandmother. Mrs. Meyer feels alienated and rejected; the nonsectarian nursing home, devoid of *Yiddishkeit,* intensifies her already profound sense of isolation and alienation.

The ancient belief that as a Jew she is one of the "chosen people" has at times given her a sense of comfort, of having been favored by God. But God and tradition seem to have failed her. When she refers to her heritage in her communication with others, they don't understand and may interpret her behavior as snobbery. Nursing staff and other residents are unaware of the tradition or its significance in Mrs. Meyer's life (Linden, 1967).

Aging and poor health engulf Mrs. Meyer in the despair of old age. The productivity of her earlier years, in which she carried out a historical tradition of laboring women, is no longer possible. Her daughter, Rose, is able to carry out tradition through her employment and uses some of her resources to aid in the support of her mother. At middle age she is torn between her regard for her aging mother and the needs of her own family. This is the struggle of many women, but for Rose there is an ethnic disposition that places particular emphasis on both relationships. She is constant in her attention to her mother, although she limits visits to "looking in" during her lunch hour. The visits are regular. On the other hand, her brother, Mark, is less attentive. He may well be considered to be neglectful except for his regular financial contribution. This behavior can be considered from the perspective of the intense mother–son interactions found in some Jewish families. There are indications that overprotective and affectionate mothers may withhold love for the purpose of discipline. The resultant stress felt by sons may, as the mother grows older, be observed in behavior similar to Mark's (Linden, 1967). He contributes regularly to her support but refuses close contact, much to Mrs. Meyer's despair. Although he accomplishes filial duty contributing to her support, his absence suggests rejection. She does not enjoy the rest and peace that she feels she would have if hers was a reverent son; neither do her grandchildren bring her joy.

The social worker who observes Bella Meyer finds an ailing elderly woman who complains of poor hearing to the extent that the staff avoids contact with her. With a grasp of the layers of understanding, one is able to expand upon this initial observation and see more of Mrs. Meyer, who is unique as an older Jewish woman in failing health who will undoubtedly resist intervention. She has been removed from the Jewish community, which has given her support and a sense of well-being, and placed in a nursing home that does not respond to her ethnic needs in any way. Her age denies her the satisfaction of work, and her children and grandchildren do not respond to her in ways that she feels are appropriate in Jewish families. This information, added to knowledge about the administrative structure and policy of the nursing home, enables the social worker to seek alternatives in health care that would respond more positively to Mrs. Meyer's ethnic needs as well as to those of other Jewish residents.

As the social worker seeks alternatives that will enhance Mrs. Meyer's life at Ashbrook Manor, there must be an awareness that one's own ethnicity may influence perspectives on the lives of others. The Meyer family cannot respond in ways that are completely familiar to the Irish, Italian, or African American social workers and must not be viewed from that perspective.

Brenda Baker and Bella Meyer both have problems that may well be alleviated through social work intervention. They will take different routes to the social worker. When their social workers and others have gained a professional perspective, which includes the layers of understanding presented here, they may be expected to become more effective in the practice, more aware of themselves and others.

## SUMMARY

This chapter has identified six of the layers of understanding necessary for social work practice. These are:

1. Social work values;
2. A basic knowledge of human behavior;
3. Knowledge and skill in social welfare policy and services;
4. An insight into one's own ethnicity and how that may influence one's perspective;
5. An understanding of the impact of the ethnic reality on the daily life of clients; and
6. An understanding that the route taken to the social worker has an impact on the manner in which social services will be perceived and delivered.

These are the first six of seven layers that lead to ethnic-sensitive practice. The final layer comprises those skills already available to the profession. They must be reviewed, reconsidered, adapted, and modified in relation to the ethnic reality. Part II addresses this seventh layer of understanding.

## REFERENCES

Epstein, L. (1980). *Helping people: The task-centered approach* (2nd ed.). Columbus: Merrill.

Garbarino, J., & Abramowitz, R. H. (1992a). The ecology of human development. In J. Garbarino (Ed.), *Children and families in the social environment* (2nd ed., pp. 11–33). New York: Aldine De Gruyter.

Garbarino, J., & Abramowitz, R. H. (1992b). The family as a social system. In J. Garbarino (Ed.), *Children and families in the social environment* (2nd ed., pp. 72–98). New York: Aldine De Gruyter.

Germain, C. B. (1991). *Human behavior in the social environment: An ecological view.* New York: Columbia University Press.

Grossbard, H. (1954). Methodology for developing self-awareness. *Social Casework, 35*(9), 380–386.

Hamilton, G. (1954). Self-awareness in professional education. *Social Casework, 35*(9), 371–379.

Johnson, L. C. (1995). *Social work practice: A generalist approach.* Boston: Allyn & Bacon.

Ladner, J. A. (1972). *Tomorrow's tomorrow: The Black woman.* New York: Anchor Books Doubleday.

Levy C. (1973). The value base for social work, *Journal of Education for Social Work, 9,* 34–42.

Linden, M. E. (1967). Emotional problems in aging. In *The psychodynamics of American Jewish life: An anthology.* New York: Twanye Publishers.

Longres, S. (1995). *Human behavior in the social environment.* Itasca, Illinois: Peacock Publishers.

Mullen, E., Chazin, R., & Feldstein, D. (1970). *Preventing chronic dependency*. New York: Community Service Society.

National Association of Social Workers. (1981). Social work code of ethics. *Social Work, 26,* 6.

National Association of Social Workers (1997). *Code of ethics*. Washington D.C.

Reamer, F. G. (1995). Ethics and values. *Encyclopedia of social work* (19th ed.). National Association of Social Workers, 893–901. Washington, DC.

Reid, P. N., & Popple, P. R. (1991). Introduction. In P. N. Reid & P. R. Popple (Eds.), *The moral purposes of social work: The character and intentions of a profession* (pp. 1–10). Chicago: Nelson Hall.

Reid, W. J., & Epstein, L. (1972). *Task-centered casework*. New York: Columbia University Press.

Schulman, E. D. (1991). *Intervention in human services: A guide to skills and knowledge* (4th ed.) New York: Merrill, an imprint of Macmillan Publishing Company.

Social work code of ethics. *Social Work, 26*(1), 6.

Staples, R., & Johnson, L. B. (1993). *Black families at the crossroads. Challenges*. San Francisco: Jossey-Bass.

Williams, S. E., & Wright, D. F. (1992). Empowerment: The strengths of Black families revisited. *Journal of Multicultural Social Work, 2,* 23–36.

Wood, G. G., & Middleman, R. (1989). *Social service delivery A structural approach to practice*. New York: Columbia University Press.

# 5

# APPROACHES TO SOCIAL WORK
# AND THE ETHNIC REALITY

The profession of social work in the United States traces its major beginnings to the late nineteenth century, a time of societal change and growth. The cities were growing dramatically as the country became urbanized. Immigration, mostly from Europe, was at an all-time high. Industrialization and the scientific revolution were proceeding rapidly. The country was still experiencing the aftermath of the Civil War. Many African Americans, former slaves, were making their way into the cities of the North. These developments brought in their wake many new social problems. Newly arrived immigrants from Europe, freed slaves, and other African Americans crowded into the new cities. New ways of responding to the emerging human need had to be found. The emergence of social work was one response.

Richmond refers to combining a "new way of serving humanity" (1917) with systemized knowledge. Reflecting on this history, Goldstein's (1990) comments point to a commitment to charity, philanthropy, and caring and suggest that "the 'social' in social work is the expression of this heritage" (p. 32).

How best to operationalize this perspective is a matter of ongoing disagreement and debate. Some believe that most human ills can be cured by changing the economy and opening up more access to resources. Others focus on a scientific perspective. Jane Addams (1910) and her colleagues emphasized reform; Mary Richmond joins those who think it necessary to enhance the new scientific perspective and to define social work as a science (Goldstein, 1990).

Another variant of this debate focuses on the differences of opinion concerning the major sources of human problems and the paths to problem resolution. Some adherents of a social-reform perspective believe that the major sources of individual and social dysfunction are to be found in inequities in the social structure and environmental problems. Those committed to this view of the human condition explain behavior in sociological and structural terms; they advocate a major focus on interventive strategies designed to effect social and environmental change (e.g., Germain & Gitterman, 1995).

Another group believes that much human functioning can best be understood by reference to psychologically based explanations of human behavior. Each of these perspectives influences the selection of helping strategies.

Yet another group seeks to understand how the interplay of social and psychological forces impinge on and shape people. Both bodies of thought are drawn on in the effort to heighten understanding and generate appropriate helping strategies.

These different viewpoints have been translated into approaches to social work practice, or what is often termed *practice theory*. Turner commented on the historical evolution of practice theory. In his view, the search for theory has been informed by the effort "to understand the complex reality of 'person in situation.'" He suggested that the test of a theory is in its ability to help and to provide quality, effective, accountable service.

Turner defined theory as "an organized body of concepts that attempt to explain some aspects of reality in a manner that has been, or is capable of being verified in an acceptable manner" (Turner, 1995). He contended that theory is used to help practitioners give meaning to and assess people's strengths, weaknesses, and resources. Theory "facilitates and gives direction to the process of decision making" in work with clients. Theory helps us to anticipate the outcomes of intervention. All intervention planning presumes sufficient understanding that action can be taken with predictable outcomes (Turner, 1996). Key elements of theory should help us: (1) to recognize the similarities and differences in the changing elements of daily practice; (2) to enhance the concept of client self-determination by focusing on the resemblance of clients to each other, as well as their uniqueness; and (3) to test concepts as practice seems either to support or refute them.

In his earlier work, Turner held firm to the conviction that explanation and description of our clients and their world should lead logically to identification of problematic behavior and to guidelines for helping (Turner, 1974). Later he entertains the possibility that a theory of intervention could be developed that is different from the theories of personality, learning, and behavior so familiar to most social workers (Turner, 1986).

The view that causal knowledge may not provide an adequate base for practice is held by a number of analysts. Fischer (1978) and Reid (1978) are among those who have presented this perspective.

Fischer makes a distinction between causal/developmental knowledge and intervention knowledge. The former answers the question *why* and aids in understanding and "diagnosing"; the latter answers the question *what* and deals with theories, principles, and procedures for induced change (Fischer, 1978). There is increasing doubt about the assumption that understanding the causes of history of problems provides clues about what is sustaining the problem, or guidelines for intervention. This view is not shared by all. Middleman and Goldberg (1974) contend that understanding the causes of a problem goes a long way toward defining it and projecting solutions.

Turner also commented on the relationship between theory and values. Anthropologists suggest that all of us must come to terms with five value orientations. These focus on the basic nature of human nature, the importance of time, the nature of human activity, and the relationships between human beings and nature. The relevance of this perspective for our present considerations is readily apparent. Cultures differ in their perspectives on time. Some focus on the present, others on the future, and some stress the past. These differences must be taken into account in intervention. For example, there are substantial distinctions between Western and non-Western conceptions of time.

Turner, who has commented on the development of practice theory in numerous publications over the past twenty years or more, suggested that the present state of practice theory is best characterized as diverse. In his view, the search for a singular unifying theory has been abandoned. Instead, we have a pluralist theoretical base. Different theories focus on different elements of the human condition and on ways of human understanding.

For example, some problems call for approaches to solving discrete problems, whereas others focus on the inner dynamics of functioning. Each of these problem-solving perspectives may be useful for work with different people.

Considerable work remains to be done in clarifying the relationship among what is known and believed about human behavior, the cause of the problems, and the way in which social work uses that knowledge.

A number of distinct, although inevitably overlapping, approaches to social work practice can be identified (see Table 5.1). For the most part, these approaches are based on the various assumptions and theories about the human condition discussed earlier.

## THE PSYCHOSOCIAL APPROACH

The concept that people are both psychological and sociological beings is synonymous with social work's perspective. Turner (1974) suggested that the term *psychosocial* is fully the prerogative of our profession. However, psychosocial therapy has come to be associated with a particular view of the human condition and approaches to practice, the meanings of which are not uniformly shared. Consequently, the configuration of ideas and interventive approaches termed *psychosocial practice* can be viewed as separate and apart from the more general view, shared by most social workers, that many of the issues with which they deal can in large measure be understood in psychosocial terms. For these reasons, we treat the psychosocial approach as a distinct perspective on practice.

The psychosocial approach has a long and honorable history. Much attention has been and continues to be focused on efforts to refine, reformulate, and specify the basic assumptions, interventive strategies, and techniques that continue to evolve.

### Assumptions

It is a basic assumption of this approach that we are in large measure governed by unique past histories and the internal dynamic generated by those histories. This view of human beings translates into a perspective on practice that emphasizes the need to maintain a dual focus on psychological and sociological man; that is, on intrapersonal man, interpersonal man, and intersystemic man (Turner, 1974).

Richmond (1917) emphasized this dual perspective in her view of social casework as involving processes that develop a personality through adjustments deliberately effected, individual by individual, between people and their social environment.

**TABLE 5.1    Prevailing Approaches to Social Work Practice**

| Approach | Leaders | Assumptions |
|---|---|---|
| Psychosocial | Hollis, Turner, & Strean | People are governed by past; people are psychological, sociological, interpersonal, intrapersonal, intersystems beings; people shape own destiny; problems stem from unmet infantile drives, faulty ego/superego functioning, current pressures; psychodynamic theory important; use others |
| Problem solving | Perlman, Compton, & Galaway | Life is a problem-solving process; capacities impaired by excess stress, crisis, insufficient resources; present important; influenced by past; eclectic theoretical stance |
| Task centered | Reed & Epstein | People have problem-solving capacity; breakdown generates capacity for change; clients define their own problems; eclectic theoretical stance |
| Structural | Middleman & Goldberg (Wood) | Environmental pressures primary cause of problems; inadequacy, usually refers to disparity between resources and need |
| Systems | Pincus & Minahan | Social work concerned with: absence of needed resources; linkage between people and resource systems; and problematic interaction between resource systems, internal problem-solving resources |
| Ecological | Germaine & Gitterman | Focus on relationship between living organisms and environment; all life forms seek adaptive balance, require resources; reciprocal environment—organism interaction at expense of others; stress = imbalance between demand and capability to meet demand; coping = adaptive effort; human relatedness essential for survival; environment = physical and social |
| Process stage approach— minority practice | Lum | Postulates that all U.S.-based people of color share experience of racism and minority values on importance of corporate collective structures, extended family, religious and spiritual values; NASW code of ethics needs modification to incorporate above |
| Ethnic-sensitive practice | Devore & Schlesinger | Individual and collective history affects problems; present most important; ethnicity is a source of cohesion and strife; nonconscious phenomena affect functioning |
| Strengths perspective | Saleeby | People have strength; deal with problems; resilience |
| Empowerment | Lee | Oppression structurally based; can analyze institutional source |

| Interventive Procedures | Attention to Ethnic Reality |
| --- | --- |
| Sustainment; direct influence; ventilation; reflective discussion of person/situation; environmental work | Stresses pathology related to class and ethnicity |
| | Adaptation to ethnic reality not spelled out |
| Ascertaining facts; thinking through facts; making choices | Calls attention to ethclass |
| | Adaptation to ethnic reality descriptive, not incorporated into interventive procedures |
| Exploring problem; contracting; task planning; establishing incentives and rationale | Major attention to ethnicity, class, and poverty |
| | Adaptation to ethnic reality not incorporated into interventive procedures |
| Stress: principle of accountability to the client following demands of client task; maximizing supports in the client's environment; least content | Major attention to problems related to ethnicity, class, and poverty |
| | Adaptation to ethnic reality not incorporated into interventive procedures |
| Help enhance coping capacity; establish people-resource linkages; facilitate interaction within resource system; influence social policy, dispense material resources | Some attention to ethnicity, social class |
| | Adaptation to ethnic reality not incorporated into interventive procedures |
| Strengthen fit between people and environments; coordinate with/link people to resources; contract with client; engage to protect client/others' vulnerability; exert professional influence at case and policy level | Major attention to ethnicity and social class |
| | Adaptation to ethnic reality not incorporated into interventive procedures |
| Focus on: culturally based stress experiences; language; social and personal aspect of problem; workers must develop ethnic competence | Attention to ethnicity, but not social class |
| | Adaptation to ethnicity incorporated into interventive procedures |
| Contact; problem identification with focus on minority issues; recognition of difficulty in seeking help; assessment with focus on ethnic identity, minority issues; intervention usual with attention to oppression, powerlessness, themes related to the minority experience | Attention to ethnicity almost exclusively on people of color; virtually none to other ethnic groups |
| | Incorporates adaptation to ethnicity/minority status into interventive procedure |
| Collaborate with client | Totally congruent |
| Use political and clinical helping technologies | Totally congruent |

A number of themes emerge. All people are thought to have both the responsibility and capacity to participate in shaping their own destiny. People are social beings who reach their potential in the course of relationships with family, friends, small groups, and the community. Belief in the capacity to choose and to make decisions from among alternatives is related to the belief that each of us is unique and unpredictable and that we all have the capacity to transcend history (Turner, 1974). Nevertheless, genetic endowment and the environment are most important in shaping actions.

In a recent formulation of the approach (Woods & Robinson, 1996), the following assumptions are identified: many feelings and thoughts "lie outside of awareness" (p. 564); personality is a dynamic combination of forces that affect behavior; even minor changes affect the entire personality and can alter thinking and feeling, as well as behavior; defenses serve functional and dysfunctional ends; symptoms represent adaptive mechanisms that serve to uncover and aid in resolution of internal conflicts; and "neurosis" has social origins and is based in experiences with social relationships. In an earlier statement, Hollis (1972) suggested that breakdown in social adjustment can be traced to three interacting sources: (1) infantile needs and drives left over from childhood that cause the individual to make inappropriate demands on the adult world, (2) a current life situation that exerts excessive pressures, and (3) faulty ego and superego functioning.

Problems stemming from persisting infantile needs and drives generate a variety of pathologies and disturbances in capacity to assume adult responsibilities. Disturbances may also be generated by environmental pressures, such as economic deprivation, racial and ethnic discrimination, inadequate education, and inadequate housing. Family conflict or loss occasioned by illness, death, or separation are also viewed as environmental or current life pressures. Faulty ego functioning is manifested in distorted perceptions of factors operating both external and internal to the individual. Breakdown is often triggered by disturbance in more than one of these areas because they tend to interact and affect functioning.

Turner (1974) suggested that the goal of psychosocial therapy is "to help people achieve optimal psychosocial functioning given their potential and giving due recognition to their value system." These goals can be accomplished through the development of human relationships, available material, and service resources, as well as through human resources in the environment. Involvement with a psychosocial therapist may effect change in cognitive, emotive, behavioral, or material areas so that there is a relief from suffering.

In summary, the psychosocial approach stresses the interplay of individual and environment, the effect of past on the present, the effect of nonconscious factors on the personality, and the impact of present environmental as well as psychologically induced sources of stress and coping capacity. Major attention is given to psychoanalytic conceptions of human behavior and how these explain the presenting difficulties.

## Assumptions and the Ethnic Reality

The definition of the ethnic reality calls attention to those aspects of the ethclass experience that provide sources of pride, a comfortable sense of belonging, various networks of family and community, and a range of approaches to coping that have withstood the test of time. At the same time, it highlights the persistent negation of valued traditions and the turmoil experienced by various ethnic groups as they encounter the majority culture. Particular attention is paid to the effects of discrimination in such spheres as jobs, housing, and schooling. A review of the major tenets of psychosocial theory indicates that the roles of ethnicity and social class are incorporated into this perspective. Hollis (1972), Turner (1974, 1978), Strean (1974), and others have emphasized the destructive effects of discrimination, poor housing, and poverty. Many have mentioned the effect of destructive stereotyping.

However, two major gaps are apparent. First, there is no clear or detailed indication as to how minority status, ethnicity, and class converge to shape individuals and contribute to the problems for which they seek help. This gap is noted by many social work analysts. A second omission, or perhaps distortion, is the tendency to stress the negative and dysfunctional aspects of the ethnic reality. Attention is commonly and explicitly called to the disabling effects of discrimination or low socioeconomic status. This is as it should be. However, the unique and often beneficial effects of membership *in* various groups are often ignored.

Good psychosocial practice should be ever mindful of those sources of identity deriving from a sense of peoplehood and those sources of difficulty that stem from systemic inequity. The consideration of past history in relation to present functioning should present positive and negative aspects of the ethnic reality. The classic statements of the approach do not help us here. There have been efforts to make these kinds of connections (Grier & Cobbs, 1969). A "test" of psychosocial theory as it applies to Chicano clients shows its usefulness in work with this group when integrated with cultural insights (Gomez, Zurcher, Buford, & Becker, 1985).

Others have carried out similar work. Lee (1997) provides many suggestions for psychotherapeutic work with Asian clients, who frequently have difficulty utilizing traditional psychotherapy. What is needed is explicit education about the purposes of questions, and how the issues dealt with may be linked to the problems people bring. Immediate psychological first aid and personal disclosure by the therapist are all strategies that are helpful and congruent with the culturally based styles and belief systems of many Asian people who are minimally assimilated to American values. Franklin (1992) suggests a series of approaches to help therapists work with African American men who may be distrustful of therapy.

The Native American perspective on time and the priority some give to kin over aspects of work is frequently cited (Attneave, 1982; Good Tracks, 1973). Behaviors related to these perspectives clash with the values of the larger society. When work schedules are not met, a job can be lost and result in much pain and turmoil.

Similarly, some Chinese fathers who, by mainstream standards, remain emotionally distant from their children may well trigger confusion and doubt in those emerging into adolescence in American society. But there is another aspect to these types of experiences: In a hostile world, kin who act in accustomed ways and who transmit powerful belief systems go a long way toward providing emotional sustenance. The loss of a job may seem negligible compared with the sense of satisfaction obtained from doing what is expected by family. Emotional distance may be experienced as rejecting and confusing, yet it provides a sense of the past or a clear sense of being dealt with in time-honored and known ways.

Our reading of the best that has been written about the psychosocial approach suggests that insufficient attention has been paid to how to use the knowledge of the ethnic reality, despite various writers having taken great care to point out that practitioners must be attuned to these differences.

## THE PROBLEM-SOLVING APPROACHES

Rather than pursue the psychosocial approach, concentrating on psychoanalytic insights, many practitioners look to the problem-solving approaches as the framework to be used for the helping process. Prominent among these are Perlman (1957), Reid and Epstein (1972), and Compton and Galaway (1989). Perlman can be considered the originator of the problem-solving framework, presented in her classic work (1957). Reid and Epstein have introduced a more structured model termed *task-centered casework.* Compton and Galaway (1989) have elaborated on this model, as have Turner and Jaco (1996).

Common to these approaches is a reliance on a wide range of theoretical stances. Few reject Freudian conceptions; however, such conceptions are not central to the approach. Ego psychology, learning theory, role theory, and communication theory are among the theoretical foundations drawn on by the proponents of the problem-solving approaches.

### The Problem-Solving Framework—Assumptions

Intrinsic to this approach is the view that all of human life is a problem-solving process and that all people have problems. Turner and Jaco (1996), quoting Meyer (1994), suggest that problem solving can be defined as a "cognitive activity aimed at changing a problem from the given to the goal state" (p. 503). Difficulties in coping with problems are based on lack of opportunity, ability, or motivation.

In the course of human growth, individuals develop problem-solving capacities that become basic features of the personality. To deal effectively with diverse problems, including recurrent life course tasks, requisite resources and opportunities must be available. Excessive stress, crisis, or inadequate resources impair coping capacity. Interpersonal conflict, insufficient resources, deficient or dissatisfying role performance, and difficulties in moving through the stages of the life course as anticipated are all viewed as problems. Compton and Galaway suggest that "troubles in living" derive from difficulties encountered in solving some of life's situations or from deficiencies in motivation or capacity (including knowledge, social skills, and biopsychosocial factors in development) and opportunity (such as access to support systems, needed resources, and helping relationships).

There is less emphasis than in the psychosocial approach on the importance of personal pathology in the etiology of problems. Equilibrium may be restored and optimal functioning regained when people are helped to function more competently and when needed social and welfare services are provided (Siporin, 1975). Past experiences, present perceptions and reactions to the problem, and future aspirations join together to form the person with a problem. Of primary importance is today's reality. Knowledge of the current living situations by which persons are "being molded and battered" provide the facts necessary for activation of the problem-solving process (Perlman, 1957). Later Perlman (1986) suggested that a major contribution of the model is its "focus upon the here-and-now" and the recognition that "each help seeker comes to us at a point of what *he* feels to be a crisis" (p. 249).

Compton and Galaway (1989) added a number of important notions. The model contains no built-in assumptions about the cause, nature, location, or meaning of the problem. Client goals are highlighted; thus, there is congruence with the view of clients' rights to self-determination and to define their own problems.

A person's response to the problem-solving process is influenced by the structure and functioning of the personality, which has been molded by inherited and constitutional equipment as well as by interactions with the physical and social environment. Blocks may impede the process, including lack of material provisions available to the client, ignorance or misapprehension about the facts of the problem and the way of dealing with it, and a lack of physical and emotional energy to invest in problem solving. An important assumption focuses on the role of the worker–client relationship in the problem-solving process. The ability of the two partners to interact to communicate is critical.

Culture and its influence on individual development is also discussed. In describing the person, Perlman (1986) presents the individual operating as a physical, psychological, and social entity—a product of constitutional makeup, physical and social environment, past experience, present perceptions and reactions, and future aspirations. Also important is the person as a whole (p. 250).

The goal in problem solving is to provide the resources necessary to restore equilibrium and optimal functioning through a process that places emphasis on contemporary reality and present problem-ridden situations. These resources are of both a concrete and an interpersonal nature.

### Assumptions and the Ethnic Reality

No contradictions exist between this model and the concept of the ethnic reality. There is considerable congruence between the notion that effective coping is contingent on the availability of adequate resources and opportunities and our view that, for the most part, the ethnic reality often simultaneously serves as a source of stress and strength. Although this approach does not neglect the dysfunctional effect of personality pathology, it places greater emphasis on restoration of competence and provision of resources in delineated problem areas than does the psychosocial approach. This is consonant with our emphasis on the systemic source of problems often faced by oppressed ethnic groups. However, few of the earlier or more recent writings specifically address the kinds of issues that must be taken into account by the ethnic-sensitive worker. For example, considerable literature suggests that the process of communication between workers and clients is affected by their respective ethnic group membership and by the client's ethnic reality (e.g., Davis & Proctor, 1989; Devore & Schlesinger, all prior editions). Neither earlier nor present work on the problem-solving perspective deals with these kinds of issues explicitly.

## TASK-CENTERED SYSTEM

The task-centered approach was first formulated by Reid and Epstein in 1972 and is closely related to the problem-solving perspective. It draws on components of structured forms of brief casework (Reid & Shyne, 1969), aspects of Perlman's problem-solving approach (Perlman, 1957), the perspective on the client task put forth by Studt (1968), and the specification of casework methods presented by Hollis (1965; Reid, 1977).

Since the inception of this approach, extensive work has been carried out to test and refine the model (Reid, 1977, 1978). It is viewed as an evolving approach to practice, responsive to continuing research and developments in knowledge and technology; its basic principles were summarized by Reid (1986).

The task-centered approach stresses the importance of helping clients with solutions to problems in the terms defined by the clients. The worker's role is to help bring about desired changes. The client, not the worker, is the primary agent of change. The approach emphasizes the human capacity for autonomous problem solving and people's ability to carry out action to obtain desired ends. Problems often are indicative of a temporary breakdown in coping capacity. The breakdown generates and sets in motion forces for change. These include client motivation as well as environmental resources. The range of problems identified is similar to that usually encountered and identified in other approaches: problems in family and interpersonal relations, in carrying out social roles, in decision making, in securing resources, and involving emotional distress reactive to situational factors (Reid, 1986).

Intervention is usually brief and time limited; this is based on the view that the greatest benefit to the client is derived in a few sessions within a limited time period. Substantial research has documented the fact that (1) short, time-limited treatment is as effective as long-term intervention and (2) change occurs early in the process.

Problems take place in the context of the individual, family, and environmental systems that can hamper or facilitate resolution (Reid, 1986). In contrast to psychosocial theory, problem-oriented theory as defined by Reid and Epstein (1972) does not focus on remote or historical origins of a problem but looks primarily to contemporary causal factors. Attention is centered on those problems that the client and practitioner can act to change. Wants, beliefs, and affects are crucial determinants of action (Reid, 1978).

The possible role of the unconscious in influencing human action is not ruled out. However, given the emphasis on the present, it is assumed that problems as defined by clients can be managed without efforts to gain insight into unconscious dynamics (Reid, 1978). "In this conception the person is seen as less a prisoner of unconscious drives than in the theories of the psychoanalyst and less a prisoner of environmental contingencies. Rather, people are viewed as having minds and wills of their own that are reactive but not subordinate to internal and external influences" (Reid, 1986, p. 270).

Theories designed to explain personality dynamics and disorders, the function of social systems, and other factors are thought to aid in problem assessment. However, these provide limited clues concerning how people perceive problems, and they do not explain the relationship between personal and environmental factors. Furthermore, there are competing theories to explain similar problems. The worker is left with limited guides for action. Practitioners are free to draw on any theory or combination of theories if they seem to add to an understanding of the situation (Epstein, 1977).

Also important in this approach is the view of poverty and of the characteristics of poor clients. These contrast with other approaches. Epstein is critical of perspectives on the poor that emphasize their negative characteristics. She suggests that given the persistent and severe inequities endemic in modern society that minimize the access to resources for so many, treatment technologies are not conducive to addressing or managing or controlling such vast influences (Epstein, 1977). Fundamental resolutions to the problems experienced by poor families will require the development of social policies to mitigate the oppressive consequences of racial, ethnic, and sex discrimination; poverty; and inadequate education, day care, and other like programs.

### Assumptions and the Ethnic Reality

The task-centered model was developed in part because of an interest in providing more effective service to the poor. We have noted the critique of certain prevailing views of the poor. The insistence on working with problems in the terms identified by the client is stressed. These thrusts are a major step in the direction of ethnic-sensitive practice as we define it (see Chapter 6). When clients truly have the freedom to reject problem definitions that do not concur with their own views, the risk of attributing personality pathology to systemically induced behaviors and events is minimized.

For example, many American Indians feel that responsibility to family takes precedence over responsibility to the workplace. Knowing this, the social worker is unlikely to characterize as lazy an American Indian who explains his failure to work on a given day as being due to family obligations. If the ethnic reality of an American Indian man is understood, it is unlikely that he will be characterized as lazy or unmotivated.

The extent to which adherence to such subcultural perspectives leads an American Indian man to lose several jobs may become the issue of concern between him and the social worker if he chooses to make it so. He is free to define the "problem" and to deal with it on his terms. Once viewed this way, consideration of various options is possible without recourse to the pathological label. For example, can his need to work regularly be reconciled with the responsibilities to family and friends as these are defined by his own group? In some instances a new "client" or group of clients can emerge. These may be fellow employees or a supervisor who understands the kinds of commitments he has and is able and willing to make adaptations in work routines that allow him to tend to family and work needs.

## THE SOCIAL PROVISION AND STRUCTURAL APPROACHES

Approaches that highlight the inequity of the social structure as a major source of difficulty have long been an integral part of the literature of social work practice. The work of Addams (1910) and Wald (1951) exemplifies this perspective. They were followed by Reynolds (1938), Titmuss (1968), Younghusband (1964), and Kahn (1965).[1]

Recent efforts to explicate the relationship between the social context and principles of social work practice are exemplified by Germain's (1979) and Germain and Gitterman's (1980) ecological approach and by Meyer's ecosystems perspective (1976). Germain proposed that practice is directed toward improving the transactions between people and environments in order to enhance adaptive capacities and improve environments for all who function within them. Out of this perspective a number of "action principles" are derived. These relate to "efforts at adaptation and organism environmental transactions...those transactions between people and environments are sought that will nourish both parts of the interdependent system" (Germain, 1979).

## THE STRUCTURAL APPROACH

A detailed model that identifies social institutional sources of stress and specifies social work actions generated by such a perspective is presented by Middleman and Goldberg (1974), and subsequently elaborated by Wood and Middleman (1989). They identified theirs as a structural approach; we will examine it in some detail.

### Assumptions

Several assumptions underpin this approach: (1) people are not "necessarily the cause of their problems and therefore are not always the appropriate targets for change efforts" (Wood & Middleman, 1989, p. 27), (2) "inadequate social arrangements may be responsible for many problematic situations" (Wood & Middleman, 1989, p. 27), and (3) environmental pressures should first be considered as a possible source of suffering and target of change.

The proponents of this approach feel that it is destructive and dysfunctional to define social problems in psychological terms. Many of the people served by social

---

[1]We acknowledge the work of Siporin (1975) in helping us arrive at this formulation.

work—minority groups, the aged, the poor—are not the cause of the problems that beset them. Consequently, efforts focused on changing them are misplaced.

Much of social work efforts are expended in working with and on behalf of people who do not adequately deal with the situations in which they find themselves. Inadequacy is a relative concept that refers to the disparity between skills or resources and situational requirements. If it is expected that people ought to be skillful and resourceful in response to the requirements of varied situations, then those lacking the necessary coping skills are perceived as inadequate. On the other hand, when situational demands are inappropriate and not sufficiently responsive to individual or collective need, then the situation is perceived as inadequate. "Thus to say that a given man is inadequate is both a description of disparity between that person and a particular situation, and a value judgment attributing blame for that disparity" (Wood & Middleman, 1989, p. 27). They put major responsibility for that disparity on inadequate social provision, discrimination, and inappropriate environments and organizational arrangements.

Based on this perspective, they conceptualize social work roles in terms of two bipolar dimensions: locus of concern (Middleman & Goldberg, 1974), the intended beneficiary of the worker's action, and persons engaged. Locus of concern identifies the reason for social work intervention. The concern may focus on (1) the problems of particular individuals, such as the members of the minority group who confront discrimination in employment and cannot find a job, or (2) the larger category of individuals who suffer from the same problem.

"Persons engaged" calls attention to those people with whom the social worker interacts in response to the problem. Those engaged may be the "sufferer" (client) and/or others. This may involve a process by which the social worker facilitates action by clients and family and community networks to help themselves and each other; or it may involve focusing attention on more explicit social change activity. This can range from efforts to effect legislative change, to organizing for specific community services, to marshaling informal community supports in time of crisis.

The major targets of intervention are always the conditions that inhibit functioning and increase suffering. Social workers intervene in an effort to enhance the nature of the relationship between people and their social environment. They try to use change or create needed social structures and resources. There are four categories of activity: (1) work with clients in their own behalf (such as in casework), (2) work with clients on behalf of themselves and others like them, (3) work with nonsufferers on behalf of clients, and (4) work with nonsufferers on behalf of a category of sufferers (such as in research, policy development, and social change activities).

## Assumptions and the Ethnic Reality

The congruence between many of the assumptions of the structural approach and our perspective on the ethnic reality is in many respects self-evident. We have established that a sense of class and ethnicity is strongly experienced in everyday life and that many ethnic groups and all minority groups are held in low esteem by various segments of the society. Not infrequently we find that certain culturally derived behaviors are viewed as deviant or inadequate by those tied to core societal values.

The basic assumptions of the structural approach are consonant with our view concerning the part played by the ethnic reality in generating many of the problems at issue.

However, like the proponents of other approaches, these authors leave the implicit impression that matters of race and ethnicity are primarily problematic. They do not call explicit attention to the particular sources of strength or to the coping capacity that such group identification often generates, nor do they tend to the fact that ethnic and class factors contribute to how people view problems.

## THE SYSTEMS APPROACH

In the introduction to this chapter, we called attention to the fact that some social work theoreticians have developed approaches to social work practice that are independent of various substantive theories derived from other domains of interest; they want to identify a "social work frame of reference" related to the basic values, functions, and purposes of the profession.

Pincus and Minahan (1973) present such a model. They define social work practice as a goal-oriented planned change process. The model uses a general systems approach as an organizing framework. It is intended for application in a wide range of settings. An effort is made to avoid the often-noted dichotomies between person and environment, clinical practice and social action, and microsystem and macrosystem change. In their view, the profession's strength and major contribution is its recognition of and attention to the connections between these elements.

### Assumptions

Two basic concepts form this approach: resources and interaction between people and the social environment (Pincus & Minahan, 1973). A resource is considered to be anything that helps to achieve goals, to solve problems, to alleviate distress, to aid in accomplishing life tasks, or to realize aspirations and values. Resources are usually used in interaction with one another. There is interdependence among resources, people, and varying informal and formal systems. The former include family, friends, and neighbors; the latter, the societal, governmental, and voluntary health, educational, and social welfare services.

This perspective helps to identify five areas of concern to social work: (1) the absence of needed resources, (2) the absence of linkages between people and resource systems or between resource systems, (3) problematic interaction between people within the same resource system, (4) problematic interaction between resource systems, and (5) problematic individual internal problem-solving or coping resources.

### Assumptions and the Ethnic Reality

The systems approach derives its basic thrust from the values and purposes of social work. By definition, this focuses attention on the many gaps in institutional life that prevent people from reaching their full potential. There is no question that the gaps related to discrimination and cultural differences have always been recognized by our profession. The emphasis on resources and environment implicitly calls attention to those problems and strengths related to the ethnic reality. However, Pincus and Minahan (1973) did not devote explicit attention to these issues, although their examples do point to problems experienced by minority people as they confront mainstream institutions.

The assumptions on which this systems or generalist approach are based are, like all the others we have reviewed, congruent with a view that takes account of the ethnic reality. However, no explicit attention is paid to these matters.

## ECOLOGICAL PERSPECTIVES

We began this chapter by pointing to the two major schools of thought regarding the relationship between person and environment that have long been an integral part of social work theory and practice.

The ecological or life model approach developed by Germain (1979) and Germain and Gitterman (1980) is a response to this historical didactic and an attempt to develop a conceptual framework that provides a simultaneous focus on people and environments (Germain & Gitterman, 1986). Some analysts view ecology as a useful "practice metaphor" that seeks to further understand the reciprocal relationships between people and the environment and to see how each acts on and influences the other. The ecological perspective is an "evolutionary, adaptive view of people and their environments" (Germain & Gitterman, 1986, p. 619). An important concept is that of "person-environment fit."

This discussion will review the basic assumptions of the ecological or life model approach as developed by Germain and Gitterman in 1980 and summarized in 1986.

### Assumptions

The ecological framework is an important and useful way of thinking about social work's societal function. Key concepts are ecology; adaptation, stress, and coping; human relatedness, identity, self-esteem, and competence; and the environment, including its layers and textures (Germain & Gitterman, 1986).

#### Ecology

Ecology is a useful concept because of its focus on the relationships among living organisms and all elements of their environments. Integral to this concept is an effort to examine the adaptive balance or goodness of fit achieved between organisms and their environments. All forms of life are involved in the process of achieving this adaptive balance. In order to develop and survive, all living forms require stimulation and resources from the environment. In turn, these living forms act on the environment, which becomes more differentiated, more complex, and able to support more diverse forms of life.

The reciprocal interactions between an organism and its environment may occasionally be at the expense of other organisms. Damage may render an environment no longer capable of supporting human or physical life forms; or conversely, failure by the environment to support individual life forms may threaten their survival. For example, social environments may become damaged or "polluted" by such cultural processes as poverty, discrimination, and stigma. Under positive environmental circumstances, individuals grow and develop in a positive manner.

### Adaptation, Stress, and Coping

Stress, defined as "an imbalance between a perceived demand and a perceived capability to meet the demand through the use of available internal and external resources" (Germain & Gitterman, 1986, p. 620), develops when there are upsets in the usual or desired person–environment fit. Stress may be positive, in the sense associated with positive self-feeling and anticipation of mastering a challenge, or it may be experienced negatively.

Coping refers to the adaptive effort evoked by stress and usually requires both internal and external resources. Internal resources refer to levels of motivation, self-esteem, and problem-solving skills. Problem-solving skills are in part acquired by training in the environment—from family, schools, and other institutions.

### Human Relatedness, Identity, Self-Esteem, and Competence

Human relatedness is essential for biological and social survival. Infants and children require extended periods of care and the opportunity for learning and socialization. The family, peers, and the institutions of the larger society are the context in which such learning takes place. Deprivation in key primary relationships is painful and may lead to fear of relationships because of their association with loss and pain. Human relationships are crucial, giving rise to a sense of identity and self-esteem. This process begins in infancy and expands to include the increasing range of social experiences that usually accompany growth. Included among the factors that shape identity and self-esteem are gender, race, and social class.

Competence has been defined as "the sum of the person's successful experiences in the environment" (Germain & Gitterman, 1986, p. 622). Individuals achieve a sense of competence when they have the experience of making an impact on the social and physical environment. Important in the development of competence are curiosity and explorative behavior. If competence is to be developed and sustained, appropriate conditions must be provided by family, school, and community.

### The Environment

Germain and Gitterman (1986) suggested that the environment consists of layers and textures. The former refers to the social and physical environment; the latter to time and space. The physical world includes the natural and the built world. The social environment is the human environment of people "at many levels of relationships." These environments interact and shape one another. Technological and scientific developments shape norms in social behavior. Illustrative are the changing sexual norms influenced by the development of contraceptive technology. Importantly, the way in which society appraises certain groups is evidenced in elements of the built environment. Germain and Gitterman (1986) made an important point when they suggested, for example, that design differences between a welfare office and a private family agency often reflect societal values. These in turn affect daily life and self-perception.

Key elements of the social environment are bureaucratic organizations and social networks. The structure and function of bureaucratic organizations give them the potential for positive or negative impact on person–environment fit. Social networks often occur naturally—though they need not—in the life space of the individual. Whether they occur naturally or are formed (as in the case of organized self-help groups), social networks often serve as mutual aid systems. Included are help with providing resources, information, and emotional support.

The physical environment is the context within which human interaction takes place. The sense of personal identity is closely related to "a sense of place." The importance attached to the degree of personal space and what is defined as crowding is influenced by culture and gender, as well as by physical, emotional, and cognitive states.

The life model views human beings as active, purposeful, and having the potential for growth. In the course of ongoing interchange with the environment, there is a potential for problems. These are termed, in the model, problems in living.

### Problems in Living

Problems in living are encountered in the course of managing life transitions, in dealing with environmental pressures, and, in some, by maladaptive interpersonal processes. Life transitions can become problematic under a number of circumstances, including when conflicting role demands are related to status changes and when life transitions and developmental changes do not coincide. Marriage may present a woman with demands to be a wife in the traditional sense at the same time as the occupational role needs to be played in more contemporary terms. The unmarried teenage mother is often not developmentally prepared for the parenting role.

Environmental pressures may result from (1) the unavailability of needed resources, (2) people's inability to use available resources, and (3) environments and resources that are unresponsive to particular styles and needs. The last point is well illustrated by the highly structured elements of many of our health and welfare systems, which do not take account of the ethnic reality of particular groups. For example, the sterile, private atmosphere of a contemporary delivery room may not be congruent with the need for communication with and presence of female relatives to which some Chicano and American Indian women are accustomed. Maladaptive interpersonal processes can arise in efforts to cope with significant environments, illness, and other stresses.

### Social Work Purpose

The distinctive professional social work purpose is focused on helping people with the problems of living; that is, it seeks to improve transactions between people and their environments or to improve the goodness of fit between needs and resources. This effort provides social work with a "core" function. The ecological framework provides one new approach to how best to carry out this function. The three major types of problems noted earlier are particularly suited to social work interventions.

## Assumptions and the Ethnic Reality

The important contribution to the practice literature made by Germain and Gitterman (1980, 1986) does much to help social workers to recognize and understand the complex person–environment interactions that have long been of central concern to the profession. It recognizes that problems are outcomes of the interactions of many factors and abandons the search for a single cause or cure (Hartman & Laird, 1983). There clearly are no contradictions between the ecological perspective and the view of the ethnic reality developed in this book.

The focus on person–environment fit and on the reciprocal relationships between people and their environment is congruent with the view that ethnicity, minority status, social class, resource availability, and societal evaluations give shape to problems in living and affect the capacity to cope with these problems. Germaine and Gitterman have repeatedly stressed the point that matters of culture and class are critical elements in the person–environment interaction. The congruence between this model and ethnic-sensitive practice has been noted by Devore (1983), who suggested that the proponents of the model "have encouraged practitioners to move beyond practice models that look within the individual for the cause of problems to one that encompasses the many facets of life" (p. 525). Clearly, the model and its assumptions can only facilitate the work of the ethnic-sensitive practitioner.

## THE GENERALIST PERSPECTIVE

During the past decade or more, increased attention has been directed to the development of the generalist perspective. The most recent version of the Curriculum Policy Statement of the Council on Social Work Education (CSWE, 1992) requires that all baccalaureate and master's level programs of social work educate students in the generalist perspective.

In Chapter 7 we review the generalist perspective in some detail. We review the work of a number of analysts who suggest that this perspective can be traced to the Milford Conference, held in 1923. At that time, a generic model of casework theory was presented (Morales & Sheafor, 1991) as a way of bringing greater unity to the several types of social casework then extant. At present, the generalist perspective is said to reflect the profession's theoretical focus on assessment, the person in situation, relationship, process, and intervention (Johnson, 1994). Others (e.g., Anderson, 1982) point to the emphasis on targeting problems at all levels: intrapersonal, organizational, community, institutional, and societal. We suggest that an ethnic-sensitive approach to generalist practice is best operationalized by the structural model discussed earlier in this chapter.

## THE EMPOWERMENT AND STRENGTHS PERSPECTIVES

The empowerment approach and the strengths perspective are recent additions to the social work practice literature. The empowerment approach (see Lee, 1996) is guided by simultaneous concern for people and their environments. This formulation is based on the work of C. Wright Mills and Schwartz's view of the integral connection between personal and public issues. Also important is the ecological perspective as developed by Germain and Gitterman (1980) and others, with its emphasis on the interdependence of all systems. Ecological perspectives are linked with a view that conflict is important "as a means of releasing the potentialities of people and their environments" (p. 230).

The authors of the strengths perspective (e.g., Saleeby, 1997) view the emphasis on client strengths and resources as a significant departure from past approaches, which were more focused on pathology. A "lexicon of strength" informs the perspective in which the key aspects of the empowerment approach are clearly embedded.

### The Empowerment Approach

#### Assumptions[2]
Oppression is a structurally based phenomenon with far-reaching consequences for both individuals and their communities. The effects of oppression range from health effects and death, for example, excessive rates of infant mortality among groups such as African Americans; to hopelessness and its behavioral sequella such as suicide for some; to despair and internalized rage.

These effects of oppression point to the importance of such social factors as good support networks and other means of developing connections and relatedness. However, most of the problems caused by oppression require a dual focus on changing the environment as well as strengthening individuals.

It is a key assumption of this approach that people are fully capable of solving their immediate problems. They can go beyond this level to analyze the institutional and structural sources that sustain their oppression. Basically, people empower themselves, and it is they, not the professional helper, who is key in the helping process. Both clinical and political helping technologies must be utilized.

### Strengths Perspectives

#### Assumptions
The lexicon of strengths is a way of directing us to words that highlight strength, including *empowerment, membership* (as in important supportive units such as families), *resilience, healing and wholeness,* and *dialogue and collaboration.* An important

---

[2] Much of the following discussion is based on the empowerment approach as discussed by Lee (1996).

concept is to "suspend disbelief in client perspectives." This relates to a long-standing criticism of traditional social work approaches in which the clients' views of their problems were often discounted in favor of the assessment made by the professional.

Other important principles are focused on the view that all people have the strength to deal with their problems and that we don't know the upper limits of people's capacity to grow. Service is best rendered in collaboration with the client and not for the client.

### Assumptions and the Ethnic Reality

There is little question that both of these perspectives are consonant with the conceptions of the ethnic reality and ethnic-sensitive social work practice.

Elsewhere in this volume we have critiqued those approaches to the needs, lifestyles, and orientations of several ethnic groups and oppressed ethnic groups that focus almost exclusively on the difficulties and pathologies facing these groups, with limited attention to their strengths and culturally based coping capacities. We welcome the focus on strength and empowerment inherent in these two relative newcomers to the social work practice literature.

Specifically, it is important to note that in her discussion of the empowerment perspective, Lee (1996) presents what she terms "bifocal vision" that must inform practice. This vision must include understanding of the history of a group's oppression and a history of policies governing the group; an ecological, stress, and coping paradigm; and ethclass and feminist perspectives. Importantly, Lee asserts (1996) that the work on ethnic-sensitive practice carried on by the present authors (Devore & Schlesinger, 1981, 1987, 1991, 1995), others (e.g., Lum 1995; Davis, 1984), and Chau (1990) "made knowledge of culture and race critical to empowerment practice."

It is a testament to the major developments that have taken place in social work's efforts to truly confront self-determination, the impact of ethnicity and class on social functioning, and the structural bases of the oppression still experienced by many groups that others join us in efforts to infuse the very core of social work practice with these assumptions and principles.

## APPROACHES FOCUSED ON CULTURAL AWARENESS AND MINORITY ISSUES

### Assumptions

Green (1995) developed an approach focused on cultural awareness because in his view social work had paid limited attention to the concerns and interests of minority clients. Green reviews a number of concepts focused on culture, race, ethnicity, and minority groups. He rejected the use of the concept of race because of its presumed pejorative connotations and suggested that it is difficult to apply social class concepts in pluralistic societies. His review of the concepts just noted led him to conclude that efforts to define them entail terminological and conceptual problems.

He asked whether there is a "concept of cultural variation that could be…useful in understanding cross-cultural social service encounters, regardless of the social characteristics or the relative power of the groups or individual involved" (p. 8). He answered his own question by suggesting that the concept of ethnicity, as developed by anthropologists, is useful.

Green (1982) contrasted two views of ethnicity. One, termed *categorical,* attempts to explain differences between and within groups and people by the degree to which distinctive cultural traits such as characteristic ways of dressing, talking, eating, or acting are manifested. These distinctive traits "are not significant except to the extent that they influence intergroup and interpersonal cross-cultural relationships" (p. 11). These elements of "cultural content" may become important as political and cultural symbols used when a group makes claims for resources or demands respect.

The second view, termed *transactional,* focuses on the ways in which people of different groups who are communicating maintain their sense of cultural distinctiveness. It is the manipulation of boundaries between distinctive cultural groups that is crucial to understanding ethnicity and its impact on life.

Ethnicity, stated Green, can be defined in terms of boundary and boundary-maintenance issues. The importance of ethnicity surfaces when people of different ethnic groups interact.

Green adopted a transactional approach to ethnicity. He suggested that in interactions between groups it is not "the descriptive cultural traits" that are important, but "the lines of separation and in particular how they are managed, protected, ritualized through stereotyping, and sometimes violated that is of concern in a transactional analysis of cross-cultural diversity" (p. 12). Those persons who mediate intergroup boundaries are critical actors in cross-cultural encounters. Social workers assume an important role as boundary mediators, given the part they play in the communication of information and in the regulation of resources pertinent to various groups.

Four modes of social work intervention with minority groups serve to identify the implications that ethnicity has for key social service activities. The first, *advocacy,* points to the inherent conflicts in relationships between a minority and the dominant group. Dominant institutions dominate minority people, and advocacy identifies with clients who are subject to domination.

In *counseling,* the individual is the target of change. Culturally sensitive counseling is not well developed. A *regulator* role is also identified. This role focuses on work with the group, usually termed the involuntary client, and is often viewed as unfair and unjust by ethnic community leaders. Examples given include the removal of American Indian children from their homes after allegations of social deprivation. As "regulators," social workers are in a position to define deviance in ways that may do violence to important group values.

In the *broker* role, social workers intervene both with the individual and with society. This role represents a "necessary response to the failure of established social service organizations to meet the legitimate needs of minority clients" (Green, 1982, p. 21). Each of these roles has different consequences for destructive or liberating interactions with minority clients.

# A MODEL OF HELP-SEEKING BEHAVIOR

Green suggested that there is a lack of "cross-cultural" conceptualization in social work and therefore turned to a medical sociological/anthropological model of help-seeking behavior. This model focuses on (1) culturally based differences in perceiving and experiencing stress, (2) language and how it crystallizes experience, and (3) the social as well as personal experience of a problem.

Client and professional cultures are distinct. Components of the model, as they pertain to cultural differences, are (1) the recognition of an experience as a problem by the client, (2) the way language is used to label a problem, (3) the availability of indigenous helping resources, and (4) client-oriented criteria for deciding whether a satisfactory resolution has been achieved. There is a basic contrast between the values and assumptions of the client and those of the service culture. Culturally aware practice requires an ability to suspend agency and professional priorities in order to be able to view services from the perspective of the client. This requires much learning and effort on the part of the worker.

## Ethnic Competence

Green (1995) proposed a number of ways of acquiring *ethnic competence*. Ethnic competence refers to a performance level of cultural awareness representing a degree of comprehension of others that involves more than the usual patience, genuineness, and honesty in client–worker relationships. It is the ability to conduct professional work in a way that is consonant with the behavior of members of distinct groups and the expectations that they have of one another. Use of cultural guides and participant observation in diverse communities are means of acquiring ethnic competence.

## Congruence of the Model with Prevailing Approaches to Social Work Practice

The model of cultural awareness reviewed here presents a useful way of thinking about social work's past tendency to minimize and neglect ethnic and cultural differences. It draws on key social work roles as a way of illustrating and highlighting some of the real dissatisfaction with which social work is viewed by some minority groups.

This disenchantment with the profession's neglect and distortions of ethnic group life led Green (1982) to identify a model of help-seeking behavior drawn from a discipline outside of social work. The key elements of that model are potentially congruent with prevailing approaches to practice. However, Green does not make the linkages. Each of the elements of the model could readily be integrated into the approaches reviewed here, assuming the kind of commitment and ethnic competence described.

## The Model as a Guide for Practice

The cultural awareness model contributes conceptual insights into ethnicity, highlights the profession's historical neglect of this area, and presents some important guidelines for acquiring sensitivity to various ethnic groups. Ethnographic interviews, participant observation, and study of ethnographic documents are all useful mechanisms for coming to an understanding of the lives of clients.

Limited if any attention is directed to how the constraints of time and agency function affect the workers' ability to take the steps that in Green's view are needed to acquire ethnic competence. A related question bears on how workers acquire ethnic competence in the ways proposed when they work in a multiethnic community.

## THE PROCESS–STAGE APPROACH

### Assumptions

Lum (1992) aimed to break new ground by focusing on key differences between the emphases in current social work practice and minority characteristics, beliefs, and behaviors. He believes that social workers' professional orientation must be reexamined from the viewpoint of ethnic minorities, and he presented a framework for ethnic minority practice by proceeding from the assumption that minorities share a similar predicament as well as values and beliefs and that practice protocols applicable to these minorities can be developed. He pointed to the relative lack of attention in social work to minority practice, which he defines as "the art and science of developing a helping relationship with an individual, family, group, and/or community whose distinctive physical/cultural characteristics and discriminatory experience require approaches that are sensitive to ethnic and cultural environments" (p. 3).

The terms *people of color* and *ethnic minority* are used interchangeably throughout this book, and they basically refer to African Americans, Latinos, Asians, and American Indians. The common experience of racism, discrimination, and segregation "binds minority people of color together and contrasts with the experience of White Americans" (Lum, 1986, p. 1).

Lum postulated a number of commonly held minority values. He proposed that social work values and the code of ethics of the National Association of Social Workers need to be modified to incorporate collective minority values that emphasize family unification, recognition of the leadership of elders and parents, and mutual responsibility of family members for one another. Certain Western values and interventive theories and strategies center on individual growth in contrast to kinship and group-centered minority culture. Minority family values revolve around corporate collective structures, including maintenance of ethnic identification and solidarity. Extended family and religious and spiritual values have extensive influence in the minority community. There are a number of generic principles of feeling and thought that cut across groups, despite the known differences in values and culture between varied groups.

Minority knowledge theory has its own intrinsic concepts. Drawing implications for practice with minorities from existing social work knowledge theories is not sufficient. Nevertheless, most theories of social work practice can be adapted for use with people of color.

### Congruence of the Model with Prevailing Approaches to Social Work Practice

Efforts to answer the question, "Is the process–stage approach congruent with prevailing approaches to social work practice?" must be divided into at least two segments: (1) review and analysis of the basic assumptions and (2) consideration of how the process and stages of practice are in keeping with procedures of social work practice.

### The Basic Assumptions

Lum (1986) proceeded from the assumption that all people of color presently living in the United States—Latinos, Asian Americans, American Indians, and African Americans—are bound together by the experience of racism, which contrasts with the experience of white Americans. He further proposed that these groups share collective minority values that emphasize family unification, recognition of the leadership of elders and parents, and mutual responsibility of family members for one another. Also important are values revolving around corporate collective structures, maintenance of ethnic identification, and solidarity. Extended family, kinship networks, spiritual values, and the importance of a vertical hierarchy of authority are said to have extensive influence. The prevailing ethics of the profession, as embodied in the code of ethics of the National Association of Social Workers, are currently oriented toward individual client rights. This code should also address and incorporate the collective minority values just summarized.

In his discussion of "ethnic minority values and knowledge base" (p. 55), Lum directed limited attention to the concept of or influence of social class. He suggested that

> *For ethnic minorities, social class is influenced by racial discrimination and socioeconomic constraints. Although people of a particular minority group may occupy different social class levels, coping with survival and the reality of racism are forces that bind people of color together.*

In our view, there are some key conceptual, empirical, and ideological flaws in the assumptions as presented.

We agree that racism is a factor that is shared by the groups identified by Lum. However, the degree to which they hold in common the "minority values" identified is subject to considerable question. The degree of adherence to these types of values, for any group or for any individual member of a group, remains a matter of empirical question and exploration with the individual member. Thus, to suggest that all people of color, in contrast with all whites, value a hierarchy of authority, corporate structures, and the same spiritual values runs counter to much of the life experience of these groups. The view neglects substantial empirical evidence that shows that the degree of adherence to these values is a function of recency of migration (e.g., Bean & Tienda, 1988) and of social class. Indeed, the accelerating current debate about the nature and source of the African American underclass (see our discussion in Chapter 2 and Wilson, 1987) casts serious doubt on the contention that issues of survival and racism bind to the degree that the conceptualization presented here would suggest. Our concept of the ethnic reality takes account of factors of social class and suggests a framework for understanding the ethnic- and class-related differences that bind as well as those that pull people away from identification with core ethnic values.

The major difficulty in identifying a minority value base that is shared by all people of color is that the effort to unify can have the effect of minimizing and distorting the important unique and rich cultures and values that are characteristic of each of the groups identified as people of color. To attribute a common set of values to diverse people already beset by racism risks a negation of uniqueness, special needs, and stereotyping.

Surely, even a brief review of the values adhered to by such groups as Navajo Indians, urban African Americans who live in the ghetto, Asian Indians, people from the Caribbean, and third- or fourth-generation Japanese women casts doubt on the view that they share spiritual values, the value on vertical hierarchy of authority, or the importance of corporate collective structures.

Importantly, many of these and related values are or have been held by many white ethnic groups. For example, the emphasis on family and group solidarity is often discussed as an attribute of Jewish people and of many Italians.

### Interventive Procedures

Each of the models of practice discussed here has developed a somewhat distinctive set of procedures. As social work practice theory and interventive modalities have evolved and grown, the distinctions between the procedures presented with different models have been muted. For the most part, the focus on the process of assessment or problem identification and on work with the client or client group in efforts to help with the problem of concern. In Chapters 7, 8, and 9, the basic procedures currently most commonly used in social work practice are delineated and adaptations in keeping with the ethnic reality are proposed.

Our analysis of these procedures intended to assess the extent to which they have taken account of ethnic-related dispositions suggests that few of the models have incorporated ethnic-sensitive procedures.

## SUMMARY

This review of some of the major approaches to social work practice indicates that, with few exceptions, the assumptions on which practice is based do not contradict prevailing understandings of cultural, class, and ethnic diversity.

The models reviewed in this chapter share adherence to basic social work values. The dignity of the individual, the right to self-determination, and the need for an adequate standard of living and satisfying, growth-enhancing relationships are uniformly noted. Differences emerge about what social workers need to know and do in order to achieve these lofty objectives.

It is quite apparent that those social workers who believe that past personal experience and nonconscious factors have a major bearing on how people feel in the present structure their practice differently from those who emphasize the importance of institutional barriers, both past and present. Both groups draw on a wide range of psychological and sociological knowledge. However, their theoretical differences influence the manner in which these are incorporated in practice.

These differences are reflected in how problems are defined, what kinds of needs are stressed, the structure of the worker-client relationship, and the type of activity undertaken.

## REFERENCES

Addams, J. (1910). *Twenty years at Hull House.* New York: Macmillan.

Attneave, C. (1982). American Indians and Alaska native families: Emigrants in their own homeland. In M. McGoldrick, J. K. Pearce, & J. Giordano (Eds.), *Ethnicity and family therapy* (pp. 55–83). New York: Guilford Press.

Bean, F. D., & Tienda, M. (1988). The structuring of Hispanic ethnicity: Theoretical and historical considerations. In F. D. Bean & M. Tienda (Eds.), *The Hispanic population of the United States* (pp. 7–35). New York: Russell Sage Foundation.

Chau, K. (1991). *Ethnicity and biculturalism: Emerging perspective of social group work.* New York: Haworth Press.

Compton, B., & Galaway, B. (1989). *Social work processes* (4th ed.). Homewood, IL: Dorsey Press.

Council of Social Work Education. (1992). *Handbook of accreditation standards & procedures for the baccalaureate and masters social work programs.* Alexandria, Virginia: Author.

Davis, L. E. (1984). *Ethnicity in social group work practice.* New York: Haworth Press.

Devore, W. (1983). Ethnic reality: The life model and work with Black families. *Social Casework, 64,* 525–531.

Epstein, L. (1977). *How to provide social services with task-centered methods: Report of the task-centered service project* (Vol. 1). Chicago: School of Social Service Administration, University of Chicago.

Fischer, J. (1978). *Effective casework practice: An eclectic approach.* New York: McGraw-Hill.

Germain, C. B. (Ed.). (1979). *Social work practice: People and environments.* New York: Columbia University Press.

Germain, C. B., & Gitterman, A. (1980). *The life model of social work practice.* New York: Columbia University Press.

Germain, C. B., & Gitterman, A. (1986). The life model of social work practice revisited. In J. Turner (Ed.), *Social work treatment* (pp. 618–644). New York: The Free Press.

Germain, C. B., & Gitterman, A. (1996). *The life model of social work practice* (2nd ed.). New York: Columbia University Press.

Gitterman, A. (1996). Life model theory and social work treatment. In Turner, F. *Social work treatment* (4th ed. pp. 389–408). New York: The Free Press.

Goldstein, H. (1990). The knowledge base of social work practice: Theory, wisdom, analogs, craft. *Families in Society. 71*(1) 32–43.

Gomez, E., Zurcher, L. A., Buford E., & Becker, E. (1985). A study of psychosocial casework with Chicanos. *Social Work, 30,* 477–482.

Good Tracks, J. G. (1973). Native American non interference. *Social Work, 18,* 30–35.

Green, J. W. (1982). *Cultural awareness in the human services.* Englewood Cliffs, NJ: Prentice Hall.

Green, J. W. (1995). *Cultural awareness in the human services.* Boston: Allyn & Bacon.

Greir, W. H., & Cobbs, G. (1969). *Black rage.* New York: Bantam.

Hartman, A., & Laird, J. (1983). *Family centered social work practice.* New York: The Free Press.

Hollis, F. (1965, October). Casework and social class. *Social Casework, XLVI*(8), 463–471.

Hollis, F. (1972). *Casework: A psychosocial therapy* (2nd ed.). New York: Random House.

Jones, D. M. (1976). The mystique of expertise in social services: An Alaska example. *Journal of Sociology and Social Welfare, 3,* 332–346.

Kahn, A. J. (1965). New policies and service models: The next phase. *American Journal of Orthopsychiatry, 35.*

Lee, E. (Ed.). (1997). *Working with Asian Americans: A guide for clinicians.* New York: Guilford Press.

Lee, J. A. (1996). The empowerment approach to social work practice. In Turner, F. *Social work treatment* (4th ed. pp. 218–249). New York: The Free Press.

Lum, D. (1986). *Social work practice and people of color: A process-stage approach.* Monterey, CA: Brooks/Cole.

Lum, D. (1992). *Social work practice and people of color.* Pacific Grove, CA: Brooks/Cole.

Lum, D. (1995). *Social work practice and people of color* (3rd ed.). Pacific Grove, CA: Brooks/Cole.

Meyer, C. H. (1976). *Social work practice* (2nd ed.). New York: The Free Press.

Middleman, R., & Goldberg, G. (1974). *Social service delivery: A structural approach to practice.* New York: Columbia University Press.

Mirelowitz, S. (1979). Implications of racism for social work practice. *Journal of Sociology and Social Welfare, 6,* 297–312.

Morales, A., & Sheafor, B. (1989). *Social work: A profession of many faces.* Boston: Allyn & Bacon.

Norton, D. G. (1978). *The dual perspective.* New York: Council on Social Work Education.

Perlman, H. H. (1957). *Social casework: A problem-solving process.* Chicago: University of Chicago Press.

Perlman, H. H. (1986). The problem solving model. In J. Turner (Ed.), *Social work treatment* (pp. 245–266). New York: The Free Press.

Pincus, A., & Minahan, A. (1973). *Social work practice: Model and method.* Itasca, IL: F. E. Peacock Publishers.

Reid, W. J. (1977). *A study of the characteristics and effectiveness of task-centered methods.* Chicago: School of Social Service Administration.

Reid, W. J. (1978). *The task centered system.* New York: Columbia University Press.

Reid, W. J. (1986). Task-centered social work. In F. J. Turner (Ed.), *Social work treatment* (3rd ed., pp. 267–295). New York: The Free Press.

Reid, W. J. (1996). Task centered social work. In Turner, F. *Social work treatment* (4th ed. pp. 617–640). New York: The Free Press.

Reid, W. J., & Epstein, L. (1972). *Task-centered casework.* New York: Columbia University Press.

Reid, W. J., & Shyne A. (1969). *Brief and extended casework.* New York: Columbia University Press.

Reynolds, B. C. (1938). Treatment processes as developed by social work. *Proceedings, national conference of social work.* New York: Columbia University Press.

Richmond, M. (1917). *Social diagnosis.* New York: Russell Sage Foundation.

Saleeby, D. (1997). *The strengths perspective in social work,* (2nd ed.). New York: Longman.

Siporin, M. (1975). *Introduction to social work practice.* New York: Macmillan.

Strean, H. S. (1974). Role theory. In F. J. Turner (Ed.), *Social work treatment: Interlocking theoretical approaches* (pp. 314–342). New York: The Free Press.

Studt, E. (1968). Social work theory and implication for the practice of methods. *Social Work Education Reporter, 16*(2).

Titmuss, R. (1968). *Commitment to welfare.* New York: Pantheon.

Turner, F. J. (1970). Ethnic difference and client performance. *Social Service Review, 44.*

Turner, F. J. (1974). Some considerations on the place of theory in current social work practice. In J. Turner (Ed.), *Social work treatment* (pp. 3–19). New York: The Free Press.

Turner, F. J. (1995). Social work practice: *Theoretical base* (19th ed., pp. 2258–2265). Washington, D.C.: National Association of Social Workers.

Turner, F. J. (1986). Theory in social work practice. In J. Turner (Ed.), *Social work treatment* (pp. 1–18). New York: The Free Press.

Turner, F. J. (1996). *Social work treatment,* (4th ed. pp. 1–17). New York: The Free Press.

Turner, J., & Jaco, R. M. (1996). *Problem solving theory and social work treatment.* In F. Turner (Ed.), *Social work treatment,* (4th ed. pp. 503–522). New York: The Free Press.

Wald, L. (1951). *The house on Henry Street.* New York: Holt, Rinehart & Winston.

Wilson, W. J. (1987). *The truly disadvantaged: The inner city, the underclass and public policy.* Chicago: University of Chicago Press.

Wood, G. G., & Middleman, R. (1989). *The structural approach to direct practice in social work.* New York: Columbia University Press.

Woods, M. E., & Robinson, H. (1996). *Psychosocial theory and social work treatment.* In F. Turner (Ed.), *Social work treatment,* (4th ed. pp. 503–522). New York: The Free Press.

Younghusband, E. (1964). *Social work and social change.* London: George Allen & Uwin.

# 6

# ASSUMPTIONS AND PRINCIPLES FOR ETHNIC-SENSITIVE PRACTICE

*This chapter presents the assumptions and principles for ethnic-sensitive practice. These principles are built on (1) select assumptions about human functioning, (2) the concept of the ethnic reality, (3) the layers of understanding, and (4) the view of social work as a problem-solving endeavor.*

*A synthesis of the perspectives presented in the preceding chapters suggests that social work practice needs to be grounded in an understanding of the diverse group memberships that people hold. Particular attention must be paid to ethnicity and social class and to how these contribute to individual and group identity, disposition to basic life tasks, coping styles, and the constellation of problems likely to be encountered. These, together with individual history and genetic and physiological disposition, contribute to the development of personality structure and group life.*

## ASSUMPTIONS

In the previous chapter, we reviewed a number of models for social work practice and considered the varying viewpoints about such matters as (1) the relative importance of the past or the present, (2) how problems are presented and viewed, (3) the importance of the unconscious, (4) the sense of strength and empowerment and, (5) the role of ethnicity in human life. From this array of perspectives, we have selected those most congruent with our views, and we present them here as basic assumptions that undergird our work. They are:

1. Individual and collective history have a bearing on problem generation and solution.
2. The present is most important.
3. Ethnicity is a source of cohesion, identity, and strength as well as a source of strain, discordance, and strife. Social class is a major determinant of life's chances.

4. The social/societal context, and resources needed to enhance the quality of life make a major contribution to human functioning.
5. Nonconscious phenomena affect individual functioning.

## PAST HISTORY HAS A BEARING ON PROBLEM GENERATION AND SOLUTION

Theorists differ in their views concerning the relationship between the origins of a problem and the mechanisms that function to sustain or diminish that problem in the present (Fischer, 1978). Nevertheless, there is little question that individual and group history provide clues about how problems originate and suggest possible avenues for resolution.

### Group History

In Chapter 2, we considered the factors that contribute to the persistence of ethnicity in social life. We reviewed how elements of a group's experience—its joys and its sorrows—seep into the very being of group members. The particular history of oppression to which many groups have been subjected was noted, as was the fact that all groups attempt to develop strategies to protect and cushion their members from the effects of such oppression. Culture, religion, and language are transmitted via primary groups to individuals and serve to give meaning to daily existence.

Crucial to a group's past is the history of the migration experience or other processes through which the encounter with mainstream culture took place. Some, like American Indians and many Chicanos, are a conquered people.[1] Others, including the early Anglo-Saxon settlers, fled religious oppression. Many came for both reasons. Others, like the Irish, came to escape starvation. The contemporary immigrants from the Far East, Asia, Latin America, Europe, and the Middle East come for many of the same reasons.

These experiences continue to affect how members of these groups perceive and organize their lives and how they are perceived by others. Howe (1975) suggested that the earlier generations of Jewish immigrants, fleeing oppression and economic hardship, were focused on seeing to it that their sons and daughters acquired the needed education in order to make it in the outer world. The "fathers would work, grub and scramble as petty agents of primitive accumulation. The sons would acquire education, that new-world magic the Jews were so adept at evoking through formulas they had brought from the 'Old World'" (Howe, 1975). And so, many Jews went off to school in the mainstream, and a substantial numbers of them quickly moved into the middle class. Jews' traditional respect for learning and the particular urban skills in which they had been schooled—a function of anti-Semitism in Eastern Europe, where they were not permitted to work the land (Zborowski & Herzog,

---

[1]Today many American Indian tribes view themselves as nations negotiating on a basis of equality with the United States.

1952)—converged to speed their entry into middle-class America. Education, success, and marriage were the serious things in life. Sensuality and attending to the body were downplayed.

There was a deeply ingrained suspicion of frivolity and sport. "Suspicion of the physical, fear of hurt, anxiety over the sheer 'pointlessness' of play; all this went deep into the recesses of the Jewish psyche" (Howe, 1975). There may be little resemblance between Jewish life on New York's Lower East Side at the turn of the century and the contemporary urban Jew. And yet, the emphasis on intellectualism persists, as does the haunting fear of persecution. There is a lingering suspicion of things physical and a tendency to take illness quite seriously. Jewish men are still considered to make good husbands—they are seen as steady, kind providers who value their families.

Mexican revolutions early in the 1900s, together with the history of American conquest, generated much family disruption. Conscription of men into the armed forces was common. Poor Mexicans migrating into the larger cities of Texas left behind a history, a way of life centered about homogeneous folk societies. In these societies "God-given" roles were clearly assigned. Women did not work outside the home, unless it was in the fields. Each individual had a sense of place, of identity, of belonging. Work was to be found tilling the soil, and education in the formal sense did not exist. Rituals of the church were an intricate part of daily life (West, 1980). These new rural immigrants whose language and belief systems were so different from the frontier mentality were not welcomed.

The history of African Americans in this country has become well known. They were brought in by slavery, an institution of bondage that lasted for 200 years. Yet the astute social worker must know that the history began before the Mayflower, on the African continent, where they developed a culture that reflected skill in agriculture, government, scholarship, and the fine arts (Bennett, 1964). Unlike the ethnic groups mentioned earlier, African Americans were unable to openly preserve their customs, religion, or family tradition in this new land. The institution of slavery actively sought to discourage all that.

Yet, present developments point to the persistence of African customs and values. Sikh immigrant parents struggle to maintain a balance between their traditions, including those focused on family, on dress, and on religious observance, while helping their children to take advantage of the educational opportunities offered here (Gibson, 1988). Although there is considerable congruence between their educational values and those found in educational systems in the United States, there is considerable struggle around other issues. The past history of oppression, imposed by the mainstream society, continues to generate problems in the present—oppression continues.

These are but a few examples of how the nature of migration and the values that people bring with them may converge with the mainstream in the United States and affect present functioning. Intervention strategies must take these into account.

The collective experience of a group affects individuals differently. Personality and life history serve as filters and determine which facets of ethnic history and identity remain an integral part of a person's functioning, which are forgotten, and which are consciously rejected. It is nevertheless unlikely that any Jew does not emit a particular shudder when reminded of the Holocaust. Japanese Americans of any generation recall the relocation experience. In a racist society, they can never be sure how they will be received, for their difference is physically visible.

### Individual History and Group Identity

Individual members of groups have a sense of their group's history. For some it is dim and for others it is clearly articulated; for each it provides a sense of identification with the group. Such identification becomes a component, an integral part of the personality. Erikson (1968) suggested that identity is a process "located" in the core of the individual and yet also in the core of his or her communal culture. The individual maintains a sense of ethnicity, and communal culture, as part of his or her personality. Events in the present that remind one of a past ethnic history may affect decisions made in the future. Such was the experience of a young African American woman who considered her past and its implications for the future. The memories were dim and called forth in response to a class assignment focused on exploring family origins:

> There were always sports persons like Joe Lewis and Jackie Robinson to be proud of but they [the media] never mentioned Paul Robeson or Marcus Garvey. I used to go to the movies and watch Tarzan kill those savages. After several movies it finally dawned on me that those savages were actually my people. Today, I go out of my way to instill racial pride in my children and make sure they are aware of Third World people.

The same assignment brought to the surface dim identifications with a Jewish tradition:

> Education was of prime importance to him [my father], followed closely by social class, religion, and background. Most of my parents' teachings influenced me in other ways. It was understood that I would attend college.... This push toward the pursuit of education and the importance of proper background influenced me in the rearing of my daughters.

In both of these instances, the personality of the mothers has been influenced by the core of the communal culture, with a connection to a clearly identifiable ethnic history. They recognize that their ethnic experiences influence the way they relate to their children.

A final example highlights the integration of the communal culture into the personality and lifestyle of two generations. In this instance the writer has adult children who, as she states, are somewhat removed from their Italian background. Nevertheless, she notes

> My grown son on occasion will request that I 'make one of them ethnic meals.'
> When my daughter visits she always tries to time her trip to coincide with some

*ethnic event. She will be coming home this weekend and will be going to New York to the Feast of San Gennaro in Little Italy. We will partake of some Italian cooking specialties and atmosphere. On these occasions I always feel proud of being Italian.*

Each individual has an ethnic history with roots in the past. Traditions, customs, rituals, and behavioral expectations all interface with life in the United States.

There are those people—on the increase among all groups—who intermarry. Often, those in such a relationship will try to preserve elements of both cultures. Their marriage ceremony may include elements of both groups' traditions. At a wedding between a Chinese American woman and a Jewish man, the bride may wear white at the ceremony that is performed by a rabbi. Then, she dons traditional Chinese wedding finery at the reception held in the Chinese tradition.

These aspects of the past have the potential of affecting perceptions of problems in the present. For those Slavs who were raised with the expectation that intergenerational support is or should be available, its absence may be particularly disquieting and in the extreme devastating. The individual and collective history of African Americans suggests that resources are available in time of trouble. Families across the social classes respond to the needs of kin, both emotional and financial. The response in either instance may rest upon an awareness, articulated or not, of the past (Stack, 1975; Krause, 1978; Boyd-Franklin, 1989). Those people who come from families with a multiethnic and perhaps multiclass background experience joy and strain. One student wrote about the experience of growing up with a Jewish intellectual father and a Puerto Rican mother who had been on welfare before her marriage. The marriage did not last, but the student recalls celebrating holidays at different times with her mother and with her father. They were occasions for joy and for sorrow. But her feeling of identification with both groups remains strong. Her own marriage to someone with a Slavic background adds to the personal mosaic. The fact of her diverse background does not, in the situation of this person at least, minimize the feeling of identity with several groups.

We assume, then, that in any situation that comes to the attention of the social worker, part of the response to that situation derives from an individual's sense of the past as it is intertwined with his or her personal history. Experience with the ethnic reality is an integral part of this history.

## THE PRESENT IS MOST IMPORTANT

The past affects and gives shape to problems manifested in the present. Social work's major obligation is to attend to current issues, with full awareness that the distribution and incidence of problems is often related to the ethnic reality. Thus, alcohol-related problems are extensive among American Indians, Latinos, and Irish Americans. A disproportionate number become alcoholics and develop the medical problems associated with chronic heavy drinking. Suicide and homicide rates among some native tribes are increasing. These problems require attention in the present. Socioeconomic well-being is threatened. The contact with the urban

United States has had particularly negative effects on American Indians. The pride and noble sense of self and tribe so intrinsic to American Indian life must be drawn upon as a mechanism and source of strength for dealing with current problems. However, there is a surge of economic growth as some communities win treaties and develop a variety of businesses.

Understanding and knowledge of the history, customs, and beliefs of different ethnic groups are required for effective practice, both at the individual and the institutional level. Appreciation for customs and beliefs is essential in response to diverse problems. These are manifest in the wishes of members of many ethnic groups to take care of their own in times of trouble. For example, the infant daughter of a paranoid schizophrenic Italian woman needs placement. The schizophrenia is the major problem. It is the grandfather's wish that a cousin adopt the child, thereby keeping her within the family. The ethnic-sensitive worker will realize that the grandfather's effort to keep the infant in the family may well be founded upon the sociopolitical history of Southern Italy. In the midst of that political turmoil, the family was the only social structure upon which an individual could depend. Survival depended upon a strong interdependence among family members that influenced all areas of life. It was a bulwark against those who were not blood relatives (Papajohn & Spiegel, 1975). Yet cousins may not be in a position to offer care in the "old country way" envisioned by the father. At the same time, workers must not only recognize this disposition but make every effort to help the family explore those family resources that will minimize an already traumatic situation.

The current problem must always receive primary attention. However, the practitioner must recognize that ethnic group history may affect present perception of the problem and its solutions.

## THE ETHNIC REALITY AS A SOURCE OF COHESION, IDENTITY, AND STRENGTH AND AS A SOURCE OF STRAIN, DISCORDANCE, AND STRIFE

In Chapter 2, the effects of ethnicity and social class were sketched in broad outline. We now focus attention on those specific components of the ethnic reality that serve as sources of cohesion, identity, and strength, as well as sources of strain, discordance, and strife.

### The Family

As one of the major primary groups, the family is responsible for the care of the young, transmission of values, and emotional sustenance. All families are expected to carry out related tasks.

The value placed on the family and the extent of commitment to involvement in the solution of diverse family problems varies by ethnicity and social class. Attention must be paid to how these same values may produce strain, clash, or conflict with the demands and prejudices of the larger society. Particular cohesive family structures can be observed in the response of members of the Navajo tribe to family problems. It is expected that aunts, cousins, sisters, and uncles will all share in the burden of childrearing and will help out with problems. Relatives do not live far away from one another. Old people give guidance to their children and grandchildren. There is strength in this bond. The family becomes a resource when the courts have questions related to child neglect and custody. Chicanos, Puerto Ricans, Asians, and many Eastern Europeans have similar attitudes toward family obligations.

The sense of family cohesion often diminishes in the second and third generation of immigrants or migrants. The family as transmitter of old values, customs, and language is often seen as restrictive by members of the younger generation.

*Zaidia Perez is a single parent, estranged from her family. She has violated a family expectation by refusing to marry the father of her children. Her Puerto Rican extended family withholds the support usually offered. The result is a life of loneliness and isolation. Additional turmoil comes from Ms. Perez's struggle with her ethnic reality. She is a poor Puerto Rican. It is her conviction that her Spanish heritage and dark coloring have denied her entrance into the middle class. In response she attempts to reject her background by refusing to associate with other Puerto Ricans in the neighborhood.*

Zaidia's struggle with the ethnic reality denies her those supports that come from affable relationships with family and neighbors. Some of that support is provided by ritual and other celebrations.

### *Rituals and Celebrations*

As Puerto Ricans celebrate *Noche Buena* (Christmas Eve), there is a feeling of relaxation, of caring, and of temporary retreat from problems. The extended family gathers with close friends to celebrate "the Good Night." The regular diet of rice and beans becomes more elaborate—yellow rice and pigeon peas are most important, as is the *pernil asado* (roast pork).

The ethnic church—Italian, Polish, and African American churches, the Jewish synagogue, and the Asian Indian temple—is where those with similar histories and like problems gather to affirm their identity and beliefs. This is enhanced by feast days, which combine reverence with ethnic tradition.

The Academy Award-winning film *The Deer Hunter* vividly depicts how rituals and the church serve to buttress and sustain. A wedding takes place in the "Russian Orthodox Church with its spirals that might well have been set in the steppes of the Urals" (Horowitz, 1979). The old Russian women carry cake to the hall for the wedding of one of three young men about to go off to war. There is joyous celebration, Russian folksinging, and "good old-fashioned patriotism." These second-generation, working-class Russian Americans have strong allegiances to this, "their native land." The wedding provides the occasion for the community's show of love and support as their young men go off to war.

There is excitement in rituals and celebrations. For weeks or days before the event, family members in many ethnic groups prepare for Rosh Hashanah, Yom Kippur, Christmas, weddings, and saints' days and *samskaras*. On each of these occasions there is the potential for stress. Each participant does not have the same perception of the event.

Sax (1979) describes his return to his parents' home for the Jewish holidays. No matter what your age, as a child you are assigned a seat at the dining room table. He is a single male, and at *shul* fellow worshipers offer condolences to his parents, who try to be stoic on the matter. But it is time he was married. Proud to be a Jew, he returns to his home for the celebration of Yom Kippur, but he has not fulfilled a communal obligation and the strain seeps through, even on this holiest of days.

Just as the ritual is an occasion for joy and celebration, it is also a time when the young are reminded of transgressions or departures from tradition. Perhaps the David Saxes will think twice about returning for the next celebration.

## Ethnic Schools and Parochial Schools

The Hebrew school, the Armenian or Ukrainian language school, and parochial schools are examples of mechanisms for the preservation of language, rituals, and traditions.

The tie to the old generation and its values is often maintained through such schools. The young do not always feel the need for such an experience. While they attend after-school programs, other children are involved in a variety of activities from which they are excluded. The feeling of strain is expressed by young adults as they recall their childhood experience. "Needing to go to Hebrew school, they felt left out of neighborhood activities two afternoons a week and Sunday morning. They couldn't belong to Little League, or play Pop Warner football or do the other things that other kids did."

Parochial schools in many neighborhoods are expected to transmit ethnic tradition and values, as are the many secular ethnic schools. They assure a continuation of the faith as well as a place in which morality and social norms can be reinforced.

In this design there are inherent conflicts as ethnic neighborhoods change. Gans's (1962) study of the Italians of Boston's West End describes such a neighborhood, in which the church and its school were founded by the Irish, who slowly moved away and were replaced by Italians. The church, however, retained Irish Catholicism. Rather than providing the solace anticipated for association with church-related institutions, discordance is quite evident.

An example of the stress that may come from such a conflict is provided by an Italian who attended such a school:

> *I like being Italian. I grew up in a mixed neighborhood. But it wasn't mixed in terms of what the authority was in relation to church and school if you were Catholic. It was Irish.... I went to a parochial school run by Irish nuns and priests. That is important to mention because there was an insensitivity to our cultural needs at the*

*time.... The Americanization of the Italians was a cultural genocide, at least when I grew up. St. Patrick's Day would come and we would all celebrate.... Obviously there were other saints who were Italian but the cultural pride was not brought in the way St. Patrick was (Frank Becallo, personal communication).*

The ethnic church, through its schools, has the ability to provoke discomfort in students and parents when it does not provide the opportunity for affirmation by all ethnic groups who attend.

## Language

Many immigrant and migrant groups are identified with a past that includes a language other than English. That language is variously used by or familiar to first-, second-, and third-generation children of immigrants. Each language generates a unique ambience and contributes to a group's *Weltanschaung* (world view) (Sotomayor, 1977). Although language can serve as a self- and group-affirming function, and the bilingual individual is to be admired, the use of the second language often generates problems. This is particularly true in those institutions that refuse to listen to anything but mainstream words. Nevertheless, the language can function as a solution in an alien place. For Chicanos, Puerto Ricans, and many Asian people, linguistic identification and affirmation can serve to ease internal stress imposed by political, economic, and social degradation.

Many groups, especially many Latinos, reject the notion that they should abandon their language and its associated culture. This is also true for many Sikhs (Gibson, 1988). Others develop a new sense of identity, as with a pan Asian group (e.g., Kibria, 1997). Bilingual education, which facilitates the acquisition of skills needed for participation in the economic sector of society, is strongly supported. Many minorities view this as essential, refusing to relinquish this basis of uniqueness. Nevertheless, "talking funny" attracts attention and increases the risk of being called a "dumb" wop, Polack, spick, or chink.

## Language—the Sounds of Discord

The effect of mainstream negation of native language has already been noted. There are those group members who consciously deny their native language as a way of "losing" their ethnicity. To speak Italian, Polish, Hungarian, Chinese, or Spanish may well cause strain for those who feel this inhibits their efforts to become American.

In the struggle to become American, Prosen (1976) did not speak Slovenian, the language of her birth, from the time she entered high school until she reached womanhood. When addressed in that language, more often than not she did not respond.

Names such as Franzyshen, Bastianello, and Turkeltaub attract attention. Asian languages and names are difficult for Europeans to hear. Teachers, employers, and new acquaintances stumble over and often resist attempts to learn how to pronounce these names, yet many maintain these names with pride.

## NONCONSCIOUS PHENOMENA AFFECT FUNCTIONING

A comprehensive body of literature has developed that addresses the extent to which social workers must attend to or be aware of the nonconscious, unconscious, or preconscious aspects of human functioning. Hollis (1972) pointed out that there is some confusion about the meaning of the unconscious and the preconscious. There is consensus that in their contacts with social workers people often refer to "hidden" feelings and vague and obscure thoughts and memories. Turner (1979) suggested that significant portions of the personality are not available to the conscious mind. Hollis's treatment of the subject is thorough. There is little question that matters of which people are unaware or that they cannot articulate affect their behavior and feelings. This position is maintained by Woods and Robinson (1996).

One dimension of nonconscious phenomena is particularly important in relation to the ethnic reality. In Chapter 2, culture was defined as involving perspectives on the rhythm and patterns of life, which are conveyed in myriad ways. Nonconscious phenomena factors not quite within awareness are operative when we speak of the routine and habitual dispositions to life that become so thoroughly a part of the self that they require no examination. These dispositions, not articulated, go to the core of the self. The rhythm of Polish community life may be conveyed through the sounds heard by children as they grow. The sounds become routine, an accepted part of life; they are not examined for meaning. They may evoke joy or sadness for reasons unknown to the listener. The Polish experience is described as follows: "The sounds emanating from our home were a potpourri of language, music and shouts. . . . We were a rather emotional and demonstrative family. Laughter and tears, anger and affection were fully given vent. . . We were often headstrong, hasty, sinning, repenting, sinning and repenting again" (Napierkowski, 1976). Recognition of cultural and other life experiences not quite within awareness is a critical component of ethnic sensitive practice.

## PRACTICE PRINCIPLES

Our review of various approaches to social work practice has shown that the profession is diverse and encompasses a variety of viewpoints about the optimal ways of achieving social work objectives of facilitating people's efforts to solve the myriad problems of daily living that are the social worker's concern. Although these approaches are varied and diverse, there is unanimity about the importance the profession attaches to the means that facilitate enactment of the profession's value base.

Our review also suggests that for the most part the approaches to practice are consonant with the view of the ethnic reality presented here. Thus, it is apparent that an understanding of the ethnic reality can be incorporated into all approaches to practice. Especially applicable, however, are those models that focus on simultaneous attention to micro and macro issues.

## Simultaneous Attention to Micro and Macro Issues

The interface between private troubles and public issues is an intrinsic aspect of most approaches to social work practice. All models identify efforts toward systemic change or "environmental work" as a component of professional function. The integration of individual and systemic change efforts is a basic component of the model of ethnic-sensitive practice presented here. Such integration is essential if practice is to be responsive to the particular needs and sensitivities of various groups and individuals. We focus particular attention on the structural source of problems and on those actions that adjust the environment to the needs of individuals (Wood & Middleman, 1989).

Practice is a problem-solving endeavor (Perlman, 1957, 1986; Turner & Jaco, 1996). Problems are generated at the interface between people and their environments. Many of the problems with which social workers deal involve economic and social inequity and its consequences for individuals. This inequity is frequently experienced at the individual and small group level.

Ethnic-sensitive practice calls particular attention to the individual consequences of racism, poverty, and discrimination. Examples are internalization of those negative images the society holds of disvalued groups and learning deficits that are a consequence of inadequate education provided for minorities.

Members of all groups experience some difficulties in their intimate relationships, become ill, and struggle to master the varying tasks associated with different stages of the life cycle. Simultaneous attention to micro and macro tasks focuses the social worker's attention on individual problems at the same time that the systemic source of and possible solution of the difficulty is recognized. Support for personal change efforts and help in altering dysfunctional behaviors is crucial.

A useful framework for highlighting the process of simulation attention to micro and macro tasks is the one presented by Middleman and Goldberg (1974) and amplified by Wood and Middleman (1989). They identify practice as bounded by locus of concern (the problem calling for social work intervention) and persons engaged (persons and/or institutions involved as a consequence of the problems being confronted). This formulation suggests an approach to intervention that follows the demands of the client task. The generalist perspective and practice model is congruent with this framework.

The social worker must look beyond the problems presented by individual clients to see if others are suffering from the same problem. The perspective also serves to call attention to those community and ethnic networks in which people are enmeshed and that they can call upon to aid in problem resolution.

Problems, as identified by the client or social worker, have diverse sources and call for a variety of systemic and individual action. This can be seen in the following example. A Jewish boy may feel torn between parental injuncture not to become involved in celebration of Christmas and his need to join the children in his public school as they trim Christmas trees and sing carols. The turmoil may result in the child becoming withdrawn and searching for reasons not to go to school. Support and counseling from the school social worker may be needed. This may be particularly true if there are few other Jewish children in the school and if alternate sources of support and identity affirmation are not available. At the same time, actions can be planned that are designed to enhance cultural diversity and respect for and knowledge of diverse customs. Suggestions that the school incorporate celebrations unique to various groups as part of the holiday celebration are part of the plan for action. The Jewish and Greek Orthodox children may share the fact that their holiday is celebrated at a different time and in some unique ways.

Social workers must be attuned to both levels of intervention as they go about the task of helping people who are caught in the clash between varying cultures.

Many of the problems with which we deal involve inequity and discrimination. Systemic actions are often called for by the presenting problems. If successfully carried out, such action can forestall or minimize similar problems for other people.

We present here a number of cases to illustrate how practice is enhanced when simultaneous attention is paid to micro- and macro-level tasks, coupled with sensitivity to the ethnic reality.

> *A Mexican American woman accustomed to delivering her babies at home surrounded by family and friends, suffers greatly when placed in the Anglo maternity ward. The sounds are unfamiliar to her and the strangers do not speak her language. She is denied privacy when she is placed in the labor room with other women. Wrapped in a towel, she gets up, searching for familiar faces and more familiar sounds. Physical force may be used to return her to bed. She may be termed an uncooperative, unappreciative patient.*

Little consideration has been given to the possibility of adapting hospital procedures to meet the needs of a large Mexican American community in the area. An understanding of Chicano childbirth rituals would enhance the experience rather than induce terror in an alien setting. A variety of actions are required in this situation, based on the assumptions and theoretical formulations previously discussed: (1) sociological insights call attention to the ethnic reality and suggest an explanation for the action of wandering out of the labor room—although the possibility of pathology must be explored; (2) the patient needs help to avoid a crisis; (3) alternatives to the alien delivery room structure need to be explored. Birthing centers may provide a more comfortable structure, one in which family members participate in the delivery process. This Chicano mother is an "involuntary" social work client. However, institutional and individual needs require the social worker's attention. The crisis nature of the situation compels quick action. Subsequent efforts to modify delivery procedures should involve Chicano women in the planning process.

> *In the midst of a city, hidden within a Latino population, is a community of old Orthodox Jews. Their life is barren. Their housing is substandard. The few clothes that they own are threadbare. Many basic necessities of living are missing from their lives. Language separates them even more from the mainstream. A Yiddish-speaking outreach worker from a community senior citizen program discovers that a significant number of the adults are in need of health care. A particular need is*

*in the area of nutrition. They do not get enough to eat. As a relationship develops, they are able, with the worker assuming a broker role, to obtain the services of a local Nutrition for the Elderly program, which will respect their dietary tradition. Such an accommodation is accomplished with the rabbi of the community. Together they attempt to work this out, realizing that the nutrition program has no basic stake in providing services for members of this religious group. This response was noted despite the fact that the program's mandate was to meet the nutritional needs of the elderly. Special meals for the orthodox add to the program's work load. However, success means that not only will this group be fed but that other ethnic groups will be more likely to have their requests heard.*

The activity has provided regular, nutritious meals that meet dietary tradition through work with the elderly, their rabbi, and the various staff members and administrators of the Nutrition for the Elderly program. The outreach worker began from a point of sensitivity to the ethnic reality.

Application of the principle of following the demands of the client task was successful in beginning a process of change in the policy of a community service program.

*Christine Taylor is a small, thin African American woman in her middle years. She has been receiving AFDC for herself and her two children, who are 10 and 8 years old. With changes in the welfare law, she is now required to work 30 hours a week cleaning bathrooms in a public facility. Her sister, Florence Jackson, lives in the same community. During the past few years, Ms. Taylor has had a number of medical problems, including a hysterectomy and a cerebrovascular accident, which caused paralysis of her left side. She feels she can't do this hard work though she doesn't mind working. She is trying to get her assignment changed. The worker doubts her story and wonders if she is cheating. The worker is aware that they have sufficient food and the children are well clothed. Suspecting a hidden income, the worker probes and discovers that Ms. Taylor is part of a community process known as "swapping." The primary participants are her sister Florence and their close friends. These women have lived on welfare for some time and have had little ability to accumulate a surplus of goods. They share food, clothing, and daily necessities. The limited supply in the community is continually redistributed among family and close friends. Without this system, the sisters, their friends, and neighbors may not survive.*

The practitioner who is aware of this survival technique, which has grown out of the reality of the experience of poor minority people, would not have assumed that deviance, illicit relationships, and perhaps fraud were at work. Knowledge of the existence of such support systems could have minimized premature suspicion and harassment.

*Hidden in the community is another support that enables Ms. Taylor to cope with the guilt and anger she feels about her handicap. Sister Sawyer is an African healer. She claims to have been born in a little village in South Africa and believes a special blessing has been given to her that enables her to remove evil spells, change luck from bad to good, ease pain, and remove unnatural illness. From Sister Sawyer Ms. Taylor receives comfort and reassurance that she is indeed a special person, as well as potions and scriptures that assist in her need for affirmation.*

In this situation two environmental supports of the type often overlooked or considered illegitimate have been identified. If the principle of maximizing potential supports in the client's environment is to be applied, then ethnic coping practices must be viewed as valid. More extensive knowledge of these practices may enable the practitioner to enhance the established structures. Swapping is a well-established custom but may be enhanced if the network is enabled to purchase in bulk from a local cooperative, known to the practitioner and used by the entire community. This would make more commodities available to the group at lower prices, thus maximizing the benefits of a well-established and useful custom.

*A young probationer was under court supervision and had strict orders to remain with responsible adults. His counselor became concerned because the youth appeared to ignore this order. The client moved around frequently and, according to the counselor, stayed overnight with several different young women. The counselor presented this case at a formal staff meeting, and fellow professionals stated their suspicion that the client was either a pusher or a pimp. The frustrating element to the counselor was that the young people knew one another and appeared to enjoy one another's company. Moreover, they were not ashamed to be seen together in public with the client. This behavior prompted the counselor to initiate violation proceedings. (Red Horse, Lewis, Feit, & Decker, 1978)*

This counselor is unaware that these young women are functioning as a support system for his client. They are in fact his first cousins, who are viewed in the same way as sisters. He has been obeying the orders of the court and staying with different units within his family network, which includes more than 200 people and spans three generations. With this knowledge of the client's ethnic reality, the system can be recognized and encouraged. Appropriate family members can be enlisted to participate in plans for the future.

*A Chinese man in his 40s, an engineer by profession, is admitted to a rehabilitation hospital following a stroke. He seems to be making a good recovery, when he makes a suicide attempt. The social worker, startled, explores the reasons with him, his wife, and literature on the Chinese experience. All agree that this is not uncommon for Chinese men facing an illness with potentially devastating consequences.*

Many additional examples could be given. Individual problems often bring to the surface the need for changes in agency policy and administrative practices. Client concerns continually highlight the need for change in existing legislation, the development of new public policy, and research on appropriate service delivery.

The examples have pointed to the need for sensitive awareness of unique cultural patterns, whether the service rendered involves one-to-one counseling with individuals or the need to adapt or develop community programs consonant with the ethnic reality. Each of these and other types of services call for an extensive repertoire of skills. The principle of following the demands of the client task suggests that client need shall determine the nature of the service rendered. In the example cited earlier of the pregnant Chicano woman who runs out of the labor room searching for a familiar face, a number of interventive tasks are suggested. On-the-spot intervention calls for the ability to help her to minimize her fears and avert a crisis. A long-range perspective points to the need to adapt hospital routines in the manner congruent both with the perspective of other Chicano women like her and good medical practice. Perhaps the solution would have been as simple as assuring her that bilingual staff are available to facilitate communication with women when they move into a period of crisis. In the case of a suicidal Chinese man, workers need to be prepared to extend many supports to seriously ill Chinese men. In the community where the hospital is located, the Chinese population is on the increase. If practitioners are to respond to diverse consumer needs, they must be aware of the range of activities commonly suggested by any one problem.

All of these activities involve extensive skill and a readiness to adapt to and learn about the multiple groups that inhabit this land and their members who find their way to social agencies.

## SUMMARY

The basic assumptions of ethnic-sensitive practice are as follows:

1. Individual and collective history have bearing on problem generation and solution.
2. The present is most important.
3. Ethnicity is a source of cohesion, identity, and strength, as well as a source of strain, discordance, and strife. Social class is a major determinant of life's chances.
4. The social/societal context and resources needed to enhance the quality of life make a major contribution to human functioning.
5. Nonconscious phenomena affect individual functioning.

In addition to these assumptions, ethnic-sensitive practice is based on a particular set of principles, which include:

1. Paying simultaneous attention to individual and systemic concerns as they emerge out of client need and professional assessment.
2. Adapting practice skills to respond to the particular needs and dispositions of various ethnic and class groups.

Those approaches most congruent with simultaneous attention to psychological and structural issues are most adaptable to the assumptions of ethnic-sensitive practice.

## REFERENCES

Attneave, C. (1982). American Indians and Alaska native families: Emigrants in their own homeland. In M. McGoldrick, J. K. Pearce, & J. Giordano (Eds.), *Ethnicity and family therapy* (pp. 55–83). New York: Guilford.

Bennett, L., Jr. (1964). *Before the Mayflower: A history of the Negro in America, 1619–1964* (rev. ed.). Chicago: Johnson Publishing.

Boyd–Franklin, N. (1989). *Black Families in therapy.* New York: The Guilford Press.

Cooke, E. H. (1986). Letter on behalf of U.S. English.

Erikson, E. H. (1968). *Identity, youth and crisis.* New York: W. W. Norton.

Fischer, J. (1978). *Effective casework practice: An eclectic approach.* New York: McGraw-Hill.

Gans, H. J. (1962). *The urban villagers: Group and class in the life of Italian-Americans.* New York: The Free Press.

Gibson, M. A. (1988). *Accommodation without assimilation. Sikh immigrants in an American high school.* Ithaca, NY: Cornell University Press.

Hollis, F. (1972). *Casework: A psychosocial therapy* (2nd ed.). New York: Random House.

Horowitz, I. L. (1979). On relieving the deformities of our transgressions. *Society, 16,* 80–83.

Howe, I. (1975). Immigrant Jewish families in New York: The end of the world of our fathers. *New York,* pp. 51–77.

Jackson, E. C., Macy, H. J., & Day, P. J. (1984). A simultaneity model for social work education. *Journal of Education for Social Work, 20,* 17–24.

Jimson, L. B. (1977). Parent and child relationships in law and in Navajo custom. In S. Unger (Ed.), *The destruction of American Indian families.* New York: Association of American Indian Affairs.

Kibria, N. (1997). The construction of 'Asian American': Reflections on intermarriage and ethnic identity among second-generation Chinese and Korean Americans. *Ethnic and Racial Studies, 20,* 523–544.

Krause, C. A. (1978). *Grandmothers, mothers, and daughters: An oral history of ethnicity, mental health and community of three generations of Jewish, Italian, and Slavic-American women.* New York: The Institute on Pluralism and Group Identity of the American Jewish Committee.

Middleman, R., & Goldberg, G. (1974). *Social service delivery: A structural approach to practice.* New York: Columbia University Press.

Mullen E., Chazin, R., & Feldstein, D. (1970). *Preventing chronic dependency.* New York: Community Service Society.

Napierkowski, T. (1976). Stepchild of America: Growing up Polish. In M. Novac (Ed.), *Growing up Slavic in America.* Bayville, NY: EMPAC.

Papajohn, J., & Spiegel, J. (1975). *Transactions in families.* San Francisco: Jossey–Bass.

Perlman, H. H. (1957). *Social casework: A problem-solving process.* Chicago: University of Chicago Press.

Perlman, H. H. (1986). The problem solving model. In F. Turner (Ed.), *Social work treatment* (3d ed.). New York: The Free Press.

President's Commission on Mental Health. (1978). *Task Panel Report.* (Vol. 3, Appendix).

Prosen, R. M. (1976). Looking back. In M. Novac (Ed.), *Growing up Slavic.* Bayville, NY: EMPAC.

Red Horse, J. G., Lewis, R., Feit, M., & Decker, J. (1978). Family behavior of urban American Indians. *Social Casework, 50,* 67–72.

Sax, D. B. (1979, September 27). A holiday at home: A widening gulf. *The New York Times.*

Sotomayor, M. (1977). Language, culture and ethnicity in the developing self concept. *Social Casework, 58*(4), 195–203.

Stack, C. B. (1975). *All our kin: Strategies for survival in a Black community.* New York: Harper Colophon Books, Harper & Row.

Turner, F. (1978). *Psycho social therapy.* New York: The Free Press.

Turner, J., & Jaco, R. M. (1996). Problem solving theory and social work. In F. Turner (Ed.). *Social work treatment* (4th ed.). New York: The Free Press.

Vidal, D. (1980, May 11–14). Living in two cultures: Hispanic New Yorkers. *The New York Times.*

West, R. (1980, March). An American family. *Texas Monthly, 8.*

Wood, G., & Middleman, R. (1989). *The structural approach to direct practice in social work.* New York: Columbia University Press.

Woods, M. E. & Robinson, H. (1996). *Theory and social work treatment.* In F. Turner (Ed.), *Social work treatment* (pp. 555–580). New York: The Free Press.

Zborowski, M., & Herzog, E. (1952). *Life is with people: The culture of the shtetl.* New York: Schocken Books.

# ETHNIC-SENSITIVE PRACTICE

Part II of this book illustrates the principles of ethnic-sensitive practice in action. Three methods of practice have been dominant in the history of social work: casework, group work, and community organization. It is within these familiar methods that we have explored the usefulness of the problem-solving method and the structural approach, among others. Each method is anchored by the unifying base of knowledge, values, and skill. In the search for an even more unifying method, the generalist method has evolved. The generalist method has been described as an approach to practice that is open to the use of a variety of techniques and levels of intervention, from the individual (micro) to the community (macro).

Practice with individuals and groups recognizes the need for knowledge related to the processes of human development and individual responses to life's difficulties at various positions in the life course. This understanding has been the base for the development of approaches to practice that emphasize the importance of the worker-client relationship and the worker's self-awareness and purposeful use of self. These are essential tools for use as client systems meet the challenges that confront them.

Social work practice and literature have always recognized that many people do not seek help readily and that personal change is difficult. The same is true for social work efforts to identify and access resources that may be useful in the change effort. Strategies developed in direct practice reflect the importance of attention to strategies for the processes of help giving and help seeking. Identifying and working on challenges and concluding the process by which client and worker come together are themes consistent with this method of intervention. In Chapter 5 these themes were examined in relation to the ethnic reality. (As we move toward a strengths perspective in our practice, we begin to identify client tensions and concerns as challenges rather than problems.)

Civil rights activities in the 1960s, the War on Poverty in the 1970s, immigration policy changes in the 1980s, and Welfare Reform of the 1990s all require that we pay attention to private troubles and public issues related to race, ethnicity, social class, and gender. Community organization was identified as the appropriate method for intervention in the 1960s and 1970s but less often in the 1980s.

The successful Montgomery Bus Boycott of the 1960s provides an example of community organization as a viable tool for social change. The War on Poverty identified the need for social workers to acquire the macro skills necessary for needs assessments, program design, and evaluation strategies. In addition a need arose for administrative skills in staffing, financial management, service monitoring, and program evaluation. The War on Poverty and Welfare Reform call our attention to issues of social class and gender. Women and their children are most often the targets of welfare reform.

Social work education has responded well to the Council on Social Work Education curriculum policy calling for the generalist perspective to be presented at the undergraduate and beginning graduate levels of education. The ecological systems theme, identification of challenges, a multilevel approach (micro, mezzo, macro), and the ability to select the most appropriate theory and intervention, together, guide generalist perspectives.

In this section we delineate the major procedures related to generalist practice in Chapter 7. In Chapter 8 we place emphasis on the provision of services to individuals, families, and small groups. Chapter 9 considers ethnic-sensitive macro practice in oppressed ethnic group communities. We consider generalist, micro, and macro practice the present spectrum of social work practice. Each looks to the practice base of knowledge, values, and skill. Each section of this practice spectrum is examined in relation to its adaptation to the layers of understanding and the ethnic reality presented in Part I.

Social work practice, for the most part, is carried out in a variety of social work agencies and other human service settings. Most of these settings are organized to respond to particular areas of need. The areas of need are extensive; however, we have chosen three for discussion here. The selection is arbitrary and related to our individual interest and expertise. In Chapter 10 we focus on work with immigrants and refugees, with special attention to the impact of policy changes and Welfare Reform legislation. Practice with families and the impact of life course theory is the theme of Chapter 11. An examination of Welfare Reform of 1998 and its impact on individual and families is presented in Chapter 12.

TANF has replaced AFDC. The considerable changes in the health care system are presented in Chapter 13. In each instance we illustrate how the principles of ethnic-sensitive practice that we have developed can be integrated with the body of concepts and themes that have special relevance for the area of practice. The social worker involved with families needs to be aware of the impact of historical, individual, and social time as they relate to the life course. Within this concept issues related to the ethnic reality may be identified. Welfare reform places time limits for the receipt of benefits with particular emphasis on work. Workers need to be well informed as policies change and continually aware of the challenges women and children face as the system, with its emphasis on work for adults, reinvents itself. Health care workers need to understand how health and illness are defined and that responses to illness are, frequently shaped by deeply ingrained cultural dispositions. In each area of practice, knowledge of prevailing policies, service organizations, and available resources is essential.

Throughout this section of the book, an effort is made to highlight generalist, micro, and macro tasks that are generated by specific client challenges and ethnic-sensitive perspectives. Case examples illustrate how an understanding of the impact of social class, ethnicity, and life course positions, as well as self-awareness and specialized knowledge, converge to aid in assessment and suggest directions for intervention.

Implementing the proposed intervention strategies requires adaptation of skills as proposed in Chapters 7, 8, and 9. In addition we call attention to the way in which the route to the social worker both constrains and enhances practice in work with immigrants and refugees, with families, with recipients of public assistance, and with persons who find themselves in need of health care. We believe that the approach to practice illustrated by these particular fields of practice can be readily adapted to any other substantive areas of practice.

# 7

# ETHNIC-SENSITIVE
# GENERALIST PRACTICE

*The Sandra Mitchell Story*

*Sandra Mitchell is a twenty-one-year-old African American single mother with four children. She has only been able to complete the ninth grade, which limits her potential for employment. At present, she receives public welfare assistance for herself and Edith who is 13 months old. Mandy is five. Jessica, who is three, lives with Sandra's parents who have custody. Although two-year-old Stella lives comfortably with her father's mother, Sandra wishes to regain custody. Sandra and her young family were referred to the Catholic Youth Organization Protective Services Division by the local child protective agency. There has been evidence of domestic violence with Sandra having been physically abused by her boyfriend. Due to her youth, she has few skills that support her in child care responsibilities. Appointments with the children's doctors are missed continually. The tasks of motherhood are overwhelming. Although she has the will to be a good mother, she does not know what it takes. In addition, she will be at risk financially with the implementation of 1996 Welfare Reform policies related to family assistance.*

## THE GENERALIST PERSPECTIVE

The initial meeting of the landmark Milford Conference was held in Milford, Pennsylvania in 1923. The primary task for this meeting of agency executives, convened by the American Association of Social Workers, was to define social casework. Difference in perspectives led to four more meetings and The Milford Report. The report provided a foundation for the development of "the generic social casework theory" (Morales & Sheafor, 1991). Leighningers's (1980) examination of generalist practice cites the Milford Conference as a symbol of the desire to bring greater unity to the several fields of social casework. The call for unity in 1929 has led educators and practitioners to the present and a curriculum policy statement (1994) that requires a generalist perspective at the baccalaureate and masters level in social work education programs. This practice perspective reflects the profession's evolutionary response to society's concerns, needs, events, and thinking (Johnson, 1994).

Johnson (1994) continued to suggest that "generalist practice reflects the theoretical heritage of the profession; assessment, person in the situation, relationship, process, and intervention" (p. 33). Anderson (1982) added that generalists have a wide range of knowledge and skills that target problems at all levels of intervention: intrapersonal, familial, interpersonal, organizational, community, institutional, and societal.

Heus and Pincus (1986) presented the creative generalist as one who "pays attention to, understands and develops expertness in the problem-solving process; discovering, utilizing and making connections to arrive at unique, responsive solutions" (p. 13). Connaway and Gentry (1987) defined generalist practice "as a constellation of social worker role sets designed to respond inclusively and flexibly to a broad range of client systems consistent with the goals and functions of the profession" (p. 3).

As perspectives on generalist practice evolve, others have added their considerations. Kirst-Ashman and Hull (1993) introduced the Generalist Intervention Model (GIM) based on the familiar foundation of knowledge, values, and skills. This is a problem-solving model in which attention is given to micro, mezzo, and macro systems as targets of change. The GIM proposes that any problem may be analyzed and addressed from a wide range of views. The problem-solving method is identified as useful given its flexibility in application. In a later work (1997), the authors present a view of generalist practice as it relates to organizations and communities. Two processes for macro intervention are identified as PREPARE and IMAGINE. The first addresses assessment; the second addresses implementation of the change effort and evaluation of macro change.

The search for a holistic view of practice was led by Maria O'Neil McMahon (1995) whose contention was that the generalist worker needs to be able to view holism as a totality in perspective, "with sensitivity to all of the parts or levels that constitute the whole and to their interdependence and relatedness" (p. 2). Health, wholeness, and the holy are terms proposed in relation to holism.

Tolson, Reid, and Garvin (1994) extend the task-centered approach developed earlier by Reid and Epstein (1972) with the addition of ecological systems theory and a generalist perspective. The result is a model that identifies systems (family, organizations, community, society) and the problems that need to be targeted.

An empowering approach to generalist practice has been offered by Miley, O'Melia, and DuBois (1998). This contribution to the generalist conversation is a framework explaining the functions and roles of generalist social workers, and a strengths and empowerment construct that assumes that "...clients have existing reservoirs and competencies to draw upon" (p. 80).

Although *The Life Model of Social Work Practice* developed by Germain and Gitterman (1980, 1996) is not presented as a generalist model, yet, it may well be viewed as the forerunner of generalist practice. The initial edition was published in 1980. The second edition provides a summary of the defining characteristics of Life-Modeled Practice. Their definition of professional function includes practice with individuals, families, groups, and communities, as well as institutional and political advocacy. Certainly this is our present thinking in relation to the functions of the generalist social worker.

This review of generalist perspectives serves to remind us that views and models related to generalist practice vary. Some elements remain clear. We do agree on multimethod and multilevel approaches with eclectic choices of the theoretical. Differences are to be found in the use of the planned change effort, an ecological systems base, or the philosophical concept of empowerment. No matter what the perspective may be, there is agreement that competent practice requires that attention be paid to the knowledge, values, and skills fundamental to our practice.

## ETHNIC-SENSITIVE GENERALIST PRACTICE

The ethnic-sensitive perspective on generalist practice builds on the structural approach to practice presented by Wood and Middleman (1989). Similar frameworks have been presented by Anderson (1982), Jackson, Macy, and Day (1984), and Day, Macy, and Jackson (1984). Each affirms the initial principle for ethnic-sensitive practice to pay "simultaneous attention to individual and systemic concerns as they emerge out of client need and professional assessment." This principle of simultaneous activity is influenced by the layers of understanding. The interaction may be seen in Figure 7.1 on page 162.

Ethnic-sensitive generalist practice is a problem-solving activity influenced by the layers of understanding as workers direct simultaneous attention to individual and systemic needs. Each presentation of the simultaneous model (Wood & Middleman, 1989; Anderson, 1982; Jackson, Macy, & Day, 1984) calls for (1) direct work with individuals and families in troublesome times; (2) work with groups experiencing similar troubles; (3) influencing informal and institutional systems out of concern for a particular individual, families, and communities with particular problems; and (4) influencing informal and institutional systems out of concern for particular individuals or families.

The generalist worker responding to the request of the child protective agency will work directly with Sandra. Her parents and Jessica's grandmother may serve as resources in the change process. The worker may seek the services of the local program for women who have been abused. Joining a support group that meets at the women's shelter will allow Sandra to relate to women with similar experiences in abusive relationships. Many young mothers like Sandra find it difficult getting to medical appointments on time or at all. The failure to keep an appointment may not be evidence of real neglect, rather the lack of child care resources for children who do not have appointments. Or the cause may be the lack of convenient transportation. This reality calls for an assessment of this single mother's needs in relation to the children's medical needs.

The advocacy role directs the worker to possible resources or to the development of services that will give assurance of better care of young children, particularly those whose parent caretakers are single.

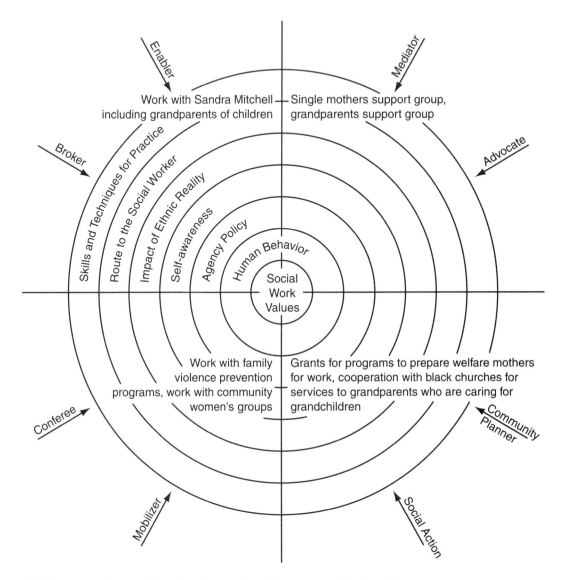

**FIGURE 7.1    A Paradigm for Ethnic-Sensitive Generalist Practice**

Attention needs to be given to grandparents who are caretakers. What services are available to them as they take on tasks that were completed earlier in their life course? Does the community center have a group for grandparents who care for grandchildren? There would be a program if there were funds available for a facilitator with skills in working with older people. Although there is clearly a tradition in the African American experience that supports the care of children by kin, caretakers often need care themselves (Smith, 1997). Given the evolving changes in welfare reform, it is essential that the worker have access to information about the most current policy in relation to the mothers and children.

### The Kenneth Novack Story

*Kenneth and Wanda Novack are second-generation Polish Americans. They rent a house in a low-income, predominately Polish community and live there with their three children: Lawrence (age 15) and twin girls Saundra and Teresa (8 years old). Kenneth graduated from high school and found employment at a local factory. The factory closed 3 years ago, and he has not worked since. Wanda works double shifts as a home health aide and is the major source of income for the family. Mr. Novack refuses to apply for public assistance.*

*The family is experiencing increasing levels of stress. Lawrence, who was an A student, is now barely passing. Last week he was caught stealing from a local convenience store. Teachers are concerned that the twins come to school without lunch or money for lunch at least three times a week. Their father had assumed child care responsibilities during his unemployment. But, during the past 3 months, he has been spending more time in bed and less time caring for the children. He believes that he has failed as a father and husband; he should be able to support his family and resents Wanda's employment. There are many family members in the city, but they are unaware of the Novacks' troubles. Concern for the children has led the school social worker to contact the protective unit of child welfare services.*

## THE LAYERS OF UNDERSTANDING

The layers of understanding are an integral part of ethnic-sensitive generalist practice. The authors, whose work was reviewed earlier, have responded to the Council on Social Work Education mandate for attention to issues of diversity that include race, ethnicity, social class, and religion. Our response to this directive has guided the development of ethnic-sensitive practice. The generalist is included among many other social workers who embrace the knowledge, values, and skills essential for practice. These respond to the need for change in the lives of individuals, their families, groups in which they may hold membership, their communities, and the institutions to which they may belong. Sandra Mitchell needs help in the care of her children. Kenneth Novack needs a job. Each may be assisted by a generalist worker who has an understanding of the layers of understanding.

### Layer 1—Social Work Values

The ethnic-sensitive generalist and other social workers who will work with the Mitchell or Novack families continue to have the *Code of Ethics* developed by the National Association of Social Workers (1996) as a value base for practice. This revised Code sets forth six ethical values and principles to which social workers should aspire.

The *service* value is guided by an ethical principle that asks that service to others be set above self-interest while drawing upon knowledge, values, and skills to help people in need and to address social problems. Social workers are called upon to treat clients respectfully, being mindful of individual differences and cultural and ethnic diversity as they respond to the value of *Dignity and Worth of the Person.* Ethical Standard 1.05 calls for social workers to seek understanding in the nature of social diversity and oppression with respect to race, ethnicity, national origin, color, sex, sexual orientation, age, marital status, political belief, religion, or mental or physical disability.

Sandra is an emerging African American adult, single, with four daughters. This description may generate assumptions related to her age, ethnicity, and the difficulty she encounters as she tries and fails to care for her children competently.

Sandra has been a mother since adolescence. Life course development theory would expect her to respond to the tasks of coping with physical and psychological aspects of puberty. Developing sexual awareness has led her to relationships that resulted in pregnancy four times, and into an abusive relationship. The social worker would do well to challenge the myth of black violence (Stark, 1993), and act with determination to understand the dynamics of Sandra's relationship with the abuser. An understanding of African American traditions in relation to family would help to explain the willingness of both grandparents to care for Stella and Jessica. Staples and Johnson (1993) explain that if it were not for strong kinship bonds, men and women would not have survived slavery. A keen awareness of kinship obligations will be evident as workers accept the plans for Stella and Jessica to remain with their maternal and paternal grandparents.

In response to the *Code of Ethics* (1.05 a), the generalist worker at the CYO will take into account the diversity characteristics of ethnicity, color, gender, age, and marital status as they impinge on Sandra's life experiences. Her experiences with the response, or lack of response, from social service delivery systems must be included as a variable as well. An understanding of the nature of human diversity and oppression as they relate to Sandra is essential as workers respond to the mandates of the Code of Ethics.

Kenneth Novack is a thirty-seven-year-old unemployed Polish American. The lack of employment lends some support to abusive humor that implies that Polish Americans are socially backward, uneducated, and shiftless. With only a high school education, another job has been difficult to find. The children are in trouble; the twins are not well fed and young Lawrence is a thief.

The generalist worker in the protective unit of the child welfare agency must respond to 1.01 of the *Code of Ethics* as it addresses the social workers' commitment to clients, declaring that the well-being of clients is the workers' primary responsibility. If indeed the client's interests are primary as the Code suggests, then attention must be paid immediately to the nutritional needs of Saundra and Teresa. Intervention in behalf of Lawrence must be considered and Mr. Novack's apparent depression must be addressed as well. As each of these tasks, and others that may be identified, are accomplished, the worker will be engaged in the promotion of the well-being of this family.

In the cases of Sandra Mitchell and the Novack family, codified social work values undergird the work of the CYO generalist and the child welfare worker. The well-being of the clients must be primary and diversity issues related to race, ethnicity, age, marital status, and social class must be addressed if self-determination is to be encouraged (1.02).

## Layer 2—Basic Knowledge of Human Behavior

The generalist perspective presented by Miley, O'Melia, and DuBois (1998) includes an ecosystems view as a part of the knowledge base for practice. Germain and Gitterman's (1996) belief that individuals confront many stressors in various aspects of life provides a framework for examining the life experiences of Sandra Mitchell and Kenneth Novack.

The life model (Germain & Gitterman, 1980, 1996) contends that the stressors include difficult life transitions, traumatic life events, environmental pressures of poverty and oppression, as well as dysfunctional processes in family, group, and community life. Life transitions include developmental and social changes in status and role. Kenneth Novack and Sandra Mitchell have lost status. Both have suffered significant losses, their roles as parents have been compromised. Kenneth has lost the employment that gave him status as head of his family. The social time concept related to the life course suggests that unexpected transitions, such as loss of job and loss of child custody, may lead each family to positive transformations or to disorganization. Kenneth's family seems to be on the verge of disorganization and Sandra's family is in the process; two of her children already live in the homes of their grandparents. Social workers who have responsibility for the children in kinship care must have an understanding of the meaning of these events to Sandra, her mother, and the children's paternal grandmother. This care from both grandparents gives support to Billingsley's (1993) contention that the extended African American family excels in informal adoptions. He continues that parents of single mothers, grandparents to the children, are generally the family members that care for children.

Germain's (1991) ecological perspective in relation to human development in the context of family and community argues that family members develop in tandem. She calls for an examination of interpersonal processes in families. Teresa and Saundra, the Novack twins, are children as are Edith, Mandy, Jessica, and Stella, the Mitchell children. Lawrence is an adolescent, Sandra is an emerging adult, Kenneth and Wanda Novack are adults. Unemployment, lack of sufficient food, school failure, and the inability to care for small children all impede family processes. Each family member, including grandparents, will respond to stressors in relation to their individual life course and family life course positions.

This knowledge of human behavior will assist CYO protection workers and child welfare generalists as they support these families in decision making in relation to joining a group for young single mothers, or enrolling in retraining programs that develop skills needed for employment in industries that plan to move into the area. An understanding of the needs of children and adolescents provides a foundation for referrals to community resources geared to after school programs or evening league sports for young men. It will also lead to thinking about child welfare policy in relation to kinship care, or alternative court systems for adolescents.

## Layer 3—Knowledge and Skill in Agency Policy and Service Influence Professional Practice

Sheafor and Landon (1987) have stated that "social work practice is inherently generalist" (p. 660). Social workers in schools and protective units of child welfare services will focus on the person and environment interaction within the context of the school and child welfare agency. Each will need to understand the administrative processes that support their work.

The social work generalists at Teresa and Saundra's school and at Lawrence's high school will need to understand that the objective of school social work "is to maximize equal opportunity for all pupils so that each child regardless of background can make the best of what school has to offer" (Allen–Meares, 1991, p. 13). The work of school generalists will be influenced by various federal, state, and local legislation that calls attention to the needs of special children. These include pupils with handicaps, bilingual children, pregnant adolescents, truants, and abused and neglected children. The Novack twins and their brother are in the latter population. There is evidence that their parents, especially their father, is not responding to his children's basic needs.

Knowledge of the law related to child abuse and neglect will be essential for school and child welfare generalists. They will need to answer important questions. Must a social worker be certain that abuse or neglect is taking place? Does the state require that school social workers report child abuse or neglect? What are the procedures for reporting abuse or neglect (Fischer & Sorenson, 1991)?

School social workers need to collaborate with school personnel, administrators, teachers, teacher aides, guidance counselors, athletic staff, and psychologists. There must be an understanding of the boundaries set by administrators. Although it is expected that school social work generalists will make home visits, conduct social developmental studies of pupils and families, and refer families to community based services (Allen–Meares, 1991), not all administrators accept these as appropriate social work activities. It becomes difficult to respond to the needs of children when such constraints are in place.

Child welfare generalists function within a more comfortable social work context. Costin, Bell, and Downs (1991) note that child welfare continues to be the one field in social welfare in which social work is dominant. The social worker assigned to the Novack family will find support in relation to a commitment to the welfare of all children. The work of protective services is clear, providing a foundation for the work with Lawrence and his twin sisters. Child protective services are authoritative and respond to complaints from family or community forces, but they must use this authority prudently. Services are directed to families in which children are at risk, and agencies must act promptly in response to community sanctions. It is expected that child protective agencies will respond to the needs of these children.

Knowledge of the function of school social work and the manner in which it is received in a particular school setting is essential for the generalist who will respond to the needs of teachers and staff, children and their families, and the community at large. The protective service generalist will understand the function of this service within the larger context of child welfare.

## Layer 4—Self-Awareness, Including Insight into One's Own Ethnicity

The Maternal and Child Health Bureau (undated) has defined cultural competence as having knowledge that cultural differences as well as similarities exist, without assigning values such as better, worse, right, or wrong to those cultural differences. Programs directed to the health of children are expected to be culturally competent. Of interest to us here is the expectation that programs will be committed to practices in which personnel assess their own cultural heritage and attitudes. This introspection is the core of this layer of understanding.

The ethnic-sensitive generalist worker realizes that media messages about the rate of adolescent pregnancies among African American teenagers must be examined closely. They will recognize that violence against women occurs at all social class levels and generally is not provoked by the female partner. Sandra Mitchell may be more a victim of physical and verbal abuse than a neglecting parent; Mr. Novack's depression could be more related to his inability to find meaningful employment than to any jokes about the indolence of Polish men.

*What do I believe?* and *How will I respond?* to questions with answers that reflect my own ethnic experience? Often a worker's experience has been influenced by two or more ethnic or religious groups. In those experiences are children honored and respected? Are they cared for within the family when the need arises? Are parents who are in need admonished for their seeming failure, or do family members rally around to help and support? The families introduced here need help as many stressors touch on their lives. The generalist workers response will be influenced by personal experiences with the ethnic reality, in addition to the experiences of the Novacks and the Mitchells.

## Layer 5—The Impact of the Ethnic Reality on the Daily Life of the Client

Sandra Mitchell and the kin who serve as caretakers of her children are African American. They are all members of the working class. Sandra receives no support payments from the fathers of the children; therefore, she receives public assistance and may be at risk as welfare reform evolves. The grandparents' resources are meager even though they care for their granddaughters. Harper and Lantz (1996) call attention to role flexibility in African American families as they respond to unemployment, poverty, and racism in the United States. Extended families have learned to share households, food, money, child-care services, and emotional nurturance

(p. 41). The ethnic reality for this extended African-American family is such that movement to a more prosperous social class position will not be easy for Sandra, who is without the skills called for in the labor market. In addition, she will continue to be responsible for the care of at least two small children.

The church, often a significant resource in the African American community, may be viewed as available to all three generations in this family. The range of services that may be offered by the black church are identified by Tolliver (1995) in a study of a church in Central Harlem, New York City. There was a sense of compassion in this congregation, with leaders committed to helping the people of the Harlem community. Congregations such as these are community resources with the ability and willingness to respond to the needs of the children, adolescent, young adult, and adults in this family. Oates–Cannon (1995) adds that a strong religious orientation is a source of strength for African American single mothers. The resources of the church and a strong religious orientation may be listed among the resources available to single mothers in African American families and communities.

Alba's (1990) examination of discrimination experienced by white ethnic groups included responses from Polish Americans who reported that the experiences were most often slurs or negative comments. Seldom were they denied a job or a place to live. This Polish experience differs from that of African Americans, who experience overt discrimination in many ways. The lack of experience with discrimination does not make the Novacks immune from other experiences related to their social class position.

The Novack marriage had been stable before Kenneth lost his job. Each family member understood that everyone in the family was to pull their own weight. The children did their part. Lawrence was a good student, achieving excellent grades. Unemployment had a significant impact on the family. Mr. Novack's image of himself changed; he is no longer unable to contribute to the family finances. His fear of dependency is compounded by the realization that his wife is employed and he is not. The mutual respect, support, cooperation, and financial and spiritual help that has been noted as a characteristic of Polish families is lacking. Lawrence's delinquent behavior has brought shame to the family (Mondykowski, 1982). Outsiders have intruded by suggesting that help is needed.

Ethnicity and social class, the ethnic reality, has had an impact on both families, Mitchell and Novack. This must be taken into consideration when they meet the generalist social worker in the school or at the child welfare agency.

### Layer 6—An Understanding of the Impact of the Route to the Social Worker

Sandra's route to the social worker has been coercive. The report of child neglect has alerted child welfare systems charged with the protection of abused and neglected children. The child welfare generalist seeks to safeguard the physical and emotional well-being of children who have been or are at risk of being neglected or abused (Stein, 1981). Earlier neglect was such that Stella is cared for by her maternal grandmother. Sandra now seeks custody of Jessica. Her chances of success are questionable given the coercive route that she has been forced to take.

The Novack's route to the social worker is totally coercive. A complaint has been made by the school. Protective service is involuntary, and the situation with the children is such that the agency is justified in "intruding" into the family's life. Someone has suggested that the Novacks are "not providing the love or basic care a child needs for healthy growth and development" (Costin, Bell, & Downs, 1991).

Teachers who are concerned about protecting children, the sanctity of the family, government interference, or the child welfare system may be reluctant to report abuse to the social worker. Part of the social workers' responsibility will be to provide information or training for all school staff so that they are alerted to the signs of neglect or abuse. It is clear that the twins are without lunch or money for lunch; they are hungry. Other neglect or abuse is not so easily identified (Goren, 1991).

Mr. Novack will resist the intrusion. However, he has been unable to carry his weight in caring for the children. Mrs. Novack is employed, so there is income, but Mr. Novack remains in bed and neglects to prepare lunch or to give the girls money for lunch.

Routes to the social worker have been difficult for these families. They do not wish to develop relationships with social workers. Social workers respond to a social mandate to care for all children, no matter what their special characteristics may be.

## Layer 7—The Adaptation of Strategies and Procedures for Ethnic-Sensitive Generalist Practice

We stated earlier that generalist social workers must direct simultaneous attention to individual and systemic concerns that emerge out of client need and professional assessment. The response will require a wide range of skills, techniques, and roles for ethnic-sensitive work with individuals, families, and small groups, and in planning, advocacy, and collaboration with natural and formal institutions. Each of these resources for intervention must be reviewed, reconsidered, adapted, and modified in relation to the ethnic reality.

A review of the social work practice literature provides adequate references for intervention at micro, mezzo, and macro levels (Brown, 1991; Shulman, 1991, 1992; Hepworth & Larsen, 1997; Netting, Kettner, & McMurtury, 1993; Breuggemann, 1996; Tropman, Erlich, & Rothman, 1995; Kretzmann & McKnight, 1993). Other works provide directives for interventions with oppressed ethnic groups (Lum, 1996; Julia, 1996; Green, 1995; Harper & Lantz, 1996; Rivera & Erlich, 1998; Logan, Freeman, & McRoy, 1990).

Ethnic-sensitive generalists need to direct their attention to functions and roles available to them as they work simultaneously with individuals, families, communities, and organizations (Miley, O'Melia, & DuBois, 1997). Wood and Middleman (1989) have suggested the roles of conferee, broker, and mediator. Hoffman and Sallee (1994), Johnson (1995), and Kirst-Ashman and Hull (1997), among others, proffer additional roles useful to the generalist including enabler, educator, advocate, behavior changer, community planner, caregiver, collaborator, and networker roles.

Miley, O'Melia, and DuBois (1998) provide greater specificity, assigning roles to particular generalist functions identified as education, consultancy, and resource management. With each function the worker may assume a variety of roles as work is accomplished at micro, mid, and macro levels.

Assuming the resource management function and the broker/advocate role, Sandra's worker may link her with the services and resources she will need, such as reliable transportation to medical facilities and convenient food pantries that will supplement the welfare grant and food stamps.

At the mid level, implementation of the convener role requires the worker to join with others in the child welfare system to develop a network that would assist single mothers. Networks have the ability to direct colleagues and their clients to new resources. If there are no community resources available that would help single mothers to develop skills that are needed for responsible child care, development of such resources is certainly the role of the facilitator. The activist role at the macro level work would require continuous attention to welfare reform regulations that would be detrimental to young mothers without marketable skills. At some later point, social action may be appropriate.

The roles of enabler, facilitator, and planner are components of the consultancy function. Mr. Novack and his family need to find solutions that will allay the stress that confounds them. How will the twins be fed? What is the best educational plan for Lawrence given his low grades and problem with the police? Does Kenneth require medical attention for depression, and does Wanda have sufficient medical coverage as a benefit of employment? As a facilitator, the school social work generalist may join with the CYO protection worker to promote better linkages between the school, the child protection division of the child welfare agency, and families in which children are at risk.

Research and planning are the strategies at the macro level of consultancy. What does the community need in the manner of resources for unemployed workers? Mr. Novack has been unemployed for three years and has few skills beyond those needed as a laborer in the industry that closed. What may be the social worker's role in the development of policy that will attract new industry to the community? Certainly there are other men and women with few skills who lost employment along with Kenneth Novack.

No matter what function or role the generalist may take, the ethnic-sensitive worker will acknowledge that for Sandra, her children, and their grandparents, racism and its impact will be evident at several points during their life course. The fourth layer of understanding calls for workers to be aware of the impact their own ethnic experiences may have on their practice. The dynamics of differences in terms of clients behavior and its impact on workers' behavioral expectations, must be considered. What might Sandra's response be to an older Italian worker given her experiences with covert and overt racism throughout her life?

Kenneth Novack is a second-generation Polish American. Polish immigration to the United States began during the American colonial era with the first wave arriving between 1608 and 1776. The Novacks' parents were part of the mass migrations of Poles during the early years of the twentieth century. Like many other Polish immigrants, they were from peasant classes who settled in industrial centers and began employment at the bottom of industries that were expanding at the time. They found themselves in the middle of the pecking order in places of employment between native born Americans, the Irish, and Germans—and black Americans who were at the very bottom (Hraba, 1994). An understanding of the history of Polish immigration, traditions, and customs provide a context for intervention with the best functions and roles. Mr. Novack is no longer able to hold the patriarchal role that has been assigned to Polish men. Three years of unemployment have taken away the power that he once held as head of the family. What might be his response to a well-educated African American woman who has been assigned by the child welfare agency?

Ethnic-sensitive intervention will be enhanced by an ethnic assessment on which to base functions and roles. A revised guide for ethnic assessment originally posed by Fandetti and Goldmeir (1988) may be found in Appendix 2. There are three levels of assessment: the person, the family or group, and the community. Each is to be viewed as one of the several components of the ethnic reality. Ethnic assessment involves consideration of cultural orientation, ethnic dispositions, family orientations, and the larger community as well as the ethnic community.

This final layer of understanding requires generalist workers to be aware of the many functions and roles that are available for intervention. Each must be used selectively in response to the ethnic assessment as individual and systemic needs are identified.

## SUMMARY

The Council on Social Work Education in its most recent policy statement (1997) requires that programs provide a generalist perspective at the undergraduate and the graduate foundation level. In addition, it requires that attention be paid to human diversity. This chapter has highlighted race, ethnicity, age, and social class along with a strengths perspective. It reviews the most current work presenting the generalist perspective. Functions and roles for this practice method at micro, mezza, and macro levels have been suggested. This perspective allows the generalist to view intervention through simultaneous activity in several systems.

## REFERENCES

Alba, R. A. (1990). *Ethnic identity: The transformation of white America.* New Haven, CT: Yale University Press.

Allen-Meares, P. (1991). The contribution of social workers to schooling. In R. Constable, J. P. Flynn, & S. McDonald (Eds.), *School social work: Practice and research perspectives* (2nd ed., pp. 5–16). Chicago: Lyceum.

Anderson, J. D. (1982). Generic and generalist practice and the BSW curriculum. *Journal of Education for Social Work, 18,* 37–45.

Billingsley, A. (1993). *Climbing Jacob's ladder: The legacy of African American families.* New York: Simon & Schuster.

Brown, L. (1991). *Groups for growth and change.* New York: Longman.

Brueggemann, W. G. (1996). *The practice of macro social work.* Chicago: Nelson-Hall Publishers.

Connaway, R. S., & Gentry, M. E. (1987). *Social work practice.* Englewood Cliffs, NJ: Prentice-Hall.

Costin, L. B., Bell, C. J., & Downs, S. W. (1991). *Child welfare policies and practice* (4th ed.). New York: Longman.

Day, P. J., Macy, H. J., & Jackson, E. C. (1984). *Social working exercises in generalist practice.* Englewood Cliffs, NJ: Prentice-Hall.

Fandetti, D. V., & Goldmeir, J. (1988). Social workers as culture mediators in health care settings. *Health and Social Work, 13,* 171–180.

Fischer, L., & Sorenson, G. P. (1991). *School law for counselors, psychologists, and social workers.* New York: Longman.

Germain, C. B., & Gitterman, A. (1980). *The life model of social work practice.* New York: Columbia University Press.

Germain, C. B., & Gitterman, A. (1996). *The life model of social work practice: Advances in theory and practice* (2nd ed.). New York: Columbia University Press.

Goren, S. G. (1991). The wonderland of social work in schools, or how Alice learned to cope. In R. Constable, J. P. Flynn, & S. McDonald (Eds.), *School social work: Practice and research perspectives* (2nd ed., pp. 62–70). Chicago: Lyceum.

Green, J. W. (1995). *Cultural awareness in the human services: A multi-ethnic approach.* Boston: Allyn & Bacon.

Harper, K. V., & Lantz, J. (1996). *Cross-cultural practice: Social work with diverse populations.* Chicago: Lyceum Books.

Hepworth, D. H., & Larsen, J. A. (1993). *Direct social work practice: Theory and skills.* Pacific Grove: CA: Brooks/Cole.

Hoffman, K. S., & Sallee, A. (1994). *Social work practice: Bridges to change.* Boston: Allyn & Bacon.

Hraba, J. (1994). *American ethnicity* (2nd ed.). Itasca, IL: F. E. Peacock.

Jackson, E. C., Macy, H. J., & Day, P. J. (1984). A simultaneity model for social work education. *Journal of Education for Social Work, 20,* 17–24.

Johnson, L. C. (1995). *Social work practice: A generalist approach* (5th ed.). Boston: Allyn & Bacon.

Julia, M. C. (1996). *Multicultural awareness in the health care professions.* Boston: Allyn & Bacon.

Kirst-Ashman, K. K., & Hull, G. H. (1993). *Understanding generalist practice.* Chicago: Nelson-Hall Publishers.

Kirst-Ashman, K. K., & Hull, G. H. (1997). *Generalist practice with organizations and communities.* Chicago: Nelson-Hall Publishers.

Kretzmann, J. P., & McKnight, J. L. (1993). *Building communities from inside out: A path toward finding and mobilizing a communities assets.* Chicago: ACTA Publications.

Logan, S. M., Freeman, E. M., & McRoy, R. G. (1990). *Social work practice with Black families: A culturally specific perspective.* New York: Longman.

Lum, D. (1996). *Social work practice and people of color: A process–stage approach* (2nd ed.). Pacific Grove: Brooks/Cole Publishing Company.

McMahon, M. O'N. (1995). *The general method of social work practice* (3rd ed.). Boston: Allyn & Bacon.

Miley, K. K., O'Melia, M., & DuBois, B. (1998). *Generalist social work practice.* Boston: Allyn & Bacon.

Mondykowski, S. M. (1982). Polish families. In M. McGoldrick, J. K. Pearce, & J. Giordano (Eds.), *Ethnicity and family therapy* (pp. 393–411). New York: The Guilford Press.

National Association of Social Workers. (1996). The code of ethics. Washington, DC: NASW Press.

Netting, F. E., Kettner, P. M., & McMurty, S. L. (1993). *Social work macro practice.* New York: Longman.

Oates-Cannon, E. W. (1995). Religiosity and successful single mother headed African American families. *Black caucus journal of the national association of social workers.* 2(1) 1–12.

Reid, W. J., & Epstein, L. (1972). *Task centered casework.* New York: Columbia University Press.

Rivera, F. G., & Erlich, J. L. (1998). *Community organizing in a diverse society* (3rd ed.). Boston: Allyn & Bacon.

Sheafor, B. W., & Landon, P. S. (1987). Generalist perspective. In A. Minahan (Ed.), *Encyclopedia of social work* (18th ed. pp. 660–669). Silver Springs, MD: NAtional Association of Social Workers.

Shulman, L. (1992). *The skills of helping individuals, families and groups* (3rd ed.). Itasca, IL: F. E. Peacock.

Smith, C. (1997). The African American tradition of kinship care in the child welfare system: Last laugh or last chance. Paper presented at New York State Social Work Association Annual Meeting, Colonie, NY.

Staples, R., & Johnson, L. B. (1993). *Black families at the crossroads: Challenges and prospects.* San Francisco: Jossey–Bass.

Stein, T. (1981). *Social work practice in child welfare.* Englewood Cliffs: Prentice-Hall.

Tolliver, W. F. (1995). At the point of need: A model for church based social services. *Black Caucus Journal of the National Association of Black Social Workers.* 2(1) 12–20.

Tolson, E. R., Reid, W. J., & Garvin, C. D. (1994). *Generalist practice: A task-centered approach.* New York: Columbia University Press.

Tropman, J. E., Erlich, J. L., & Rothman, J. (1995). *Tactics and techniques of community intervention* (3rd ed.). Itasca, Ill.: F. E. Peacock Publishers.

Wood, G. G., & Middleman, R. R. (1989). *The structural approach to direct practice in social work.* New York: Columbia University Press.

# 8

# ADAPTING STRATEGIES AND PROCEDURES FOR ETHNIC-SENSITIVE PRACTICE: DIRECT PRACTICE

### The Jones Family

*Ernestine and Joseph Jones and 18-month-old Ellen have been referred to the social worker serving the inpatient pediatric unit of a large, suburban hospital located in the Northeastern United States. The department provides services to the families of children who are hospitalized for a variety of medical problems. Many of the children currently hospitalized in such facilities are suffering serious difficulties. Services include help in planning for posthospital care, especially in locating and using a variety of community-based resources, such as home nursing care, counseling to help children and families cope with the social and psychological consequences of the illness, and communicating with doctors, nurses, and other members of the hospital staff.*

*A family history, shared with the hospital by a local agency serving young people infected with the human immunodeficiency virus (HIV), showed that the Joneses are a middle-class, African American family. Mr. Jones is employed as a postal worker and Mrs. Jones as a clerk in the local office of the Motor Vehicle Bureau. Both are high school graduates who had always worked hard and hoped that their children would go to college and make a good life for themselves. They had three children. Two are college graduates who live some distance away. Ellen lives with her grandparents, Ernestine and Joseph, aged 44 and 46, respectively.*

*Ellen was 18 months old at the time of the referral and was born with acquired immunodeficiency syndrome (AIDS). Her mother, Jan, who had been addicted to drugs, died of AIDS a few weeks before Ellen's present hospitalization.*

*Beth Jacobs is the social worker to whom the Joneses have been referred. She has an M.S.W. and has been out of school for 5 years. The increase in the number of situations involving HIV- and AIDS-infected children has led her to develop considerable knowledge about the usual medical and psychosocial difficulties being experienced by these children and their families.*

> *The Joneses had broken off contact with Jan. Her addiction and welfare status had upset them. When she was dying of AIDS they took in Jan and her child.*

In this chapter we present the social work strategies and interventive procedures most commonly used by social workers in direct practice and discuss how these strategies and procedures can be adapted to take account of ethnic and class diversity. We continue the pattern established in the discussion of generalist practice of viewing the social worker's activity as a series of thoughts and actions that can be subsumed under the concept "The Layers of Understanding" in Chapter 4. As we consider the strategies and skills of direct practice, we draw extensively on the situation of the Jones family to illustrate the major concepts. We show how the social worker aims to help them to cope with Ellen's hospitalization: from anticipating the needs of her day-to-day care after discharge to confronting her impending death. We draw as well on other case material, especially the case of Doris Cheng.

## PART 1: THE LAYERS OF UNDERSTANDING

In this first part of the chapter we consider the situation of the Jones family, as well as that of other people, within the first six layers of understanding: (1) social work values; (2) knowledge of human behavior; (3) knowledge and skill in using social welfare policies and services; (4) self-awareness and management of the worker's own ethnic reality; (5) the impact of the ethnic reality on the daily life of clients, and (6) understanding the route to the social worker.

The worker–client encounter is composed of many facets of thought, action, and feeling. When these encounters are described and analyzed, they are of necessity presented as if all events and thought take place in chronological order. In fact, much thought and action is occurring simultaneously. Some take place before work with the client begins. For example, in the following pages we suggest that workers draw on their basic knowledge of the theories of human behavior as they try to assess the situation before them. We also consider the importance of a high degree of self-awareness and how that awareness can aid the worker in responding with sensitivity to the client. Anticipation of client resource needs is also expected.

### Intervention and the Layers of Understanding

#### Social Work Values
Basic adherence to social work values quickly becomes an integral part of the social worker's functioning. Respect for the client's right to self-determination, to basic resources, and other values becomes habitual in the sense that practice is imbued and guided by values. Nevertheless, there are times when a worker's commitment to values is tested. There are instances where the worker's own beliefs run counter

to client lifestyle. And so it is important that we begin this discussion of direct intervention with a reminder that workers must constantly reflect on the importance of values, and consider possible approaches when adherence becomes especially difficult. In the following pages, we will be following the case of the Jones family and Doris Cheng. In both these situations, value issues may arise because the families' belief systems may run counter to those to which workers are accustomed. For example, Mrs. Jones is a born-again Christian who aims to draw the worker into her own belief system. Doris Cheng, a highly educated Chinese woman, uses a folk healer. Respect and acceptance of these kinds of client decisions become extremely important if intervention is to be empathic and effective.

### Knowledge of Human Behavior

In working with different clients, social workers draw on the repertoire of knowledge they have acquired through the years of their schooling and practice experience. Not all that they know is applicable to every situation. There are some general guidelines in how best to draw on one's store of knowledge.

For example, in preparing to work with Mrs. Jones and Ellen, the worker knows that this is an African American family that has shown much strength in the face of considerable difficulty, caring now for a grandchild with AIDS, following the death of a daughter who had so disappointed them. Some examples follow.

*Personality theory* draws attention to ego strength; the conceptions of *the ethnic reality* helps to focus on the likely experiences of this middle-class African American family caught in the contemporary crisis of AIDS, coupled with a strong tradition of religiosity, a source of comfort to many African American families.

The available evidence suggests that they indeed have a lot of strength. This has been demonstrated in their capacity to overcome the obstacles of racism, surely an element of the experience of most African Americans. Despite modest economic circumstances, they have managed to help two children to acquire a college education.

They surmounted their disappointment and anger brought on by Jan's addiction and illness in order to care for Jan before her death, and are now preparing to do the same thing with her dying child. Part of the worker's task is to recognize the strengths of the family members as they once more "gird their loins" to meet the present challenges. Other situations are illustrative. There is, for example, the situation of Doris Cheng.

### Doris Cheng

*Doris Cheng is a 30-year-old engineer at a large communications firm. She and her husband are both natives of Taiwan and were educated there. They came to the United States shortly after graduating from college and marrying in Taiwan. Mr. Cheng is an unemployed computer programmer. They have a 3-year-old child and are presently separated.*

*Ms. Cheng seeks the help of the company's Employee Assistance program when her husband continues to come around, threatens physical abuse, and blames his present lack of employment on her. On seeing a psychiatrist, he refused to go back, believing the psychiatrist was really an FBI agent.*

> *Exploration reveals that Doris has a history of petit mal seizures and that her son, Don, barely weighed 5 pounds at birth. Her husband's family fears that her seizure disorder may be inherited and related to the son's low birth weight.*
>
> *Both sets of parents have moved to this country, although they also retain a home in Taiwan. Doris spends a great deal of time with her husband's parents. They do not believe their son has a psychiatric problem and want Doris to return to him. She refuses to return unless he seeks further psychiatric help.*
>
> *Her ability to work is suffering given all of the physical and psychiatric pressures.*

**Personality Theory.**   This situation ultimately calls for complex differential psychiatric and physical diagnoses, as well as assessment of personality functioning. Important is the knowledge to distinguish between perceptions of mental health and illness as viewed in the United States and in traditional Chinese culture.

The situation of the Jones family also calls for other kinds of understanding.

**Family and Individual Life Cycle Theory.**   The Joneses are approaching middle age. At this stage of life many people no longer have child care responsibilities. They have worked hard and had hopes that by now they would be able to enjoy the fruits of their labor.

When grandparents are in the position of having to assume total responsibility for the care of infants, the ordinary ebb and flow of their life is disrupted. Not only is the expected cycle of life disrupted and "out of sinc" with usual expectations, but there is enormous physical strain. Toddlers, especially if they are ill and require a great deal of attention, strain the physical capacity of many people.

**Other Theories of Human Behavior.**   Other theories and areas of knowledge are needed as workers begin the process of engagement, assessment, problem formulation, and problem solving.

Practitioners need to be familiar with the prevailing trends in family life and with the concerns of those who find themselves in troubled family situations. The daily traumas of marital conflict may be compounded by a sense of personal failure, hostility, the threat of desertion, or limits on mobility. Those who work in schools need to be familiar with theories of learning disability and must learn who is at particular risk for developing school-related problems. These are examples of the kinds of knowledge that social workers must have.

Also of extreme importance is understanding of how organizations function and the responsibilities and feelings of others who work in the organization. This is particularly relevant in interdisciplinary settings. Workers employed in school systems where they function on teams of psychologists, teachers, and physicians must familiarize themselves with the kinds of problems usually brought to the team and how each discipline views its role.

### Knowledge and Skill in Using Welfare Policies and Services
One of social work's unique contributions among the helping professions is the social worker's understanding of the importance of resources in people's lives, as well as knowledge of available resources and skills in helping people to access these.

It is crucial, therefore, that social workers draw on this knowledge continually. For example, in working with the Jones family, knowledge of shifting and new resources can go a long way toward making life easier for this burdened family.

### Self-Awareness and Managing One's Own Ethnic Reality

A key component of any practice is the worker's capacity to bring to bear a disciplined understanding of self or what is commonly known as *self-awareness.* Elsewhere we have suggested that "the disciplined and aware self remains one of the profession's major tools. Involved is the process of discovering 'Me—not always nice, sometimes judgmental, prejudiced and noncaring' and making use of such insight to further empathic skills" (Devore & Schlesinger, 1986, p. 514). A key component of the aware self is awareness of one's one ethnic and cultural background and how these experiences have contributed to personal strength and trauma. Most important is the capacity to integrate the personal experience of self and ethnicity in the disciplined process of understanding how these impact on other people, especially the clients whom social workers serve. The response of Beth Jacobs, the social worker who is working with Mrs. Jones, is illustrative of the need for disciplined awareness of self and awareness of one's own ethnic background.

> *Beth Jacobs is a young Jewish woman. She was raised in a Jewish family that identified themselves as cultural, nonreligious Jews. They consider the Jewish people to be an ethnic group, with a proud history, that has experienced considerable oppression. Beth, like her parents, does not believe in God. Approaching life from a rational, nonspiritual perspective, she has difficulty in understanding and being empathetic with deeply devout people. As she read the record about how devout Ernestine Jones is, she knew she would need to be aware of her tendency to ignore these matters. Intellectually she understands that their beliefs are a great source of comfort for the Jones family.*

Sometimes it is difficult to manage one's own ethnic reality, even if one is a member of the same ethnic group.

> *The worker at the Employee Assistance Program assigned to Doris Cheng is a seasoned marital therapist, herself a Chinese woman. A longtime resident in the United States, she is aware of Chinese belief systems regarding health and mental health, yet she is thoroughly immersed in the perspective on health and mental health that is dominant in the United States.*
>
> *Her own parents are dead; she is married to a German American man. Although she respects the Chinese tradition of paying homage to the elderly, she no longer guides her own life by these precepts. Indeed, in the past, in working with young Chinese people who clung to the old ways she found herself experiencing a sense of disdain. As she anticipates working with Doris Cheng, she recalls these past thoughts and reminds herself that this pejorative and judgmental stance will get in the way of working effectively with Doris Cheng and her family.*

Many other examples of needed self-awareness can be given. As is implicit in the discussion of the feelings experienced by Ms. Cheng's worker, workers who themselves are members of the ethnic group being served have much "inside" knowledge. This is often a plus in working with people. At the same time, they must be aware of and guard against the possibility of overgeneralizing from their own experience or of holding out particularly stringent expectations for behaviors they believe are related to their own ethnic group. For example, Puerto Rican social workers in a school system may have particular awareness of the strain and pulls evoked by bilingualism. They may understand the special comfort children get from speaking Spanish to their peers and how hurtful are the taunts of teachers who admonish children to speak only English. As young people they may have accompanied their own mothers to the school, the welfare board, or the landlord to serve as translators. They may have experienced the frustration of trying to convey accurate meaning in a different language.

They must guard against approaching the situation by a stance that says, "I made it, why can't you?" Such tendencies are not uncommon. Irish social workers, because they know that alcoholism is a particular problem for some Irish people, expect Irish alcoholics to "shape up." Also instructive are the experiences of one of the authors (E.G.S.):

> *Shortly after beginning practice as a young hospital social worker, I was asked to talk with the orthodox Jewish mother of a 3-year-old boy admitted to the hospital with an infected rash all over his leg. The doctors thought that the rash may have been exacerbated by dirt. They thought the child was seldom bathed.*
>
> *I immediately informed them that I would check, but that it was most unlikely because Jewish children were not dirty. This was indeed a unique referral involving a Jewish family. I told her that Jewish mothers fussed a lot over their children.*
>
> *Subsequent exploration showed that the doctors had indeed been correct. Not only did I feel chagrined but insulted that a Jewish mother should treat her children so.*
>
> *The initial stance, derived from my perception of "proper Jewish behavior," slowed the process of helping the mother come to grips with the problem; the family's orthodox Jewish neighbors and relatives had a disposition similar to mine. To help her to deal with the problem meant that a particular sensitivity to the failure she perceived had to be injected.*

The tendency to deny negative aspects of the actions of members of one's own ethnic groups—especially in relation to behavior that violates certain precepts—is persistent and not limited to particular individuals. At least 25 years after the episode reported above, a hospital-based social worker asked me to explore elements of physical neglect that had been noted in an orthodox Jewish community located not far from the university. The local Board of Health had identified a few clusters of homes where it appeared that the children were not properly being cared for. I approached the situation by informing a rabbi of my acquaintance of the situation. This rabbi was also a social worker and had ties to the community from which the reports were being issued. His response was to declare that this was "impossible," a "mistake," and to pursue the matter no further. We do not help effectively when we deny negative aspects in the behavior of our own people.

### The Impact of the Ethnic Reality

In Chapter 2 we described and discussed the ethnic reality and how a combination of factors—different for each group and different for different subgroups at different points in history—impact on the problems people experience and their response to these problems.

The struggles of the Jones family are in many ways not unique. Families experience internal strain and discord between family members. The estrangement from daughter Jan that the Joneses experienced until shortly before her death is a sadness experienced by many families when disagreement reaches a point of crisis.

The Joneses are, by most standards, middle-class people who have acquired this status in the face of considerable racism, at considerable personal cost. Such status is often tenuous. Many African American people are deeply religious. Many African American women are said to be especially strong and the leaders of their families (Boyd-Franklin, 1989).

The family's experience with AIDS is unfortunately one that they share with many other African American families. AIDS has impacted on the African American community with special force. The Joneses' experience in becoming parents to grandchildren is not uncommon.

Minkler and Roe (1993) report the experiences of the grandmothers who raise the children of the crack cocaine epidemic and focused on a particular subset of that group, African American women. They suggested that the "historic inkeeping role of the black grandmother gives the newer role a special salience in the African American community." They pointed to historical accounts that have traced the pivotal stabilizing role of elders in black life.

"In our own study, grandmothers' despair over the crack involvement of their sons and daughters often caused still deeper pain and anguish around the assumption of the caregiver role. Although the women we interviewed willingly and lovingly accepted full-time caregiving as an alternative to having their grandchildren neglected or removed from the family and placed in foster care, many expressed anger, resentment, and depression over the prospect of 'second-time around' parenthood under these circumstances" (Minkler & Roe, 1993, pp. 5–6).

Whether or not Ernestine Jones expresses the sentiments of distress implied by those who have studied women like her, it is highly likely that she shares some of these feelings.

The role of the church in the African American community has received considerable attention. Lum (1996) and others have suggested that the church has long played a powerful role in aiding African American people to cope in the face of profound oppression and its accompanying problems. Mrs. Jones especially is most devout. She has told the people at the other agency how important the church is to her.

### The Route to the Social Worker

In Chapter 4 the concept of the route to the social worker was discussed in some detail. It was pointed out that many social work clients do not seek services voluntarily. Many have limited choice about whether to use these services. Others, such as prisoners or families whose children are wards of the state because of parental neglect or abuse, must use the services.

> *Mrs. Jones has some choice about whether to accept the social worker's offer of service. She could, if she chose, tell Beth Jacobs that she and Mr. Jones will manage with Ellen and that she needs no help. Indeed, that might be true. Between her husband and her friends, they likely can manage.*
>
> *But it is unlikely that Mrs. Jones will refuse contact with the social worker once it is offered. She is facing some major difficulties and will unlikely scoff at any offer of assistance.*
>
> *However, other factors need to be considered. African American people, especially those with limited resources, have reasons to be suspicious of a variety of health and welfare institutions. Although Ernestine Jones may doubt that Beth Jacobs can be of much help, past experience suggests that refusal might be misconstrued as lack of cooperation. And such lack of cooperation might have negative consequences. So it is to be expected that she will agree to work with Beth Jacobs.*

On the surface, Doris Cheng seems to be coming voluntarily. However, although the record may not reflect it, it is possible that Ms. Cheng's superiors at the communications company have let her know that her work is "not up to snuff." Despite pledges of confidentiality, she has substantial fear that her job will be at risk if she does not follow through with the service. Other situations can be cited that underscore the importance of understanding the route to the social worker.

> *Mr. Garcia, a recent immigrant from Columbia, is referred to the local Child Protective Agency because of allegations of child abuse. A hard-working, unskilled laborer seeking desperately to find his way in this country, Mr. Garcia cannot believe anyone would accuse him of child abuse. He learns that his custom of disciplining his young son through the use of a strap has come to the attention of the school the child attends. The teacher has found bruises. Otherwise, the child seems content and well cared for. The investigation shows that Mr. Garcia's use of a strap to discipline the child was customary in his country. When the worker suggests this is not done here, he agrees and says, "I guess I cannot rear up my son the way I was reared up."*

> *Mr. Reilly is a well-paid truck driver, and a member of the union that protects his wages and working conditions. He is getting on in years and lately takes a nip before driving "just to take away some of the aches." His superiors detect alcohol on his breath when he reports for work, although there have been no accidents. He is given a warning and told to see "one of the social workers" the company hired to help get the guys over some rough spots. If he does not see the social worker and they find he has been nipping before coming in, the union cannot protect him.*

These situations highlight the fact that the route to the social worker is often taken involuntarily and more often than not entails threat or fear. Not infrequently, the client's understanding of his or her world, based in part on the ethnic reality, is at odds with myriad social institutions with which people must interact. We must be extremely sensitive to these kinds of situations as we work to try to establish trust.

# PART 2: WORK TO BE DONE BEFORE MEETING WITH CLIENTS

In this second part of the chapter we present the social work strategies and interventive procedures most commonly used by social workers in direct practice. Several levels of work get done before worker and client meet.

## Basic Knowledge Acquisition

We refer here to all the effort to acquire relevant knowledge, such as that considered earlier in this chapter.

## Understanding Your Community and Your Organization[1]

### Learning about Your Community

Another level of work, which we term understanding your community and understanding your organization, refers to the responsibility of learning as much as possible about the community and about the organization in which the work is carried out.

Communities vary in many ways and inevitably impact on the work of the agency. The resources available, the population characteristics, the availability of resources, the type of government, the availability of transportation, and the prevailing community- and ethnic-based networks are but a few of the factors that bear on the ability to render service. Communities are different in many ways. They vary along ethnic and class dimensions in the availability of services, in general ambience, and in style. A variety of tools can facilitate the process of becoming familiar with the community. Use of census material, publications about the community, and interviews with community leaders are but a few of the available resources. It is incumbent upon agencies and practitioners to make use of these resources in order to develop a community profile.

### Identifying Community Needs

Lum (1986) identified a series of tasks that go beyond the development of a community profile. These include conducting a study of the needs of minority clients, service programs, and staffing patterns. As will be gathered from review of the community profile, it is essential to determine whether the network of social agency and other institutions have sufficient staff who, if necessary, are bilingual and/or sensitive to the needs of the diverse community groups served.

---

[1]See sample outline for developing a Community Profile in Appendix 1.

*When it comes time for Beth Jacobs to see the Joneses, the information she has acquired about the community will stand her in good status. She knows that 20 percent of this city's population of 50,000 is African American. The church of which the Joneses are members, as well as other African American churches, have a reputation for providing considerable social support to parishioners when crises arise. The church has yet to develop a formal AIDS service structure.*

### Learning about Organizations

Organizations that provide health and human services are diverse and complex. Some are small and neighborhood based and are operated by segments of the ethnic community (e.g., Jenkins, 1981); some are large and multidisciplinary intended to serve diverse peoples. Some institutions are operated for the specific purpose of providing social work services; a case in point is the family counseling agency. Others, are multidisciplinary and usually termed host settings. This is true for hospitals, schools, and prisons, which typically provide service by social workers. Social workers will want to know early in their affiliation with any agency which discipline or individual typically exerts power and influence. They need to know how various groups are generally received. It is important to know whether members of minority groups feel welcomed or find the atmosphere demeaning.

Also important is the effort to learn how others who work in a system think, feel, and behave. This is particularly relevant in interdisciplinary settings. For example, workers employed in school systems where they function on teams of psychologists, teachers, and consulting psychiatrists must familiarize themselves with the kinds of problems usually brought to the team and how each discipline views its role. They should be clear about the linkage function between school, home, and other resources. They need to be aware of how they, as children, may have experienced problems in their own school work. If, as children, they had difficulty, are they likely to "overidentify"? Or, conversely, if their own school careers were extremely successful, how can they use this experience to help those in trouble? How can they learn to understand?

Those who provide service in the criminal justice system need to know something of the adversary system and the law and how people experience encounters with these institutions. The same is true of work with families in the public social services and in health care.[2]

### Adaptation to the Ethnic Reality

In approaching the work situation, the particular class and ethnic disposition (the ethnic reality as it pertains to the issues and problems that regularly surface in the work setting) must be considered. There is a substantial body of literature on the impact of race in the helping process. Although the research findings are equivocal, there is some suggestion that communication is enhanced when workers are members of the same group (e.g., Jones, 1978; Turner & Armstrong, 1981). Davis and

---

[2]See Chapters 7, 12, 13, and 14 for more detailed treatment.

Proctor (1989) have reviewed the literature on the relationship between race and treatment. There is some evidence that racial dissimilarity may threaten clients' ability to talk about their problems. At the same time, there is some evidence that experienced and sensitive workers can work effectively with racially dissimilar clients. Workers must be ready to consider how their own ethnic and class backgrounds affect responses. Experienced and sensitive workers can and must work effectively with ethnically and racially dissimilar clients (Schlesinger, 1996; Davis & Proctor, 1989). Efforts to achieve "ethnic competence" as described by Green (1995) are pertinent here. The reader will remember that the emphasis is on "a...level of cultural awareness...that surpasses the usual injunctions about patience, genuineness and honesty in client–worker relationships."

If workers are members of the ethnic groups usually served in the setting, they may have much inside knowledge. At the same time, they must be aware of and guard against the possibility of overgeneralizing from their own experience or holding out particularly stringent expectations for behaviors that they believe are related to their own ethnic group.[3]

When workers are not members of the ethnic and class groups usually served, they have an obligation to familiarize themselves with the culture, history, and ethnically related responses to problems. Among the suggestions made by Green (1995) about the processes that may prove useful in developing "ethnic competence" are strategies of participant observation in communities of interest, which are used by anthropologists in studying ethnographic material about the community.

When workers meet their clients, they need to have developed emotional and intellectual awareness, to be ready to listen, to help evoke meaningful responses, and to draw on diverse resources. This readiness is derived from experience, from a conceptual stance that aids in thinking about the problems, and from awareness of the range and types of reactions usually evoked by members of different ethnic groups.

## Work before Meeting with Any Particular Client

Information available on any client varies substantially.

> *A considerable amount of information had been made available on Ellen Jones and her family from the medical and nursing staff. The worker knew a great deal about the diagnosis, problem, and predicted course of medical events. She knew that this family has experienced much disappointment but has demonstrated considerable strength. They overcame great pains and disappointments and took in Jan and Ellen. They are now mustering their strength to cope with Ellen's difficulties.*
>
> *Beth Jacobs hopes that the Joneses' church will provide spiritual as well as concrete support, such as help with the child.*
>
> *The worker who saw Doris Cheng for the first time had limited information at her command. It remains up to her to attempt to sort out various questions that come*

---

[3]See earlier discussion of the kind of pitfalls sometimes encountered.

*up: (1) How much is understood about Doris's seizure disorder, and is she receiving proper treatment? (2) Is Doris's 3-year-old son all right or was the low birth weight indicative of any serious difficulties? (3) How much of Mr. Cheng's difficulties can be attributed to serious mental illness? (4) How much of the difficulty represents a conflict that Doris may be experiencing between the expectations held out by Chinese tradition that she will pay homage to the elderly, especially her husband's family, and her beginning challenge of these strongly held traditions? Answers to these questions will have to await the assessment process.*

### Adaptation to the Ethnic Reality

As workers cull through such information as is available in preparation for meeting the client, attention also must be focused on ethnic and class matters.

The worker should obtain all possible information about the ethnic reality. If no information about ethnic group membership is available, this should be determined if possible. This knowledge will enable the worker to think ahead, anticipating any special needs or areas of sensitivity that are often associated with ethnic memberships and the help-seeking/help-getting process.

The fear of racist or prejudiced orientations is never far from the minds of most minority or other disadvantaged people. Practitioners must be constantly alert to this possibility. This is particularly important when the clients are members of minority groups and the workers are members of the majority group.

To simply know that someone is white is insufficient. The enormous differences between the various white ethnic groups can affect the work. Examples are the well-known volatility in relation to physical illness of many Jewish and Italian people, as contrasted with the stoicism of "old Americans" (Zborowski, 1952).

Social class data and information about what people do is essential. In Chapter 3 we commented on the relationship among social class, the kind of work people do, and their sense of autonomy and capacity to control their own lives.

The images that people have of themselves and those held by others may have great bearing on how they approach problem resolution. Class data provide clues about socioeconomic wherewithal, the kind of work people do, and broad stances on life's problems.

## PART 3 INTERVENTION

### Problem Identification and Assessment

As worker and client meet, there are many matters to consider. The worker needs to be sure to create an environment as comfortable as possible—and to use those skills and procedures likely to set the helping process in motion. The client may be worried, fearful, anxious about the difficulty confronting him or her, as well as wondering if this is the person and the place where help is likely to be forthcoming.

Traditionally, social workers have termed the first stage of worker/client interaction the process of problem identification and assessment. In discussing this step of the interventive process, we distinguish between "entry skills"—those skills focused on "launching the interaction process" and creating a comfortable environment for the interview—and those skills focused on the interviewing process itself, the nature of questioning, problem identification assessment, and intervention. In fact, these are not distinctive stages; rather, various elements of the process are overlapping and recurring. Middleman and Goldberg (1974) include (1) stage setting, (2) tuning in (Middleman & Goldberg, 1974; Shulman, 1984), (3) attending (Egan, 1975), and (4) preparatory empathy (Shulman, 1984; Hepworth & Larsen, 1993).

### Stage Setting: Privacy, Creating Comfortable Spaces Accommodating to the Setting

Stage setting involves attention to the physical setting in which the interaction is going to take place and takes account of positioning vis-à-vis clients. The purposive use of space to enhance communication is basic. There is little question that the prevailing norms of American society suggest that privacy is urgent. It is assumed that most people will feel more comfortable discussing their problems if they are not in danger of being overheard by strangers. Often, people don't want other people in the family to know they are discussing certain matters with the social worker. By and large, people are more comfortable if there is sufficient physical space to permit them to maintain some physical distance from each other; they may move closer together if the situation warrants. Settings that provide at least a minimal degree of physical comfort are thought to be essential. Comfortably cushioned chairs, pleasantly painted, cheerful rooms, and a place to stretch one's legs are seen as highly desirable if not essential.

A mental review of many of the places where social workers meet their clients quickly leads to the realization that these generic guides to stage setting are often honored in the breach. Hospitalized patients who are unable to leave their beds usually share rooms with others. A curtain is the most deference to privacy that can be offered. When clients are visited in their homes, relatives, friends, or neighbors may be present. Large segments of the client population—particularly those served by underfunded public agencies—often encounter the worker in large offices occupied by many other people. At best there may be glass-enclosed cubicles in which the partitions do not reach the ceiling. Visits may be made in community center playrooms, libraries of prisons, or empty cafeterias of residential centers. Each of these spaces is likely to be frequented by others. Many of these are regrettable structural facts that emerge out of society's low regard and lack of respect for those who are at the "bottom of the ladder."

There are circumstances in which interaction is most comfortable if carried out in natural or convenient settings. These include seeing the child in the playground or seeing concerned relatives in a parking lot or restaurant during a lunch hour. Time may not permit a visit to the office. Some natural settings tend to preserve anonymity or privacy where needed.

Social workers who are sensitive to the facts of space will learn to make adaptations. When the interview with the hospitalized patient calls for as much privacy as possible, workers will draw the curtain and sit close. This closeness may be a compromise with the desire to maintain a comfortable physical distance, usually important in the early stages of building a relationship. Other compromises with privacy may be seen in the example of talking with youngsters in the community center lounge or with the residents in the institutional cafeteria. Workers will try to gauge to what extent they can create a "do not disturb" ambience by positioning; but by doing so, they must be careful not to embarrass those who are seeking or being offered service. Privacy should be guarded, but not at the expense of avoiding needed contact or in a manner that publicly singles out a particular person. A conversation between two or more people in the midst of a crowded room can be more private than one held in a distant but readily spotted part of a public room. The worker's first meeting with Mrs. Jones is an example.

> *Mrs. Jones was referred to Beth Jacobs by the attending physician in the Pediatric Clinic. He was planning to admit Ellen, who was suffering from severe diarrhea and vomiting. She had recently stopped speaking. On pediatric rounds held earlier in the day, the physician shared with the social worker the facts earlier noted, Ellen's mother's recent death, the family's involvement with the church, and their distress with the daughter who had died. Thinking about how and where she might best make initial contact with Mrs. Jones, Beth Jacobs looked for her in the waiting area of the x-ray department. They sat in a private area of the hallway, with no one else around. Ellen was in her grandmother's arms and had just finished with x-rays. When Beth Jacobs walked up to them, Ellen started to cry, clung to her grandmother's neck and hid her face. Beth Jacobs: "Mrs. Jones, my name is Beth Jacobs, and I am with the Social Work Department. Dr. W. asked me to speak with you about your granddaughter. Is this a good time?" Beth Jacobs is honoring Mrs. Jones's need for convenience as well as for privacy.*

### Adaptation to the Ethnic Reality

The degree to which every effort should be made to adhere to the tenets of privacy vary considerably by ethnic group membership. Many Eastern Europeans (e.g., Czechoslovakians, Estonians, Hungarians, Poles, and Ukrainians) are particularly "shamed" at having to ask for help (Giordano & Giordano, 1977). The same is true for many Asians (Toupin, 1980; Hooyman & Kiyak, 1988; Lum, 1992). For members of these groups and others with similar dispositions, particular effort should be made to assure privacy and/or anonymity. When people who share these feelings are seen in the hospital, it would be wise to take off the white coat if it is customarily worn. After people have been engaged in a private conversation with the curtain drawn, they may decide how to answer their neighbor's queries about who the "nice young woman was" who came to see them. They are then free to identify her as a family member, neighbor, or the social worker.

When the pain of getting help is almost as intense as the problem that generates it, a number of concessions to privacy should be considered. Is a prearranged home visit for an intake interview for public assistance feasible? Can workers park their cars around the corner? Can workers dress in a manner that does not readily identify them? Can the mother of a disturbed youngster be seen in the school court-yard amidst a crowd? Is the sign on the van advising everyone that this is the "Senior Citizens' Nutrition Project" or the local "Economic Opportunity Corpora-tion" really necessary?

The situation at the Employee Assistance Program of the communications company is an ideal setting for initiating the contact with Doris Cheng. Substantial literature supports the view that Chinese people, like many other Asian persons, are uncomfortable about seeking the kind of help offered by social workers and mental health facilities in the United States (Ho, 1987). The worker knows this and on meeting Doris Cheng maintains an air of formality, uses last names, and remains seated behind her desk as she and Doris begin to work together.

Not all possible concessions to privacy and anonymity can be spelled out. How-ever, it is crucial that workers be aware of these possibilities and behave in a manner that opens up options. Some Slavics, Asians, and others may feel comfort-able about being interviewed within earshot of their neighbors. However, unless people are given the choice on these types of matters, workers may find that, despite sincere offers to help plan for care problems, their clients were most uncommunicative.

There are other people who do not seem to mind discussion of certain private matters when others, unrelated to them, can hear. Many Jewish and Italian people are quite voluble and seem ready to express discomfort and pain publicly; some are given to reaching out for a sympathetic, interested ear (Zborowski, 1952). Dominick and Stotsky (1969) described Italian nursing home residents who are always ready to converse with visitors about rooms, belongings, anything at all. Schlesinger (1990) suggested that the same is true for many elderly Jewish people.

People with this disposition may gain some satisfaction from the public visi-bility provided by the social worker's concern and attention. Caution must be exer-cised to guard against assuming that satisfaction gained by visible attention to physical problems will not carry over to situations in which an application for pub-lic assistance, food stamps, or publicly subsidized housing is to be filed, or if a youngster has developed problems with the law. This may represent loss of face or much highly valued financial independence. In such situations, generic rules of privacy apply. Efforts to learn what types of people require privacy and anonymity are crucial.

## "Tuning In"

Tuning in has been defined as "development of the worker's preparatory empa-thy" (Shulman, 1984). Citing Schwartz, Shulman suggested that tuning in includes the worker's efforts to "get in touch with those feelings which may be implicitly or directly expressed in the interview." Although the process should begin before the encounter, it is ongoing and continues throughout the interaction. Shulman sug-gests that tuning in can take place at several levels. Several of these have been noted in other contexts. They include the acquisition of basic knowledge of human behavior, articulation of that knowledge with the problems at issue, and the unique response of worker and client. The following case situation illustrates the articulation of several levels.

> *Jim Brown, a social worker, knows that a 13-year-old boy has been referred because he is disruptive in school and is reading several years behind his grade level. The boy has recently transferred to the school as a result of moving into his third foster home this year. In synthesizing, tuning in, and processing these facts, the worker draws on his general knowledge about the possible reasons for learning difficulty, family systems, how families absorb new members, and the dynamics involved in foster parent–foster child relationships.*
>
> *In tuning in to the child, he should consider the possibility that the reading deficit may be a function of poor education, perceptual difficulty, or emotional distress. He needs to "think and feel" in advance about how alienated, isolated, lonely, and rejected this boy might be feeling. Perhaps the worker can recall an analogous experience he may have had. Did he go to summer camp when he really did not want to? Was there ever a time when he was afraid his own parents had abandoned him? Did he ever experience a similar school failure?*

> *The life of Beth Jacobs and that of the Joneses are worlds apart. She is young, single, and healthy. Her parents are still sufficiently young so that they have not yet developed the kind of health problems that beset people in their later years. She has experienced few losses; there is little in her own experience that can help her to get in touch with the feelings that may be experienced by the Joneses.*
>
> *She struggles, and it is a struggle she will encounter throughout her career. No one worker can experience as much as the large variety of clients he or she will encounter. As Beth Jacobs struggles, she thinks of her own people, so many of whom perished in the Holocaust. Her mother talks about it all the time and cries. Some African Americans—rightly or wrongly—perceive the disproportionate number of AIDS victims in their community almost as a deliberate act of genocide. She has difficulty accepting this intellectually, but she can nevertheless get in touch with the feeling of despair it evokes. A young child in her family nearly died a year ago from a bout of childhood leukemia. Perhaps she can anticipate for herself at least some of the kinds of feelings that Mr. and Mrs. Jones must be experiencing.*

> *Doris Cheng's worker, herself Chinese, remembers how resentful she was when as a young woman she was expected to do what her then Chinese mother-in-law said. She began to feel the rage again and began to feel guilty, for this is not an appropriate feeling for a young Chinese woman. So, she started thinking that she might come close to how Doris might be feeling.*

### Adaptation to the Ethnic Reality
In tuning in, as in other steps of the helping process, it is essential that workers draw on knowledge about themselves, their client's ethnic group, and the impact these have on the response to the helping encounter. The distinction between *emic* and *etic* is useful (e.g., Lum, 1992; Schlesinger & Devore, 1995). Emic focuses on the

specific characteristics of the group, whereas etic suggests that all people and groups are alike in some major respects. From this perspective, it is likely that the worker can draw on that which is unique to the client's group while finding the universal common themes. These and many other examples indicate the varying processes involved in tuning in and in developing preparatory empathy.

Hepworth and Larsen (1993) made an important contribution to the skills of "communicating with empathy and with authenticity." Being empathetically attuned involves not only grasping the client's immediately evident feelings, but in a mutually shared, exploratory process, identifying underlying emotions and discovering the meaning and personal significance of feelings and behavior (pp. 86–87). They identified five levels of empathic response ranging from communicating limited awareness of even the most conspicuous client feelings to the capacity to reflect each emotional nuance "attuned to the client's moment-by-moment experiencing..." (pp. 96).

Processes similar to those described above are involved in tuning in and responding empathetically to the meaning of the helping encounters to members of various ethnic groups. In the situation of Jim Brown, who was working with an adolescent boy, it is important to know that the young client is an African American child of underclass background whose foster parents are African American, middle-class, professional people living in a community composed predominantly of white people.

As a white male, Jim Brown, the worker, needs to review his knowledge about the African American community and what he understands about how class differences within that community manifest themselves. He needs to recognize that African American people living in a predominantly white neighborhood may be experiencing substantial strain. At an emotional level he needs to "feel through" his reactions to African American people, particularly adolescent boys. Is he afraid of physical aggression and does he associate African American youngsters with aggression? Does he tend to expect less academically from an African American boy? Is he possibly feeling that the white middle-class school has been invaded? Does he have a feel for how African American children might experience the white world? Does he understand the particular sense of distrust, inadequacy, and fear of not measuring up felt by many young blacks? The fact that he was able to draw on his own past fear of abandonment is illustrative of the emic perspective.

Other illustrations of the various levels of tuning in to ethnic dispositions can be given. Repeated reference has been made to the frustrations of those whose command of the English language is limited. Many approach human service agencies, fearing that their culture and way of life are not respected. There may be distrust of practitioners, particularly those who are not members of their own group. Such matters should always be tuned into before and during an encounter. As workers prepare themselves to tune in and to respond empathically, they need to become even more sensitive to and knowledgeable about ethnic components. How does the person feel about having a worker of a different (or the same) group? Davis and Proctor (1989) suggested that this is almost always a consideration. Is the person comforted or threatened by that? What about the very pain of being there? Should that be acknowledged—with Asian people, with American Indians? And perhaps to those inclined to respond to help positively—middle-class Jews and many well-educated professionals—can something be asked about whether they were relieved to be finally coming for help?

## *Attending Generically*

*Attending* refers to purposeful behavior designed to convey a message of respect and a feeling that what people are discussing is important. Attending skills include the ability to pay simultaneous attention to cognitive, emotional, verbal, and non-verbal stimuli, deciding "what is the main message" (Middleman & Goldberg, 1974, p. 100) and focusing attention on that message. In the process of focusing on the key elements of the situation, it is important to be aware of and refrain from communicating inappropriate judgmental attitudes.

Appropriate use of body language and dressing in a manner considered appropriate by clients are also examples of attending. The other person should be faced squarely, and open posture should be adopted and good eye contact maintained. The practitioner should lean toward "the other." These aspects of physical attending let the clients know of the worker's active involvement and aids the practitioner in being an active listener. This type of posture helps in picking up both verbal messages and nonverbal clues. Under most circumstances it is important to maintain a relaxed, natural, comfortable position and to use those spontaneous head, arm, and body movements that come naturally to workers in most interactive situations. Wood and Middleman (1989) have suggested that the worker avoid sitting behind the desk. Coming out from behind the desk and sitting at "right angles" to the client facilitates focused attention. Maintaining comfortable eye contact is customary in many contexts. In professional as well as personal interaction, the use of friendly greetings is expected.

Put simply, when the encounter begins it is crucial that initial approaches are made in a professional but human manner that is attentive to the concerns of the other.

> *After Beth Jacobs introduces herself to Ms. Jones, they continue to sit in the quiet area of the waiting room of the x-ray department. Beth Jacobs: "My name is Beth Jacobs. I'm with the social work department. Dr. W. asked me to speak with you about your granddaughter. Is this a good time?"*

The worker, respectful of the fact that Ms. Jones is here primarily to have x-rays taken, pays attention and lets Ms. Jones know she does not want to interfere. Her demeanor is natural and comfortable but cognizant of the serious situation at hand.

> *Beth Jacobs: "I won't keep you long. I just wanted to see the baby, meet you, and talk a little bit about what kind of support services we might help you with after she leaves the hospital. I am aware of the situation. Has the doctor explained to you why he wants her admitted?"*

### Adaptation to the Ethnic Reality

There are some groups whose members find it difficult to respond to the type of spontaneity and physical posturing suggested by Egan and others. Many people believe eye contact is shameful. Toupin (1980) suggested that even acculturated Asians are likely to consider eye contact as shameful. This is particularly true for women who believe "only street women do that." Many American Indians view the matter similarly. Eye contact may be indicative of lack of respect.

There are situations that call for modification of other aspects of attending. Those groups (e.g., many working and underclass minority people) who view workers as authority figures may, especially in the initial contact, be more comfortable when there is more formality than Egan's proposals imply. This is also true for those who are most uncomfortable about expressing feelings or who feel shamed about needing help (e.g., some Slavs and Asians). It is important in this connection that workers understand that for many people failing to respond to eye contact, sitting demurely, or not readily revealing feelings are not indicative of pathology or resistance. Rather, they are accustomed ways of responding, given the circumstances.

Practitioners who truly attend will modify their behavior according to the knowledge they gain about the disposition of various groups. The skills, and approaches to launching the interaction process just discussed are used in conjunction with the process of questioning. At this point, some comments about the nature of questioning and listening are in order. These will be touched on here only briefly. There are many excellent works that treat the matter in detail, including the effects of race on the interview process.

### The Nature of Questioning: The Ethnic-Sensitive Interview

The social work interview is one of the most critical elements of practice. It is through the interview that the client/worker relationship is developed and sustained, and that critical information is shared by the client with the worker, and vice versa. The very process of the interview can be, and often is, intrinsically therapeutic.

A great deal has been written about the social work interview. Many excellent works treat the matter in detail. The object here is simply to identify some of the major principles and to suggest how basic interview processes and strategies can and must be adapted to take account of client ethnic reality.

In the minds of many people, the process of questioning, a basic component of the social work interview, is equivalent to social work itself. It is through this process of asking questions, reflecting on the answers, and giving feedback about the matters discussed that much of social work gets done. There is a considerable body of literature on the social work interview (e.g., Kadushin, 1995). Social workers question many people about their situations. Some questions are focused on fact, some on feeling. Some questions are asked to obtain simple, precise factual answers. Others are intended to evoke feeling.

### Identifying the Source or Locus of the Problem

Both factual information and theoretical perspectives play a part in identifying what the source of a problem seems to be. In our review of approaches to practice (see Chapter 5), we summarized divergent theoretical views. Although these differences exist, a number of basic principles cut across the divergent perspectives.

The client's perspective on the source of the difficulty should be given primary consideration. Pottick and Adams (1990) have recently discussed putting this concept into action. Doing so requires much skill, patience, and restraint. Workers are trained to think in theoretical terms, to synthesize, and to make assessments. It is not easy to be nonjudgmental when people attribute all of their difficulties to external matters or perhaps to supernatural forces. Workers who are eager to "put their knowledge to work" need to be self-disciplined. Sensitive workers will ask and listen before they make a judgment.

If the problem is systemically based, individuals should not be held responsible for the situation. The list of inadequate resources to deal with problems is endless. When clients complain about welfare budgets, workers must acknowledge the trauma of trying to survive with so little; perhaps they even need to cry with people before going on to help with budgeting designed to stretch the impossible. The budgeting process may be necessary as a survival technique. But to suggest to such people that they are not getting along because they do not know how to budget is blaming the victim.

At the same time, we must help people to take responsibility for their actions and, importantly, to help them to surmount even the most devastating systemic barriers. As suggested earlier, being sure to identify racist, sexist, or other sources of oppression can avoid a "blaming the victim stance."

For example, a Puerto Rican woman may consider it her duty to "serve" her husband—she has a sense of *marianismo.* However, he is not working, yet does not assume housekeeping responsibilities. Exploring the woman's feelings, without violating cultural imperatives, is important.

The sudden, unexplained deaths of many Hmong men after arriving in the United States may be related to the difficult immigration transition.

### Adaptation to the Ethnic Reality

The principles and associated skills discussed here apply in work with all people. They become even more important when one is dealing with ethnic, minority, and other oppressed people.

The ethnic-sensitive worker has a particular responsibility to be aware of the systemic sources of many problems. Attributing systemically induced problems—those derived from racism, poverty, and prejudice—to individuals is harmful. It adds to their burden. Lum (1992) identifies many of the systemically induced problems that bring minority people to social agencies. Racism, manifested as a negative reaction to minority people in a wide spectrum of situations, is a case in point. African Americans are disproportionately unemployed and underemployed, contributing to negative self-image and interpersonal problems. These experiences of low status, low income, and exploitation yield feelings of powerlessness. Recent immigrants (e.g., Vietnamese and Laotians) experience dislocation as they try to make sense of the new culture. The relatively high levels of depression found among African American men (Gary, 1985) may be related to the frequency of stressful events they are more likely to encounter. These include changes in residence, job changes, physical illness, and arrests, all found with greater frequency among African American men. Helping to identify the links between systemic problems and individual concerns is a crucial component of ethnic-sensitive practice.

With some notion of the nature and source of a problem established, worker and client can begin to consider how they will work on the problem. Contracting is an important move in that direction.

## Contracting: Some Preliminary Considerations

The literature on contracting is extensive (Compton & Galaway, 1989; Fischer, 1978; Maluccio & Marlow, 1974; Middleman & Goldberg, 1974; Pincus & Minahan, 1973; Reid & Epstein, 1977; Seabury, 1976). Central to much of this work is the assumption that people can contract to explore their interpersonal relationships, to confront dysfunctional systems, and to make use of health and welfare systems as these are currently organized.

Many groups do not share the rational conceptions of problem solving implicit in the concept of contracting. Many lack trust in the health and welfare delivery systems. Some are loath to be designated *client,* which some views of contracting imply. Indeed, Reid (1986) suggested that some people cannot and will not engage in this form of worker–client engagement.

Much that is understood about the world view of the various American Indian cultures points to the fact that some view any act of manipulation or coercion with mistrust. This applies to psychological as well as physical behaviors. Good Tracks (1973) pointed out that suggestions concerning appropriate behavior, whether conveyed subtly or in the form of an outright command, are viewed as interference. Interference in others' behavior is considered inappropriate. This holds true for the way parents teach their children, the actions of children, and the demands made by organized institutions. Good Tracks suggested that for these reasons many major social work techniques are ineffective with Native Americans.

Contrast this with certain dispositions common to many Asian Americans. Several themes recur in the literature. According to Toupin (1980) and Ho (1976, 1987), general characteristics of the model Asian personality can be identified. Many Asian people are likely to express deference to others, to devalue themselves and their family to others, and to avoid confrontation. Shame—for insensitive behavior, for behavior subjecting the family to criticism, and for causing embarrassment—is extensively drawn on in socialization practices. They preserve the family honor by not discussing personal problems outside the family. Expression of emotions may not bring relief because it may reflect negatively on the family. There is deference to authority, and therapeutic personnel are viewed as authority figures.

In commenting on the social worker's potential ability to be helpful without violating cultural precepts, Good Tracks (1973) suggested that "patience is the number one virtue governing relationships with American Indians. A worker who has little or no patience should not seek placement in American Indian settings.... The social worker's success may well be linked with his ability to learn 'Indian time' and adjust his relationships accordingly" (p. 33). He pointed out that the workers will be observed, and people may seem indifferent. It may take considerable time, perhaps a year or more, before they are trusted.

Workers' efforts to provide a variety of concrete services will be observed. At some point a member of the community may bring a problem of a more personal nature to a worker. Technique alone will not speed up this process.

The principle of contracting is crucial when it is related to client autonomy and self-determination. When viewed primarily as a technique for rapid engagement of clients in the helping process, the danger exists that class and ethnic dispositions will receive insufficient attention.

### Approaches to Contracting

The approach to contracting that follows is guided by the preceding considerations.

*Contracting* refers to the process by which workers, clients, and others engaged in problem-solving activities come to some common agreement about the respective work to be done, the objectives sought, and the means by which these objectives are to be attained. By its very nature, the process involves clients and others in setting the terms by which the work of problem solving is to be carried out. Various writers (e.g., Compton & Galaway, 1984) have stressed the fact that contracting involves a partnership. When social worker client interaction is approached from this perspective, workers are less likely to impose their definition of the problem or task on the client.

Many definitions of the contract have been offered. In social work and other interpersonal helping endeavors, the contract can be viewed as consensus between the involved or concerned persons about why they are working together, how they will work together, and what they hope to achieve. Translated into the "gut and heart" of day-to-day practice, what does this mean? It means that workers and clients deliberate, and often struggle, to come to decisions about the focus of the work to be done. This is affected by the various contexts in which services are rendered and the point in time when decisions about the work to be done are made. Some people can make such decisions quickly; others waver and need considerable time.

The social worker assigned to the outpatient clinic of a hospital is asked to find out why so many people do not keep essential follow-up appointments. In exploring the matter, she learns that people are "fed up" with being told to be there at 9:00 in the morning and not being seen until 11:00 or 12:00. They lose time from work, and lose patience as well. In checking to see what happens elsewhere, the worker finds that the same kind of people come much more regularly if there is a staggered appointment system. In this instance, she first contracts with the hospital administration to explore the issue. She then shares her information with the administration and patients. Does the administration want to institute a staggered appointment system? Should she ask her patients how they would feel about it?

In this process, an effort is made to maximize the possibility of involvement in problem solving by those concerned: the patients and hospital administration.

In considering the relationship between the context and contracting, a number of generic principles can be stated:

- When clients have little or no choice about being there, a clear-cut statement about the help and the options available, despite the constraints, is essential.
- The range of services available should be spelled out clearly, with an emphasis on the role the client and worker each will play.
- The contract should not focus on "people changing" when system changing is in order (e.g., only if the staggered appointment system in the outpatient clinic is not successful should the social worker talk to patients about their appointment-keeping behavior).

The limitations of time and agency function should be clearly spelled out (Compton & Galaway, 1979).

**Adaptation to the Ethnic Reality.**   There is little doubt that members of minority groups, those who do not speak English, and those who have a long history of negative experience with health and welfare institutions are particularly sensitive and fearful about what might happen when they get to the agency. Continuing attention and sensitivity to these matters must be evident. The skill of helping people who feel particularly defeated to recognize and believe that they can play a part in determining why and how something is to be done is one that needs to be continually sharpened. Gomez, Zurcher, Buford, and Becker (1985) have demonstrated the positive effects of this approach with some Hispanic clients.

The injustice done to American Indians by the massive removal of children from their homes to "boarding schools" has been documented repeatedly (Byler, 1977). The assumption that minorities and the poor are not articulate and cannot constructively engage in therapeutic encounters involving active verbalization has been challenged. The difficulty of conveying affect and sensitive factual information through an interpreter is well known. Despite this, some American Indians abuse their children, and some poor minority people need help with basic survival needs before they can engage in the process of examining interpersonal relationships. Bilingual or indigenous workers are not always available.

The basic rules of contracting must then be expanded to include the following points:

1. Consider the basic meaning that involvement with this setting is likely to have for different people. For instance, an American Indian family may be quite ready to consider placement of a child with someone in the extended family once its members have been assured that the child is not going to be torn from the fold of the community.
2. Consider the implications of what is being suggested, given the client's ethnic reality.

## Working on the Problem

Recently, one of the authors of this book visited an agency to review a student's progress. In reviewing the student's progress recording, it was evident that the student deflected the client's attention from the problem at hand on a number of occasions. As soon as her clients seemed ready to discuss an emotionally sensitive matter, the student changed the subject. When this was pointed out, the insightful student said, "I know, but if they really tell me I might have to do something about it. And I don't really know how. Those people have terrible troubles, and they won't go away. I can't really change anything for them." This is a common dilemma, not only for the student but also for the more seasoned practitioner. Part of the dilemma arises out of the seeming intractability of the problems for which help is sought. Part of the problem is related to lack of skill, and part to the inherent difficulty entailed in forging ahead, on a sustained basis, with efforts to help.

> *Beth Jacobs has been talking to Mrs. Jones about the baby and how they manage to provide for her care.*
>
> *But Mrs. Jones seems to want to talk about her dead daughter and her hope that she found Jesus before she died. Beth Jacobs has some reluctance, but Mrs. Jones comes back to it.*
>
> *Beth Jacobs: "It must be very painful for you. But it sounds like you have a strong faith to help you through this."*
>
> *Mrs. Jones: "Yes, I surely do. I just pray every day and read my Bible to find the strength and wisdom. I just praise God that my daughter got to know him before she died. You need to find God yourself, dear."*
>
> *Beth Jacobs: "I struggle my own way. The important thing now is, are you and your husband able to talk about this?"*
>
> *Mrs. Jones: "Not much. He's not much of a talker. But we understand each other. I know how he feels."*
>
> *Mrs. Jones begins to cry. She and Beth Jacobs just sit there quietly.*
>
> *After a few moments, Mrs. Jones says she must be getting along home now and tend to a few things.*

> *Worker: "Doris, have you been able to talk to your mother-in-law about getting your husband back to see a psychiatrist?"*
>
> *Doris (hesitant, lowering her head): "I just can't bring it up."*
>
> *Worker: "Perhaps she'd talk to me. We're the same age. Perhaps she would consider me like family."*
>
> *Doris (quite relieved): "Could you please call her?"*

Once the work has begun, workers and clients truly become involved in the work of problem solving. The phases of this process can be identified. With some variation, these phases ensue whether work is focused on problems of interpersonal relationships with individuals or groups, on planned community or other efforts toward changing systems, or on a variety of planning endeavors. They include (1) conducting an ongoing reassessment of the problem, (2) partializing the problem into manageable parts, (3) identifying obstacles, (4) obtaining and sharing additional information, (5) reviewing progress or setbacks, and (6) terminating the process. Environmental work is critical. The problem-solving process goes on. No single work can possibly do justice to the various strategies and skills involved in the problem-solving process.

We approach the matter by suggesting, for a number of select areas, how the work of problem solving may differ from the beginning phases.

### Ongoing Reassessment of the Problem

The process of ongoing reassessment calls attention to many facets of the situation. External changes may take place that can dramatically alter the course of events. Life can be measurably altered if a job is lost or obtained, if the child of a couple experiencing marital difficulty becomes seriously ill, or if the neighborhood that is organizing for better service is scheduled for demolition. Ongoing review and reappraisal is essential. Too often, workers become so caught up in the preparatory work that, upon seeing people, they forget to review. Setting aside some time to learn what happened this week, yesterday, or an hour ago is an essential component of interaction.

> *The conversation with Mrs. Jones shifts between intense, affective exploration about her daughter's death, as was the case a moment ago, to the more immediate concerns of how to deal with day-to-day needs.*
>
> *Beth Jacobs: "How do you and your husband manage? I know you both work. Who stays with the baby?"*
>
> *Mrs. Jones: "I work at night and my husband works during the day."*

> *Worker (the next day; calls Doris at home): "Doris, I have called your mother-in-law. She has asked me to come to her house for tea. We will chat then. I have found this approach helpful sometimes."*
>
> *Doris: "I am relieved. Perhaps she will understand what you mean; how important it is for my husband to see a psychiatrist (she starts to sound as if she is beginning to weep). Do you think it will be O.K.?"*
>
> *Worker: "Let's take one thing at a time. I'll arrange to see your mother-in-law. And when can you come in to see me?"*

### Partializing the Problem

In these and many other types of situations, multiple problems present themselves. In this reassessment phase, as the work proceeds, the initial agreement needs to be reviewed.

> *Mr. and Mrs. Jones are worried about the baby. Beth Jacobs wants to let them know that she is ready to help them think through the long-range outlook for Ellen.*
>
> *Mrs. Jones: "You know my husband is still so upset about Jan's death. And every night he comes home and he worries about Ellen. Do you know very much about AIDS?"*
>
> *Beth Jacobs: "I don't know a great deal, but I am learning and I can ask medical people for the answer. Do you have something specific in mind?"*
>
> *Mrs. Jones: "My husband says babies like ours who have this condition don't last long. Do you know if that's true?"*

> Beth Jacobs: *"We don't really know how long they can live. Especially with infants. What we do know helps children like her is to keep them well nourished with plenty of rest. If she is weakened she has more chance of getting infections. You are doing the right thing. You are taking such good care of her. Are you worried that she will also die?"*
>
> Mrs. Jones (trying to keep from crying): *"Yes! Oh Lord! Maybe the Lord wants it that way. But why? What did we do? So many black babies out there. I have a few friends in the church...."* (she begins to cry).
>
> Beth Jacobs sits there quietly grieving with her. After a few moments Beth Jacobs puts her hand on Mrs. Jones' arm, asks her if she could use a cup of coffee and says: *"Sometimes it helps to cry."*
>
> Mrs. Jones: *"Yes, thanks. I have to go soon."* She sips some coffee and then gets up.
>
> Beth Jacobs: *"Would you like to talk again when you come to see the baby tomorrow?"*
>
> Mrs. Jones: *"O.K."*


> Doris Cheng: *"Did you see my mother-in-law?"*
>
> Worker: *"Yes, I did. She was upset. But she is beginning to understand. She will try to persuade him to go to a psychiatrist they know from China. Doris, what about you? Have you seen a doctor about your seizures? How is work coming?"*
>
> Doris: *"From China? They don't understand. She's just putting it off."*
>
> Worker: *"Please give it a chance. Have you seen a doctor?"*
>
> And so the worker tries to help Doris to deal with a number of her issues and tries to help her to recognize the cultural differences between herself and the rest of the family.

### Identifying Obstacles

Obstacles come in the form of emotions, entrenched behavior patterns, discrimination, language barriers, environmental deficits, and so on. Despite this, an understanding of barriers or obstacles can help to overcome or minimize them.

Will Doris Cheng be able to recognize that she needs to take her husband's and in-laws' version of events into account as she tries to deal with her problem?

**Adaptation to the Ethnic Reality.**    Plans made in the privacy of the worker's office or in locales in other ways removed from the network of church, community, and kin may flounder when others become aware of what is going on. A Catholic woman planning a divorce may talk to her priest, who suggests she reconsider. The members of an African American neighborhood improvement group may encounter explicit and implicit racism when they meet with the mayor and other city officials. A Chicano woman who has obtained employment may encounter the wrath of her husband, who feels his very being threatened by her action.

These and like obstacles derive from deeply ingrained attitudes. Some members of Mrs. Jones's church do not feel she should trust that social worker. The next time that Beth Jacobs approaches her she may be less open. Perhaps Beth Jacobs will need to talk with Mrs. Jones about the fact that they are members of different ethnic groups.

> *Beth Jacobs approaches Mrs. Jones while she is visiting the baby. She asks whether she wants to talk with her in the lounge or in her office. Mrs. Jones agrees but is a little distant. They sit in the lounge.*
> *Beth Jacobs: "It must be hard talking about all that's facing you with a stranger like myself—a young white person; you might wonder whether I really understand what you're going through."*
> *Mrs. Jones (hesitantly): "Well, you're a nice lady; but some of those people of the church did say there's no point in talking to you."*
> *Beth Jacobs: "Did they say why?"*
> *Mrs. Jones: "You know, like you said, they thought what's the point. You're not one of us. You can't know what this AIDS epidemic is doing to us."*
> *Beth Jacobs: "Would I be asking too much to ask you to help me to under-stand . . . I really need to learn, you know."*
> *Mrs. Jones: "Maybe. And it really did help when you sat here quietly while I cried."*

When cultural dispositions serve as obstacles to moving ahead, the following principles are suggested: (1) explore the source and nature of the difficulty care-fully and gently, and (2) consider whether the obstacles are of an individual or a collective nature. For example, is the Catholic woman devout and basically com-mitted to staying in any marriage, or is she simply reporting the question raised by the priest? Mrs. Jones was only partly influenced by the members of her church. Is the Chicano woman the only one in her community to have taken a job? If not, have other women encountered similar problems? Is it possible to organize a Chicano women's support group? How can outreach help the elderly to overcome obstacles to use of service? Starrett, Mindel, and Wright (1983) found that increased informa-tion about and use of social services by the Hispanic elderly were related to the kind of information available in their community networks.

### Obtaining and Sharing Additional Facts and Feelings
Throughout the worker–client encounters there is the process of factual and emo-tional feedback. A client may tell the worker that conversations with her boss about a new assignment are going well. She took the worker's advice and did some relaxation exercises before approaching her. They will meet next week to talk about her newly acquired word processing skills. The worker complements her.

**Adaptation to the Ethnic Reality.**   It is possible that culturally sensitive matters may not have surfaced earlier in the helping process. Or there may be other matters not yet discussed. This is the case with Doris Cheng.

*The day after their conversation about whether Beth Jacobs could really understand the situation of this African American family, Beth and Mrs. Jones begin to chat after Mrs. Jones has visited Ellen.*

*Mrs. Jones is distressed. The baby does not seem well. She was sniffling and crying a lot.*

*Beth Jacobs: "I see you're really upset with her condition today. You must get depressed."*

*Mrs. Jones: "Yes, but I pray—I go to church."*

*Doris Cheng and the worker are meeting in accord with the agreement made at their last meeting.*

*Worker: "Today I think we really need to get to work to see how you are doing. Have you been having any seizures? Have you seen your doctor about medication?"*

*Doris (squirming a bit, reluctant): "I have to tell you something. I am embarrassed. I went to this other kind of doctor. You know, not an American doctor; a Chinese man who dispenses herbs. He gave me something, and it's helping."*

*Worker: "I didn't know you believed in this. I thought you had given that all up."*

*Doris: "You never know."*

*Worker: "The herbs probably won't hurt. And if you like going there it's O.K. But I've never known them to cure seizures. Let's talk about how you might get help from the herbalist, a neurologist, and perhaps a therapist."*

There are situations in which the basis for lack of progress as related to ethnicity may be shared. Only when the matter is discussed does the work progress.

A young Slavic woman was assigned an African American worker to help her think through her job troubles. The young woman was working at a semiskilled clerical job and was dissatisfied. The worker's efforts to try to identify the specific problem were yielding a very fuzzy picture. One day the young client blurted out in a rather embarrassed manner, "You know what's really bothering me on the job is my supervisor. But I never told you about that because she's black like you, and I thought you'd get mad at me." Only when the worker accepted her feeling and told her it was acceptable not to like any particular African American person were they able to move on to realistically consider the young woman's situation.

Ethnicity as a variable in the problem being considered may become evident during a later phase of contact. Mrs. Miller, a 25-year-old college graduate, had crossed out all sections pertaining to background on the form requesting service for marital counseling. The worker, respectful of her right to privacy, did not ask. The conflict as originally presented involved the couple's differences about having children. Mrs. Miller wanted to have children; Mr. Miller did not.

One day Mrs. Miller came in particularly distraught, and said, "I thought we had it all worked out before we got married. But yesterday he told me he doesn't want children because I'm not Jewish. He'll have children if I convert. I told her before we were married I couldn't do that."

Sometimes people are not aware of how important their ethnic background is until such basic issues as childbearing arise. And so the client shares a bit of information not previously known, perhaps even to herself.

### The Phasing Out of the Worker–Client Relationship

Strean (1978) suggested that the termination of any meaningful worker–client relationship will induce strong and ambivalent feelings. Others (Compton & Galaway,
1979) addressed the dynamic generated by the separation process, the sense of loss
or support that can be experienced in transfer or referral, and the heightened affect
sensed by both worker and client as the end of the relationship approaches.

Shulman (1984) suggested a number of principles to be considered in the termination phase: (1) identifying major learning, (2) identifying what is to be done
in the future, (3) synthesizing the ending process, and (4) considering alternative
sources of support to those obtained from the worker. For the ethnic-sensitive
worker, the last principle has particular significance. Alternative sources of support are often lodged in kinship and neighborhood networks, in the church, or in
a newly heightened sense of ethnic identity. These and other principles are major
considerations, requiring particular sensitivity to the possibility that clients may
view termination as rejection or may be fearful about going on alone.

Most of the skills reviewed earlier—stage setting, attending, tuning in, and
identifying areas of concern—continue here. The stage is now set for departure,
and all need to articulate what that means.

### Termination

> Seven days after the conversation between Mrs. Jones and Beth Jacobs about
> whether Beth Jacobs could understand, Beth arrives on the pediatric floor. She has
> been told that the baby is doing better and is ready to go home. She wants to be
> sure that the Joneses are prepared.
>
> Beth Jacobs: "Mrs. Jones, I hear Ellen is well enough to go home."
> Mrs. Jones: "Yes, bless the Lord! We're so happy—we'll have her with us."
> Beth Jacobs: "Are you ready?"
> Mrs. Jones: "Well, I told you the schedule we're on."
> Beth Jacobs: "Sometimes it gets tough, especially if she keeps getting sick. I
> brought you some information about support groups for families with children like
> your granddaughter. Do you think that might be something you would like to do?
> I also brought you some brochures."
> Mrs. Jones: "Yes, I'd like to know about them."
> Beth Jacobs: "They're in your town. Both meet at your local hospital. And you
> know I'm here. And there are other people in the department if I am away."
> Mrs. Jones (sadly): "Thanks. I think we got along O.K. I'm afraid I'll be back
> when the baby comes back. I'll look for you."
> Beth Jacobs: "Thank you for our conversations. I've learned a lot from you. I,
> too, know that you will be back. I am sorry that that will be likely. I hope we can
> talk again."
>
> A week after their previous meeting, Doris Cheng and the worker are meeting again.
> Doris has followed the worker's advice and has gone to see a neurologist, who
> put her on anticonvulsant drugs. She has talked with her mother and mother-in-

*law. She is willing to meet regularly with her husband and talk about a reconciliation if the psychiatrist can assure her there will be no more threats of abuse.*

*She thinks she needs long-term counseling to help her think through her life. The worker agrees and together they will try to find someone. Perhaps another Chinese woman, someone who understands both worlds. She will still see the herbalist.*

*Her supervisor is pleased that she now comes in on time; she cannot drive but has arranged for regular transportation.*

*Doris thanks the worker. They will miss each other. Each has learned something about how to incorporate the old ways into the new world.*

And so the work goes on. Worker and client assess, reassess, and move on. Mrs. Jones will return. There is little doubt Ellen will become ill again.

Doris Cheng has moved on to other helpers. Her work with the Employee Assistance Counselor may be done.

The process of help giving and help taking is much affected by ethnic and cultural factors. It also has its own momentum and procedures that cut across a wide variety of groups and problem areas.

## SOCIAL GROUP WORK

*A group consisting of gay male couples in committed long-term relationships in which at least one partner has AIDS has been meeting weekly for 1½ hours for over 5 years. Some 20 couples have been involved during the whole time of the group's existence. Some have left due to breakups or dissatisfaction with the group. Others have died.*

*There are whites representing various ethnic groups, African Americans, and some Latinos. Most of the members would be characterized as middle class.*

*When we are introduced to the group, they are discussing a request that they invite some women and some heterosexual male drug users who have AIDS to join the group.[4]*

We conclude this chapter on direct practice with a brief overview of group work approaches. The response of a group of gay men to the request that they include non-gay people in the group is used to illustrate some key principles and strategies of social group work. Glasser and Garvin (1977) and Brown (1991) traced the origins of group work to the period of social upheaval that accompanied the Industrial Revolution. Earlier we pointed to the role of the early settlement house movement and to workers such as Jane Addams who were instrumental in developing approaches that recognized cultural diversity and the importance of understanding the role of

---

[4] The excerpt from the group being described here are from a group that meets at the Gay Men's Health Crisis in New York City.

ethnicity and culture in U.S. life. Recent literature (e.g., Gitterman & Shulman, 1986) highlights the role of mutual aid groups in working with people with diverse needs who are at varying stages of the life cycle and who are experiencing diverse problems. There is evidence that groups can play an important part in helping people to cope with a variety of problems such as addiction to alcohol and other serious life difficulties.

Considerable other evidence points to the importance of the group as a vehicle for helping people to cope with a variety of life's issues. Most people are familiar with the increasingly important role played by self-help groups in helping people to struggle through such problems as addiction to alcohol and other drugs. A variety of groups are available for people experiencing all sorts of disabling and disruptive chronic health problems. And then there are the less formal groupings in the community and in the workplace: the community and neighborhood networks and other unstructured group processes that enable people to turn to others, similarly situated, who may be available for assistance of one kind or another. Our attention here is focused on those groups that are organized by social workers and closely related professionals.

Incorporating an understanding of the ethnic reality into practice has received increasing attention. A recent work edited by Davis (1984) shows how important group modalities can be in intervention with people from different ethnic minority groups.

There are a number of group work models. Adams and Schlesinger (1988) have identified and summarized the following approaches: (1) the social goals approach (Vinter, 1974); (2) the socialization approach, focused on enhancing the social development of voluntary participants in groups; and (3) resocialization or remedial approaches that assume the existence of a problem or deviance. The group then has the objective of "remedying" or "resocializing" those whose behavior is considered in some way deviant or improper. Brown (1991) identified treatment groups, socioeducation groups, and social action groups.

Despite variations in objectives, conceptual underpinnings, and style, a number of elements are common to most approaches. Included are efforts to achieve group objectives through sharing, the development of cohesion, and viewing the group as a mutual aid system.

## The Layers of Understanding

In the preceding section considerable attention was paid to how to use the layers of understanding as a framework for approaching case situations. The same holds true in work with groups. For example, knowledge of the dynamics of group process and function is essential. In working with a group such as the gay men's AIDS group, workers need to understand a great deal about how AIDS affects people, about stigma, and about how people approach death and terminal illness. Garvin (1981) and Brown (1991) have identified the phases of work with groups. These are analogous to the process of direct intervention with individuals just reviewed.

### The Pregroup Phase

Both the title and contents of a recent book on social group work, *Group Work with Populations at Risk* (Greif & Ephross, 1997), suggest that group work is closely related to the issues of concern in ethnic-sensitive social work practice. Many members of oppressed ethnic groups are especially vulnerable—to major illness, to disenfranchisement, and to loss of power. Those who are members of the lower socioeconomic strata are especially vulnerable to the vagaries of the economy and the market. Our earlier discussion of the Route to the Social Worker (see Chapter 4) suggests that many people who find themselves in disadvantaged positions in society are likely to find their way to social agencies by mandatory and coercive routes. Some of the groups discussed in the above mentioned book are people who are vulnerable by virtue of their ethnic and/or oppressed status. They include the unemployed (Lytle-Viera, 1997), victims of ethnoviolence, African American youth in the criminal justice system (Harvey, 1997), and others.

Also of importance are those groups that are focused on people with major illness such as cancer (e.g., Daste, 1997, and many others).

Who would benefit from involvement in a group and how to go about developing a group are major questions. Obviously, much more is involved than simply deciding that a group would be a good way in which to serve a particular population group.

There are several issues involved and steps to be taken. Some assessment must be made as to whether there is sufficient interest in a group for people to take the necessary time and energy to attend and to become engaged in the work of the group.

> *The social worker in a clinic serving developmentally disabled children and their families had the idea that the siblings of the developmentally disabled youngsters had many issues to confront, including taking on extra responsibility for the affected sibling, some sense of embarrassment and shame, and for the older ones, wondering about their long-run responsibilities when their parents could no longer care for their siblings.*
>
> *She wrote letters and invited a number of the siblings from her caseload to come to a meeting.*
>
> *For several weeks, only one or two attended and were rather uncommunicative when they did come.*
>
> *Sensing a lack of interest, the worker abandoned the project.*

Subsequent work suggested that the siblings were interested, but embarrassed; that they might have come if they had been approached individually first, and in these conversations learned that there were other siblings out there with similar experiences. Much has been written about the whys and hows of forming a group. Important to the present consideration is the discussion of taking into account what Shulman (1984) referred to as finding some common ground between members. Group purposes will affect group composition. For example, a group of African American adolescent boys organized for the purpose of helping with the particular problems of this age and minority group will not want to include young white men or women of any age. On the other hand, a group that wants to tackle the issue of racism in society will need to include members of different groups. The gay men's group already in existence ponders group composition.

> *Leader: "We will be adding some new couples to the group in the next few weeks and would like to hear what your feelings are about having a woman or someone who is heterosexual join the group."*
>     *John: "I don't like it at all. This is a group for gay men and should stay that way."*
>     *Gary: "I feel that it is the only place in the world where I can feel absolutely safe and where other people really understand me."*
>     *Paul: "I wonder if maybe they might not feel the same way because they have AIDS. After all, they are ostracized, too."*

### Planning a Group

In planning a group, scheduling becomes important. Pottick and Adams (1990) pointed out that scheduling time for intervention needs to take account of the problems on which people are working. Once the decision has been made to plan a group, many additional factors need to be considered. These include agency auspice and cooperation, scheduling, and further attention to group composition. For example, when pregnant adolescents are being encouraged to stay in school, it is inappropriate to schedule services during school time. In a hospital setting, such as an oncology ward, it is important to recognize that members will give priority to treatment needs. In the case of family members, they will give priority to how their family member is feeling, to work needs, and to other external situations. Workers need to be flexible in response to lateness or nonattendance.

It is critical that attention be paid to administrative sensibilities. For example, a hospital social worker thought it was a good idea to start a group of patients as a way of helping them to air some of their concerns about their care in the hospital. She hoped to use such a group as a way of conveying the members' mutual concerns to floor and hospital management. Both had been quite responsive to her suggestions, as well as to patient suggestions about areas needing improvement.

She was, therefore, quite surprised, when there were all sorts of barriers put in her way about forming the group. Other staff raised issues of time, interferred with treatment plans, and were afraid she would be neglecting some of her other patient care responsibilities if she started this group.

Further inquiry revealed that a group similar to this, started by a young African American social worker, had surfaced complaints from African American patients at a time when negative practices as perceived by the African American community near the hospital were already receiving attention. The unspoken fear was that in organizing groups she would select African American patients, though she had clearly demonstrated commitment to serving all of the patients.

**Adaptation to the Ethnic Reality.**   In thinking about whether and how to organize a group, the social worker must take the ethnic reality into account. For example, many Asian people are said to be uncomfortable in discussing their problems with strangers. Groups may run counter to that sentiment. When professional judgment nevertheless suggests that a group may be appropriate, ethnic-sensitive strategies may help. For example, Lee, Gordon, and Hom (1984) pointed out that the group may be viewed as a place where family secrets are exposed. They suggested that one way of overcoming this fear is to have workers work toward becoming accepted by the family network as being a member. They cited the following case to illustrate the point.

> *An 8-year-old Chinese boy with temper tantrums and difficulty in peer relationships is referred to a children's clinic. He has a close, clinging relationship with his mother and poor social skills. Preparatory work with the mother was carried out to introduce her to the importance of group therapy. The day the boy was to enter the group, he continued to cling to his mother and demonstrated considerable anxiety.*
>
> *The mother encouraged him to go and murmured to him: "It's O.K. Go with Uncle."*
>
> *She was identifying the group leader as if he were a trusted member of the family.*

## Starting the Group

Shulman (1993) suggested that the process of work with the group is analogous to beginning work with individual clients. Consequently, as the worker starts the group, the process of tuning in considered earlier in this chapter becomes most important.

It is essential that members have the opportunity to express their feelings about whether there is a fit between their purposes and those of the agency. It is also important to confront obstacles that may stand in the way. For example, if the group's members are involuntarily in prison or if the school has insisted that they join the group, anger and resentment may well be present. People need to be encouraged to express their distress and feelings of tension about being there.

It is also important to clarify tensions and expectations. In some situations it is important that the worker spell out what the group can and does expect and what is beyond the group's or group leader's capacity to control. This is especially relevant when group participation has been mandated, as in the case of people in difficulty with the law. The following case example is illustrative.

> *Leader (after explaining attendance rules and expectations of participation by members, as well as the mandatory reporting role of the group leader): "I'm sure it is possible to follow all these rules and not change, not open up to facing yourself or to the other men here. You can probably get through this group and not really change. That's up to you. The judge may order you to be here or your wife may be saying that she won't come back unless you get help. And as I have said, we require your anger diary and regular attendance in order for you to stay here, but no one can reach into your mind and heart and order a change. That's where you have complete control." (Gitterman & Shulman, 1986, p. 28)*

### Adaptation to the Ethnic Reality

The lack of congruence between some of the interventive modalities used in social work with the long-standing experiences of many ethnic groups has been frequently noted. We have pointed out that many Asian people, many Latino people, many American Indians, and others are accustomed to dealing with their troubles within the family. Living as they do in U.S. society, many find themselves in a situation of wanting or needing many of the interventions offered within the U.S. health and welfare system.

It is clear that when recent immigrants are asked to be involved in such areas of intervention as group therapy, discussion groups to consider problems, or political action groups, workers need to begin by saying something to the effect that this may be a new or possibly an uncomfortable experience. The social work concept of "starting where the client is" is a helpful starting point. A good way to do that is to ask people whether they are familiar with the process of getting people together in formal groups to deal with family problems, political action, or other purposes. Asking how people in their country or their group usually do things is important. Workers should feel free to admit that their knowledge is limited.

It is also important to help people express distress about being there. This is the case with many people, especially those whose route to the social worker has been at least somewhat coercive. It may become evident that people are there because they have no choice or feel that they have no choice.

## The Work Phase

As we have seen, in the beginning of a group process people have a variety of concerns, fears, and hopes. Communication is especially difficult in the beginning. Clearly, if people continue to come, they experience some increasing comfort; this is certainly likely to be the case if they have any choice about being there. Nevertheless, communication difficulties are likely to continue. For many people, it remains difficult to share matters of deep concern publicly with others, and some people, terribly worried about their own situations, become impatient at the need to defer to the problems of others.

Thus, as the work of the group continues, the worker needs to continually clarify and to help people to express themselves and use the group in a way helpful to them. Shulman (1993) pointed out that at the beginning of each meeting the worker needs to find ways to help individuals present their concerns to the group. Issues may involve a number of matters. Some people always try to capture the group's attention solely for their own purposes. This is a threat to the group's continuation and its achievement of its purpose; consequently, it must be dealt with. At the early part of each session, workers need to clarify, with the group, the focus for that session. Also important is attention to the underlying message being conveyed. For example, a subcommittee of the local health and welfare council has been asked to develop approaches for developing greater sensitivity to prejudice and to the needs of different minority groups in the community's health and welfare agencies. There have been a lot of complaints.

> *The group asks one of the members to turn to experts in race relations to help develop strategies. As different plans are brought in, the council keeps rejecting them, finding them wanting. Finally, it is evident that the real purposes are being subverted. The idea of the presence of racism or prejudice is rejected. One member says, "What we really need is to help people to be more polite." The chairperson agrees.*

It is much more comfortable to let it be. Perhaps the complaints will go away. Perhaps if the issue surfaces again, next month or next year, the group will be able to confront it. Although group members may verbally agree to focus on a particular topic, they may, and often do, veer from it. Questions then need to be asked about the connection between the group and the subject actually being considered.

Characteristic role structure emerges in a group, as does the inevitable power structure. The worker must analyze the power structure and seek to reduce or eliminate detrimental uses of power.

### Adaptation to the Ethnic Reality

In attending to matters concerning the ethnic reality during this phase of group work, a number of issues deserve special attention. In the case of the health and welfare council, the group is struggling with one of the major issues confronting society. It is not easy.

In the situation of multiethnic, interracial groups, attention must always be paid to the dynamics of interaction between members of different groups. For example, as communication patterns emerge and sociometric structuring becomes evident, it is important to consider whether social and communication groups have developed around ethnic group membership. Do all of the African Americans sit together? Do whites have the power? If so, what is the reaction of the African Americans? How are group goals being effected? Are the African Americans being intimidated? Or, conversely do the African Americans have power? Are whites afraid to object and raise questions because they are afraid of being called racist?

> *The group of gay men continues to struggle.*
>
> *Paul: "I keep thinking about what someone said last week—if a woman came here to a gay men's agency, she'd have to have thought about what it would be like. And if she wanted to come into a group with us, she would most likely be pretty accepting. I would be willing to try it."*
>
> *John: "I don't know. I think I might leave. I want to be with my own kind. One of the things that I really like is the social contacts here. I can't imagine that I would want to become friends with some hetero woman and her drug user hubby."*

And so the group continues to split on basic group purposes and tasks. For some the issue of AIDS and how that affects other people is overriding. They will expand on group purposes. Those who view the group primarily as a support group for gay men who happen to have AIDS are unrelenting in their desire to keep other tasks at bay. The health and welfare council members are not yet ready to see racism and how to combat it as part of their task.

Ethnic-sensitive practice means attending to those matters that interfere with people's comfort and capacity to solve problems. Much in the lives of members of minority and other ethnic groups relates to the prejudices and inequities associated with such group membership. There may be times where a worker will need to turn to the outside community in the effort to obtain resources or minimize discomforting, prejudiced environments. The health and welfare council will again be asked to consider the issue of racism and bigotry. A school social worker dealing with youngsters with reading problems may well find that the difficulty, especially in the case of minority children, rests less with the children than with the school. The school may simply not be providing adequate instruction and supports to help these youngsters learn how to read. Engaging the system on behalf of the youngsters in the group then becomes an important adaptation to the ethnic reality.

## Termination

When and whether a decision is made to terminate a group will depend on a number of factors. For some groups, the amount of time is predetermined: the end of the summer in camp, the end of the school year. Others will leave the matter up to the group members, ending the group when they have achieved a goal or goals. Some groups, such as those in acute care or other short-term treatment hospital settings, may be available indefinitely, although the composition of the group may be in constant flux.

Garvin (1981) and Brown (1991) suggested that all endings entail some loss and some anxiety. People are likely to have invested energy, time, and affection in the group. He also contended that whatever the reason for termination, the worker has certain obligations as the group experience is drawing to a close. The worker needs to try to help members with a number of issues, including evaluating goal achievement; dealing with feelings about termination; trying to maintain positive changes; and using the skills, knowledge, and changed attitudes acquired as a result of the group experience. Shulman (1984) identified the following skills associated with sessional endings and transitions: summarizing, generalizing, identifying next steps, and exploring the reasons for "doorknob comments."

Both transitional endings and termination entail the responsibility of stopping to acknowledge that something has happened, that it is about to be over—permanently or temporarily—and that it is useful to review and assess the meaning of the experience. The meaning and implications for the next stage may be useful, or it may have turned out to "be a bust." Either needs to be acknowledged.

### Adaptation to the Ethnic Reality

How issues concerning the ethnic reality are handled at termination or at the point of transition will clearly be related to what the group's issues were and how related issues were dealt with to that point. We offer the following suggestions. If dealing with matters pertaining to intergroup issues was part of the group's goals, it is of the utmost importance that the group takes time to consider what happened. That means reviewing the positives and the negatives. If racism and bigotry were evident, it is important to review the process, examining where the expression might have originated, how it was handled, and what the members of the group have learned.

Where a group of people from the same group were struggling with issues that relate to their membership in a particular ethnic or minority group or social class group, it is important to review whether their understanding, sense of self, self-esteem, and sense of empowerment have been enhanced.

> *The gay men's couple's group continues. Their struggle to decide whether to include nongay people was resolved in favor of allowing other people in. In the case of this group, several issues were considered. They included the ethnic reality of these men, most of whom were middle-class whites, Hispanics, and African Americans. The newcomers—drug users and perhaps some street people—were likely to be of a different class. It was not an easy struggle.*

## SUMMARY

The practice skills presented in this chapter represent a composite of many identified in the social work literature, both in direct practice with individuals and in work with groups. Ethnic-sensitive practice requires adaptation or modifications in keeping with knowledge about prevailing group dispositions to issues such as privacy, the use of formally organized helping institutions, stances concerning self-disclosure, discussion of intimate matters outside of the family, and the context in which service is or should be offered. Flexibility is necessary in determining where service is to be rendered and the speed with which workers seek to engage clients in contracting. Simultaneous attention to interpersonal and institutional issues is always of concern.

## REFERENCES

Adams, A. C., & Schlesinger, E. G. (1988). Group approach to training ethnic-sensitive practitioners. In C. Jacobs & D. Bowles (Eds.), *Ethnicity and race: Critical concepts in social work* (pp. 204–216). Silver Spring, MD: National Association of Social Workers.

Boyd-Franklin N. (1989). *Black families in therapy.* New York: The Guilford Press.

Brown, L. B. (1950). Race as a factor in establishing a casework relationship. *Social Casework, 32,* 155–160.

Brown, L. N. (1991). *Groups for growth and change.* New York: Longman.

Byler, W. (1977). The destruction of American Indian families. In S. Unger (Ed.), *The destruction of American Indian families.* New York: Association on American Indian Affairs.

Chen, P. N. (1970). The Chinese community in Los Angeles. *Social Casework, 51,* 591–598.

Comas-Diaz, L. (1984). Content themes in group treatment with Puerto Rican women. In L. Davis (Ed.), *Ethnicity in social group work practice* (pp. 63–72). New York: Haworth.

Compton, B. R., & Galaway, B. (1979). *Social work processes.* Homewood, IL: Dorsey Press.

Compton, B. R., & Galaway, B. (1984). *Social work processes* (3rd ed.). Homewood, IL: Dorsey Press.

Compton, B. R., & Galaway, B. (1989). *Social work processes* (4th ed.). Belmont, CA: Wadsworth.

Daste, B. M. (1997). Group work with cancer patients. In *Group work with populations at risk.* New York: Oxford University Press, pp. 15–27.

Davis, L. E. (Ed.). (1984). *Ethnicity in social group work practice.* New York: Haworth.

Davis, L. E., & Proctor, E. K. (1989). *Race, gender and class.* Englewood Cliffs, NJ: Prentice-Hall.

Devore, W., & Schlesinger, E. (1986). Ethnic-sensitive practice. In *Encyclopedia of social work* (1st ed.). Washington, DC: NASW.

Dominick, J. R., & Stotsky, B. (1969). Mental patients in nursing homes IV: Ethnic influence. *Journal of the American Geriatric Society, 17*(1).

Egan, G. (1975). *The skilled helper: A model for systematic helping and interpersonal relating.* Monterey, CA: Brooks/Cole.

Fandetti, D. V., & Goldmeir, J. (1988). Social workers as culture mediators in health care settings. *Health and Social Work, 13*(3), 171–180.

Fischer, J. (1978). *Effective casework practice: An eclectic approach.* New York: McGraw-Hill.

Gambino, R. (1974). *Blood of my blood: The dilemma of the Italian-Americans.* Garden City, NY: Anchor Books, Doubleday.

Garvin, C. D. (1981). *Contemporary group work.* Englewood Cliffs, NJ: Prentice-Hall.

Gary, L. E. (1985). Depressive symptoms and black men. *Social Work Research and Abstracts, 21*(4), 21–29.

Ghali, S. B. (1977). Culture sensitivity and the Puerto Rican client. *Social Casework, 58,* 459–468.

Giordano, J., & Giordano, G. P. (1977). *The ethnocultural factor in mental health: A literature review and bibliography.* New York: American Jewish Committee.

Gitterman, A., & Schaeffer, A. (1972). The white professional and black client. *Social Casework, 53.*

Gitterman, A., & Shulman, L. (Eds.). (1986). *Mutual aid groups and the life cycle.* Itasca, IL: F. E. Peacock.

Glasser, R. H., & Garvin, C. D. (1977). Social group work: The developmental approach. In *The encyclopedia of social work.* Washington, DC: National Association of Social Workers.

Gomez, E., Zurcher, L. A., Buford, E., & Becker, E. (1985). A study of psychosocial casework with Chicanos. *Social Work, (30),* 477–482.

Good Tracks, J. G. (1973). Native American non-interference. *Social Work, 18* (6), 30–35.

Green, J. W. (1982). *Cultural awareness in the human services.* Boston: Allyn & Bacon.

Green, J. (1995). *Cultural awareness in the human services: A multi-ethnic approach* (2nd ed.). Boston: Allyn & Bacon.

Greif, G. L., & Ephron, P. H., (Eds.). (1997). *Group work with populations at risk.* New York: Oxford University Press.

Harvey, A. R. (1997). Group work with African-American youth in the criminal justice system: A culturally competent model. In G. L. Greif & P.H. Ephross (Eds.), *Group work with populations at risk.* New York: Oxford University Press.

Hepworth, D. H., & Larsen, J. A. (1990). *Direct social work practice: Theory and skills* (3rd ed.). Belmont, CA: Wadsworth.

Hepworth, D. H., & Larsen, J. A. (1993). *Direct social work practice.* Pacific Grove, CA: Brooks/Cole.

Ho, M. K. (1976). Social work with Asian Americans. *Social Casework, 57,* 195–201.

Ho, M. K. (1987). *Family therapy with ethnic minorities.* Newbury Park, CA: Sage.

Hooyman, N. R., & Kiyak, H. A. (1988). *Social gerontology.* Boston: Allyn & Bacon.

Jenkins, S. (1981). *The ethnic dilemma in social services.* New York: The Free Press.

Jones, E. E. (1978). Effects of race on psychotherapy process and outcome: An exploratory investigation. *Psychotherapy: Theory, Research and Practice, 15,* 226–236.

Kadushin, P. (1995). Interviewing. In R. Edwards, (Ed.), *Encyclopedia of social work* (19th ed. pp. 1527–1537). Washington, D.C.: National Association of Social Workers.

Leashore, B. R. (1981). Social services and black men. In L. E. Gary (Ed.), *Black Men* (pp. 257–268). Beverly Hills, CA: Sage.

Lee, P. C., Gordon, J., & Hom, A. B. (1984). Group-work practice with Asian clients: A sociocultural approach. In L. Davis (Ed.), *Ethnicity in social group work practice* (pp. 37–45). New York: Haworth.

Lewis, R. G., & Ho, M. K. (1975). Social work with Native Americans. *Social Work, 20*(5), 379–382.

Lopata, H. Z. (1976). *Polish Americans: Status competition in an ethnic community.* Englewood Cliffs, NJ: Prentice-Hall.

Lum, D. (1986). *Social work practice and people of color: A process–stage approach.* Monterey, CA: Brooks/Cole.

Lum, D. (1992). *Social work practice and people of color: A process–stage approach* (2nd ed.). Monterey, CA: Brooks/Cole.

Lytle-Viera, J. E. (1997). Group work with unemployed people. In G. L. Greif & P. H. Ephross (Eds.), *Group work with populations at risk.* New York: Oxford University Press, pp. 306–317.

Maluccio, A. N., & Marlow, W. D. (1974). The case for contract. *Social Work, 19*(j), 28–37.

Mercer, J. R. (1972). Career patterns of persons labeled as mentally retarded. In E. Freidson & J. Lorber (Eds.), *Medical men and their work: A sociological reader.* Chicago: Aladin-Atherton.

Middleman, R., & Goldberg, G. (1974). *Social service delivery: A structural approach to social work practice.* New York: Columbia University Press.

Minkler, M., & Roe, K. M. (1993). *Grandmothers as caregivers: Raising children of the crack cocaine epidemic.* Newbury Park, CA: Sage Publications.

Mokuau, N., & Matsuoka, J. (1986, March.) *The appropriateness of practice theories for working with Asian and Pacific Islanders.* Presented at the Annual Program Meeting, Council on Social Work Education, Miami, Florida.

Mondykowski, S. M. (1982). Polish families. In M. McGoldrick, J. K. Pearce, & J. Giordano (Eds.), *Ethnicity and family therapy* (pp. 393–411). New York: Guilford Press.

Pincus, A., & Minahan, A. (1973). *Social work practice: Model and method.* Itasca, IL: F. E. Peacock Publishers.

Pottick, K. J., & Adams, A. (1990). *Bringing providers and clients together by delivering comfort, understanding and respect.* Unpublished manuscript.

Reid, W. J. (1986). Task-centered social work. In E. J. Turner (Ed.), *Social work treatment* (3rd ed., pp. 267–295). New York: The Free Press.

Reid, W. J., & Epstein, L. (1977). *Task-centered casework.* New York: Columbia University Press.

Rio, A. T., Santisteban, D., & Szapocznik, J. (1993) Family therapy for Hispanic substance abusing youth. In R. Sanchez-Mayers, B. L. Kail, & T. D. Watts (Eds.), *Hispanic substance abuse.* Springfield, IL: Charles C. Thomas.

Seabury, B. A. (1976). The contract: Uses, abuses and limitations. *Social Work, 21*(1), 1–5.

Schlesinger, E. G. (1990, June 15). *Ethnic-sensitive social work practice: The state of the art.* Presented at the Annual Field Institute, School of Social Work, Rutgers, the State University of New Jersey, New Brunswick, NJ.

Schlesinger, E. G. (1996). *Are there circumstances in which the helping professional must be of the same ethnicity and gender as the client? No.* (1996). De Ande, D. *Controversial issues in multiculturalism,* (pp. 206–211). Boston: Allyn & Bacon.

Schlesinger, E., & Devore, W. (1995). Ethnic-sensitive social work practice: The state of the art. *Journal of Sociology and Social Welfare,* XXII(1) March, pp. 29–58.

Shulman, L. (1993). *The skills of helping individuals and groups.* Itasca, IL: F. E. Peacock.

Shulman, L. (1984). *The skills of helping* (2nd ed.). Itasca, IL: F. E. Peacock.

Shulman, L. (1986). Group work method. In A. Gitterman & L. Shulman (Eds.), *Mutual aid groups and the life cycle* (pp. 23–54). Itasca, IL: F. E. Peacock.

Starrett, R. A., Mindel, C. H., & Wright, R. (1983). Influence of support systems on the use of social services by the Hispanic elderly. *Social Work Research and Abstracts, 19*(4), 35–40.

Strean, H. S. (1978). *Clinical social work practice.* New York: The Free Press.

Toupin, E. S. W. A. (1980). Counseling Asians: Psychotherapy in the context of racism and Asian-American history. *American Journal of Orthopsychiatry, 50*(1), 76–86.

Turner, F. (1995). Social work practice: Theoretical base. In R. Edwards (Ed.), *Encyclopedia of Social Work* (19th ed., pp. 2255–2265). Washington, DC: National Association of Social Workers.

Turner, S., & Armstrong, S. (1981). Cross-racial psychotherapy: What the therapists say. *Psychotherapy: Theory, Research and Practice, 18,* 375–378.

Vinter, R. D. (1974). The essential components of group work practice. In P. Glasser, R. Sarri, & R. D. Vinter (Eds.), *Individual change through small groups* (pp. 9–33). New York: The Free Press.

Wood, G. G., & Middleman, R. R. (1989). *A structural approach to direct practice in social work.* New York: Columbia University Press.

Zborowski, M. (1952). Cultural components in response to pain. *Journal of Social Issues, 4*(8).

# 9

# ETHNIC-SENSITIVE MACRO PRACTICE

*The Saragosa Tornado*

*"Under rainy, funereal skies, dazed residents of this tiny West Texas town trickled back to a community that barely exists after a devastating tornado Friday night"* (Applebome, 1987).

*The tornado struck Saragosa, a Hispanic farming community of about 350 second-generation residents. Everyone in town is related, interwoven with each other by family and community. When the tornado struck, about 100 residents were in the community center attending a Head-Start graduation ceremony. Six young graduates were killed along with 29 other persons. Five of the six public buildings were destroyed, as were more than half of the homes. Damage was estimated at $6.4 million.*

*The president made federal aid available. Residents were eligible for low-interest loans; low-income persons could receive grants up to $5,000. Churches made special appeals for help. The Red Cross reported $470,000 in pledges. (Applebome, 1987)*

## DEFINING MACRO PRACTICE

Social work intervention responding to the devastation of the Saragosa community requires workers who have the knowledge, values, and skills that will support macro interventions. Our social work history provides evidence of attention paid to communities in need. Weil and Gamble (1995) examine the roots of community work, identifying the settlement movement, charity organizations, and grassroots organizing as significant contributions to our professional history. They recognize the polluting influence of racism and prejudice which denied oppressed ethnic groups full participation in society. These experiences led oppressed groups to build their own survival, self-help, and community change organizations. Two such organizations will be examined in this chapter.

The generalist model for practice, which is required for undergraduate and first year masters social work programs, provides the opportunity to explore simultaneous work at micro, mezzo, and macro levels, which includes practice with organizations and communities. Community may be identified as a neighborhood, city, or small rural town such as Saragosa. It may be defined as a group of towns known as a county, or a geographical region such as Central New York.

Netting, Kettner, and McMurtry (1993) describe macro practice as intervention designed to bring about planned change in communities or organizations. Rivera and Erlich (1995) provide an approach to practice with people of color. A paradigm is presented to help practitioners to arrange their skills and strategies in ways that are goal-oriented. A three-tier process, which may be conceptualized as contact intensity at several levels of community development identified as primary, secondary, and tertiary contacts, is suggested.

The primary level, the most intimate, requires racial, cultural, and linguistic identity with the community. These characteristics allow for entry into ethnic communities. At the second level language is not an essential, the functions at this level include that of liaison with outside institutions and a technical resource with ethnic-sensitive skills. The final tertiary level may be occupied by an "outsider," who works for the common interests and concerns of the community. The social worker with community macro skills may be active at each level (Rivera & Erlich, 1995).

In *Strategies of Community Intervention,* the editors (Rothman, Erlich, & Tropman, 1995) have gathered articles related to macro practice, which include the familiar locality development, social planning, and social action models for community intervention. Brueggemann (1996) identifies the many roles macro workers may assume in the intervention process. Included are researcher, social activist, program developer, social planner, and administrator.

Long and Holle's (1997) enlightening exploration of macro practice is related to life course positions, providing examples of practice with young mothers and infants, young adults, as well as senior citizens who are assisted in organizing a response to a questionable community policy decision. Kretzmann and McKnight (1993) lay out a path that may be followed as the worker identifies and mobilizes community assets. Social workers responding to the needs of the Saragosa community, and other communities in need, have available many perspectives on macro practice that will support their intervention efforts.

## THE LAYERS OF UNDERSTANDING

The layers of understanding guide ethnic-sensitive community workers. Social workers involved in the rebuilding of Saragosa must recognize that the several strands that held the community together have been stretched and sorely stressed. Some survivors questioned the Church; has God forsaken us? Language, which binds them together, is now a barrier in relationships with those who come to help.

Social workers moving through the layers of understanding must begin with a knowledge base that includes a profile of Saragosa that affords them an understanding of the uniqueness of this small ethnic community. Other layers will require that attention be directed to policies related to applications for federal and local assistance, an understanding of the impact of the ethnic reality on families and the community at large, as well as the skills and techniques that support macro models for intervention.

The Saragosa tragedy gained considerable media attention. Little media attention is directed to other communities with social problems that have persisted for years.

### The CURN Story

*The South Side community is predominantly African American. The neighborhood has many substandard dwellings, high rates of crime and violence, drug abuse, and alcoholism. There is little evidence of high academic achievement and therefore few models for children and youth to relate to as they look to the future. The neighborhood adults recognize the need to support their children and youth in the development of self-esteem and the modes of resilience that will assist them as they combat negative community pressures.*

*Communities United to Rebuild Neighborhoods (CURN) began in Mrs. Geneva Hayden's living room as a children's library. This was a "safe place" for neighborhood children. A computer was added, a donation from Cooperative Extension, a grant provided the funds for a printer.*

*Adult residents joined Mrs. Hayden and expanded the work so that it became an advocate for young and old in the area. With this community action thrust in mind, block captains were selected to represent their immediate neighbors as needs were identified. Initial tasks for the entire group included cleaning the neighborhood, rummage sales as fund-raisers, and block parties for everyone. A stipend from a community foundation supported participation in a leadership development program for Mrs. Hayden.*

*As the organization grew, they joined with the city park department and developed a community garden. A request for funding for a summer program was granted by a foundation that supports the mission work of a church. Donated funds supported a summer time trip to Philadelphia for elementary school children; the mayor was among the donors. Children earned sneakers for participating in a summer reading program. The work was under way.*

*The next goal was to acquire and rehabilitate a house in the community. Such a dwelling will provide a safe place for children, a program and service center, as well as an office/home for the group. Plans are under way.*

Our discussion of the layers of understanding will consider practice in the two communities described: Saragosa, destroyed by a sudden storm; and the CURN neighborhood, beset by poor housing, crime and violence, and substance abuse.

## Layer 1—Social Work Values

Social workers who respond to the immediate needs in Sarasoga are guided by the Code of Ethics as they act to provide appropriate services in public emergencies to the greatest extent possible (*Code of Ethics* 6.03). In both communities, social workers are expected to seek to ensure that all people have equal access to the resources, employment, services, and opportunities they require to meet their basic human needs (*Code of Ethics* 6.04). Tornado survivors will need all of the federal funds that are available, Red Cross donations, along with donations from churches. CURN will need continued support from the city, the state, and philanthropic organizations if they are to rebuild the neighborhood.

The Code of Ethics, passed by the Delegate Assembly of the National Association of Social Workers (NASW) in 1996, is the profession's commitment to a set of values that guide day-to-day practice. It is based on the premise that all persons have worth, dignity, and uniqueness. It is difficult to respond to this value in positive ways when there is evidence of continued child abuse and neglect, family violence, or drug abuse in a neighborhood. It is easier to work actively to "expand choice and opportunity for all people, with special regard for vulnerable, disadvantaged, oppressed, and exploited people and groups" (*Code of Ethics* 6.04).

Macro practice certainly holds to the values of the profession, but as community workers respond to need in distinctly different communities they will respond to those sections of the Code of Ethics that seek to restore responsibility to clients as well as those calling for ethical responsibility to society.

## Layer 2—Basic Knowledge of Human Behavior

### Knowledge of the Community and Organizations

The community of interest must be understood as a place, set within often loosely defined geographical boundaries. The boundaries of Saragosa are clear in that it is a small town. Neighborhoods such as CURN have more fluid boundaries within city limits. Locations of these neighborhoods are often identified by geography: the North, East, South, or West Side. Other neighborhoods may be identified as ethnic enclaves, often referred to in negative ways that demean residents who are members of majority or minority ethnic groups. Names such as Jew Town, Chinatown, Little Italy, or Black Bottom identify these enclaves. Terms such as kike, wop, nigger, or dumb pole characterize residents in degrading ways.

Saragosa was an ethnic community, a closely knit enclave with about 350 residents. This Hispanic enclave offered its citizens the comfort of family and friends, a church, and a community center. The tornado damaged every component of the community.

The community workers' need for knowledge about community organizations is not limited to those delivering human services but must include political and social organizations and religious organizations. These span mainstream tall-steeple churches to storefront congregations. Few such organizations were to be found in Saragosa before the tornado. After the disaster, responses came from organizations in other cities. Among those responding was El Paso Senior Opportunities Services (EPSOS), an organization whose mission is service to the Hispanic elderly.

Social workers aligned with the CURN neighborhood are aware of the tensions that exist in relation to many social service agencies that have failed to respond to community need. Much can be accomplished with groups who are committed to change in the community. At present these include the American Red Cross, Cooperative Extension, a community philanthropic foundation, and neighborhood schools. Although the literature speaks of the work and the power of the church in African American communities (Frazier, 1964), such is not the case in this neighborhood. Rather, a supportive relationship has been established with a church in a nearby suburb.

### Resources and Power

Mondros and Wilson (1994) view power as a process attained through concrete activities that may be measured as outcomes. They call attention to the distinctions between actual power and the feeling of being powerful. Empowerment is seen as a psychological state with a sense of competence, control, and entitlement. Propelled by the disposition, the community is allowed to pursue concrete activities aimed at becoming powerful.

The macro social worker must understand that power may be destructive or productive as the process generates ideas and community concerns and builds a community (Rivera & Erlich, 1995). In the Saragosa and CURN communities, power may be experienced in positive and negative ways. Delays in processing the low-interest loans to residents of Saragosa engender feelings of powerlessness against the forces of a very large governmental system. In the South Side CURN neighborhood, there is a sense of accomplishment and power as they join with the city in the development of a garden that will provide some food, and an abundance of flowers, as well as the opportunity for the adults to teach the young the secrets of good gardening.

If a community is to enter into the empowerment process, then the worker must be aware of the resources available. Many of these may be identified through the process of mapping suggested by Kretzmann and McKnight (1993). This activity identifies the many resource assets that a community may have. At the micro level, there are individuals with special gifts. There is a grandmother who is willing to watch the children as they play, and an artist who is willing to paint the signs for the weekend block party. Churches and citizens groups, such as those who respond to the Saragosa tragedy, are at the mezzo level of resources that are distant from neighborhoods at the institutional-level schools, libraries, community colleges, as well as four-year universities, businesses, or recreational facilities that may be found in parks. As social workers and community people work together in mapping, they are able to identify resources not ordinarily considered. An understanding of the processes in acquiring power and empowerment, and the ability to identify the assets a community will have, are basic to the change effort.

### Community Disaster Behavior

Social workers are often present in times of community disaster, fires, floods, earthquakes, or tornados. Knowledge of disaster behavior is essential if professional responses are to be competent. Siporin (1987) submitted that competent communities respond to disaster in a collective manner and are able to mobilize for mutual aid as emergency welfare systems emerge. They are also able to cope with the onslaught of media and government investigations, as well as volunteers and professionals who come to help. Vulnerable communities are unable to cope with disaster and follow a downhill path from which they may not recover. Saragosa is a competent community.

Knowledge about individual and family behavior in disaster must be joined with knowledge about community behavior. Unique crisis experiences requires knowledge that reaches beyond familiar crisis intervention perspectives and incorporates considerations of disaster syndrome or post-traumatic stress syndrome.

### Understanding Community Social Problems

The dual perspective introduced by Dolores Norton (1978) presents the individual at the center of nurturing and sustaining systems. Both systems are expected to support the development of individuals. Unfortunately, neither can be depended on to be consistent in nurturing or sustaining. An understanding of this dual perspective provides the macro worker with tools to examine a community.

Social problems, such as family violence, substance abuse, disruptive marriages, or teenage mothers, may be found in the nurturing system. These are in evidence in the CURN neighborhood. Problems in Saragosa may be addressed by the sustaining system with federal grants for the rebuilding of the community, low-interest loans, and gifts from community churches. In the first instance, the nurturing system struggles to care for its own, while the sustaining system responds in positive ways to the community in crisis.

## Layer 3—Knowledge and Skill in Agency Policy and Services Influence Professional Practice

### Macro Level Roles and Ethnic Social Services

Planner, activist, and outreach are appropriate roles for macro practice within the community to be used with strategies such as research and planning, social action, and community education (Miley, O'Melia, & DuBois, 1998). Social workers are expected to have an understanding of agency policy and services in order to determine the appropriate use of each role and strategy. Advocacy and brokerage are roles that may be added to ensure success in the change process.

Not only must a worker understand and appreciate the policies and services of their own agency, but of other institutional resources as well. The ethnic-sensitive worker will be familiar with ethnic agencies in the community. The Urban League is committed to service as a change agent in African American communities. Jewish Communal Service has a similar focus in serving Jewish communities. Polish American Clubs and Hungarian Community Centers are additional resources in many communities.

An examination of social services related to oppressed ethnic groups (Inglehart & Becerra, 1995) describes ethnic social services as those provided by members of ethnic groups for members of the group. They add that such services are not limited to the array of oppressed ethnic groups; Jewish, Italian, Catholic, Irish, and Slavic groups may be included as well.

Ethnic-sensitive practitioners understand that ethnic agencies such as EPSOS address the needs of the Hispanic elderly, as they respond to the problems identified in Saragosa. Elderly citizens were trained to identify and respond to individual and community needs. The South Side Family Center, an African American multiservice center, assists CURN when transportation is needed for field trips. An awareness of ethnic-agencies, their policies and services as well as their constituencies, extends the reach of the macro social worker.

## Layer 4—Self-Awareness and Insight into One's Own Ethnicity

Local newspapers and evening television news regularly report on the violence in the CURN neighborhood. The sound of gunshots at night are ordinary. An eighteen-year-old male shot in the front of a church adds to community grief for the loss of another neighborhood child. Many travelers are fearful when they drive along major streets that pass through the neighborhood.

In the aftermath of this reality, workers may be questioned, "How can you walk on those streets?" "Does your agency expect you to go *there*?" These questions and others are related to safety and community social problems. They are asked by friends and the general public who have legitimate concerns.

In our initial discussion of this layer, self-awareness was a central theme. "Who" questions were presented to help social workers to catch self-awareness. Workers were asked to begin to think and feel through the impact of their own ethnicity on their perception of themselves and others.

McMahon (1990) asked students to think about the ethnic groups that lived in their home environment when they were growing up. The follow-up question asks for recollections of family relationships with other ethnic groups, majority and minority. Students are asked to think about their communities and the messages their families gave about who lived next door or on the block. These attitudes have an impact on perceptions of what a community is, who should live there, and the power they may have in relation to others within and outside of the community. Thinking and feeling through the responses to McMahon's queries help the macro worker to provide answers to "why" questions.

## Layer 5—The Impact of the Ethnic Reality on the Daily Life of the Community

Saragosa and CURN are lower income communities. Ethnic minority status is a powerful force in each place. We have posited that the ethnic reality is the intersect at which social class and ethnicity meet. It will determine lifestyle and life chances of individuals and families. In this discussion we add the community.

In the United States the oppressed ethnic community often finds itself in the lower income stratification. In a review of the African American community in the 1990s and beyond, Blackwell (1991) presents racism, patterned oppression, and the systematic exclusion from equal participation in the life and culture of American society as continuing consequences of ethnic group membership.

Lack of access to health services and health insurance, little knowledge of good health practices, more hazardous occupations and environmental exposure, children's exposure to lead, and genetic factors such as sickle cell trait place African American families and communities at risk for health and health-care–related issues (Thomas, 1992).

Daily life was a struggle in Saragosa before the tornado. The residents were poor farmers with little contact beyond their borders. The storm generated feelings of anger and loss of community identity and intensified personal problems. Certainly this was an exceptional natural event, and the ethnic reality, oppressed ethnic group, and low-income status confounded the experience.

Like the African American community, Hispanic communities find that racism and discrimination are barriers to community development. Immigration policies prompt the search for illegal aliens, persons without documentation that permits residence in the United States. Sentiment against these persons is such that in 1994 the citizens of California voted to deny education and health services to illegal aliens who were most often identified as Hispanic.

Experiences in education and unemployment are elements of a community's ethnic reality. Although a wide range of positions may be held in the labor force, there remains a significant difference between Hispanic and non Hispanic salaries, with the minority workers earning lower salaries (Garcia, 1990).

Workers who respond to problems in low-income oppressed ethnic group communities need to understand that the consequences of the ethnic reality present daily conflicts. Residents continually find themselves in marginal, powerless positions in relation to their desire for social change.

### Layer 6—An Understanding That the Route to the Social Worker Has an Impact on How Social Services Are Perceived and Delivered

Routes to the social worker can be coercive or voluntary in nature. These routes may be easily identified in direct practice. Individuals and families may be coerced into the helping process with an obligation to work on problems identified by others. The voluntary route is taken by those who have identified problems to be addressed and at least initially are seeking solutions.

In macro practice, routes to the social worker are seldom clearly defined. Neither the courts nor social service agencies have the ability to require communities and neighborhoods to enter into professional relationships with social workers. Families in this neighborhood, like families in many inner cities, experience poverty, mental illness, divorce, single parenting, unemployment, and continuing poverty. These private troubles become public issues and thereby generate professional concerns when practitioners represent the interests of the larger society.

By assuming the outreach role, macro workers may provide this public with accurate information related to conditions in low-income communities such as CURN. In addition, they are active in providing information to the community in need of resources that may be available. Of equal importance is the recognition that many resources are not available. This recognition calls forth the advocacy role that may highlight the need for a viable route to social workers who are able to understand community as client, rather than relying on the more limited micro system view. These workers join with residents in the planning and implementation of social action activities.

In their presentation of the social action role, Connaway and Gentry (1988) identify social problem and cause as concepts that call for social action. The problems, individual and community problems enumerated earlier, are best addressed through collective action. The need for social action may be the impetus that places a community on the route to the social worker.

For the CURN community, the route to the social worker is through the appreciation of the value of their children who are too often injured by the destructive behavior of their adult caretakers. The CURN community has made a commitment to their children, particularly the young ones. The task is preventive intervention, which is accomplished through programs directed toward improving reading and study skills, field trips, journal writing, and building relationships with elderly members of the community. The route is voluntary as the community acts in their own interests and the field of practice identified as macro or community work.

Attention to the unmet needs of individuals, most often children, and families result in macro responses that encourage the community as a whole to question the behavior of the sustaining system.

### Layer 7—The Adaptation of Strategies and Procedures for Ethnic-Sensitive Macro Practice

In earlier editions we have placed particular emphasis on very familiar strategies for intervention. We have presented the planning, administration model, evaluation, community organization, as well as the collective and partisan models (Devore and Schlesinger, 1991, 1995). These modes of practice have proved to be the foundation for our practice with communities and organizations.

We are enriched as new publications advance our understanding of individuals, their communities, and the social structures that impinge on their lives. The *Journal of Poverty* (1997) calls attention to the impact of poverty on individuals and communities; the *Journal of Community Practice* (1995) addresses organizing, planning, development, and change. Publications such as these provide the ethnic-sensitive macro practitioner with recent innovations in practice, as well as the result of studies related to community work.

The editors of *Controversial Issues in Communities and Organizations*, Michael Austin and Jane Isaacs Lowe (1994), present some of the continuing debates related to this area of practice. Shillington, Dotson, and Faulkner (1994) respond to the question: "Should only African American community organizers work with African American neighborhoods?" McMurtry, Kettner, Daley, and Netting address the question "Is community organizing dead and is the future organizational practice?" In yet another edited work, Adams and Nelson (1995) recognize that families and communities must continually face urgent and growing problems. They propose that we "reinvent human services" as we develop a community- and family-centered practice.

The influence of macro systems and macro practice is addressed by Long and Holle (1997), presenting a life course perspective in relation to macro practice as a method of intervention. The case studies presented provide examples of the administrative role in macro practice, the combining of group work and community work, and the immigrant experience, among many others. We are led to a greater understanding of the influence macro practice may have on individual movement through the life course from infancy to later adulthood.

The contribution that relates most to the ethnic-sensitive macro practice is an anthology edited by Rivera and Erlich (1992, 1995, 1998). Contributors to *Organizing in a Diverse Society* have addressed community work in various communities of oppressed ethnic groups, including African American, Native American, Puerto Rican, and Chicano, among others. Building upon the editors' paradigm for organizing people of color and profile of the community organizer, contributors provide examples of macro practice related to community change. We applaud this work and view it as a significant contribution to our practice literature.

Their paradigm for community intervention requires that ethnic-sensitive macro practitioners consider the levels of intensity and influence that are most appropriate in their work with an oppressed ethnic group community.

### Evolving Models of Community Practice

In the nineteenth edition of the *Encyclopedia of Social Work* (1995), Weil and Gamble review the roots of community practice beginning with the settlement movement and adding grassroots organizing and rural community organizations. They continue with a new constellation of models for community–macro practice. Eight models are presented: (1) neighborhood and community organizing, (2) organizing functional communities, (3) community social and economic development, (4) social planning, (5) program development and community liaison, (6) political and social action, (7) coalitions, and (8) social movements.

**The Community Social and Economic Development Model.** Discussion highlights the community social and economic development model. The social work roles suggested are negotiator, promoter, teacher, planner, and manager. These support the ethnic-sensitive social worker associated with the members of CURN and the wider neighborhood. The anticipated outcome of the work is the development of plans for change from a grassroots perspective. This organization has grown out of the community with scant help from institutional structures, and expects that, through their own efforts, community children will be able to recognize the gifts they possess as resources to be used not only for their own development, but for the enrichment of the community as well.

The residents of this low-income, marginalized community are concerned with the education of their children and the development of skills that prepare adults for more than marginal labor as domestics, janitors, and construction helpers. Skills needed for leadership are developed when block captains assume responsibility for a small portion of their community.

Additional concerns relate to the lack of police protection, limited resources for adult leisure, an unresponsive city public works department, and the need for a safe environment for the children. The community social and economic development model identifies banks, foundations, external developers, and community citizens as targets for change. Each has resources that are able to address concerns identified by the community.

Given the national and local need for affordable housing, significant investment in the rehabilitation of the many boarded-up houses would be an important change in behavior of both banks and other mortgage brokers.

The ethnic-sensitive practitioner, in the role of negotiator, recognizes that institutional racism is often at the core of neglect in relation to this section of the city. Myths related to African Americans' ability to work and earn incomes that would support loans can lead to redlining, or drawing invisible red lines around certain neighborhoods. Bank policies such as this must be questioned if CURN is to fulfill its goal of rebuilding the neighborhood.

The CURN experience has received the support of local foundations and churches. Social workers will need skills in needs assessments and research to assist residents to determine realistic goals, and to identify the resources that are available within the population and the larger community. Goals must be developed with ethnic-sensitivity. Celebrations of Juneteenth or Kwanzaa call the community together in the affirmation of the African American experience in the United States. Experiences with racism, sexism, or classism cloud visions of possibilities for change. Goals must be framed, recognizing that these "isms" may present barriers to the development of goals that will enrich the individual, family, and community experience.

## SUMMARY

This chapter has examined the layers of understanding as they relate to macro, or community practice. We have recognized the value of models for community practice that form the foundation for emerging models of practice. One of these models is the community social and economic development model that responds to the realities of many communities and neighborhoods in which oppressed ethnic groups reside. The experiences of two of these communities are presented to highlight the work of ethnic-sensitive macro practitioners in rural- and inner-city settings.

## REFERENCES

Adams, P., & Nelson, K. (Eds.). (1995). *Reinventing human services: Community- and family-centered practice.* New York: Aldine de Gruyter.

Applebome, P. (1987, May 24). After a twister: Coping with a town that isn't there. *The New York Times,* pp. 1, 22.

Austin, M. J., & Lowe, J. I. (Eds.). (1994).*Controversial issues in communities and organizations.* Boston: Allyn & Bacon.

Blackwell, J. E. (1991). *The Black community: Diversity and unity* (3rd ed.). New York: Harper Collins.

Brueggeman, W. G. (1996). *The practice of macro social work.* Chicago: Nelson-Hall.

Connaway, R. S., & Gentry, M. E. (1988). *Social work practice.* Englewood Cliffs: Prentice Hall.

Daley, J. M., & Netting, F. E. (1994). Is community organizing dead and is the future organizational practice? No. In M. Austin & J. I. Lowe (Eds.), *Controversial issues in communities and organizations.* Boston: Allyn & Bacon.

Faulkner, A. O. (1994). Should only African American community organizers work in African American communities. In M. Austin & J. I. Lowe (Eds.). *Controversial issues in communities and organizations* (pp. 1132–139). Boston: Allyn & Bacon.

Frazier, E. F. (1964). *The Negro church in America.* New York: Schoken.

Garcia, A. (1990). The changing demographic face of Hispanics in the United States. In M. Sotomayor (Ed.), *Empowering Hispanic families: A critical issue for the '90s.* (pp. 21–38). Milwaukee: Family Service Association.

Inglehardt, A. P., & Becerra, R. M. (1995). *Social services and the ethnic community.* Boston: Allyn & Bacon.

*Journal of community practice.* (1995). Binghamton, NY: The Haworth Press.

*Journal of poverty.* (1997). Binghamton, NY.: The Haworth Press.

Kretzmann, J. P., & McKnight, J. L. (1993). *Building communities from the inside out.* Chicago: ACTA Publications.

Long, D. D., & Holle, M. C. (1997). *Macro systems in the social environment.* Itasca, IL: F. E. Peacock Publishers.

McMahon, M. O. (1990). *The general practice of social work: A problem approach.* (2nd ed.). Englewood Cliffs, NJ: Prentice-Hall.

McMurtry, S. L., & Kettner, P. M. (1994). Is community organizing dead and is the future organizational practice? Yes. In M. Austin & J. I. Lowe (Eds.), *Controversial issues in communities and organizations* (pp. 97–103). Boston: Allyn & Bacon.

Miley, K. K., O'Melia, & DuBois, B. L. (1998). *Generalist social work practice: An empowering approach.* (2nd ed.). Boston: Allyn & Bacon.

Mondros, J. B., & Wilson, S. (1994). *Organizing for power and empowerment.* New York: Columbia University Press.

Netting, F. E., Kettner, P. M., & McMurtry, S. L. (1993). *Social work macro practice.* New York: Longman.

Norton, D. (1978). *The dual perspective.* New York: Council on Social Work Education.

Pollard, W. L. (1978). *A study of Black self help.* San Francisco: R. & E. Research Associates.

Rivera, F. G., & Erlich, J. L. (1995). *Community organizing in a diverse society.* (2nd ed.). Boston: Allyn & Bacon.

Shillington, A. M., & Dotson, W. L. (1994) Should only African American community organizers work in African American communities? Yes. In M. J. Austin & J. I. Lowe (Eds.), *Controversial issues in communities and organizations* (pp. 128–132). Boston: Allyn & Bacon.

Siporin, M. (1987). Disaster and disaster aid. In A. Minahan (Ed.), *Encyclopedia of social work* (18th ed., Vol. 1, pp. 438–449). Silver Springs, MD: National Association of Social Workers.

Thomas, S. B. (1992). The health of the black community in the twenty-first century: A futuristic perspective. In R. L. Braithwaite & S. E. Taylor (Eds.), *Health issues in the black community.* San Francisco: Jossey-Bass.

Weil, M. O., & Gamble, D. N.(1995). Community practice models. In *The encyclopedia of social work* (19th ed., Vol. 1, pp. 577–593). Washington, DC: National Association of Social Workers.

# 10

# ETHNIC-SENSITIVE PRACTICE WITH REFUGEES AND NEW IMMIGRANTS

## The Kim Family

*After a recent breakup with her boyfriend, Lily Kim, 14½ years of age, attempted suicide and was hospitalized briefly. The hospitalization led the family to a local community health service agency for family counseling.*

*The entire family agreed to participate in the intervention process. Lily has two brothers: Alex, 20, and John, 17. Mr. Kim, age 48, and Mrs. Kim, age 39, have been married for 20 years. They emigrated to the United States in 1979 and settled in California. The couple met and married in Korea when he was a middle school history teacher and she was a student. Before coming to the United States she was a full-time homemaker.*

*Mr. Kim is about average height for an Asian man, although he is slightly overweight. He dresses in clean, wrinkled, and faded slacks, shirt, and sports jacket. His hairstyle is conservative. He appears to be weary and tired.*

*In contrast, Mrs. Kim is slender, attractive, and youthful. She wears a becoming, fashionable, tight dress and matching high heels. She has been a waitress in a local Korean restaurant for the past 11 years and has been the major bread winner.*

*Alex, the eldest son, is a sophomore in college and continues to be on the honor roll. He works part-time in the college library and spends much of his time away from home. When at home he receives the privilege of the elder son. When the English language is used he acts as spokesperson for the family. The younger brother John is an athletic-looking adolescent who is friendly and helpful. John has problems with sleep but his parents do not seem to be concerned about it.*

*Their attention is focused on their youngest child and only daughter, Lily, who is tall and fully developed. She is self-conscious about her appearance and is dressed in a tight red top and black leggings with a lot of jewelry, heavy makeup, and highlighted hair.*

*Although Mr. Kim tries to speak as "head of the family," his wife and children are impatient and continually interrupt him as he attempts to tell the family story. He does cut short his response and seems apprehensive with little facial expression as he stares at the wall hangings.*

*A language deficiency and a lack of job skills for the vicinity has resulted in Mr. Kim's unemployment. Several attempts at small business have failed. Traditional Asian values cause Mr. Kim to feel that he has failed to protect his family from Western corruption. Most particularly he is ashamed of the conduct displayed by his wife and daughter. He is unwilling to talk about his fear that his family does not respect him because he has not made much money; suspicion that his wife has been unfaithful plagues him.*

*As Mrs. Kim tries to tell the family story her husband interrupts or corrects her. She impatiently expresses hopelessness about the family situation. A few months ago, despite Mr. Kim's objections, she enrolled in an ELS (English as a Second Language) class hoping to improve her language proficiency and her employment opportunities. Health problems seem apparent as she speaks of chronic stomach aches and her husband's regular medication.*

*As the family story is told, Alex accepts affirmation from both parents for his academic accomplishments. He appears to have a quick temper and does not have a good relationship with either his father or his sister. John, on the other hand, is friendly and helpful. He keeps eye contact with the family members as the story unfolds. A high school senior, he has a B average and works part-time in a local fast food store. The earnings are given to his mother in an effort to avoid family fights. These efforts seem to have little influence. Unlike his brother, he gets along with all of the family members, listening to their problems and helping out when he can. He garners little response for the difficulty he has in falling asleep, a problem that has persisted for several months. (Y. E. Lu, personal communication, September 23, 1994)*

## KOREAN IMMIGRATION

The members of the Kim family are among those immigrants designated as the new immigrants prompted by the Immigration and Naturalization Act of 1965. The Act opened the way for the entry of many from Asian nations with previously low quotas. When the new law went into effect in 1968, millions began to arrive from Asia, Mexico, the Caribbean, and other Latin American countries. Movement continued into the 1970s and it is estimated that about one third of the immigrants came from Japan, China, Korea, the Philippines, and smaller Asian countries (Dinnerstein, Nichols, & Reimers, 1990).

Koreans were the third largest group, Mexicans and Pilippinos being the first, who arrived after 1970 (Min, 1988). Mr. and Mrs. Kim came in 1979. Many Korean professionals who immigrated at the time were looking for better economic opportunity and educational resources for their children.

# THE ACCULTURATION EXPERIENCE

Movement from their home in Korea to the United States presented few initial hazards for the Kim family. They were apparently well situated. Mr. Kim was employed in education, and Mrs. Kim remained in the home assuming the roles of wife and mother in a traditional manner.

Min's (1988) discussion of the Korean American family suggested that despite previous education and employment levels most Korean immigrants have serious problems with the English language. This is only one of Mr. Kim's problems, but it has limited his employment opportunity. Many other Koreans have been successful in small family businesses (Lorch, 1992; Kim, 1987), but Mr. Kim's entrepreneurial attempts have failed. For the past 11 years Mrs. Kim has been employed as a waitress in a prosperous Korean restaurant. This places her in the position of primary bread-winner, a role that makes her husband uncomfortable. This income, along with income from the part-time employment of Alex and John, allows the family to maintain a reasonably comfortable lifestyle within the community.

Lily, the Kims' youngest child, was born in the United States. It would seem that the process of migration and assimilation would not have affected her life. However, as assessment evolves, one can see the impact of this experience on the entire family and on Lily most particularly. The family's ethnic reality is challenged as comfortable traditions encounter unfamiliar practice in the family interaction. Mrs. Kim, the mother, does not hold to a traditional role. She is employed and seeks to extend her education (Kitano & Daniels, 1988). Her style of dress and that of her daughter suggest that she admires Western styles. Alex and John are able to contribute to the family income, even though John finds it makes little difference to the family climate.

Lily has attempted suicide. Suicide is the third most common cause of adolescent death. In addition, it is believed that the rate among new immigrants is high (Germain, 1991). Lily's father wishes to hold on to the old ways. He finds that his wife is successful in the labor market, although this was not ordinary for women in Korea (Min, 1988) or other Asian countries. Lily's parents argue about Mrs. Kim's exploring ESL study in a community college for better employment. Other Asian immigrant women have reported the loss of emotional support when entering the labor force, even though their positions are often marginal (Benson, 1990; Strober, 1994).

We suggested in Chapter 3 that two tasks of adolescence are coping with sexual awareness and development of relationships with peers of both sexes. In the Kim family assessment, one must add the variable of assimilation as parents are wedged between their own traditional values and those of their U.S. children. Could it be that Lily has been dating a U.S. schoolmate? And could it be that her father does not approve of this relationship?

Although the custom of arranged marriages has diminished in the United States, many parents still attempt to maintain influence in mate selection (Sho & Ja, 1982), and although evidence shows an increase of out-marriage, they hope for marriage that will maintain family and national traditions (Min, 1988).

The evolving ethnic reality for this family and the intersection of ethnic dispositions and social class finds this family with some stability in relation to income, which provides working-class status, but also brings changes in status due to changing gender roles. Their minor sons, contrary to Korean practices, work to support themselves and the family (Kitano & Daniels, 1988). Lily has confronted adolescent relationship problems unfamiliar to her parents. Schafer (1989) provides some understanding of Lily's dilemma in his explanation that many young Koreans born in this country face culture conflicts common to any first generation in a new country. Her father can speak English but not well enough to ensure him continued employment so he struggles with unfamiliar gender roles. Lily, as a U.S. adolescent, has opportunities for relationships that clash with the Korean traditions of courtship and marriage. She is at significant risk. John's sleeplessness may be an indication of stress in the acculturation process.

## THE LAYERS OF UNDERSTANDING

We continue the discussion of the refugee and immigrant experience, adding cases related to the experiences of Cambodian and Soviet Jewish refugees. Experiences differ, but there is a similarity as each group moves through the stages of migration and acculturation (Drachman, 1992; Strober, 1994).

Chapter 4 presented the layers of understanding, particularly as they relate to ethnic groups presently in the United States. Here we are concerned with recent arrivals. Many have yet to become acculturated as they continue their adaptation to a new environment. Decisions to leave home were made under duress resulting from the traumatic experiences of war in Cambodia, Laos, or Vietnam.

In the Soviet Union, antisemitism limited social, educational, and employment opportunities for Jews. Many decided to seek more accepting environments. Changes in communist policy led to *glasnost* (openness) and *peristroika* (restructuring), which relaxed and revised immigration policy (Simon, 1992). The fall of the communist government accelerated immigration because living conditions in the new Russian state declined. Food shortages, housing difficulties, lack of secure employment, civil unrest, the potential for civil war, and a lack of trust in government exacerbated the effects of antisemitism for Russian Jews' experiences.

### Phavey Nong

*Phavey Nong, age 27, and her family have settled in Central New York. She arrived with her mother and other refugees from Cambodia in 1981. Although she is employed as a social work assistant providing services for other Asian refugees, she is reluctant to speak much about her own marriage, which causes her much distress.*

*Phavey and her husband Vannah, age 29, appear to have made a good adjustment to life in the United States. However, they continue to carry the burden of childhood and adolescent experiences. Their lives were disrupted by a war that finally forced them to become political refugees. A problem presents itself in that*

*Souvahn, their 7-year-old son, wishes to change his name to Justin so that he will fit in better with his first-grade friends. Vannah is distressed by the request, and Phavey wonders about Souvahn's need for the name change.*

*The war began when Phavey was 7 years old. Her prosperous family, compelled to leave their home in Phnom Penh, was forced to work in the fields planting and harvesting rice. For 13 years, they, along with many other families, were continually relocated, and became victims of torture, violence, and starvation. Eventually, many were able to trudge from Kampot, on the South China Sea, to a refugee camp in Thailand. Despite inhumane treatment there the family was able to get to the Philippines and then to the United States.*

*According to Cambodian tradition, Phavey was married to Vannah when she was 16. The marriage, arranged by her mother, did not please Phavey, who felt sure that it would not have pleased her deceased father. Phavey's father, in defiance of Cambodian customs for gender assignment, had wished for her to find a place in the medical profession. A learned man, he spoke five languages fluently and taught his eldest daughter well.*

*She made it clear before the marriage that she would not tolerate beatings or abuse, a practice accepted in silence by most Cambodian women. Vannah, though a kind husband who is gentle and a tireless worker, makes it difficult for Phavey to reach her several goals. He has made some accommodations in that he washes dishes and cleans house.*

*Phavey uses work to escape from her marriage. She compares her life to pre-1970 Cambodia. Then, women were powerless, losing their identity at 16, expected to marry, give their parents grandchildren, and care for their husbands as servants. She feels sure that her father would have protected her, but he died during the war. Phavey's relationship with her mother is marred by resentment. "She is the one who put me in this predicament!"*

*The couple discuss their differences at home but are reluctant to seek counseling. Cambodian women are reluctant to talk to social workers about their problems, preferring to "work it out in their heads." Social workers are unknown in Cambodia and are not seen as a resource for relief from individual and/or family stress.*

### Tatjana and Mila Mankov

*Tatjana Mankov, age 35, and her 13-year-old daughter Mila live in a Soviet Jewish enclave in a large eastern city. Tatjana was divorced from her husband several years ago and lived with her mother in a small apartment in Moscow. Her mother, feeling that she was too old for change, stayed behind. With this decision she forfeited her role as grandmother, one highly prized in Russia.*

*Although Tatjana misses her mother and feels the loss of friends and her career, she feels positive about immigration. Mila will have the advantage of education that will lead to employment. In Russia many young people are no longer assured of placement after schooling.*

*At times Tatjana was anxious about her prospects and asked for extra help, but for the most part she was eager to make a good life for her daughter. Both worked hard to learn English and explore the resources of the city for entertainment and culture. It was difficult for Tatjana to accept that services available in the Soviet Union such as housing, health and dental care, and employment were not available here in the same manner.*

*With support from a resettlement agency and a comfortable, familiar community, mother and daughter have settled in. Tatjana has employment in a hospital. Sometimes she is invited to play the piano in a neighborhood restaurant, where a very cosmopolitan clientele appreciates her musical expertise and she can supplement her income. Despite significant losses, this family is optimistic about their new life.*

## Layer 1—Social Work Values

The Social Work Code of Ethics continues to be the foundation on which social work practice is based. As it provides guidelines for the daily conduct of social work professionals, particular attention is directed to the social workers' ethical responsibility to clients. It is established that the clients' interests are of primary concern, and issues of discrimination are addressed:

Section 1.05 of the revised *Code of Ethics* states: "Social workers should obtain education about and seek to understand the nature of social diversity and oppression with respect to race, ethnicity, national origin, color, sex, sexual orientation, age, marital status, political belief, religion, or mental or physical disability."

Work with refugees and recent immigrants requires that we acknowledge the discrimination that is too often found in communities as new residents arrive and their national origin is called into question. Residents are frequently concerned about deep differences in race, culture, and religion (Ryan, 1992). Goode (1990) described tensions in a Philadelphia neighborhood in which newcomers are Korean, Puerto Rican (citizens viewed as foreigners), and Colombian, and newcomers from other Central and South American countries. Unwelcomed as well were Asian Indians, West Indians, and refugees from Cambodia and Vietnam. Southeast Asians often practice Buddhism, which increases the level of discrimination against them.

African American and Korean relations suffer in many communities, particularly because of cultural clashes between Korean merchants and African American customers. Protest and boycott have led to what Alex J. Norman (1994) has described as "shouting and shooting." Employing social work values, Norman has developed a culture model for mixed group dialogue to facilitate a Korean/African American dialogue.

If we are to respond to immigrants and refugees in an ethnic-sensitive manner, we must be aware of discrimination practices related to race, gender, religion, and national origin of those who become our clients in a manner that makes evident our devotion, loyalty, and determination as we provide services with skill and competence.

## Layer 2—Basic Knowledge of Human Behavior

The Kim family, Phavey Nong, and Tatjana and Mila Mankov have had separate experiences in their travels to the United States. If we are to understand them and others like them, we must have an understanding of the migration experience and the impact it will have on the lives of children, adults, and the elderly.

Mr. Kim persuaded his family to leave Korea and come to the United States. The need to persuade suggests that this was not an easy decision for a family with two young children to make. The Nongs are Cambodian refugees whose lives were disrupted. War destroyed their homes and took family members. A change in political climate supported Tatjana Mankov's decision to leave Russia with her daughter Mila. Previously this decision to leave would have been met with hostility and would have put those left behind at political risk. Relaxed policy will permit them to visit relatives in Russia when they are able (Drachman & Halberstadt, 1992).

Social workers and other professionals who have worked with immigrant and refugee populations have determined that as individuals and families leave home, their experience may be examined using a three-stage framework that is generic for all immigrant groups or specific as it applies to particular groups (Drachman, 1992; Drachman & Halberstadt, 1992; Frye, 1993; Strober, 1994; Pickwell, 1989).

The initial stage of the framework addresses preimmigration and departure. The second addresses transit and the third resettlement. This framework has been viewed as a psychosocial history with a chronological approach (Lee, 1988). The history provides indications of stress and trauma accompanying the initial loss. It also recognizes accommodations that must be made as newcomers resettle.

The following stage-of-migration framework provides a foundation for consideration of the migration experience. We must understand that experiences and responses will vary according to family composition; social class status of the family (whether they are from rural or urban environments); level of education and employment; beliefs and religious traditions; and social supports available during each stage of migration (Drachman, 1992).

> *Premigration experiences:* Social and political forces (war, political unrest, fear of violence or persecution, loss of family members, loss of home) leading to the decision to leave. Who goes and who remains. Loss of community, family, and friends.
>
> *Transit:* Perilous journeys of short or long duration fraught with hunger, rape, attack by pirates, fear of death. Short or long stay in detention center or refugee camp. Loss of friends/family members en route. Wait for decision of immigration process by host country.
>
> *Resettlement:* Reception by host country. Conflict of traditions, values, and other cultural issues. Individual responses related to age, gender, and role. Dissonance between expectations and reality of the host country. Opportunity structure of host country (Drachman, 1992; Lee, 1988).

Cambodian refugees endure more stress than any other refugee group. Frye (1993) confirms Phavey Nong's cumulative experience of loss of home, separation from family and friends, and torture in refugee and reeducation camps. It may be assumed that her father lost his life in one of these camps. His accomplishments did not shield him from the terror of war. More rural Cambodians [Khmer] were less fortunate. They were poor rural farmers, illiterate in their own language (Frye, 1993). They have suffered at each stage of the migration process.

At resettlement they have poor language skills, a barrier between them and the health-care system, which they need for physical and mental health problems. During the first and second years of resettlement, Southeast Asian refugees are reported to have high levels of physical and psychological dysfunction manifested in feelings of depression and anxiety. Vague somatic distress is experienced as abdominal pain, chest pains, dizziness, flatulence, headaches, fatigue, low back pain, and sleep disturbance (Pickwell, 1989). Phavey's resettlement is much richer, yet her working day is filled with the distress of other Asian women refugees.

Tatjana and Mila did not have to endure the pre*glasnost* Soviet mindset that leaving was a betrayal of country. Familiarity with changing political climate prepared them for a less stressful preimmigration experience. Separation from her mother and profession was difficult, but the economic environment was familiar. Resettlement required that she accept marginal employment, but she found a niche in an ethnic community that welcomed her musical skills.

We have little knowledge of the Kims' migration process. We know that he wished to migrate and that there was some resistance, but the family did leave their home in Korea. No doubt parents, siblings, and special friends were left behind. More is known about the years following resettlement. Mr. Kim had problems with employment. Mrs. Kim's employment as a waitress followed the trend in which immigrant women work in marginal positions. Phavey Nong's training and work is an example of more recent opportunities for immigrant women in more highly skilled positions (Pedraza, 1991).

### Religion and Health Beliefs

Listed among the critical variables to be noted during the resettlement stage of migration are cultural issues (Drachman, 1992). Pickwell (1989) described culture shock in the third stage and a greater need for health care among Southeast Asian immigrants. Providers of health and social services need to be familiar with folk healing methods and allow them to be practiced in conjunction with Western medical practices. "Cupping" and "coining" are used to relieve minor ailments such as headaches, stomach aches, or fevers. Cupping involves creating a vacuum on the skin's surface to draw out the fever or pain. Coining requires the rubbing of a coin or spoon over the skin to draw out the illness or spirit causing the illness. The bruises left by these practices have in some cases led to accusations of child abuse (McInnis, 1991).

Other health practices that may be observed include consultation with the shaman believed to be able to contact the spirit world to appease angry spirits or return lost souls to ailing individuals (McInnis, 1991; Pickwell, 1989).

The Kims and the Nongs seem to have accepted more Western modes of health care. After her suicide attempt, Lily was treated in a hospital and the family now looks to a social work agency for help. Phavey Nong has become part of the health-care system. However, significant numbers of immigrants from Southeast Asia hold to health and religious traditions from their preimmigration world.

Buddhism provides the major spiritual support for immigrants from Cambodia, Laos, and Vietnam. Christian churches offer similar support for Koreans in the United States. Catholic and Presbyterian mission programs in Korea responded to the suffering imposed by war in the 1800s, and Koreans adopted the Christian faith. Korean churches in the United States provide a resource for newly arrived immigrants; a place for religious involvement and identity; and a sanctuary for peace of mind and self-improvement (Kitano & Daniels, 1988).

Religious beliefs held in Buddhism provide strength for Southeast Asians who suffered during the transit stage and during resettlement and after. The sense that catastrophe and suffering are a normal part of the human condition allows believers to accept terrible experiences and find ways to cope with them (Lee, 1988).

Teachings in Buddhism declare that human existence is filled with suffering as long as people hold to desires that cannot be fulfilled. To overcome suffering, individuals must learn a correct lifestyle and meditate. In immigrant communities, Buddhist temples have become centers for community activity. Monks provide religious assistance, traditional healing, and a variety of support services to families in need. According to custom, monks may not receive payment for services. Members of the community provide food, shelter, and other necessary supports (Canda & Phaobtong, 1992).

Postcommunist Russia has permitted the Russian Orthodox Church to reclaim its position in the lives of its citizens. Cathedrals that have been neglected for years are being rebuilt and worship is a public event.

Tatjana and Mila are Jews and have suffered from antisemitism during their preimmigration stage. Jews were not able to engage in religious activities, so many young Soviet Jewish immigrants have little religious knowledge or sentiment. Their ethnic identity as Jews was realized through negative experiences in education and employment (Gold, 1992). Experiences denying Jews a sense of self led Soviet Jews to invest in their careers, with status being attached to professional achievement (Hulewat, undated). Tatjana's musical career may well have been such an investment. After resettlement, she has been able to reclaim her interest in music with affirmation from her ethnic community and the general public.

This layer of understanding requires sensitivity to the stages of migration and the impact that each has on the lives of individuals. Service provision in resettlement will be influenced by earlier stages. The ethnic-sensitive worker must consider the political and social climate, age, gender, family composition in the United States, family left behind, social class, and religious practices in the assessment process.

## *Layer 3—Knowledge and Skill in Immigration Policy and Services Service*

Several areas of social policy are essential to this layer of understanding. Social service agencies may continue to provide services needed by recent immigrants as they move through the acculturation experience. Language can be a significant barrier to communication, so it is incumbent upon deliverers of service to this population to have bilingual staff available. Experience with resettlement programs for Russian immigrants has led agencies to understand that Russian-speaking workers are able to establish relationships with immigrants more rapidly than struggling English-speaking staff. Often, bilingual workers are from the ethnic community and participate as indigenous paraprofessionals with training and supervision (Ivry, 1992). Phavey Nong's facility with language helps the Catholic family agency to provide services to Asian refugees more efficiently.

### Immigrants and Welfare Reform

The ethnic-sensitive worker can be confounded by evolving legislation and regulations related to immigrants and welfare reform. The need for welfare reform has been a part of political debate for some time. With the passing of The Personal Responsibility and Work Opportunity Reconciliation Act of 1996 (P. L. 104–193), immigrants became a part of the welfare reform debate. The act placed restrictions on immigrants' access to previous benefits, such as food stamps and Supplementary Security Income (SSI). It was expected that this policy would provide a federal savings of about $23 billion. Advocates for immigrants questioned this policy and were able to generate relief through the Balanced Budget Act of 1997, which restored SSI and Medicaid benefits to elderly and disabled immigrants (Fix & Tumlin, 1997). These two pieces of federal legislation have altered immigration policy significantly. Our review of immigration policy in Chapter 1 highlights changing attitudes about immigration and immigrants and the resulting policy.

The 1980 Refugee Reform Act provided mechanisms for determining who is a refugee and how many persons will be allowed to enter once refugee status is determined. The Immigration Reform Control Act of 1986 was to be the beginning of a new era of immigration policy. The six provisions of this Reform and Control Act signaled the beginning of enforcement of immigration policy. The initial provision granted amnesty for certain undocumented immigrants. The second was a program for foreign and seasonal agricultural workers. The sanctioning of employers who knowingly hired illegal immigrants became part of three of the provisions, while the fourth and fifth provisions called attention to antidiscrimination policy and increased enforcement capabilities of the Immigration and Naturalization Service. Finally states were granted Legalization Impact Assistance Grants (Le-Doux & Stevens, 1992).

The Personal Responsibility and Work Opportunity Act of 1996 (PRWORA) significantly changed the locus of immigration policy from the federal government to each state and localities within each state. Fix and Tumlin (1997) argue that this policy fragments previously uniform national law set by Congress and the courts in relation to benefits available to persons who were not citizens. States now have greater power to deny benefits to noncitizens. Welfare reform deepens the rift between citizens and immigrants that has been evident in the past. The question posed is, "who has full membership in our society?" This animosity is evident in the passing of California's Proposition 187 in 1994 which limits services available to undocumented individuals; children are disproportionately affected by the policy.

With restrictions on legal immigrants' eligibility for benefits, U.S. immigration policy shifts from one that has historically treated legal immigrants and citizens alike in this arena to one that excludes legal immigrants from means-tested federal programs. States may now discriminate against legal immigrants in the administration of public benefit programs, now and in the future.

It will become essential for those persons who work with immigrant populations to be in touch with developing policy. The Kims, Phavey Nong, and the Mankovs do not seem to have a need for assistance at this time, but others in their various ethnic communities might, particularly those who are elderly or disabled in some manner. Ironically, the adolescents and young adults in these families will remain eligible for federal higher education assistance and services provided by the Job Training Partnership Act. Younger children will remain eligible for Head Start and other means-tested programs.

A review of the New York State Welfare Reform Act of 1997 presents an array of policies that may change, given the ability of states to make determinations as to eligibility. Similar policies will be developed in other states. It has been estimated that about 150,000 immigrants in New York State have faced the loss of federally funded food stamp benefits. The New York State Welfare Reform Act of 1997, given the ability of states to make their own determination, authorized the creation of state and locally funded food stamp programs for elderly and disabled immigrants. Given the option for participation, all counties in the state have not adopted this policy, giving credence to Fix and Tumlin's (1997) concern about the unevenness of policy in states and between states (Western New York Law Center, 1997).

It is clear that welfare reform and immigration policy are linked and are still being formulated and revised. Ethnic-sensitive workers will understand that clients will be caught up in *historical time* as policy evolves. Individual time will be augmented with unanticipated experiences in relation to basic needs. It will be necessary for agencies and social workers who serve immigrant populations to be alert. It is also a time to reflect on Code of Ethics standards related to social welfare. The Code states that "social workers should promote the general welfare of society, from local to global levels, and the development of people, their communities, and their environments" (6.01). Promoting the advocacy role, the Code asks social workers to "facilitate informed participation by the public in shaping social policies and institutions" (6.02). Advocacy and broker roles will be needed as more stressful experiences are added to the acculturation process.

## Layer 4—Self-Awareness, Including Insights into One's Own Ethnicity

Benefits for legal immigrants and welfare reform have been joined together in legislation at the national and local level. Many media outlets—radio, television, newspapers, and news magazines—tell the stories of the impact of this legislation. They also report that the level immigration has been sustained. The 104th Congress was not eager to reduce the high level of legal immigration. Entry into the United States is still valued.

Given the complexity of current policy, it is appropriate for social workers to ask several questions, "Where do I stand on this policy?" "What about my immigrant history?" "Do I value the contributions that immigrants have made as residents in this country?" The answers may not come immediately, but they need to be asked if we are to respond to the needs of individuals and families whom we have invited to be with us and have welcomed in the past.

## Layer 5—The Impact of the Ethnic Reality on the Lives of the New Immigrants and Refugees

Resettlement is an arduous task that requires daily attention. The stage-of-migration framework presents critical tasks of the resettlement stage. These are the cultural issues confronting changes in the living environment, neighborhood, and reception in that environment, exploring the opportunity structure, recognizing the discrepancy between expectation and reality, and managing accumulated stress (Drachman, 1992).

New immigrants and refugees are outsiders in the United States. Xenophobia, the fear of the foreigner, generates reactions that cause loneliness for the immigrant, communication problems, scarcity of housing, and unemployment or underemployment in positions much below skill level (Mayada & Elliot, 1992).

Southeast Asians from rural areas without literacy in their own language are closer to the margins than are others who held higher status. Lee (1988), in working with adolescents, asked that attention be directed to problems generated by difficulties with language, school adjustment, and academic demands.

Family members at each position in the life course must face culture shock. Mr. Kim tries to hold on to the role of adult male head of family, a part of Korean culture. In his study of older immigrants from El Salvador, Gelfand (1989) explained that with the loss of familiar environment older Salvadorans attempt to maintain traditional role structures. Their children find it difficult to sustain these roles in a new place. When Phavey Nong's mother insisted that her daughter marry at 16, she was holding onto Cambodian tradition. As a new immigrant, Phavey distanced herself from her mother. The clash between tradition and the new reality had damaged the relationship.

In the social space created by class and ethnicity, we find the ethnic reality. Our growing experience helps us recognize that activity at this convergence is different for new immigrants and refugees. Southeast Asians, Soviet Jews, Salvadorans, West Indians, and Eastern Europeans are among the newcomers who will hold differing beliefs in the way a family relates to various members and responds to social institutions: how one worships various gods, how one finds healing for physical and emotional pain, and what is appropriate dress for women and men. Negative responses to these differences may be manifested in institutional discrimination, a task that may be confronted for years after successful resettlement.

Immigrants arriving with skills useful in the economy have little difficulty finding a place in the middle class. Unskilled, illiterate farmers from rural farming areas have little income and hold marginal positions in the economy. The ethnic reality for them is Asian low income, and their daily life experiences will reflect that position.

## Layer 6—An Understanding That the Route to the Social Worker Has an Impact on How Social Services Are Perceived and Delivered

The routes to the social worker taken by new immigrants and refugees vary between voluntary, somewhat voluntary, highly voluntary, or totally voluntary routes. Phavey Nong has stated that she does not wish to see a social worker, and she expects that discussions with her husband Vannah will solve their marital problems. The Kims follow a social worker's suggestion and arrange for a visit to a family service agency. Tatjana and Mila Mankov find support and direction from a Jewish service agency with a resettlement program.

Work with Cambodian refugees shows that the severe psychological stress experienced in preimmigration and transit stages leads to a slower acculturation rate in resettlement. The somewhat voluntary route to the social worker may be explained by a lack of ethnic community supports and discomfort with existing community agencies. Buddhism encourages acceptance of loss and little expectation of better times. Individuals suffering in silence are not likely to follow the highly voluntary route to the social worker (Strober, 1994).

Refugee settlement programs ready to work with immigrant populations may or may not be successful. Problems arise when Soviet Jewish emigres expect that the voluntary route to social services will lead to entitlements such as housing, employment, medical care, and job training as provided in the former Soviet Union. Lack of familiarity with the mode of service delivery presents barriers to assistance as well (Drachman, 1992).

## Layer 7—The Adaptation of Strategies and Procedures for Ethnic-Sensitive Practice with New Immigrants and Refugees

Practitioners who have worked with Southeast Asian newcomers provide guidelines that direct our practice. The work before involvement requires attention to the migration process. Social workers need to understand that no matter what the conditions may have been in the preimmigration period, individuals and families will have a sense of loss. Terrors in transit included illness, hunger, death, robbery, and rape. Terrors may linger and present as physical symptoms of depression with the diagnosis of posttraumatic stress disorder (Pickwell, 1989).

Sharon McQuaide (1989) called for tuning in with empathy, allowing oneself to imagine what experiences may have been. The life model of social work practice (Germain & Gitterman, 1980) called for anticipatory empathy accomplished through a four-step process. The first step, identification with what the client may be feeling, is particularly difficult. How may a worker feel or sense the loss of all that is familiar (language, clothing, values, rules)? Can we imagine not knowing if parents, siblings, or friends are alive? Can we imagine the refugee camps that continue the torture rather than providing a safe haven (McQuaide, 1989)? Can we incorporate these feelings as if they were our own? Do we have any experiences in our own lives that reverberate in a like manner to facilitate our understanding? Rational, objective analysis is possible but difficult (Germain & Gitterman, 1980).

Ethnic-sensitive practice calls for the adaptation of familiar skills and techniques. Probing in the work phase is ill advised. "Don't dig and dig. They won't tell you. You're not family," becomes a directive for practice (McQuaide, 1989). Directives from other practitioners can be useful in work with Southeastern Asians.

1. Assess the need for concrete services such as allowances (Land, Nishimoto, & Chau, 1988; McQuaide, 1989).
2. Involve family and friends; be aware of and include informal caregivers (McQuaide, 1989; Sherraden & Martin, 1994).
3. Assess and support family strengths, work toward keeping family together (Strober, 1994; Land, Nishimoto, & Chau, 1988; Lee, 1988).
4. Be available for home visits and make yourself useful; participate in community events (McQuaide, 1989).
5. Understand health beliefs and practices that may appear to be abusive (Land, Nishimoto, & Chau, 1988; Pickwell, 1989; McInnis, 1991).
6. Plan for short-term work; limit the scope of the problems to be addressed (Lee, 1988).
7. Support groups provide a model for practice that is nonintrusive and may empower refugees for acculturation (Lee, 1988; Strober, 1994; Sherraden & Martin, 1994).
8. The traditional importance of the family supports work with families for assessment, intervention, and education (Lee, 1989; Strober, 1994).
9. Buddhist ritual and monks, when present in a community, provide support; when possible work with traditional healers (Frye, 1993; McQuaide, 1989).
10. Interpreters need to be incorporated into the agency structure and used judiciously for they may facilitate or inhibit work with clients. Ideal staff members are former refugees (McQuaide, 1989; Hulewat, undated; Ivry, 1992).

## SUMMARY

This chapter has presented three examples of the immigrant and refugee experience. It is evident that as immigration policy changes the immigrant population changes with the latest immigrants coming from Asia. Changes in Soviet Russia has made immigration less complicated for Soviet Jews. Ethnic-sensitive practice requires knowledge of changing policy and community responses to newcomers, a review of the layers of understanding, and careful adaptation of strategies and procedures for intervention.

## REFERENCES

Benson, J. E. (1990). Households, migration, and community context. *Urban Anthropology, 19,* 9–27.

Canda, E. R., & Phaobtong, T. (1992). Buddhism as a support system for Southeast Asian refugees. *Social Work 37,* 61–67.

Dinnerstein, L., Nichols, R. L., & Reimers, D. M. (1990). New York: Oxford University Press.

Drachman, D. (1992). A stage-of-migration framework for service to immigrant populations. *Social Work, 37,* 68–72.

Drachman, D., & Halberstadt, A. (1992). A stage migration framework as applied to recent Soviet emigres. *Journal of Multicultural Social Work, 2,* 63–78.

Fix, M. E., & Tumlin, K. (1997). Welfare reform and the devolution of immigrant policy. *The Urban Institute.* Retrieved from the World Wide Web.

Frye, B. A. (1993). *The Cambodian refugee: Planning and delivering culturally sensitive care.* Presented at the 121st Annual Meeting of the American Public Health Association Asian Caucus.

Gelfand, D. E. (1989). Immigration, aging, and intergenerational relationships. *The Gerontologist, 29,* 366–372.

Germain, C. B. (1991). *Human behavior in the social environment: An ecological view.* New York: Columbia University Press.

Germain, C. B., & Gitterman, A. (1980). *The life model of social work practice.* New York: Columbia University Press.

Gold, S. J. (1992). *Refugee communities A comparative field study.* Newbury Park, CA: Sage.

Goode, J. (1990). A wary welcome to the neighborhood: Community responses to immigrants. *Urban Anthropology, 19,* 125–153.

Hulewat, P. D. (undated). *Resettlement: An opportune crisis.* Cleveland, OH: Jewish Family Service Association.

Ivry, J. (1992). Paraprofessional in refugee resettlement. *Journal of Multicultural Social Work,* 2(1), 99–117.

Kim, I. (1987). The Koreans: Small business in the urban frontier. In N. Foner (Ed.), *New immigrants in New York* (pp. 219–242). New York: Columbia University Press.

Kitano, H. H. L., & Daniels, R. (1988) *Asian Americans: Emerging minorities.* Englewood Cliffs, NJ: Prentice-Hall

Land, H., Nishimoto, R., & Chau, K. (1988). Interventive and preventive services for Vietnamese Chinese refugees. *Social Service Review, 62,* 468–483.

Le-Doux, C., Stephens, K. S. (1992). Refugee and immigrant social service delivery: Critical management issues. *Journal of Multicultural Social Work,* 2, (1), 31–62,

Lee, E. (1988). Cultural factors in working with Southeast Asian refugee adolescents. *Journal of Adolescence, 11,* 167–179.

Lorch, D. (1992, January 12). Ethnic niches creating jobs that fuel immigrant growth. *The New York Times,* A1, Metro, 20.

Mayada, N. S., & Elliot, D. (1992). Integration and xenophobia: An inherent conflict in international migration. *Journal of Multicultural Social Work, 2,* 47–62.

McInnis, K. (1991). Ethnic-sensitive work with Hmong refugee children. *Child Welfare LXX,* 571–580.

McQuaide, S. (1989). Working with Southeast Asian refugees. *Clinical Social Work, 17,* 165–176.

Min, P. G. (1988). The Korean American family. In C. H. Mindel, R. W. Haberstein, & R. Wright, Jr. (Eds.), *Ethnic families in America patterns and variations* (pp. 199–229). New York: Elsevier.

Norman, A. J. (1994). Black-Korean relations: From desperation to dialogue, or from shouting to sitting and talking. *Journal of Multicultural Social Work, 3,* 87–99.

Pedraza, S. (1991). Women and migration: The social consequences of gender. *American Sociological Review 17,* 303–25.

Pickwell, S. (1989). The incorporation of family primary care for Southeast Asian refuges in a community-based mental health facility. *Archives of Psychiatric Nursing, 3,* 173–177.

Ryan, A. S. (1992). Preface. *Journal of Multicultural Social Work, 2,* xiii–xiv.

Shafer, R. T. (1989). *Racial and ethnic groups* (4th ed.). HarperCollins.

Sherraden, M. S., & Martin, J. J. (1994) Social work with immigrants: International issues in service delivery. *International Social Work, 37,* 369–384.

Sho, S. P., & Ja, D. Y. (1982). Asian families. In McGoldrick, M., Pearce, J. K., & Giordano, J. (Eds.), *Ethnicity and family therapy.* (pp. 208–228). New York: The Guilford Press.

Simon, M. L. (1992). U.S. immigration policies, 1798–1992: Invaluable texts for exploring continuity and change in racism and xenophobia. *Journal of Multicultural Social Work, 2,* 53–64.

Strober, S. B. (1994). Social work interventions to alleviate Cambodian refugee psychological distress. *International Social Work, 37,* 23–25.

Western New York Law Center. (1997). New York State Welfare Reform Act of 1997 fact sheets. No. 12—Legal immigrants and food stamps, No. 13—Immigrants and Medicaid, food stamp alert.

# 11

# ETHNIC-SENSITIVE PRACTICE WITH FAMILIES

## The Sarah Clemons Story

*When 37-year-old Sarah Clemons presented herself at the Central Family Service Center, she was at her wits end, thoroughly exhausted. Richard, her Irish Catholic husband of 17 years, was drinking again, although she was unable to locate his "stash." He had recently been intoxicated at family social events. This had made her feel crazy because people looked to her to explain his behavior. Sarah had threatened to leave him 13 years before if he did not stop drinking. He promised never to drink again and there was a reconciliation. He did not attend to issues related to his drinking, but he was a committed husband and father and attended church regularly.*

*Sarah's Polish American father used alcohol daily. He died suddenly 5 years ago of liver cancer. After his death her relationship with her brothers, also daily drinkers, changed. She is close to her English American mother.*

*Sarah and Richard were married when she was very young. She needed to get away from her father, who questioned her relationships and blocked her goals for higher education. Maternal relatives were more nurturing, particularly her grandmother, who died when Sarah's daughter was very young.*

*In most ways Sarah is comfortable with herself. There are problems with attempts to control her weight and she struggles to fit the pieces of her life together. She and Richard have sought counseling when she took the initiative, but he was less than cooperative. Although she remains committed to the marriage, she wonders if it can be improved. Friends and career provide the intimacy and contact that she wishes were a part of her marriage.*

*Two years ago, Richard's mother moved in with them, and they were able to afford a larger house. The move served to protect the elder Mrs. Clemons, who continued to fall in her own home. She also called in the middle of the night just wanting to chat. It appeared that she was drinking at the time, but the family has not discussed this problem.*

*This living arrangement has caused Sarah some distress. She provides all of the nurturing and physical supports for her mother-in-law, who is abusive and criticizes the housekeeping and meal preparation. Drinking is a part of her daily activity. Richard provides social supports for his mother but offers Sarah no protection from his mother's abuse.*

This chapter examines evolving life course perspectives. Particular attention is paid to multiracial families, interreligious families, and the experiences of single (never married) men and women.

## THE FAMILY LIFE COURSE

### *Defining the Family*

While definitions of family are elusive in the present, it has been generally accepted that the family is the basic unit of emotional development, providing an atmosphere in which individuals at various positions in the life course are concurrently existing and experiencing their lives (Armour, 1995).

Aldous (1978) noted that family membership was based on mutual consent, blood or adoption, and a common residence. She adds the concepts of marriage, parenthood, and role traditions to the definition. This is a familiar, comfortable definition that provides a universal view, describing a unit that can be trusted to carry out the tasks and functions assigned. However, in a closer examination of these universal definitions, we would find them lacking in attention to an array of family constellations found in many of our communities: childless couples, unmarried cohabiting couples, same-sex partners with or without children, single-parent families, extended families, and families with fictive kin (Germain, 1990). Persons who have never married cannot be found in definitions of families; without a partner or children they are omitted from consideration.

Germain (1990) and Billingsley (1968) examine the family as a social system. Germain's discussion considers the family as a subsystem of the community. Billingsley's focus is on the African American family and is based upon Talcott Parson's concept of a social system. Added are concepts of ethnic subsociety, family structure, and function. His discussion of family structure, based upon the African American family experience, may be considered in discussions of other ethnic families as well. Definitions of nuclear, extended, and augmented families invite us to reflect on Germain's caution about the limitation of universal definitions of the family.

In an early consideration of social work practice with families, Richmond (1917) defined family as "all who share a common table," identifying parents and children as the "most important members of the group" (p. 134). More recently, Hartman and Laird (1983) have commented on the difficulty in finding accurate definitions of *family.* They explain that definitions of family tend to set practice norms and directions. If we accept universal definitions, then those who do not meet this standard may be considered to be divergent or deviant, and in spite of their own ethnic reality, may be encouraged to move toward a more universal, acceptable family lifestyle. This speculation adds much to the discussion of definitions and proposes two categories of families: the first is "clearly biologically rooted," the second "may or may not be built on legal marriage or biological parenting" (p. 30).

Seldom do definitions of family exhibit attention to the "rich pluralism of racial, cultural, and ethnic diversity, and the wide variety of lifestyle choices that differentiate American families" (Hartman & Laird, 1983, p. 27). This omission limits the scope of our practice with families, particularly those who do not reflect universal definitions.

We can be led, however, by those who add to the traditional definitions of family as they discuss the experiences of various ethnic groups in the United States. Johnson (1985) explains that although Italians may use the word *family* in many contexts, it refers to "a specific constellation in a household, an extended group of relatives, or, in the broadest sense, the blood ties with many individuals in this country and in Italy" (p. 15).

Hispanic families are described similarly as "an interdependent and interactive network that allows for mutual and reciprocal help among its members" (p. xiv). Mexican Americans are described as family-oriented, extended, and intradependent; maintaining the family in ethnic neighborhoods known as *barrios* (Sotomayor, 1991).

An American Indian family may be a network that includes several households who may live in close proximity, assuming village-type community characteristics, or it may consist of several households in each of several states, forming an interstate family structure. These families, village or interstate in structure, are active kinship networks that include parents, children, aunts, uncles, cousins, and grandparents. The lateral extension, including several households, is unlike other American nuclear families. The openness of the structure allows for the incorporation of significant nonkin as family members with responsibilities equal to those of all other family members (Red Horse, 1980).

This openness also can be seen in African American families, which have been described as "an intimate association of persons of African descent living in America, who are related to each other by a variety of means which include blood, marriage, formal and informal adoption, or by appropriation; sustained by a history of common residence; and are deeply imbedded in a network of social structures internal and external to themselves" (Billingsley, 1990, p. 86).

Mothers, fathers, grandmothers, grandfathers, and other kin were included in the work of Hurd, Moore, and Rodgers (1995) as they sought to identify trends and themes in African American families. Three trends were identified: substantial parental involvement, support from external caregivers, and considerable male involvement. Among the themes that emerged were connection with family, emphasis on achievement, respect for others, spirituality, self-reliance, education, teaching coping skills, self-respect, and racial pride.

Although deficit definitions of the African American family are readily available, these authors call for an awareness of the involvement of parents in children's activities, the availability of child-rearing support by external caregivers, the positive male role models who are available, and that parents are likely to attempt to transmit honorable values and teach responsible behaviors.

The experiences of many Puerto Rican, Mexican American, African American, and families of other oppressed ethnic groups have been influenced by historical time during which family members' individual time stories include HIV/AIDS. This illness generates "fear and tears, stigma, pity and rejection, loneliness, hatred, anger, alienation and abandonment, dishonor, shame and guilt, frustration, disfigurement, hostility and loss of health, anxiety, depression and discrimination, secrecy and denial, reduced self-esteem, and death" (Morales & Bok, 1992). Responses to this litany of distress will vary in relation to each ethnic group and their experiences with racism, poverty, and other forms of oppression. The eventuality of death will change family structures that become more familiar; grandparents with orphaned grandchildren; aunts, uncles, siblings, and fictive kin adapt to include orphaned children. In other instances, persons with AIDS will return to their family of origin for care and nurture. Our interest here is related to the consequences of the ethnic reality for these families. Low income, poverty, racism, and homophobia converge to generate Morales and Bok's litany.

## *Defining the Family Life Course*

Rhodes (1977), Golan (1981), Carter and McGoldrick (1989), and Winton (1995), among many other social workers and sociologists, adhere to family life cycle models that assume universal, fixed, sequential stages through which families pass. It is assumed that individuals, heterosexual men and women, will join together in marriage, have children, launch them into the larger world, and experience transition into postparenthood. Some couples will separate, and/or divorce; still others will remarry following divorce.

Hill (1986), Rowland (1991), Wijnberg and Holmes (1992), and Rice (1994) have made contributions to the study of the family life cycle by examining the impact of divorce on the family life course. Slater and Mencher (1991) note that the family life cycle discussion has begun to include the influence of ethnicity, the single-parent family experience, divorce, and remarriage. But, they posit that there is a need to articulate a lesbian family life cycle. Although the discussion centers about the lesbian experience, they note that gay male families have been excluded as well. It is clear that our perspectives on family life cycles are expanding. However, Germain (1990, 1991) considered universal, fixed, sequential models of the family life experience to be meaningless because human lives are not cyclical.

Germain (1994) has suggested that a more appropriate way to look into individual life experiences is to consider development in relation to historical time, individual time, and social time. (See Chapter 3.) This perspective is continued as she viewed families, feeling that this model is closer to the experiences of contemporary families than earlier fixed stage models. We believe that the ethnic reality, and ethnic-sensitive practice that flows from it, respond to the call for the incorporation of individual, cultural, and environmental diversity into thinking about the families' movement through time.

### The Mario Mangano Story

*Mario, an Italian American, 13 years old, is unhappy. This is evident to his group worker at the Catholic Charity after-school program. Mario is sure that his family is weird. Everything is confusing to him. There are so many people in his house. His friends have grandfathers, but they do not live in the house with them. Their grandfathers live in the neighborhood but not in their houses.*

*The group worker learns that indeed there are many people in the Mangano house, in fact three generations are there. There are Mario's parents Frank and Marie, his immigrant maternal grandfather John Alba, his maternal uncles Dave and Paulie, his cousins Anna age 6, Emily age 8, and Julia age 12. The cousins give him the most trouble. Their mother, his mother's sister, died of cancer. Her kids moved in and became the family favorites. He wants to complain. When he does his mother says, "You have a mother, they don't." This is small comfort to a confused 13-year-old.*

*Mario has other concerns as well. He thinks that he wants to be a priest. His parents are sure that he will grow out of it. The priests who are his teachers are not so sure. The social worker will be available if Mario wants to talk about his weird family or going to seminary when he is older.*

## THE LAYERS OF UNDERSTANDING

No matter what size the client system may be or what particular population they may represent, the ethnic-sensitive social worker needs to recognize the value of the layers of understanding. Work with families requires an examination of professional values as they relate to expanding definitions of family; an understanding of dynamics related to individuals and their families moving in tandem; agency policy and services; self-awareness; the impact of the ethnic reality on family life; the route families may take to the social worker; and strategies and procedures useful in the helping process.

### Layer 1—Social Work Values

Hartman and Laird (1983) presented questions that must be considered when practice responds to the needs of families. "Is an unmarried and committed couple a family? A single parent and her or his children? Is a divorced father who doesn't support and rarely visits a part of the family?" (p. 26). Social workers who believe that the "real" family is the nuclear family with a married couple and their children become perplexed. Any other lifestyle may be viewed as damaging to the children and of questionable moral value.

Among the ethical standards cited in the *Code of Ethics* is "Cultural Competence and Social Diversity." The mandate is for social workers to understand cultural competence and recognize the strengths that exist in all cultures, most particularly the culture of their clients. Adherence to the Code's standard for education about, and an understanding of "social diversity and oppression with respect to race, ethnicity, national origin, color, sex, sexual orientation, age, marital status, political belief, religion, or mental or physical disability," (1.05) will make the ethnic-sensitive worker better able to respond to changing definitions of family. Each ethnic group will have values related to family, and the position of family members in relation to age or gender. Gay and lesbian parents and their children will be subjected to the homophobia present in all ethnic groups; single parents, mothers or fathers, are viable family units.

The Clemons and the Mangano families are members of several ethnic groups, yet they present problems related to family constellation. They are traditional nuclear families that have opened their boundaries to include other family members who have a need for protection.

## Layer 2—Basic Knowledge of Human Behavior

Family life course perspectives provide an assessment tool valuable to the ethnic-sensitive social worker. Individual and family social histories give information about social and individual time. These histories provide information about the significance of race, ethnicity, language, and cultural strengths as well as experiences of discrimination or oppression. Patterns of family interaction related to the ethnic reality give indications of a family's ability to manage the various challenges they will need to face (Miley, O'Melia, & DuBois, 1998). Mario lives with his parents, his maternal grandfather, and two uncles, as well as three cousins who are younger. There are three generations present in this household. As the eldest member of the family, Mr. Alba's story will reflect his individual time experiences, which include immigration to the United States as a young man. His lack of facility with the English language reflects that experience. Mrs. Mangano's care for him may be considered to be a response to the Italian ethnic disposition of commitment to family. Providing a home for Ann, Emily, and Julia is further evidence of this disposition.

Germain (1991), Longres (1995), and Norlin and Chess (1997) have provided social work students with work focused on human behavior, and the social environment content required by policy statements of the Council on Social Work Education. Each afford the opportunity to consider families and communities in relation to ecological and social systems theory. Ethnic-sensitive students and practitioners have at their disposal content related to family and roles, the family as a social institution, and family life in racial and ethnic communities.

The world of Sarah Clemons may be considered in the light of her Irish Catholic, Polish, and English ancestry. Role expectations of adult members of the family are unclear and family interaction is difficult. What is an appropriate response to the older Mrs. Clemons behavior in the family? Is there support available to her from her Irish Catholic community? Answers will be found in knowledge about families and the behaviors of various members in relation to their experiences in historical, individual, and social time.

### Biological—Maturational and Social Transitions

Our discussion thus far has indicated that we question the usefulness of certain family life cycle perspectives, particularly when they are related to the age of the oldest child. Life course perspectives related to historical, social, and individual time are more useful to the ethnic-sensitive social worker in that the ethnic reality may be incorporated, thereby expanding the possibilities for the examination of family stories as an assessment tool. We offer a perspective that observes family movement from a biological–maturational, social transition viewpoint. Five points at which the family is most vulnerable are highlighted. Each transition occurs within the context of the ethnic reality and will influence family members in relation to their age, gender, physical abilities, and other diversity characteristics:

> Joining together (couples without children);
> Families with young children;
> Families with adolescents;
> Families as launching centers for emerging adults; and
> Together again (later adulthood).

The perspective for single-parent families would be similar with a reminder that a single parent may be a mother or a father who has never married or is divorced or widowed:

> Becoming a parent;
> Single with young children;
> Single with adolescents;
> Launching adolescents or emerging adults; and
> Single again.

The life cycle of the single-parent family has been examined by a variety of social scientists and social workers (Hill, 1986; Wijnberg & Holmes, 1992; Rice, 1994). Together they call our attention to the variations in family life created by divorce. Rice's research examines the deficit model suggested by Hill. As we define family in relation to two adults, father and mother and children, other models are found wanting. Single-parent families created by divorce are regarded as deviant, given the label of broken, or disintegrated. Maladjustment of family members is assumed, the family is regarded as dysfunctional, problematic, and adequate.

Social class, ethnicity/race, and gender are variables to be considered in the discussion of single parents. African American single parents are measured by the standard of intact white ethnic families, flawed as they may be. In reference to Hines (1989), Rice (1994) challenges the description of the African American family as having a more truncated life cycle, female-headed with extended family, and a life cycle interrupted by many unpredictable life events and related stress, with few resources available supplemented by governmental support. Frameworks such as this present female-headed households as positive ethnic disposition for African Americans; such is not the case in reality.

Transitional activity related to divorce and separation is delineated by Wijnberg and Holmes (1992). We find that it responds well to our thinking related to social transitions. While they offer three role orientations, traditional, modifier, and career directed, we proffer the traditional for consideration in that it is similar to universal models of family development. The traditionalist model is based on the experiences of women who sense their family needs as more important than their own, find primary satisfaction in the roles of wife and mother, and have a desire to keep the family intact. However, if indeed divorce does occur, the traditional woman must relinquish roles that have been satisfying and take on the tasks that will redefine her status:

> Preparation for divorce: perspectives unclear, resists divorce, wishes to maintain home;
>
> Actual separation: remains child/home centered, holds to mothering role;
>
> Family system reorganization: difficult, stressful time, needs extra time to reorganize;
>
> Family system redefinition, stabilization: resolution involved, reduction in mother role expectations.

Hill (1986) makes the assumption that the economic conditions of single parenthood are such that remarriage is attractive. This decision places the family life cycle back "on schedule," divorce having placed the family "off schedule." The universal stage model, dependent on the age of the eldest child, is seen as the norm. This constellation is believed to be the most stable and livable for successful family development. The task of remarried families is to accommodate the needs of each family member in relation to biological and maturational needs.

### Family Functions and Tasks

The Clemons and Mangano families have economic and affectional responsibilities that will be carried out in relation to the ethnic reality. The Clemonses will be influenced by Polish, English, and Irish ancestry. Undoubtedly, the varied dispositions have blended. Richard Clemons remains devoted to the church even as his marriage fails. He is devoted to his mother often at the risk of damaging his marriage further.

The struggle with alcoholism does not keep Richard from fulfilling the primary instrumental task of providing food, clothing, shelter, and health care for his family. With more than adequate resources, the family is able to live in a middle-income suburban neighborhood that provides a good school for his daughter. He is less than adequate at expressive tasks that require him to establish patterns of communication with a wide range of emotions, from aggression to affection. Drinking keeps him from becoming involved with his wife in ways that satisfy her need for intimacy.

Changes in family life occur in relation to individual time experiences of each member. Mr. Alba and the older Mrs. Clemons belong to birth cohorts that experienced immigration to the United States. He has not been able to grasp the intricacy of English, which at times is a barrier to communication with family members, particularly his grandchildren. Mrs. Clemons expects a relationship with her son similar to her mother's experiences in Ireland. Their social time converges with the social time of younger family members.

Traumatic events changed family patterns in both families. The sudden death of Sarah Clemons's father changed her relationship with her brothers. Alcoholism is a barrier to satisfactory communication patterns. The death of Mario's aunt influenced his family's use of two resources: space and time. The home environment is even more crowded with three more people.

Germain (1994) spoke of the family's need to manage space and time resources. Time needs to be organized and schedules set. Mario's distress relates to shrinking resources. Cousins take up space and make demands on his mother's time, which she gives freely. The family's resolution of the older Mrs. Clemons's health problems increased the number of persons in the household, but at the same time provided resources for a larger house. Each family is influenced by their own and their group's ethnic history.

**Joining Together.**    Chapter 1 presented a discussion of intermarriage. The Clemons family is an excellent example of this practice. Sarah's mother's ethnic heritage is English, her father's was Polish, and her husband's heritage is Irish. Alba (1990) argued that ethnicity among whites in the United States is in the midst of a fundamental transformation with unclear outlines. How will Sarah's daughter identify herself given the ethnic history of her maternal grandparents and her own parents?

As individuals join together, they set in motion a portion of their own family history. Courtship may lead to living together as a family without marriage. In other instances, courtship will be followed by engagement and a wedding. Each phase of the joining together process will be influenced by family and ethnic and religious tradition. The wedding celebration will provide opportunities for families to affirm their common heritage and values (Carter & McGoldrick, 1988).

**Families with Young Children.**    When Mario was born, space was allocated and housing arrangements made to accommodate his arrival. More adaptations were necessary when Anna, Emily, and Julia moved in. The working-class status of the Mangano family provides adequate financial resources to incorporate the three children. Mr. Mangano and his brothers-in-law are all employed and share family expenses including those incurred by Mr. Alba; they now also help support their nieces. Young oppressed ethnic group families with lesser means would find it difficult to add three children to an already beleaguered household.

**Families with Adolescents.**    Family exchanges with the outside world increase as children move on to adolescence. Individual time will be influenced by the increase of exchanges with the outside world. All of the children in the Mangano family attend school, but Mario increases his exchanges as he approaches adolescence; he attends a parochial middle school, participates in an after-school program, plays ball with his buddies in the neighborhood, and with his father belongs to a father and son airplane club that builds and flies miniature airplanes.

Family success at time of launching young adults will depend on the manner in which critical issues have been addressed. Children may experience strain as they move from childhood into adolescence. Ethnic messages related to gender expectations may be confused with continued intermarriage.

Consider the ethnic implications of Sarah Clemons's marriage. The rush to launching through marriage was related to her Polish father's expectations about women and education; she appeared to receive other messages from her English mother.

When these family members leave, a social transition related to biological maturation and role status occurs; adolescents are now young adults with the responsibilities that come with the new status. Remaining family members may have more space available for activities; children no longer need to share sleeping space. More recreational space may be available.

Financial responsibilities of the family remain; housing needs continue. A consequence of transition is the reallocation of maintenance chores; younger children assume more responsibility, taking on family maintenance chores once held by departed siblings. Expressive tasks continue for remaining members.

The leaving may not be a joyful one, particularly if it is a traumatic event related to addiction or substance abuse, adolescent pregnancy, or criminal activity. In order to cope with these life stressors, the family must modify its functioning and reconsider its self-perception.

**Moving on—Together Again.**    Adults in age-condensed families must wait for launching and moving on. The traditional family life cycle events do not occur readily. Youthful grandmothers continue to care for adolescent daughters and their children. They have complex family experiences, as mothers and daughters who must care for aging parents. They may wonder if they will ever be able to move on.

### The Life Course of Never Married Single Persons

#### Andrea's Reflections

Andrea is an adult, a single, never married woman. Friends and family have questioned her decision not to be married. Several men have been interested in marriage; she did not respond and her family accuses her of rejecting men for "no reason at all."

> *I do not believe that I would make a good wife because I hate everything about what "wife" means in USA culture. My response to those who ask, "Don't you get lonely?" is, "Of course I do." But, I still prefer to be single. I like myself and appreciate my own company. It is hard for me to be in a crowd for very long, particularly very large crowds like a Rolling Stones concert in the Dome. I love my friends and treasure their company, but I do like solitude. Breakfast is my favorite meal of the day. I spend the time thinking, figuring out stuff, and planning the day. My kitchen is so much a part of me that I find it hard to share with another person. The only time I shared a home with a man was with a friend, who relinquished the kitchen to me. He hardly ever entered. I think that a husband is work. I have a job that I like very much. I do not need another one. I am a writer and know writers who are married, even some who are married to other writers. I admire how they manage this, though much of their time is spent alone. Still they have been able to*

*incorporate mates and even children into their lives. I know that I would not be able to do this myself, but I think it's a great thing to do nonetheless.*

Single persons, male or female, include the divorced, separated, widowed, and never married. Andrea is among the many adults who have chosen not to marry. She finds her life to be very satisfying at midlife. Although she has maintained a good reputation in the Italian community, she has not become a wife as expected (Scarpaci, 1981). Literature related to the Italian family usually presents marriage as primary among the family's interests. The process of mate selection and marriage, and roles assigned to bride and groom as they become husband and wife, are very clear. There is no mention of remaining single as an alternative lifestyle (Alba, 1984; Rotunno & McGoldrick, 1981).

This void in the literature related to single Italian Americans transcends ethnic groups. To be single is to be "deviant" in the larger community, adulthood cannot be attained outside of marriage. Singles who do not conform to cultural norms question the validity of the ideal that everyone should marry (Keith, 1980). A developing literature begins to examine the status of never-married men and women.

Rowland (1991) has added the never-married to a life cycle classification of households headed by adults, but implies that they do not experience family life cycle stages. Women who have never married have described the process of not getting married. This hidden event is among a series of events and transitions that occur during childhood and young adulthood. A "combination of events related to family, friends, education, work, residence, and health interacted to limit opportunity or desire to marry" (Allen, 1989, p. 77). Four themes emerged from this qualitative study: "my mother needed me," "I had to take care of myself," "broken hearts," and "I had other things to do."

Unmarried African American female college students begin to express Allen's latter theme, related to "other things to do." Fifteen percent of the women in Porter and Bronzaft's (1995) study did not plan to stay home and raise children. While these young women preferred to date African American men, they did not rule out relationships with men from other ethnic groups.

Andrea presents the advantages of singleness for her. Mid-life men cite three advantages of being single:

Maintaining personal freedom and liberty;
Keeping options open; and
Avoiding problems in relationships.

Among the disadvantages cited:

No one to share experiences with daily;
Times of loneliness;
Lack of long-term planning and building; and
"Nagging uncertainties." (Waehler, 1996)

Social workers will need to realize that unmarried persons engage in role development, negotiation of relationships, and transitions as do married persons. And, they will experience the benefit, conflict, and role strain for doing so. It is difficult to make projections about singleness in American ethnic groups. We do, however, understand that marriage is the expected transition in young adulthood or adulthood. Those who do not meet the expectation may experience ridicule through labels such as "old maid," which imply failure in not being married.

## Layer 3—The Impact of the Ethnic Reality on the Daily Life of Families

### The Susan Wakefield Story—The Multiracial Adolescent

*Susan Wakefield is an adolescent, ready to move into emerging adulthood. Like many adolescents, she sends conflicting messages about her well-being. At times she is troubled by self-doubt, at other times she is purposeful and self-assured. She has the capacity to accomplish the tasks assigned to adolescence. However, she is perplexed at times when she considers her ethnic identity.*

*Susan's parents were divorced when she was but one year old. She remained with her mother. John Wakefield was biracial with African American and Cherokee ancestry. Marilyn Wakefield is of Italian, Dutch, and Scottish ancestry. During her childhood Susan's maternal grandfather transmitted the ethnic messages of European ancestors. The home represented the Scottish past with furniture that had been in the family for generations. Meals represented the Italian and Dutch cuisine. She knew little of her paternal family, having only a few photographs of her father that reflect his African American roots.*

*Feelings of exclusion, not belonging, surfaced during her elementary school years. Children continually questioned her ethnic identity. How could she have a white mother if she was black? Unable to provide a reasonable answer, Susan began to identify herself as Black, an African American. This does not always please her mother. But, she has felt unable to identify herself in relation to her Italian, Dutch, and Scottish heritage. Susan's complexion, black, leads most people to assume that she is Black/African American. Her difficulty stems from her seeming rejection of her European background, and her great respect for her mother, grandfather, and other relatives. They have been a significant part of her life, present when there was no paternal connection. Can you be externally black and internally white? The school social worker is concerned. Although there are no apparent academic problems, Susan seems to be very sad a great deal of the time.*

## Layer 4—Knowledge and Skill in Agency Policy and Services Influence Professional Practice

The Central Family Agency provides a wide range of services to individuals and families. There is a family preservation unit, an adoption and foster care unit, as well as a unit that provides services purchased by local public agencies. Orientation and staff development and training provides an ethnic-sensitive perspective that will respond to Sarah Clemons's ethnic reality. Her social worker, a staff member on the family service unit, understands the policies of the agency that are reinforced by her supervisor. If Richard is willing to join Sarah, she will be able to work with them as a couple. There is little mention of their daughter, but the social worker understands that if necessary she may be added to the counseling process.

Catholic Charity after-school programs are but one of an array of services offered by the agency. The group worker has access to any program that will address needs he may identify. These may include drug education, parenting classes for teenage mothers, and family counseling. At present, recreation is the only service that Mario needs, perhaps later he will want to talk about becoming a priest.

## Layer 5—Self-Awareness, Including Insight into One's Own Ethnicity and an Understanding of How That May Influence Professional Practice

Each social worker's family of origin experience will differ according to its constellation and ethnic reality. Life in a family with a single mother will not provide a clear picture of the impact that Sarah and Mario's father have had on their movement into adolescence and adulthood. The "Who am I?" question may present itself as the media and legislators question the value of single-parent families.

Ethnic and family messages may have given Sarah Clemons the idea that she should not trust outsiders, particularly in relation to family problems (Mondykowski, 1982). But, as she looks for help to relieve her distress, this ethnic message is discarded. Her Jewish worker must understand that unlike Jewish Americans, many families and individuals do not look to authority figures or experts as relevant problem solvers (Herz & Rosen, 1982). She cannot expect that Sarah will be as verbal as Jewish American clients may be.

An awareness of her own ethnic messages helps this worker and others to listen and respond sensitively to Sarah Clemons, whose distress may come from her husband's ethnic response to his elderly mother. The Mangano Italian commitment to family can be respected within the Jewish reverence for family. Thinking and feeling the impact of one's own ethnicity leads one to a greater ethnic sensitivity in practice.

Susan belongs to a group of adolescents who have become more visible in our communities. She is multiracial with at least five American ethnic groups in her background. Two of these groups, American Indian and African American, are oppressed ethnic groups. Public attention has been focused on a multiracial young man, Tiger Wood, the golf champion. He affirms his European, African American, Indian, and Asian heritage. Popular culture reminds us of the quandary as they examine issues of racial identity and interfaith marriages (Morganthau, 1995; Adler, 1997).

Susan's school social worker must recognize the complexity of the ethnic reality in the lives of Susan and other multiracial adolescents. There has been very little to assist workers in the past. Individuals were expected to identify with one group as Susan has chosen to do, but the cutting off on other portions of her identity is troublesome. Racial identity development has been defined as pride in one's own racial and cultural identity. It shapes attitudes about one's self, persons from other oppressed ethnic groups, as well as members of majority ethnic groups. In addition, this development dispels myths about the sameness of all ethnic groups (Poston, 1990).

A model of positive biracial identity has been suggested by Poston (1990). Perspectives such as these will provide the social worker with a model by which to gauge the work with Susan. As they work from personal identity to integration, it is hoped that Susan's sadness will abate. The intervening steps are: choice of group categorization, enmeshment/denial, and appreciation.

> *Personal identity:* Adolescents have a greater sense of ethnic identity than has been thought.
>
> *Choice of group:* At this stage individuals are pushed to select an identity, usually one ethnic group. Susan has made this decision, but it offers scant comfort.
>
> *Enmeshment/Denial:* Confusion and guilt are characteristics of this stage, resulting from having to select one ethnic identity that is not fully expressive of one's background. Guilt, self-hatred, and lack of acceptance from one or more groups are problems. Adolescents may be ashamed and fearful of having friends meet the parent who is different from the community norm, and then feel guilty about the feelings. Anger and guilt will need to be resolved as they begin to appreciate the racial disposition that each parent holds, or they may remain at this stage of anger and guilt. Susan is in the process of moving on. The process will be enriched if the social worker and Mrs. Wakefield are able to generate community support.
>
> *Appreciation:* Appreciation is the marker for this stage as adolescents begin to recognize the value of their multiple identity. They begin to learn about their own racial/ethnic heritage and culture and may become involved in culturally relevant activities.
>
> *Integration:* Arrival at this stage will be reflected in a sense of wholeness as they recognize the value of each ethnic identity.

A review of the developing literature related to multiracial and biracial families and children will provide the ethnic-sensitive worker with a knowledge base that will support the work with Susan and other multiracial children and adolescents. Contributions vary in perspective. Kerwin, Ponterotto, Jackson, and Harris (1993) describe their qualitative work with biracial adolescents and their parents. Major themes for the parents were labels, in essence, "what do we call ourselves?"; in preparation for anticipated discrimination, some parents sought actively to prepare their children to deal with prejudice, while others sought to protect them; the location theme poses the question of where shall we live in order to be comfortable. Major themes for the adolescents were labels, self-description, and racial awareness.

Francis Wardel (1989, 1992) calls for the nation's schools to make accommodations for the increasing number of biracial and multiracial children who are entering school systems. Research findings related to these children are affirmed as the struggle for a label is identified. Is the appropriate term biracial, interracial, multiracial, or multiethnic? The goal of integration of ethnic identity is supported with an explanation that biracial children have more than "dual identity"; rather, they hold a rich heritage. An individual child's heritage may include "Asian, Native American, African, West Indian, European, and American ancestry" (p. 166). Wardel's significant contribution to teachers and social workers are suggestions for activities.

We have developed ethnic-sensitive interventions based on suggestions made to teachers in support of biracial children.

- Develop a family tree going back as far as you can on each side of the adolescent's family (genograms).
- Encourage and support discussion about individual differences.
- Encourage consideration of physical characteristics.
- Encourage reflection on the family situation through comments, questions, and discussion with creative supports.
- Support parents' right to be a partner in a multiracial marriage, assist them through suggestions for exposing children to the richness of their heritage.
- Encourage parents and children as you provide them with the tools— "language"—to defend and protect themselves from racism, discrimination, and various assaults from the community.

These interventions, linked with an understanding of the development of ethnic identity, provide the ethnic-sensitive worker with some direction as more and more children with many streams of ethnicity follow various routes to the social worker.

The ethnic reality of the Clemons family is working class, Irish Catholic, and Polish. They are among the increasing number of white ethnic Americans who are transforming ethnic identity (Alba, 1990). The Mangano family is Italian working-class who live in an Italian neighborhood that provides the comfort of church and school close at hand. Mr. Alba can find older Italians with similar experiences in historical time. Andrea is middle-class Italian and single; Susan Wakefield is middle-class, multiethnic, and represents an evolving ethnic group in ways similar to the Clemons; however, race is salient in her story.

Each family and individual will experience the ethnic reality within the context of the historical, individual, and social time of each person. Mario's childhood experiences occur in tandem with his grandfather's aging in the home of his adult children. Susan's social time reflects changing attitudes about marriage between the races. Andrea has remained single into middle age. Family and community may despair that she has not taken her appropriate place in the family life course, failing to respond to the Italian disposition calling for women to marry and become mothers and wives.

## Layer 6—An Understanding That the Route to the Social Worker Has an Impact on How Social Services Are Perceived

Sarah Clemons's route to the social worker was voluntary; Mario's will be voluntary if he decides to talk to the group worker about the people in his house; Susan's route will be somewhat voluntary as the school social worker assumes the outreach role.

In each case the route to the social worker is voluntary. Social workers that respond will need to understand that this route will not assure complete cooperation. Will Sarah's Polish roots cause her to hesitate in confronting her husband in relation to her need for more of his attention (Mondykowski, 1981)? Susan is not familiar with the responsibilities of a school social worker. She will need to understand that there may be benefits if she begins to address the sadness she feels as she struggles with her identity. The subtle message that Mario received tells him that he will find resources in the family. Even though his mother appears to pay more attention to his cousins, he knows she will be available to him if he really needs her (Johnson, 1985). The group worker will be a secondary source of help. His role is to provide a healthy environment for Mario and his friends who attend the after-school program.

## Layer 7—The Adaptation of Strategies and Procedures for Ethnic-Sensitive Practice

There is a significant body of professional literature to guide us as we work with families. To increase our ethnic sensitivity, we need to pay particular attention to the impact of the ethnic reality, the convergence of ethnicity and social class. McGoldrick, Pearce, and Giordano (1982) acknowledge that "ethnicity remains a vital force in this country, a major form of group identification, and a major determinant of our family patterns and belief systems" (p. 3). Social workers are expected to respond to this reminder and be purposeful in the assessment phase when working with individuals and families. The guide for ethnic assessment at the three levels of practice provides some direction (see Appendix 2).

At the micro level of assessment, ethnic-sensitive workers must acknowledge the issues presented in relation to problem identification. Mario may not have significant problems as he thinks about becoming a priest. His Italian Catholic cultural environment, home, and school will support him. His grandfather will be excited about the decision as well.

Susan and her mother Marilyn will need help as they confront the worry that Susan has as a biracial adolescent. "Who am I?" is a question many adolescents ask. Susan's answer will be influenced by a review of her Scotch, Irish roots, as well as a more in-depth assessment of her African American heritage. The social worker will need to develop an understanding of the dilemma faced by biracial and multiracial children, who will continue to enter into the school system.

The essential adaptation required for intervention with families is consideration of a life course perspective instead of the familiar stage model. This perspective requires ethnic-sensitive workers to tune into the social, cultural, and environmental aspects of individual and family life. Immigration experiences of older members of the family provide data related to historical time. Certainly there has been considerable social change since Mr. Alba and Mrs. Clemons arrived in the United States. Country of origin places the barrier of language before Mr. Alba, who is most comfortable as he moves about the neighborhood; he is less able to communicate with his grandchildren, who are the second-generation Americans.

We must understand that individual time reflects the life stories of family members in each generation. There are many stories to be told. Each must be heard and considered in relation to the others. It is the social time perspective that most often leads families along a route to the social worker. The timing of life transitions and life events in families may often generate stressful situations. Mrs. Clemons's move into her son's home added to Sarah's role of family nurturer. Mario's pondering about career choices presents the potential for transition difficulties. Will his grandfather and parents appreciate and support his choice of vocation?

## SUMMARY

We have suggested that family life cycle perspectives are a limited resource for the ethnic-sensitive worker. A family life course perspective enriches our examination of families as they move through time. The life course of single persons, as well as the development of racial identity for biracial/multiracial adolescents, are noted. In each instance, families and individuals do not move through time in stages; rather, they move through social time together.

## REFERENCES

Adler, J. (1997, December 15). A matter of faith. *Newsweek.* pp. 49–55.

Alba, R. (1990). *Ethnic identity: The transformation of white America.* New Haven: Yale University Press.

Alba, R. D. (1984). Italian Americans: Into the twilight of ethnicity. Englewood Cliffs: Prentice-Hall.

Aldous, J. (1978). *Family careers: Developmental change in families.* New York: John Wiley & Sons.

Allen, K. A. (1989). *Single women/family ties: Life histories of older women.* Newbury Park: Sage Publications.

Armour, M. A. (1995). Family life cycles stages: A context for individual life stages. *Journal of Family Social Work 1*(2), pp. 27–40.

Billingsley, A. (1968). *Black families in white America.* Englewood cliffs, NJ: Prentice-Hall.

Billingsley, A. (1990). Understanding African-American family diversity. In J. Dewart (Ed.), *The state of Black America* (pp. 85–108). New York: National Urban League.

Carter, E., & McGoldrick, M. (1989) *The changing family life cycles: A framework for family therapy* (2nd ed.). Boston: Allyn & Bacon.

Carter, E. A., & McGoldrick, M. (1988). *The changing family life cycle: A framework for family therapy.* New York: Gardner Press.

Germain, C. B. (1990). Life forces ad the anatomy of practice. *Smith College Studies in Social Work, 60,* 138–152.

Germain, C. B. (1991). *Human behavior in the social environment: An ecological view.* New York: Columbia University Press.

Germain, C. B. (1994, May). Emerging conceptions of family development over the life course. *Families in Society,* 259–267.

Golan, N. (1981). *Passing through transitions: A guide for practitioners.* New York: The Free Press.

Hartman, A., & Laird, J. (1983). *Family-centered social work practice.* New York: The Free Press.

Herz, F. M., & Rosen, E. J. (1982). Jewish families. In M. McGoldrick, J. K. Pearce, & J. Giordano, (Eds.), *Ethnicity and family therapy* (pp. 364–393). New York: The Guilford Press.

Hill, R. (1986). Life cycle stages for types of single parent families: Of family development theory. *Family Relations 35,* pp. 19–29.

Hines. (1989). (see Rice).

Hurd, E. P., Moore, C., & Rodgers, R. (1995). Quiet success: Parenting strengths among African Americans. *Families in Society,* pp. 434–442.

Johnson, C. L. (1985). *Growing up and growing old in Italian-American families.* New Brunswick, NJ: Rutgers University Press.

Keith, P. M. (1980). Two models of singleness: Managing an atypical marital status. *International journal of sociology of the family 10* (July-Dec.), pp. 301–310.

Kerwin, C., Ponterotto, J. G., Jackson, B. L., & Harris, A. (1993). Racial identity in biracial children: A qualitative investigation. *Journal of Counseling Psychology 40*(2), pp. 221–231.

Longres, J. F. (1995). *Human behavior in the social environment* (2nd ed.). Itasca, Ill.: F. E. Peacock Publishers.

McGoldrick, M. (1981). Ethnicity and family therapy: An overview. In M. McGoldrick, J. K. Pearce, & J. Giordano (Eds.), *Ethnicity and family therapy.* New York: The Guilford Press.

Miley, K. K., O'Melia, M., & DuBois, B. L. (1998). *Generalist social work practice: An empowering approach* (3rd ed.). Boston: Allyn & Bacon.

Mondykowski, S. M. (1982). Polish families. In M. McGoldrick, J. K. Pearce, & J. Giordano (Eds.), *Ethnicity and familial therapy.* New York: The Guilford Press.

Morales, J., & Bok, M. (1992). Cultural dissonance and AIDS in the Puerto Rican community. *Journal of Multicultural Social Work 2*(3), pp.13–26.

Morganthau, T. (1995, February 13). What color is Black? *Newsweek,* pp. 63–69.

Norlin, J. A., & Chess, W. A. (1997). *Human behavior and the social environment* (3rd ed.). Boston: Allyn & Bacon.

Parsons, T. (1954). *Essays in sociological theory.* Free Press: Glencoe, IL.

Porter, M. M., & Bronzaft, A. L. (1995). Do the future plans of educated black women include black mates? *Journal of Negro Education 64* (2), pp. 162–170.

Poston, W. S. C. (1990). The biracial identity development model: A needed addition. *Journal of Counseling & Development 69,* pp. 152–155.

Red Horse, J. C. (1980). Family structure and value orientation in American Indians. *Social Casework* (Oct.).

Rhodes, S. (1977). A developmental approach to the life cycle of the family. *Social Casework* (May).

Rice, J. K. (1994). Reconsidering research on divorce, family life cycle, and the meaning of family. *Psychology of Women Quarterly 18,* pp. 559–584.

Richmond, M. E. (1917). *Social Diagnosis.* New York: Russell Sage Foundation.

Rotunno, M., & McGoldrick, M. (1981). Italian families. In M. McGoldrick, J. K. Pearce, & J. Giorando (Eds.). *Ethnicity and family therapy.* New York: The Guilford Press.

Rowland, D. T. (1991). Family diversity and the life cycle. *Journal of Comparative Family Studies XXII* (1), pp. 1–12.

Santomayor, M. (1991). *Empowering Hispanic families: A critical issue for the '90s.* Milwaukee: Family Service America.

Scarpaci, J. V. (1981). *La Contadina:* The plaything of the middle class woman historian. *The Journal of Ethnic Studies 9*(2), pp. 21–37.

Slater, S., & Mencher, J. (1991). The lesbian family life cycle: A contextual approach. *American Journal of Orthopsychiatry 61*(3), pp. 372–381.

Waehler, C. A. (1996). *Bachelors: The psychology of men who haven't married.* Westport, CT: Praeger.

Wardel, F. (1989). Children of mixed parentage: How can professionals respond? *Children Today* (July-August) pp. 10–13.

Wardel, F. (1992). Supporting biracial children in the school setting. *Education and Treatment of Children 15* (2), pp. 163–172.

Wijnberg, M. H., & Holmes, T. (1992). Adaptation to divorce: The impact of role orientation on family-life-cycle perspectives. *Families in Society,* pp. 159–167.

Winton, C. A. (1995). *Frameworks for studying the family.* Guilford, Conn.: Dushkin.

# 12

# ETHNIC-SENSITIVE PRACTICE IN THE PUBLIC SECTOR: FROM AFDC TO TANF

*Anne Reinhard*

*Anne Reinhard is a 23-year-old mother of two children, John age 7, and Nancy age 8. They were born when Anne was in high school. Anne did not stay in high school during her two pregnancies. That would have been too much for her parents, a second-generation German American working-class couple, and their other two children. Nevertheless, Anne stayed with her parents for the first few years after the children were born. The family has been helpful to Anne with concrete supports and supplements to the welfare allowance; however, they have made it quite clear that they disapprove of the behavior that led to the birth of the children. Her siblings have gone off to form their own families. Anne retains cordial relations with her parents and siblings; however, there is some emotional distance and she feels that they do not approve of her lifestyle.*

*The children's father, a fellow high school student at the time the children were conceived and born, had some early involvement. On graduating from high school, he left town—a medium-sized community in the Midwest—and has not been involved in the lives of Anne and the children. He does not send any child support. After a few years, Anne and the children moved into their own apartment. Since the birth of the children, Anne has been receiving support under the former AFDC program for herself and the children. She is enrolled in one of the programs that offers job search and placement services and the promise of some assistance in providing vocational education. The program also makes possible extension of Medicaid and child-care benefits for a limited period after entry into the labor market.*

*Jim Green is the case manager assigned to work with Anne Reinhard. He is a young German man, also. Anne's school performance has always been excellent. She took Scholastic Aptitude Tests and scored well. If interested and able, she is likely to gain admission to a good college. She would like to become a school teacher. John Green tells her that the program will likely only support her through a vocational training program for high school completion. She tries to find ways to get around this restriction.*

*Anne, like many others in her situation, had found it difficult to support two children on the AFDC allowance, and paying the rent is always difficult. She and a group of other former AFDC mothers, with the help of some community-based church workers, are looking into the possibility of obtaining some grant funding to build a residence where a number of them could live together, sharing expenses and cooperating with each other with child care.*

### Joan Black

*Joan Black, an African American woman now 25, has had three children in short order since she left high school. Somehow she kept believing that the men with whom she was involved would love her forever. She expected that each relationship would last. So far, none of them has persisted. She lives with her mother. Joan's mother is a single parent as well.*

*Joan's children are 7, 5, and 4. The oldest, Jimmy, is extremely hyperactive and probably has attention deficit disorder. Joan has been trying to get the school and the clinic where Jimmy is treated to make a definitive diagnosis so that she can get some help for him. Then she could attend school and go to work.*

*When the kids were first born, Joan managed on odd jobs while her mother took care of the kids. Now her mother is getting older and cannot keep up with the kids, especially with Jimmy.*

*Joan has been thinking about her situation. Despite the fact that she paid little attention in high school, she knows she is good in math and would like the opportunity to make up for lost time, to become a computer programmer, or perhaps an accountant. The caseworker at the local Board of Social Services offers little encouragement that she will be able to marshal the needed support. With the new law, entry into the labor force is the order of the day. She tries to persuade the caseworker that she will never be able to properly care for Jimmy and the others unless she gets help in acquiring an education and can earn enough money to do so.*

*She is ever optimistic that one of her new relationships with one of the men in her life will work out. "He'll help me get to school," she tells Jim Green about the current man in her life who comes around on weekends. She now is very careful not to conceive another child. But she keeps bouncing in and out of disappointing relationships, and wishes she could find a man who would be a father to her children.*

*She knows that marriage and education are her best bets for getting off the welfare track.*

This chapter focuses on one subset of poor people—young families—many of whom are headed by single mothers who used to receive AFDC.

In past editions of this book, our focus has been on young women like Anne Reinhard and Joan Black, and many others in similar situations who, since the mid-1930s, had been entitled to receive assistance under a program known as Aid to Families of Dependent Children.

That program, first established by the Social Security Act of 1935, enabled states to aid needy children without fathers. States were required to submit plans as to how the program would be implemented; over the years, the program expanded in a number of ways. For the most part, coverage under Medicaid, the federally based health-care program, was available. At some point, families with working fathers who met financial criteria could enroll. Essentially, all families who applied and who met the basic eligibility requirements set in their states, were entitled to receive assistance. With some exceptions, states were permitted to set their own benefit levels.

We limit our attention to those young families who experience little, if any, pathology such as involvement with drugs, major crime, or serious mental illness. The situations of those families requires discussion beyond that possible here.

Over the years the program came under increasing criticism. Many did not distinguish between those young women and their children caught in a web of poverty, poor education, and unfortunate personal circumstances, and those enmeshed in major pathology.

Accounts such as the following readily roused public and political attention. In 1994 *Time* reported an incident in which police in Chicago found 19 children alone, living in "wretched squalor." A former Secretary of Education responded to this account and was quoted as follows:

> *Body count, yes, body count. Kids dying, kids abused, kids cut up, kids burned with cigarettes, kids whose brains are so poorly developed they can't function in school. This isn't child neglect, it's child endangerment...*
>
> *The government should not hand out welfare and food stamps and counseling. It should cut off aid, take the children away, and place them in foster care and orphanages.*

Those on the other side of the spectrum, who were committed to the development of programs that would reduce poverty levels and enhance self-sufficiency, had other concerns. Those with liberal and progressive views were distressed about inadequate allowances that usually fell well below designated poverty levels. As the AFDC rolls grew, and the number of single mothers well surpassed the widowed mothers first targeted as the major beneficiaries of the program, strident criticism increased.

This was compounded by several factors. A substantial proportion of the recipients were single, young, unmarried African American women. The women's movement and economic factors had propelled many mothers of young children into the labor force. The young mothers, a number of whom were teenagers, were viewed as lazy by contrast with the growing cohort of working women. The program was viewed as antithetical to the work ethic, fostering dependency and limiting the power of the states to determine how to provide assistance at the local level. Abuse, neglect, and drug abuse were among the "evils" attributed to the program or its recipients.

Some of the criticism was virulent and came from persons in high level government positions. One criticism was focused on the extent to which reform legislation would reduce or eliminate the safety net, that is, eliminate the basic guarantees that the most needy would receive assistance.

Despite its flaws, there was little doubt that the AFDC guaranteed the provision of basic need. A number of factors, to be elaborated on below, led to the persistent call for the reform of the welfare system, primarily AFDC. That "reform" has now come to pass in the form of legislation signed by President Clinton in August 1996, known as the Personal Responsibility and Work Opportunity Reconciliation Act of 1996 and TANF (Temporary Assistance for Needy Families). This legislation will profoundly impact the young, poor families that are the focus of interest in this chapter.

The layers of understanding for ethnic-sensitive social work practice provide the framework for analysis of policy and practice issues that must be considered by social workers working with this group of families. The new legislation poses major challenges. The situations in which Anne Reinhard and Joan Black find themselves are illustrative of some of the conceptual, philosophical, and practice issues that frequently arise in practice in the public sector. We draw on their experience, as well as that of other persons, in considering the issues in this chapter.

There is a strong myth in U.S. society that all able-bodied persons—men and women alike—who want to work will find work and that work will pay them enough to sustain themselves and their dependents. History, as well as the present, belies the myth. For example, a study of families conducted by the Institute for Social Research at the University of Michigan (Institute for Social Research, 1987) found that one in four Americans had lived in a family that needed welfare assistance at least once during a 10-year period.

In the optimistic period after World War II, it almost seemed as if poverty had disappeared. Harrington's *Other America: Poverty in the United States* (1962) revealed otherwise. Harrington characterized the poor as invisible, undereducated, underprivileged, and lacking medical care. Poverty, he suggested, "twists the spirit." That truth remains with us today.

Members of all ethnic and minority groups are found among the poor. A disproportionately large number of people of color are poor. Decades, perhaps centuries, of discrimination—the legacy of slavery—of conquest, and of continuing treatment as second-class citizens result in a life of economic and social deprivation for many people of color.

The poor turn to public agencies for support. Some can manage with transitory help for limited periods. Others, a relatively small number, remain poor and receive public assistance for extended periods.

## THE LAYERS OF UNDERSTANDING

### Layer 1—Social Work Values

As we begin this discussion of the Federal Responsibility Act of 1996 and TANF, it is well to recall social work values, for these values are especially important in a field of practice in which the clients are vulnerable, stigmatized, and too often treated as if they were society's least important people. But most of the people on whom this chapter is focused are young people—young mothers and their children. When young people are neglected and demeaned, the consequences for them, and for the society of which they are a part, are profound. Lack of education, lack of respect, and poor health care compound and intensify the situation that brought these families into the welfare system in the first place.

Our professional values are focused on the view that people are intrinsically valuable and have the capacity to grow and to develop the skills for problem solving. The importance of self-realization is stressed, as is equality of opportunity. A major thrust of social work has always been that people need to be treated in a way that maximizes their opportunities for self-direction.

As social workers carry out their work in the new program, their values will be challenged and questioned. As has already been suggested, many public assistance recipients are poor members of oppressed minority groups, and some are considered to behave in ways not thought appropriate by many in society. For all these reasons, the ethnic-sensitive social worker, imbued with social work values, must understand the complexities of the clients and the organizational structure that serves them.

The importance of the value base may seem to get lost in the maze of the public assistance structure. Welfare clients' worthiness is questioned continually by the mainstream society as well as by other agency staff members. The work ethic constantly generates the question, "Why don't you have a job?"

As is evident from review of the new legislation that follows in the next few pages, the emphasis on work and self-reliance has become paramount, even for mothers who have responsibility for the care of very young children. The law challenges some long-held beliefs on how children are to be raised. The mother, once thought to be the bedrock of the family whose presence is required in the home, now is not exempt from work requirements in many states.

*When Anne Reinhard went to see her case manager, she often expressed the feeling that people would forever think ill of her because she had conceived those kids in high school and was "on the dole." Her parents managed to remind her periodically. Young, attractive, and bright, Anne was beginning to let herself go. She was getting a bit heavy and was otherwise not taking care of herself. She was getting discouraged.*

*When John Green would talk to his friends—lawyers, school teachers, business people, and some fellow social workers—about his clients, he was besieged with questions about their morality, their "laziness," and their poor mothering habits. "Look at you and your wife," they would say. "You have the same background. I bet you wouldn't go on welfare." They all knew people who were managing to go to school on their own without relying on all that public money. Couldn't her folks help her out? Couldn't she get a loan?*

*It became increasingly difficult for John Green to find answers that reflected the social work commitment to valuing people on their own terms.*

*He quoted figures on how much money was needed to cover basics like food, rent, clothing, medical care, and child care. And he compared these figures with the reality of how much a single mother with minimal education could earn. The two sets of figures did not match up.*

*He told them about Anne's agony about being in this spot, about how it goes against the grain of the work ethic of her German Protestant upbringing, and about how she would do O.K. if the system would just help her get to school. If we had family allowances like most European countries, she would not be singled out as a single parent on the dole. And if we had a national health system, or a child-care system—also found in many European countries—she probably could manage with very little special assistance.*

*John Green kept trying. But sometimes he did wonder whether Anne was trying hard enough. He found that it was becoming harder and harder to stand up against all that antiwelfare sentiment.*

*Joan Black's caseworker, May Smith, herself an African American woman, was aware of the same kind of antiwelfare sentiment that was being expressed everywhere. She knew all the arguments. Years of oppression, poor education, not enough jobs for everybody.*

*But as she prepared herself for work with Joan Black, she could not help thinking that here was another one that was caught in the intergenerational cycle of poverty. Why couldn't they break out? Damn it, this Joan Black is smart, she wants to go to college. May would do her best to help her get out.*

As these questions come up, over and over, social workers must recognize the individual recipient's responsibility for his or her actions, while at the same time understanding that systemic failures perpetuate the cycle of poverty. Social work values compel us to ask, despite much frustration, "How do I help make a difference?"

## Layer 2—Basic Knowledge of Human Behavior

The welfare system serves all kinds of people. One of four U.S. families have been shown to need some form of public assistance within a 10-year period. This suggests that people from a range of social classes, as well as from a spectrum of ethnic and cultural groups, find themselves receiving public assistance at some time. As the discussion that follows also shows, people who receive public assistance are primarily poor and often unskilled. People of color are found on the welfare rolls in disproportionately large numbers. Consequently, it is most important that social workers who work with recipients of public assistance understand the nature of the economic system and the forces that keep substantial numbers of people unemployed or underemployed.

There are conflicting theories about what keeps people poor. Some of these trace the source of poverty to the economy and to structural factors. Others look to cultural and psychological explanations. It is critical that social workers inform themselves of these varying perspectives, without taking a stance that some term "blaming the victim" of unfortunate circumstances for the circumstances that led to the difficulties.

## Layer 3—Knowledge and Skill in Agency Policy and Service Influence Professional Practice

Perspectives on social welfare and on policies governing how best to meet the needs of a society's poor people are at the heart of the discussion of social work in the public sector. Opinion has long been divided on how a society should respond to its poorest, disabled, and disadvantaged citizens.

### Conceptions of Social Welfare

Two basic conceptions of social welfare can be identified. One, the residual conception, is based on the belief that people are expected to look to institutional supports only after the normal structure of supply—the family and the market—have broken down. The institutional conception considers welfare a "proper, legitimate function of modem industrial society, helping individuals to achieve self-fulfillment" (Rothenberg, 1984, cited in Karger & Stoesz, 1990). As will be quite clear when we review the new law, the residual conception prevails.

> It's not so bad being poor,
> If you don't mind
> That you can't really help the way you are
> 'Cause you haven't had the proper socio-Economic upbringing.
> Your skin's too dark, your hair is too curly
> And your father never married your mother. (Sermabeikian, 1975)

The stigma and hurt associated with being poor as expressed by the child who speaks in the poem are further compounded at the present time. All people in the United States have become aware of urban violence, drug abuse, and child abuse and neglect.

The Chicago incident (cited earlier) that elicited the virulent response from a former Secretary of Education rightfully brings public uproar in its wake. This kind of behavior is not tolerable. But the sensational reporting of such incidents buries the day-to-day problems and the realities of life on welfare for the Anne Reinhards, the Joan Blacks, and others.

> When Joan Black reads this account she is extremely distressed. When she goes to the store, or rides the bus with the kids, she figures everybody has her marked for "one of those people." She cringes when hyperactive Jimmy runs all over the bus. His behavior will compound the funny way people look at her.
>
> Under the new law, Joan has given up hope of going to college. Joan feels despondent. "They tell me to go to work, but I can't earn enough until I get to school to get trained for a decent job. Sometimes I feel it's a no-win situation," she says.

> *Joan feels a double burden. As a welfare mother she feels scorned, demeaned, and at the same time finds that her efforts to get out are not being rewarded with just enough help to enable her to make the shift.*
>
> *She also feels the double burden of being an African American welfare mother. People look at her as if she indeed were one of those Chicago mothers who had left their children in squalor. Will she ever be considered just an ordinary woman and mother, with more than the usual sets of troubles? Jimmy really is a handful.*

As the May Smiths and John Greens struggle to help their welfare mother clients to struggle, it is important that they are correctly informed about the nature of the welfare system, the present trends, and what the potentials and pitfalls are. We turn next to a discussion of data on the welfare system.

### The New Welfare System: The Personal Responsibility Act of 1996 and the Temporary Assistance to Needy Families (TANF)

In August 1996, following years of debate, President Clinton signed into law the Personal Responsibility Act of 1996 and Temporary Assistance to Needy Families (TANF) (Fact Sheet, 1997). This historic legislation generates a number of major changes in the welfare system. As stated in one of the federal documents that describes and analyzes this legislation, this law transforms large parts of the nation's welfare system. The most important change is that the entitlement to cash welfare under title IV-A of the Social Security Act is ended. The law has as its major goal the reduction of time spent on public assistance as a "safety net" for families experiencing temporary financial problems.

Some aspects of the legislation were implemented under waiver programs in several states; these have positive features that may enable mothers to acquire skills and work experience needed for enhancing the quality of life. Many states increased resource limits and "earnings disregards" to make it more financially feasible to return to work. Child care benefits were extended to families as an aid in transition after they leave the rolls. Federal documents describe substantial efforts that began well before the new legislation was enacted. All are, in one way or another, aimed at reducing dependency, enhancing parental support, and encouraging labor force participation (Fact Sheet, 1997, 8, 12).

However, given the vagaries of the economy, shifting unemployment rates, and regional differences, the stringent time limits and work requirements seem punitive and unrealistic. It is too early to be certain, but there is good reason to worry that the least skilled and most vulnerable will suffer greatly. The resignations of some of the president's closest aides in response to his signing of this bill were based on some of these considerations.

The legislation derives from the view that permanent welfare guarantees generate dependence on welfare. The basic character of the program is being altered by the temporary and provisional nature of benefits.

The law created two block grants. One provides grants to the states to provide cash and other benefits to help families needing assistance in supporting their children. This support simultaneously requires families to make efforts that can be documented to leave "welfare for work" and to avoid out-of-wedlock births. States are allowed to use funds from this block grant to encourage the development and maintenance of two-parent families.

The second grant is intended to be used by states to subsidize child care for welfare families, for those leaving public assistance, and for low-income families at risk for joining the welfare rolls in the future. The law limits the receipt of cash benefits from the block grant to five years. Approximately 20 percent of any state's caseload may, but need not necessarily, be exempt from this provision.

All "able-bodied adults" on public assistance for more than two years are required to become involved in some activity intended to help them become self-supporting. Work standards are in place, and at full implementation of the act, half of all recipients will be required to participate in work programs for 30 hours a week. The law also focuses on increasing child support payments from noncustodial parents.

### Data on Poverty and Public Assistance

The statistics on the numbers of people who are classified as poor and of those among them who receive public assistance are in constant flux. Further, they vary by which factors are taken into account in making the estimate as well as by state and region of residence.

Using data for two types of states (those receiving AFDC program waivers and those that do not), The Council of Economic Advisors (1997) reports closely related information: the percentage of the population that received AFDC in 1996 in the former at 4.7 percent and the latter also 4.7 percent. Data for 1996 show an unemployment rate of approximately 5.4 percent and 5.5 percent.

In 1987, 32.5 million Americans, or 13.5 percent of the population, were living in poverty. Of the 32.5 million poor, 66 percent were white, 30 percent were African Americans, and the rest were members of other groups. Rates for some Latino groups and American Indians are also high (Rodgers, 1986). Looking at the data by the numbers of involved families, we find that 7 million, or 10.8 percent, of all families are poor.

Although two-thirds of all poor people are white, the chances of being poor are much greater for African Americans. For whites, the chances are 11 out of 100 and for African Americans, one of three. Forty percent of the poor are children under 18 years of age. Despite changes in family structure, husband/wife households remain the norm and account for eight of 10 families. The female-headed household, of which we hear so much, is still the exception: The Council of Economic Advisors (1997) reports that in 1996, states without major statewide waivers had rates of 17 percent while in waiver states the rates were 15.7 percent. Nevertheless, the actual number of female-headed households has increased substantially in the past three decades. A child's risk of poverty in a female-headed household is one in three.

The link between family size and poverty and that between family size/race and poverty is clear and has existed for years. But the link between family size/ race/female-headed households and poverty is the most compelling of all poverty data. A white mother with one child has a 30 percent chance of poverty. Her black counterpart has a 42 percent chance. A white mother with four children and no husband present has a 73 percent chance of poverty. A black mother similarly situated has an astonishing 87 percent chance. These poverty rates exist after all income transfers (Dear, 1989, pp. 23–24).

The process described here has been characterized as the feminization of poverty. The reasons are complex. Some are related to the dramatic increase in divorce and separation, the substantial increase in the number of out-of-wedlock births, the low level of child support by absent fathers, and the lower wage levels earned by poor women when they are employed (Rodgers, 1986).

**Number of People on Assistance.**   Data on the number of recipients of AFDC have been changing dramatically over the past decade. In the earlier period sharp increases were reported, followed by recent substantial declines. Zippay (1993) reported that between 1988 and 1992 the number of families receiving AFDC jumped from 10.9 million to 14.2 million. Two-thirds of the 14.2 million persons on the AFDC rolls in 1992 were children. These increases were unprecedented in the history of the program and are attributed to an increase in out-of-wedlock births and to a weak economy. Between 1992 and 1997, the number of people on the welfare rolls dropped by 20 percent or 2.75 million. Efforts to account for this change are ongoing.

The Council of Economic Advisors (1997) points to several possible factors. Between 1993 and 1997, many new jobs were created. Also important may have been the expansion of the Earned Income Tax Credit (EITC) that took place in 1990 and 1993, as well as the increase in federal and state spending on child care. These may have facilitated entry into the labor market for some people who otherwise might have opted for application for welfare.

During this same period, there was another development that likely affected the significant downward shift. Between 1993 and 1996, the federal government granted waivers from prevailing welfare policies to 43 states. In their study, the Council of Economic Advisors focused on the effect of the following six waivers: termination, work requirements, reduced opportunities to participate in JOBS (Job Opportunities and Basic Skills) exemptions, increased JOBS sanctions, family caps, and increased earnings disregards. The waivers are focused on limiting the time on welfare, instituting negative sanctions if work and training requirements are not met, and controlling family size.

The 1997 analysis made by the Council of Economic Advisors suggests that between 1993 and 1996

> *A robust economy and federal waivers allowing states to experiment with new welfare policies have made large contributions towards reducing the rate of welfare receipts…that over 40 percent of the decline in welfare receipt between 1993 and 1996 may be attributed to the falling unemployment rate, and almost one-third can be attributed to the waiver. (p. 181)*

In considering that almost 3 million fewer people were on welfare than there were when the waivers were initiated, and *before* the new legislation became law, social workers must look beyond these figures to look ahead and plan a strategy for how best to serve young families. In the years ahead, including the period that began in 1997 when the new law went into effect, social workers and their clients will be working within a structure that emphasizes entry into the labor force, mandatory rules and regulations, and few—if any—guarantees that assure minimum standards.

At date of writing (late fall, 1997), it is too early to know the true effect of the waivers; whether they were productive, helping young families to mobilize themselves, or punitive, causing great hardships. We also do not yet know what will happen if and when there is an economic decline.

**Myths and Realities about Welfare Recipients.**   Many accounts focused on welfare mothers suggest that they are largely minority, teenage mothers who make welfare a way of life. The data suggest otherwise. Only 8 percent of children in AFDC families live in families headed by teenage parents. The rest are headed by mothers in their twenties and thirties. The biggest increase in out-of-wedlock births is taking place among unmarried women between ages 25 and 29.

Data on the length of time women spend on welfare are as follows: one-half of some AFDC recipients left welfare within two years. The other half tended to be long term, and close to half of this group remained on the rolls for ten years or more. Among the group that left within two years, few "climb high on the socio-economic ladder" (Zippay, 1993, p. 5). Some may have entered and exited from the rolls as they worked on developing stable employment and child-care arrangements.

> *Anne Reinhard could not finish school due to her pregnancy. Although the high school she attended had a program for pregnant mothers, her family—unused to having one of its teenage daughters get pregnant—had not permitted her to continue school with her first and then her second pregnancy.*
>
> *She has been hearing about the proposal to cut her off welfare in two years, but she knows she needs more time than that to finish high school and get some other schooling. What will happen to her ambitions to become a school teacher? It seems she keeps getting trapped over and over again.*

> *Joan Black is a high school graduate. But what can a high school graduate who wants to be a computer programmer or an accountant do with that education? Could she possibly get a computer degree in two years? She and May Smith are looking into the programs in the local community college. Maybe they fall under the rubric* vocational education.

### Factors Leading to the New Welfare Law

In her 1993 analysis, Zippay outlined the history of the AFDC program. The program is traced to the early 1900s, when the inroads of urbanization were leaving a number of women widowed at an early age. The initial response to mothers who were alone and needed to support themselves was to send their children to orphanages. Subsequently, the idea of providing funds for these mothers so that they could remain at home to take care of their own children emerged. These grants came to be known as mothers' pensions and were widely supported by a number of community groups. Some consider these pensions to have been the precursor of the AFDC program, which was initiated during the New Deal. Benefits were limited; and even before the eruption of the present controversy, "a careful eye was kept on the behavior and lifestyle of the recipients" (Zippay, 1993, p. 3). However, the poor widows and other women who were alone were considered worthy of assistance.

Over the years the nature of the population receiving public assistance began to change. More and more recipients were divorced or never-married women. A disproportionate number were women of color. And generally, there were increasing numbers who stayed on welfare for many years. Thus, increasingly, the behavior of the women on welfare was viewed as morally suspect.

> *Anne Reinhard could see it in her parents' eyes when they looked at the kids. They loved them all right, but somehow she knew that their old Protestant upbringing made it impossible for them not to look at these kids as somehow the products of sin.*
>
> *When she met with John Green, Anne would talk about this. John would help her to think through the fact that this was a different world, that not only she, but the children's father, had together produced these children. Perhaps instead of blaming herself she should review his role, go after him again for child support. This is now essential. Why should the woman take the blame, feel herself to be inferior, while he does not come around and sends no money. Getting after fathers to pay their fair share is a major feature of the new welfare law.*

> *Joan Black could not help worrying that people were seeing her as part of that awful group of people who do not take care of their kids. She knows she takes good care, but it is hard not to fall into their trap.*

Anne's and Joan's sense that they are somehow suspect is based in reality. Growth in the welfare rolls coincided with an increase in the number of young mothers entering the labor force. A number of factors had converged (e.g., the women's movement, an economic decline), which sent many women to work who heretofore would have stayed home with their young children. And so the basic premise of the AFDC program—to enable young mothers to stay at home to take care of their children—was being questioned.

A recent article in *New York* (Kasindorf, 1995) illustrates the plight of many women like Anne and Joan. The article focuses on women representing various ethnic groups: Latino, African American, Irish American, and others. There are few jobs, and programs are often not what the descriptions suggest.

They speak of the difficulty in finding jobs when education is limited and jobs are scarce. "I've waited all day for one test for any kind of job—working on trains, cleaning—there were thousands of people in line" (Kasindorf, 1995, pp. 30–31).

They reflect on the men in their lives, and they speak of the contradictions in which they get caught trying to collect support from their men. Another says, "If you come from violence or you come from a drug addict, you don't want him to know where you are. You go to the child-custody office, and they start asking you, 'How tall is he?' If he's six feet two, [you say] 'Well, he's about five feet one inch.' He's 200 pounds, you say '150.' 'Do you know where he is?' 'No'" (p. 33).

Welfare reform is about these women and others like them. The rhetoric is that they are welfare cheats, lazy, and having more and more babies as a way of retaining welfare eligibility. The situation is more complex than that. The majority of teenage mothers who had been on AFDC have been sexually abused as children (Landers, 1995). Some of these youngsters do feel deprived, needy, of a "cute thing to love" (see, e.g., Kasindorf, 1995).

**Research Foundation for Welfare Reform Legislation.**   The Manpower Demonstration Research Corporation (MDRC) of New York has been conducting studies of welfare reform efforts for many years. Zippay (1993) reported that a number of studies, primarily those conducted by MDRC on eleven work demonstration projects, laid the foundation for the work and training requirements of the existing legislation. Most participants work willingly. The training programs yielded earning gains of 10 to 35 percent. Recipients with low skills and education do not benefit in any meaningful way from short-term training programs. These programs are cost effective and can usually recoup their costs over five years. Those workfare programs, in which recipients work off the value of their benefits in community service jobs, show no meaningful impact on earnings or employment.

A 1992 report by MDRC (Riccio & Friedlander, 1992) focuses on the reports of a study of California's Greater Avenues for Independence (GAIN) Program. Begun in 1985, it was then the largest welfare-to-work program that emphasized basic education, particularly for long-term welfare recipients, as well as job-seeking activities. The study sought to determine the program's short-term effects by following the welfare receipt and work behavior of 33,000 people eligible for the program. Findings were similar to those noted earlier. That is, there is a pattern of earnings gains and welfare savings for single mothers, as well as for heads of two-parent households.

## Layer 4—Self-Awareness, Including Insight into the Impact of the Ethnic Reality on Professional Practice

We begin this part of the discussion by presenting a poem written some years ago by one of our students, a white man who had experience on welfare:

> *The Black*
> *Welfare woman says,*
> *"Don't you know that you're*
> *White and*
> *Blond and*
> *Blue-eyed?*
> *Don't you know that you can*
> *Get a job easily?*

*You can't get on welfare.*
*No Way!"*
*So,*
*How come I can't get work?*
*So,*
*How come I have no money for*
*Bread and mustard*
*Sandwiches?*
*For milk and baby food for*
*The babies?*
*How come? I'm white…but I'm poor. (Brown, 1974)*

The poet feels the attack of the social worker, who makes assumptions that in his position as a white man he should have no problem finding the employment he sorely needs. The worker and others who find themselves in similar positions must look closely at attitudes and assumptions they hold that may interfere with the helping process.

The examination of self and others in this setting involves many questions; among them is the pervasive question, "Why can't they get jobs?" Why are so many African Americans unemployed when there are so many more opportunities than there were in the past? When are they going to learn to speak English and stop using their children and friends to interpret? With all the birth control available, why do they keep having babies? Some of them are only babies themselves. I'm like them (African American, Puerto Rican, American Indian). I'm working, why aren't they? Why are their grandmothers, mothers, and daughters all without husbands?

Social workers will feel badly when they have these kinds of thoughts. They have learned about racism and about the forces that keep the underclass locked in the center-city urban ghettos. And they know how hard it is to acquire the skills needed in an increasingly competitive society that looks more and more for technological know-how. It was hard for some of them.

They need to think hard. And to feel hard. Perhaps if they are members of one of the disvalued ethnic and racial groups, they really need to think about how sometimes they almost did not make it. And if they are members of more advantaged groups, they need to think about how sometimes they almost did not make it. And if they are members of more advantaged groups, they need to think about times that they should have done better but somehow did not make it; those good grades they did not get because they did not feel up to doing the work. It all seemed so overwhelming. And they need to think about helping people to grow rather than judging them. Faced with such intransigent problems and a society that calls you a brainless softie because you have that social work job—that is not always easy to remember.

*It is especially hard for John Green to keep remembering his professional values when he works with Anne Reinhard. He has read earlier editions of this book, and he has read the poem by Brown about the double whammy sensed by some white people on welfare. And yet, damn it, she's smart and young; she could go to work; and he knows there is nothing wrong with her; she is not mentally ill or anything like that.*

*He struggles to keep this discomfort from interfering. He would like to get his hands on that guy who just walked out on her, went on with his life while he left her stranded.*

*He does recognize that she needs a lot of support for the efforts at independence that she makes; perhaps she and her mother need to have a talk, get that long-simmering tension under control. God, her mother is still young enough to help take care of those kids while Anne goes to school.*

*Slowly, as he struggles with his own biases, he begins to formulate an approach to helping Anne to rethink her situation.*

*May Smith has been trying to find a program for Joan Black that could possibly help get her the training to be a computer person. But it is hard to find. And every time she works on the situation, whenever she knows that Joan is coming in, May remembers that nobody sent her to social work school. She just worked and worked; and of course she restrained herself and did not have kids and did not do all that fooling around. Does the state really owe it to her?*

*However, if we do not let her have it, we will keep paying over and over again.*

## Layer 5—The Impact of the Ethnic Reality on Daily Life in the Public Sector

We have defined the ethnic reality as "eth-class" in action. Throughout this book, we have described the class and ethnic factors that converge to generate comfort or stress at different times and for different population groups.

As a group, the young families of interest are not well regarded in American society. They are poor, many as a consequence of lacking the education and skills needed for work in our increasingly technological society. A substantial number are members of oppressed ethnic groups. Some, the recent immigrants among them, have limited knowledge of English. Some, though by no means all, have serious physical or mental problems. And a sizable number find themselves at the lower, stigmatized end of our social class spectrum at a time or in a place where there simply is not enough work to go around.

Earlier, we cited recent unemployment figures. Those are quite low at present, but nevertheless still represent a sizable number of people. For example, the unemployment rate for blacks was double that for whites in 1994 (Bennett & DeBarris, 1997). The poverty rates for blacks are distressing. Bennett and DeBarris (1997) present data to show that in 1993, one-third of all blacks were poor and that half of those were related to children under 18. Among poor persons over age 15, 35 percent of blacks work. Black women are especially disadvantaged, there being 1.5 million more black women than men among the working poor.

These findings bear on our discussion of the ethnic reality in a number of ways. First, high unemployment rates put people at risk for dropping down into welfare eligibility income levels. The poverty rates suggest that, for many people, going on welfare simply compounds the experience of living at marginal levels for extended periods of time. A sense of apathy, despair, and self-doubt can seep into people's hearts and souls, compounded by the sense of negation and stigma experienced by many of these young families. There is a high level of suspicion that the new stringent laws, the new work rules, are targeted at African American women. Opal Caples is the subject of a recent article on welfare reform (*The New York Times Magazine,* August 24, 1997):

> *"Ooo, I was mad," Opal Caples says. "They said we had to start working for our welfare check! I didn't feel it was right...And as a black woman...[she] detected a hidden agenda. No one talked about work rules in the 1930s when welfare was made for middle-class white women."... "They're just targeting the black woman."*

As we saw in Chapter 2, education is a major indicator of the potential to fare well in the labor force. Young mothers on welfare are, as a group, not well educated. About half do not have a high school diploma (U.S. Census, Mothers Who Receive AFDC). Earlier (see Chapter 2), we presented data showing continuing gaps in education levels between Blacks and Hispanics.

As we consider the impact of the ethnic reality on the two young women whose situations we have been discussing throughout this chapter, an interesting phenomenon emerges. Somehow, if you find yourself on welfare, you are "damned if you do, and damned if you don't."

> *Anne Reinhard is the daughter of one of the more high-ranking ethnic groups: German Protestants. Her people are considered to be hardworking, morally upright, and of the "right stock." And so Anne Reinhard is stigmatized for her behavior. Her parents, she herself, her caseworker, and others all puzzle over the fact that this young woman finds herself in this position. It was not expected of her; and so, somehow she has failed.*

> *Joan Black is a single, African American mother on welfare. The number of African American welfare mothers is disproportionately high. And yet, by following in her mother's footsteps, she is enacting the negative stereotypes that many of her people have. When people think in terms of these stereotypes, they tend to forget a number of the factors that account for the disproportionately high numbers of young African American women who are in the same position as Joan Black. Repeated reference has been made to some of the factors: poor education, in large matter a function of discrimination; high unemployment rates among the unskilled; a dearth of eligible men; and other factors.*

We have said often in this book that ethnicity serves as a source of cohesion and comfort, as well as a source of stress and strife. It seems that when it comes to welfare mothers, all of the negative elements come to the fore.

It is important that we learn to marshall those elements of ethnic history and pride that can serve these young women. Hines and Boyd-Franklin (1982) and English (1991) remind us of the strengths of African American families. They point to the reliance of strong kinship bonds, family support networks, and the strengths of African American women. It is these strengths that come to the fore in most circumstances, especially when allowed to flourish with some much needed supports.

German people are reluctant to claim their heritage. We have observed this in our classes as we ask students to identify themselves as members of ethnic groups when we teach the elements of ethnic-sensitive practice. Winawer-Steiner and Wetzel (1982) made the same observation. The legacy of the Holocaust leaves many German people uncomfortable about who they are.

When these matters are set aside, it is possible to identify some characteristic German features. One is what Winawer-Steiner and Wetzel (1982) termed the "polarity of emotional restraint and sentimentality" (p. 255). Neither affection nor anger is readily shown. The work ethic is highly valued. There is an emphasis on the "balance between entitlement and obligations in the household."

These characterizations explain a bit of the family's reaction to Anne Reinhard. They are supportive, but not overtly so. Anne is uncomfortable because she feels that somehow she has let them down. And perhaps one of the ways they feel that she has let them down is that she really does not work now. Perhaps as she pulls herself together and manages to get to school and work, as she will have to do given the new law, some of the unspoken tensions will diminish. Perhaps, for her, it will be better.

## Layer 6—An Understanding That the Route to the Social Worker Has an Impact on How Social Services Are Perceived and Delivered

There is little doubt that both Anne Reinhard and Joan Black got to the social worker—to the local welfare office—via coercive routes. It is clearly expected that any welfare recipient will be assigned to a case manager who may be a social worker. The case managers, or case workers as they are often called, are expected to help welfare clients through the process of getting off welfare and becoming self-sufficient. This has been true in all the states where waiver programs have been in effect and as the new law is being implemented. These responsibilities signal a major departure for past practices in which the major functions were focused on determining eligibility.

The work culture has not been conducive to these efforts. Gurwett (1997) suggests that major transformation of the approach in working with these young women is needed if welfare reform is to have a chance at success.

As families, usually young women, come in to the various offices, they do so because they must. Clearly, there is a high element of coercion. Beyond the inevitably coercive element, there is also a demeaning quality to relationships.

A series of focus groups were conducted to learn what welfare recipients believe they need to become self-sufficient (Kraft & Busch, 1996). The conveners report that, almost universally, the recipients perceived a negative attitude about their worth.

"Whether it was the caseworkers' direct treatment of recipients or the operational standards of the organization, recipients felt disrespected and demeaned by their experiences. This was complicated 'because you feel bad enough to get on welfare, and then they (caseworkers) make you feel even worse.' The recipients reported that their interactions with the caseworkers had given them an 'attitude'" (p. 26). What they describe is a reciprocal process that begins when clients view their caseworkers as nonsupportive because of the disrespect they perceive. In turn, they develop an "attitude" and, as one says, "If they're going to degrade you, then you degrade them back" (p. 27).

There are other barriers to constructive efforts at becoming self-sufficient. Language—for Latinos from Mexico and Central and South America, Russians, Haitians, all people who do not speak English—for all of them a great deal of effort is needed to surmount language and cultural barriers. Sometimes there is a fine line between constructive rules as guides to action and a coercive style that is demeaning. The former may be useful in helping people to take a much-needed step. Next, when we discuss interventive procedures, we will briefly consider some constructive approaches.

At the point when this fifth edition was being completed, the new welfare legislation had been in effect for less than a year. Virtually no systematic information on the response of the affected families has been available in the professional literature. Newspaper accounts variously report positive effects in some sites where young women are pleased to receive help in job search or training programs. There have been reports that some workers don't fare well when community service projects force women into taxing jobs, such as cleaning public bathrooms.

The results of studies carried out to measure earlier welfare reform efforts may provide some clues as to how the new legislation will work. Earlier in this chapter we reported the results of one of the more comprehensive evaluations, California's GAIN Program. For the most part, there were reports of modest gains in earnings and modest decreases in overall welfare expenditures. During the period 1993–1996, the numbers of people on welfare substantially declined. At least one group of analysts concluded, after careful investigation, that about one-third of that drop could be attributed to the various waiver programs, another third to a good economy, and the rest to other factors.

Other kinds of information provide more qualitative information (Kraft & Busch, 1996): interviews of young mothers. They found that young mothers who have been on public assistance are not resentful of the emphasis on work. This holds true for "workfare" or community service, where clients work for their welfare checks. Some are conflicted about the new approach. Opal Caples never surrenders her contention that, with the strict new work rules, something dangerous and unfair is under way. Yet, it turns out, she enjoys her work (De Parle, 1997, p. 32).

The women who met with Kraft and Busch were, in their words, "motivated to achieve self-sufficiency." Many of the women who were working through a community work experience program expressed a desire to work. Few would argue with the fact that it is not good to be on welfare. There is a convergence of poverty and of being treated coercively and disrespectfully.

Those charged with the responsibility for implementing the new law must be aware of the counterproductive effects of traditional negative approaches.

## *Layer 7—The Adaptation of Strategies and Procedures for Ethnic-Sensitive Practice in the Public Sector*

In Chapters 7, 8, and 9 we considered a number of interventive approaches. In the chapter on generalist practice, we presented the structural, or four-quadrant, simultaneity model, which identifies the range of social work intervention. These included work with individuals around their difficulties; work with groups of individuals experiencing similar difficulties; advocacy, administrative work, policy analysis, and others. In Chapter 8 we addressed the strategies of direct intervention, and in Chapter 9 key elements of macro practice were delineated.

Each of these approaches to intervention can be brought to bear on the situation of young women and their children receiving public assistance. The structural model serves to focus our attention on the integral relationship among various levels of individual functioning, societal response or failure to respond, and possible avenues for social work intervention.

When we introduced the situation of Anne Reinhard, we mentioned that she was involved with a project that was looking into developing cooperative housing as well as child-care collaboration among some mothers receiving public assistance. This kind of effort arises logically out of the model. What is suggested is that, although one-to-one supportive work with these women is clearly necessary, some problems will not be solved at the casework/counseling level. At this level of intervention, it is not possible to raise allowances to the level that makes it easier for the women to manage their rents.

Collaboration in such a group—suggested by the second quadrant in which people work together to solve common problems—can have secondary benefits beyond the hoped-for achievement of the goal: building a residence. Sharing of work and effort often leads to sharing of problems and mutual support.

Also of importance is social work effort to effect policy changes and to advocate. In the long run, the Anne Reinhards will benefit themselves and society if given some help to get the education they so sorely need to become self-sufficient.

Much of the same holds true for Joan Black and others in her situation. As the effects of the new welfare legislation become more evident, it will take macro level practice strategies to assess as well as to advocate for needed changes.

Some issues calling for advocacy and, possibly, legal action have already arisen. Among welfare change efforts, one that is particularly controversial is the Family Cap. This provision, enacted in New Jersey some years ago, limited allowances for children to those conceived before clients went on welfare. This provision is being challenged as unconstitutional in *Sojourner A. vs. The New Jersey Department of Human Services* (1997). In this legal action the plaintiffs contend as follows:

> *The Child Exclusion prevents plaintiff parents from being able to adequately feed and shelter their children, creating a severe risk to needy children's health and*

*safety. In so doing, the measure denies plaintiff children their constitutional rights to equal protection by creating an irrational classification and violates plaintiff constitutional right to privacy." (p. 46)*

In thinking about Joan Black, one needs to think beyond her to the other women in her situation: minority mothers on welfare, a stigmatized, much maligned group. Individual social work effort will go a long way in helping her as an individual to achieve her maximum potential, to help her to raise her children. The worker must work with the school and the mental health system to get help for her youngster, who has attention deficit disorder. But beyond that, social change efforts that serve to reduce those negative forces that put so many young women like Joan in the position of needing welfare are essential.

At this point in history, when, as was suggested earlier, there is a war on welfare mothers, social workers must be in the forefront of those who lobby against this move that ultimately hurts so many young children.

### Case Management

Many of the interventive modalities discussed earlier can be adapted to work with this group. Two avenues of action are envisioned. The first focus will necessarily be on helping families to cope with the new law while they maximize such opportunities as are entailed. A second aim is advocacy, monitoring, and action at the policy level to maximize its negative effects.

## SUMMARY

In this chapter we have focused on the poor, with an emphasis on that group of people commonly known as welfare mothers. The myths that burden an already burdened existence were reviewed, as were the components of the principles of ethnic-sensitive practice that can facilitate effective social work intervention.

The new welfare law needs considerable monitoring by social workers. They need to maintain ongoing vigilance to prevent even further erosion to the "safety net." The impact on the most vulnerable groups—many of them people of color— warrants special scrutiny. At the same time, the potential for positive effects—as more women take their place in the labor force—are not to be overlooked.

## REFERENCES

Atkins, C. M. (1986). 20,000 choose paycheck over welfare check. *Public Welfare, 44,* 20–22.

Bane, M. S., & Ellwood, D. (1986, Winter). Slipping into and out of poverty: the dynamics of spells. *Journal of Human Resources, 21*(1), 1–23.

Bennett, C. E., & DeBarris, K. Y. (1997). *The Black Population.* U.S. Census Bureau (May).

Brown, S. E. (1974). From "Poetic expressions of white urban family." Submitted in partial fulfillment of course requirements for The Urban Family, Rutgers University, School of Social Work, Fall.

Carrera, J. (1986). Aid to families with dependent children. In *Encyclopedia of social work* (18th ed., pp. 126–132). Silver Springs, MD: National Association of Social Workers.

Chen, Pei-Ngor. (1970). The Chinese community in Los Angeles. *Social Casework, 51,* 591–598.

Chestang, L. (1972). *Character development in a hostile environment.* Chicago: The School of Social Service Administration, The University of Chicago.

*Council of Economic Advisors Report: Explaining the Decline in Welfare Receipt, 1993–1997.* (1997). Publications.

Dear, R. B. (1989, June). What's right with welfare? The other face of AFDC. *Journal of Sociology and Social Welfare, 16*(2), 5–44.

De Parle, J. (1997). Getting Opal Caples to work. *New York Times Magazine* (August 24), p. 33.

Dickinson, N. S. (1986). Which welfare strategies work? *Social Work, 31,* 266–272.

Duncan, G. J. (Winter 1986–87). Welfare use in America. *Institute for Social Research Newsletter, 5.*

Duncan, G. S., & Hoffman, S. D. (1987). The use and effects of welfare: A survey of recent evidence. (Mimeo).

English, R. A. (1991). Diversity of world views among African American families. In S. Everett, S. Chipungu, & B. R. Leashore (Eds.), *Child Welfare: An Africentric Perspective.* New Brunswick, N.J.: Rutgers University Press.

Fact Sheet. (1997, August 12). The Personal Responsibility and Work Opportunity Reconciliation Act of 1996. Washington, DC: Department of Health and Human Services.

Federico, R. C. (1980). *The social welfare institution—an introduction.* Lexington, MA: D.C. Heath.

Finder, A. (June 3, 1990). When welfare pays the rent. *The New York Times,* p. 6.

Findings on State Welfare Employment Programs. (January 1987). New York: Manpower Demonstration Research Corporation. (Pamphlet).

Ghali, S. B. (1977). Cultural sensitivity and the Puerto Rican client. *Social Casework, 58,* 459–468.

Gibbs, N. (1994). The vicious cycle. *Time, 143*(25), 24–33.

Goodban, N. (1985). The psychological impact of being on welfare. *Social Service Review, 59,* 403–422.

Goodwin, L. (1981). Can workfare work? *Public Welfare, 39,* 19–25.

Gueron, J. M. (1987, Fall). Reforming welfare with work. *Public Welfare, 45*(4), 13–26.

Gurwitt, R. (1997, March). Cracking the casework culture. *Governing,* pp. 27–30.

Harrington, M. (1962). *The other America—poverty in the United States.* Baltimore: Penguin Books.

Harrington, M. (1984). *The new American poverty.* New York: Holt, Rinehart, & Winston.

Hines, P. M., & Boyd-Franklin, N. (1982). Black families. In M. McGoldrick, J. K. Pearce, & J. Giordano (Eds.), *Ethnicity and family therapy* (pp. 84–107). New York: The Guilford Press.

Ho, M. K. (1976). Social work with Asian Americans. *Social Casework, 57,* 195–201.

Institute for Social Research. (1987). Ann Arbor, Mich. *Into the Working World: Research findings from the Minority Female Single Parent Program.* New York: The Rockefeller Foundation.

Karger, H. J., & Stoesz, D. (1990). *American social welfare policy: a structural approach.* White Plains, NY: Longman.

Kasindorf, J. R. (1995). Welfare reform at ground zero. *New York, 28*(6), 28–35.

Katz, M. B. (1989). *The undeserving poor: From the war on poverty to the war on welfare.* New York: Pantheon Books.

Kerpen, K. S. (1983). Working with refugees. *Public Welfare, 41,* 18–22.

Kerpen, K. S. (1985). Refugees on welfare—is the dependency rate really a problem? *Public Welfare, 43,* 21–25.

Kitano, H. H. L. (1976). *Japanese American* (2nd ed.). Englewood Cliffs, NJ: Prentice-Hall.

Kraft, M. K., & Busch, I. R. (1996). *Women on Welfare: What they have to say about becoming self-sufficient.* New Brunswick, N.J.: Rutgers University Press.

Krause, C. A. (1978). *Grandmothers, mothers, and daughters: An oral history study of ethnicity, mental health, and continuity of three generations of Jewish, Italian, and Slavic-American women.* New York: American Jewish Committee.

Landers, S. (1995). Untangling welfare debates' web of myths. *NASW News,* January 1995.

Leighninger, R. D. (1989, June). Editorial. *Journal of Sociology and Social Welfare, 16*(2), 3–4.

Lemann, N. (1986). The origins of the underclass. *The Atlantic Monthly, 257,* 31–56, and *258,* 54–68.

Mass, A. I. (1976). Asians as individuals: the Japanese community. *Social Casework, 57,* 160–164.

Mauch, J. (Summer 1972). Voices never heard, faces seldom seen. *Public Welfare, 30*(3), 16–17.

Mencher, S. (1967). *Poor law to poverty—economic security policy in Britain and the United States.* Pittsburgh: University of Pittsburgh Press.

Morales, A., & Sheafor, B. (1989). *Social work—a profession of many faces* (2nd ed.). Boston: Allyn & Bacon.

Murillo, N. (1970). The Mexican-American family. In C. Hernandez, M. J. Haug, & N. N. Wagner (Eds.), *Chicano—social and psychological perspectives.* St. Louis: C. V. Mosby.

Papajohn, J., & Spiegel, J. (1975). *Transactions in families.* San Francisco: Jossey-Bass.

Patino, D. X. (1986, Winter). Finding work for the poor in Arizona—job skills are the key. *Public Welfare, 44*(1), 16–17.

Peretti, P. O. (1973, Winter). Enforced acculturation and Indian-White Relations. *The Indian Historian, 6*(1).

Petit, M. R., & Wilcox, L. A. (1986). Inestimable— but tangible—results in Maine. *Public Welfare, 44*, 13–15.

REACH Case Manager Training. (1987). *Considerations for assessment and assignment to program components.* New York: Manpower Demonstration Research Corporation (Mimeo).

REACH Regulations. July 25, 1989. New Jersey Department of Human Services.

Reich, R. (1983). *The next American frontier.* New York: Time Books.

Rein, M. (1972). Work incentives and welfare reform. *Urban and Social Change Review, 5*, 54–58.

Riccio, J., & Friedlander, D. (1992). GAIN. New York: Manpower Demonstration Research Center.

Rochefort, D. A. (1988). Toward a work-oriented welfare system: New Jersey's REACH Program. (Mimeo).

Rodgers, H. R. (1982). *The cost of human neglect.* Armonk, NY: M. E. Sharpe.

Rodgers, H. R. (1986). Poor women, poor families: the economic plight of America's female-headed households. Armonk, NY: M. E. Sharpe.

Rofuth, T. W. (1987). Moving clients into jobs. *Public Welfare, 45*(2), 10–21.

Rothenberg, R. (1984). *The neoliberals.* New York: Simon & Schuster.

Rubin, A. (1986). Case management. In *Encyclopedia of social work* (18th ed., pp. 212–222). Silver Spring, MD: National Association of Social Workers.

Ryan, A. S. (1985). Cultural factors in casework with Chinese-Americans. *Social Casework, 66,* 333–340.

Sermabeikian, P. (1975). What's so bad about being poor? In *A little piece of the world.* Submitted in partial fulfillment of course requirements for the urban family, Rutgers University, School of Social Work. Fall.

Sklar, M. H. (1986). Workfare: Is the honeymoon over—or yet to come? *Public Welfare, 44,* 30–32.

Staff. (1986/1987). *Institute for social research newsletter.* Ann Arbor, MI: University of Michigan.

Stoesz, D., & Karger, H. J. (1990, March). Welfare reform: from illusion to reality. *Journal of the National Association of Social Workers, 35*(2), 141–148.

Swoap, D. B. (1986). Broad support buoys California's GAIN. *Public Welfare, 44,* 24–27.

*Time.* (August 29, 1977). The American underclass.

Weil, M., & Karls, J. M. (1985). *Case Management in Human Service Practice.* San Francisco, CA: Jossey-Bass.

Welfare Reform Demonstrations (1996) from the World Wide Web.

Wider Opportunities for Women. (1989, June). *Literacy and the marketplace: Improving the literacy of low-income single mothers.* New York: The Rockefeller Foundation. Report on a conference.

Wilensky, H. L., & Lebeaux, C. N. (1958). *Industrial society and social welfare.* New York: Russell Sage Foundation.

Willie, C. V. (1974). The Black family and social class. *American Journal of Orthopsychiatry, 44,* 50–60.

Wilson, W. J. (1987). *The truly disadvantaged: the inner city, the underclass, and public policy.* Chicago, IL: The University of Chicago Press.

Winawer-Steiner, H., & Wetzel, N. A. (1982). German families. In M. McGoldrick, J. K. Pearce, & J. Giordano (Eds.), *Ethnicity and family therapy,* (pp. 247–268).

Work and Welfare. (1988, January). *U.S. general accounting office, analysis of AFDC employment programs in four states.* Fact sheet for the Committee on Finance U.S. Senate.

Zippay, A. (1993). Welfare reform. Presented at the First Forum on Welfare Reform. Sponsored by School of Social Work, Rutgers University Alumni Association and National Association of Social Workers. New Jersey Chapter.

# 13

# ETHNIC-SENSITIVE PRACTICE IN HEALTH CARE

This chapter reviews the health problems before us and integrates them with key elements of ethnic-sensitive practice. It presents concepts of health and illness as well as health policies, especially as they relate to the ethnic reality. Case examples illustrate the principles of ethnic-sensitive social work in health care.

### Marie St. Claire

*This 25-year-old Haitian woman was referred to the social worker at a local hospital on the Eastern shore of the United States because she seemed to be behaving somewhat strangely after undergoing a mastectomy for breast cancer. She speaks no English, only French. The medical staff wanted to be sure that she would be all right when the time came for her discharge. No one had been able to communicate with her after the surgery. A man, also Haitian, had brought her to the hospital. He spoke some English. However, since the surgery he had not been seen. Marie St. Claire was assigned to a French-speaking social worker.*

*Now 25 years old, this woman came to the United States without a visa from Haiti several years ago. Her status is that of an illegal immigrant.*

*On meeting with Marie, the worker learned that Marie had come to the United States mainly to be with her boyfriend, Jacques, who had come a year or two before that and had promised to send for her. Work was increasingly hard to find. She left two children, ages 3 and 5, with her mother, expecting that as soon as she had her immigration status straightened out she would send for them.*

*She and Jacques live in a small apartment. He is erratically employed as a janitor. She works in a restaurant run by Haitians in the community where they live. There are substantial numbers of Haitian people in this community.*

*Things had been going pretty well until she found this lump in her breast. She found a French-speaking doctor who told her she needed to go to the hospital. She barely understood what was happening to her; they took off her breast. She was distressed about this; but what seemed to distress her even more is that Jacques had stopped coming by after he learned about her surgery.*

*Another thing she did not understand is why the nurses kept covering her up. She is most comfortable when the breast is uncovered. The nurses did not seem to want her to do that.*

### Norman Sankowitchia

*Norman is a 65-year-old man of Czechoslovakian descent. He is in the terminal stages of cancer of the pancreas and is expected to die shortly. He is in a freestanding hospice. His wife Jean was referred to Cancer Care for counseling because she seemed to be experiencing a great deal of guilt about having agreed to have him admitted to the hospice rather than having him at home.*

*Norman and Jean have been married for close to 35 years. They have two grown children. One daughter, married with one child, lives nearby, and a single son lives in a community at some distance.*

*The situation was referred to a local office of a cancer care organization in the Midwest. The referral was made because Jean felt extremely guilty about having sent him to the hospice.*

*After some surgery, Norman was discharged to his home, where Jean took care of him. Although he was quite ill, she refused any home health visits.*

*He remained very difficult to care for. As he got more sick, uncomfortable, and occasionally disoriented, he also became verbally and physically abusive.*

*Jean, knowing he was going to die, was reluctant to have him institutionalized. But his behavior was taking its toll. She agreed to have him sent to the hospice.*

In this chapter, the focus is on social work in health care. We follow the pattern established in previous chapters. The layers of understanding for ethnic-sensitive social work practice provide the framework for analysis of knowledge, theory, policy, and practice issues. The situations of Marie St. Claire and Norman Sankowitchia are drawn upon to aid in illustrating a series of concepts and strategies. Health care is a vast and complex area. Consequently, several other case situations are introduced in some detail as we consider several problem areas.

Social work's involvement in health care has a long and honorable history. It has been suggested that the roots of social medicine, medicine that looks beyond the diseased body to the social antecedents and consequences of illness, are to be found in social work in health care (Rosen, 1974).

*Medical social work,* a term more commonly used in the past than in the present, was introduced at the turn of the century by Dr. Richard Cabot (1915). Well ahead of his time, Cabot early recognized the importance of the social components of illness. He identified work pressures, political organization, and inadequate income as factors that affect health and illness. A man of vision, he understood well before others the complexity and depersonalization of modern health care as it was emerging in the United States. In 1905 he invited Ida Cannon to begin a social work department at Massachusetts General Hospital. Cabot looked to social work to help identify and intervene in those social factors that were behind individual suffering.

Since those early beginnings, dramatic changes have taken place in the health problems confronting the United States and other industrialized nations and in the way health care is delivered, organized, and financed. Health care has become more complex, more specialized, and more fragmented. Unprecedented advances in technology hold out hope for cure and relief of distress. Advances in medicine and public health have contributed to longevity. But cures are nevertheless elusive. Many people survive major illness with varying degrees of disability and require extensive assistance with many aspects of daily living. The specialization that accompanies technology intensifies the likelihood that many health care providers will focus their energies on diseased organs, having limited training and time to look beyond that organ at the person suffering from the disease. Psychosocial problems often precede, accompany, or follow illness. Health-care social work is focused on these concerns as well as on issues of access and equity in health care. Issues concerning access are paramount at a time such as now when managed care is growing. The extent to which this mode of financing and organization facilitates or hampers access is not yet clear.

## THE LAYERS OF UNDERSTANDING

### Social Work Values

Social work values have profound importance for the social worker in health care who is constantly in a position to consider issues within a values framework. The importance of self-determination comes up over and over again as social workers help the most profoundly debilitated and disabled people to participate in decision making concerning their care, as well as those that involve the very continuance of life. Vulnerable, ill people are often totally dependent on available resources. Advocating for health-care resources is a constant concern for social workers in the United States. The United States has the dubious distinction of being in the same category as South Africa by not having a system of health insurance that is accessible to all regardless of ability to pay. Important also is the intrinsic value placed on human beings and their capacity to grow.

Ethical issues loom large as more and more people question the prolonging of life when people are barely if at all conscious or are in other ways not able to function. The value system will serve the social workers who work in this arena.

> *The situation facing Ellen Brown, the worker who works with Norman Sankowitchia, is instructive. Mr. Sankowitchia is quite ill and dying. But Ellen Brown has spoken with his wife, who needs help in confronting her guilt about letting him be admitted to a hospice.*
>
> *Ellen Brown finds it hard to contain her anger at this man. For years, Mrs. Sankowitchia put up with verbal and some physical abuse. When he became ill, this got worse and worse. It is not easy to maintain a sense of respect and regard for all people. Some of them just do not deserve it. Social work or no.*
>
> *But she keeps talking to herself. And she realizes that he is a man from a different place and a different time. She has to help Mrs. Sankowitchia through a difficult period. Getting angry at him will not help in carrying out her task.*

## Self-Awareness, Including Insight into One's Own Ethnicity and an Understanding of How That May Influence Professional Practice

In an earlier chapter we pointed out that the disciplined and aware self remains one of the profession's major tools. The ability to be nonjudgmental, to reach out, and to make use of self-awareness to help others to cope is essential. In health care, self-awareness is focused on understanding one's own feelings about physical disability, pain, emotional turmoil, disfigurement, the changes in quality of life engendered by much illness, and death itself. Also important is a sense of professional identity, for health-care social work is an interdisciplinary endeavor that inevitably challenges the social worker's sense of identity and competence.

> *Marianne Dupres, the social worker assigned to work with Marie St. Claire, is herself Haitian. However, she comes from an educated, upper-class family. Her background and experience are different from that of Marie.*
>
> *She knows intellectually that young women often need to leave their children behind, that there is a lot of poverty in her country. But she has a difficult time with her response to Marie. She realizes that she really is uncomfortable about the fact that Marie left her children in Haiti. How could a mother do that. O.K. She knows about the political turmoil, and the unemployment and all that. But she does find it hard.*

> *Ellen Brown is a young Englishwoman. She understands that it is not easy for Mrs. Sankowitchia to discuss her feelings about the present situation; her husband's impending death, their difficult life together.*

As we consider the various people whose situations we have and will be presenting in this discussion of health-care social work, we need to remember that each of the workers will need to struggle with themselves as they try to reach out to the people confronting them. If they are members of the same ethnic group as the client, they will need to reach into their own background as a way of understanding. They will need to guard against a defensiveness or a stance that says, "I did it, why can't you." If they are members of another group—as is often the case— they will need to draw on those elements of their own experience as members of ethnic groups to recognize the powerful impact of ethnicity in matters of life, death, and severe turmoil.

## The Health Problems before Us: Theories, Concepts, Issues

In this section we consider the major types of health problems that confront the people of the United States. In considering these it is important to begin with some historical notes on the development of public health and medical technology.

## Public Health

Public health approaches cut across the work of a variety of health-care workers and are an essential component of social work's history and perspective in health care. Public health is focused on the prevention of disease and promoting health. The importance of the availability of comprehensive health care is also stressed.

Public health efforts can in part be traced to the beginnings of industrialization and urbanization. These processes were accompanied by the arrival of large numbers of diverse people into the cities, where they were often crowded into inadequate housing and worked many hours under less than optimal sanitary conditions. In the beginning, these efforts were focused on contaminated water supplies and on fast-spreading infectious diseases. Early on, it became evident that social factors were implicated in public health problems. As a number of social factors served to improve living and working conditions, there were dramatic reductions in some of the diseases and deaths associated with the early problems of urbanization. It has been suggested that the decline in infant mortality rates and in some of the infectious diseases predates modern medical discoveries and can be attributed to improvements in working and housing conditions. Early in the twentieth century social workers were involved in work to prevent tuberculosis, infant mortality, rickets, and scurvy. A public health perspective remains an important component of health care social work practice.

An important public health concept relates to populations at risk, that is, those population groups especially likely to develop certain health problems. Those with special responsibilities for reducing the health problems that beset many members of minority groups find the concept and related strategies most useful. This and other public health perspectives continue to play an important part in promoting the public health.

### The Case of Mrs. Green

*Mrs. Green, a 40-year-old, African American woman who has hypertension and is obese is told she must take her antihypertensive drugs regularly. She is also advised to reduce her salt intake and to lose weight. She feels healthy and is employed at night as a nurse's aide. Her husband takes over with their three children when she goes to work. A review of her dietary habits indicates that, in her hectic schedule, one of Mrs. Green's great pleasures is to stop at the local fast food store for hamburgers, French fries, and soft drinks. She also snacks a lot on the job.*

*Weekends are happily spent with gatherings of the family, to which all bring food.*

*As a nurse's aide, Mrs. Green sees many sick people; she has little trouble understanding the consequences of her disease and takes her medication regularly. But she fears that losing weight and reducing salt intake will take a lot of the pleasure out of her life. "What am I going to do?" she asks the social worker, in a half-joking, half-dejected manner.*

*Together she and the social worker arrive at an idea. A lot of people in this community eat at the fast food store. How about asking them to reduce the salt used in cooking their food? And what about a family discussion concerning the weekend*

*get-togethers? For Mrs. Green has discovered that many of her friends and rela-*
*tives also have hypertension.*

*This situation illustrates that efforts to alter dysfunctional health behaviors,*
*especially those that arise from immersion in long-standing habits and customs*
*from which people derive comfort, must often involve individual as well as com-*
*munity and systems efforts.*

### Medical Technology

Most people are familiar with the dramatic technological advances that recently
have been made in medicine. The list is long and includes improvement of surgical
techniques and anesthetic procedures, the discovery of antibiotics, renal dialysis,
transplants, the use of lasers for many kinds of surgery, and the development of
psychotropic drugs that have been instrumental in effecting a dramatic reduction
in the symptoms experienced by people with severe chronic mental illness. Also
important is the development of neonatal intensive care units and other technologies that save the lives of premature and other fragile infants.

Effective use of technological breakthroughs requires extensive, specialized
training. Each provider tends to become an expert at diseases of an organ or a part
of an organ. Often the whole person gets lost among a series of highly specialized
health-care providers who have limited knowledge or interest in the whole person.
Such specialization tends to lead to fragmented care, which causes people difficulty.
This is especially true for elderly people, people who are poor, and people whose
understanding is limited. Recent immigrants may not understand the health-care
system, may have limited if any command of English, and may have come from a
society with a different set of health beliefs and practices.

Data on the health of children fall into the same kind of pattern. The Children's
Defense Fund (Hughes, Johnson, Rosenbaum, & Liu, 1989) data point to the following highlights: (1) poor children are 36 percent less likely to be considered in good
health; (2) poor children are more likely to suffer from lead poisoning; (3) poor children are less likely to be immunized than children from more affluent homes; and
(4) African American children die four times as often as white children from prematurity. In 1994 the Children's Defense Fund continued its analysis of the state of U.S.
children, stressing the need to find ways to reduce violence and adolescent pregnancy and strengthen family life (Children's Defense Fund, 1994).

Efforts are ongoing to trace the mechanisms involved in the relationship between
infant and child health and poverty and minority status. A great deal remains to be
known. But some matters are clear. They relate to the impact of certain policy initia-
tives on these kinds of health indicators. Starfield (1989) pointed out that mothers
who participate in the WIC (Women, Infants and Children Nutrition Program) program have fewer premature infants. Prematurity, of course, is one of the leading
causes of infant mortality. Other programs have historically been shown to have a
positive impact on the infant mortality rate. These are Medicaid, Social Security, and
a number of special programs devoted to maternal and child health.

The implications of these data for the ethnic-sensitive social worker are clear.
At the individual level there is an obligation to help to refer mothers at risk to those

programs known to increase child health. At the same time, there is an obligation to be ever vigilant at the systemic level via organizations such as the National Association of Social Workers, the Association of Black Social Workers, and others in a position to attempt to affect policy directions.

**The Health of Minorities.**    The situation with respect to the health care of minority groups in the United States is as discouraging as the situation with respect to infant mortality and child health.

In most areas of health, members of minority groups fare badly when compared with other groups. This is true for most major health problems. The Office of Minority Health of the Public Health Service of the U.S. Department of Health and Human Services publishes a newsletter, *Closing the Gap*. A recent (undated) series of these newsletters discussed some of the areas in which minorities are at greater risk than others: diabetes, cancer, heart disease, stroke, homicide, suicide, and chemical dependency (U.S. Dept. of Health and Human Services, no date).

The reasons for these major disparities are not completely clear. Whatever genetic factors are involved, it is clear that the excess in deaths and illness is related to deprivation, to relative difficulties in getting access to health care, and to discomfort in using the health-care system.

Another set of problems arises with respect to some of the newer immigrant groups. Zane, Takeuchi, and Young (1994) pointed to the development of certain problems that appear to be related to acculturation. One example is the development of obesity and rates of diabetes among Asian Pacific Americans. These rates begin to approach those of African American men, which are quite high. The increases appear to be associated with the adoption of Western lifestyles (Crews, 1994).

Ethnic-sensitive social workers have an obligation to familiarize themselves with both the morbidity and mortality rates prevalent for the populations with which they work and with the interventive strategies that have been documented or are thought to be useful. A few examples will highlight these issues. African American women have the highest death rates related to diabetes. Many people with diabetes can control the course of the disease with adequate diet and, if necessary, with medication. Clearly, outreach programs need to be developed to help these women cope with their disease. Hypertension, which puts people at risk for heart disease and stroke, is especially prevalent in the African American community among its men. Hypertension too responds to medication, diet, and exercise. The situation of Mrs. Green, whose case was presented earlier, is an example of the kind of effort that can be undertaken. Social workers need to, and have, joined with the medical care system and with community-based organizations such as churches to engage in a hypertension reduction program. Asthma has become endemic in a number of Latino communities (Corn, Hamrung, Ellis, Kalb, & Sperber, 1995).

Many Asian Americans are at special risk for a number of health problems. Japanese American men are at particular risk for strokes, American Indians have a greater risk for alcoholism and related problems, and Hawaiians smoke excessively. Each of these groups has distinct cultural habits that may contribute to these problems. Some are clearly behavioral, such as smoking and drinking. Approaches for prevention involve simultaneous attention to individual need and systemic efforts to reduce the problem.

### Alcoholism

#### Jose Montero

*Jose is a 35-year-old Mexican American man. He is a college graduate who works for a large bus company and is responsible for the routing and general running of buses servicing a large geographic area.*

*For the past several years Jose has had difficulty controlling his drinking. He has also taken to having a few snorts of cocaine with buddies on the job.*

*His wife has left him and taken their 3-year-old daughter, the apple of his eye. He has also received some warnings on the job, as managers have noted some lateness. On one or two occasions it seemed that he came to the office after having had too much to drink.*

*He has been warned by management and advised to seek the services of a counselor who is provided via the company's Employee Assistance Program.*

Anderson (1995) presented basic information on alcoholism. An estimated 10 million Americans are considered heavy drinkers, according to recent national household surveys on drug abuse. In an earlier work, Anderson (1986) reported that the rates are higher for Catholics, Protestants, and people reporting no religious affiliation. Rates for Jews then low, are now increasing. There are a number of subgroups of the population whose alcohol use is of special concern. A significant number of the elderly are alcoholic (about 10 percent). Among minority groups, those most seriously affected by alcoholism are American Indians. African American women are more likely to drink heavily than are white women. However, overall alcoholism rates among African Americans are below those for Latinos and most white groups. A study of alcohol use among Latino groups in the United States compared Mexican Americans, Puerto Ricans, and Cubans (Caetano, 1988). Of the three groups, Mexican Americans were found to drink more and to have more problems than either of the other groups.

The drinking patterns of other ethnic groups have received some attention. Zane and Kim (1994) suggested that Asian Americans abuse drugs and alcohol at lesser rates than do other minority groups. However, these authors suggest that much further research into these problems is needed. Some analysts have given attention to prevention.

With some exceptions, minority communities are at a disadvantage in respect to alcohol problems. Researchers are attempting to understand the dynamics by which factors such as the nature of the original encounter with American society, cultural dispositions, and experiences in the host society converge to minimize or exacerbate the likelihood of drinking problems.

### Drug Abuse

Gray (1995) pointed out that it is extremely difficult to define *drug abuse*. Some definitions and data on use are offered. She suggests there are many dimensions to drug use and abuse, which is a term used when the involved persons are using substances in a way that is detrimental to various aspects of their lives. There are various ways to think about drug or substance abuse, including a social framework, a pharmacological framework, and a mental disorders framework. There is a tendency to interchange the terms *drug abuse* and *substance abuse.*[1]

Accurate data on drug dependence are difficult to obtain. Gray (1995) suggests that one can consider data on drug use by looking at the overall rate of illicit drug use, by examining age differences, and by comparing people of different sexual orientation or mental illness status.

The lifetime and recent prevalence of dependence on illicit drugs were, by age, as follows: 17 percent for those ages 18 to 29, 4 percent for those between 30 and 59, and less than 1 percent for those over 60. A number of psychosocial factors, including discrimination, put gays and lesbians at risk for substance abuse, and there are some suggestions that the rates are higher than for the population as a whole within these groups.

A somewhat complex situation exists in respect to substance abuse by various ethnic groups, especially oppressed minorities. Taken as a whole, fewer African Americans than whites or Latinos abuse drugs. In the drug-using group over 35, however, African Americans are more likely than whites or Latinos to use drugs. As a result, drug use is among the leading health and social problems in African American communities.

Latina women tend to use fewer drugs than Latina men, though this may be changing as women become more involved in mainstream life in the United States. Some drugs are part of the various American Indian cultures; indeed, some hallucinogens, such as mescaline used in religious ceremonies, have been exempt from some legal prohibitions against drug use. Limited information is available about the use of substances in the Asian communities.

Clearly, drug-related problems—especially those found in African American communities—are of special concern to social workers and warrant special attention from ethnic-sensitive practitioners. The negative effects of drug abuse hardly require detailed delineation.

### Acquired Immune Deficiency Syndrome (AIDS)

AIDS is a modern, if not postmodern, epidemic with far-reaching ramifications of a biomedical, public health, psychosocial, cultural, legal, ethical, political, and economic nature (Appel & Abramson, 1989). It is a growing phenomenon, the dimensions of which are still not fully understood. The social and economic costs are extremely high because people with the disease require extensive care. Progress has been made in finding medication that seems to prolong life, although this finding too is questioned. The medication is costly, as are other elements of treatment. As is the case with so many other health problems, this disease is also highly

---

[1]Much of the material in this section has been abstracted from Gray, Muriel D. Drug abuse. In *Encyclopedia of Social Work* 19th ed., 1995. Washington, DC: National Association of Social Workers, pp. 795–803.

related to poverty and the oppression of racism. Yankauer refers to the three plagues: poverty, drug addiction, and AIDS.

AIDS is a severe, contagious, virus-caused disease that used to lead automatically to death. Major breakthroughs in drug therapy now suggest that it can now be considered a chronic disease. It destroys a good portion of the body's immune system. Three major routes of acquiring the disease have been identified, all involving the sharing of bodily fluids: sexual relationships; needle sharing, as in drug use; and transfusion by blood infected with the virus.

Between June 1981 and June 1994 the Centers for Disease Control reported that 401,749 people had been diagnosed with AIDS. Of that number, 240,323 had died. World wide 12.9 million had been infected with HIV by 1992. It is expected that by the year 2000 38 million adults will become infected. Others project the likelihood of much higher numbers of people being infected (Taylor-Brown, 1995). As is so often the case, minority groups are overrepresented. Fifty-three percent of people with HIV disease are gay men, 33 percent are African American, and 20 percent are Hispanic. The majority of women and children with HIV are African American or Hispanic.

Taylor-Brown (1995) stressed the importance of viewing AIDS as a chronic infectious disease that is a social illness with global impact. Some studies of the situation among Asian and Pacific Island populations show that although the dimensions of the problem are relatively small, there have been substantial increases. Gock (1994) showed that the rate parallels that of other racial and ethnic minority groups. In those areas of the country where there are large concentrations of Asian Pacific Americans, the incidence of AIDS was reported as doubling every 10 months. This suggests that preventive strategies as well as further study is in order. Once again, the United States's most disadvantaged groups are at substantial risk for one of the more devastating health problems that the world has experienced in recent times. Considerable work is being done to develop strategies for AIDS prevention, especially with vulnerable minority groups.

### The Elderly

In beginning this discussion of the population of elderly people, it should be stated that *the elderly* are not viewed as a problem in the same sense as the health problems discussed in the preceding sections. However, a discussion of the elderly is appropriate in this section because this segment of the population has extensive needs for health care.

The technological and public health progress reported in the beginning of this chapter is related to the increase in the population of the elderly. Hooyman and Kiyak (1988) present some important data. In 1900 only 4 percent of Americans were over age 65. By 1985 that figure had climbed to almost 8 percent. Fewer deaths from acute illness as well as a reduction in infant mortality rates have contributed to the longevity of an increasing segment of the population. There are proportionately fewer elderly minority people in the population than there are younger people. By 1984, 13 percent of whites, but only 8 percent of African Americans, 5 percent of Hispanics, and 6 percent of Asians were over 65. The differences are related to the higher fertility and the higher mortality rates in the minority population.

More minority elderly than other elderly are living below the poverty level. The Hispanic elderly report many health problems and yet high rates of life satisfaction (Hooyman & Kiyak, 1988).

Many elderly, especially American Indians and Asian Americans, find themselves caught between conflicting cultural precepts about their status. Whereas these cultures had traditionally placed great value on the elderly, respected their wisdom, and found a place for them in society, acculturation processes have diminished these traditions. Young people are likely to leave the extended family, and older people become isolated, lonely, and confused about the new state of affairs.

For some time it has been thought that many of the ethnic elderly—those of European origins as well as Hispanics, Asians, American Indians, and others—could expect substantial support from their families and extended support networks. Markides and Mindel (1987) make a comprehensive analysis of family structure and support relationships among African Americans, Hispanics, Native Americans, Japanese, Chinese, and those of European origins. They conclude that this is essentially still the case. Among African Americans, kin serve as a strong support system, frequently beyond the confines of the nuclear family. Data bear out the notion that Hispanics "take care of their own." This does not mean that there are no changes. As an example, Markides and Mindel suggested that the family will not always be able to support or care for the elderly within its confines. And so, an increasing number will probably need to spend their waning years in an institution hardly known in their countries of origin or in their earlier days: the nursing home.

Considerable effort has been made to explore alternative ways of providing care to the elderly (U.S. Department of Health and Human Services, 1985). Many of the elderly, although requiring medical care, are in as great or greater need of supportive care so that they can remain in their own homes or with their families. They need help with shopping, housework, and some of the activities of daily living. Above all, limited in their mobility and often isolated and afraid, they need ways of socializing. Ethnic communities, as Markides and Mindel (1987) suggested, provide extensive support to the elderly.

Mechanic (1978) made a succinct statement on the issues confronting the elderly:

> *While aging is experienced as a personal crisis, it is largely socially caused. Since it is unlikely that we have the capacity or will to set back social trends, remedies must lie in developing group solutions that build the resources, coping capacities, supports and involvement of the aged. While the United States invests vast resources in the medical care of the aged, these are devoted almost exclusively to staving off the infirmities and disabilities of old age or to long-term institutional care. Only meager resources are invested to maintain the social integration of the aged, to protect them from loneliness and inactivity, to insure adequate nutrition, or to assist them in retaining a respectable identity.*

## Health Policies, Organization, and Financing

In the introductory comments to this chapter we noted that the United States is the only major industrialized nation that does not have some kind of comprehensive system of national health insurance or other ways of assuring access to care to all regardless of ability to pay. Many had hoped that with the support of President Clinton, Congress would pass a national health bill in 1994. That did not come to pass.

Some important health legislation has been enacted. The Balanced Budget Act of 1997 (Public Law 105–33) commits spending $24 billion over five years for children's health. New funding enabling states to expand coverage under Medicaid to provide health insurance for children under a newly created title XXI of the Social Security Act is also being provided.

Financing for health care in the United States involves a variety of private and public mechanisms. The sources of funding continues to be complex, ranging from voluntary contributions, to such publicly sponsored programs as Medicare and Medicaid, to reimbursement through private insurance carriers (e.g., Blue Cross/ Blue Shield, Major Medical).

## Managed Care

One of the most significant changes in health-care organization and financing has taken place during the past five to ten years. This is commonly referred to as *managed care.* There is consensus that this movement grew as a result of escalating health-care costs. There are many definitions of managed care, as well as considerable variation in the particular organization and payment structure entailed.

The primary intent of managed care is to limit unnecessary health service use by altering treatment processes in ways that include budget restriction, utilization controls, incentives for limiting service, and a major role for primary caregivers in controlling access to more costly specialized services. It is estimated that by the year 2000, 90 percent of private medical benefits will be administered by managed care organizations (Berkman, 1996).

Managed care organizations are operated by insurance companies, hospitals, corporations, and others. A number of options include Health Maintenance Organizations, traditional fee-for-service options with tightly regulated payment schedules, and others.

Much worry surrounds how this new, "bottom line" cost-conscious approach would affect health-care access generally and, especially, those already underserved and poorly served vulnerable groups, including oppressed minority groups. Computer searches revealed limited information about the effects to date on specific population groups. There are some signs. One possibly positive effect is that many states now require Medicaid recipients to enroll in managed care associations. Though concerns were and remain about this as a coercive measure, people on Medicaid have found access that had heretofore been denied. Managed care companies pay providers the same amount regardless of who foots the bills. Under the traditional Medicaid system, many health care providers barred Medicaid patients because of low reimbursement rates.

Thought is being given to bringing knowledge about the specific health problems of various groups to bear on planning efforts. Examples of what this type of "population based" planning might accomplish have been suggested. Lavizzo-Mourey and Mackenzie (1997) writing in the *Annals of Internal Medicine,* a highly respected medical journal, published an important article entitled, "Cultural competence: Essential measurement of quality for managed care organizations" and make a number of suggestions that are applicable to our work. They suggest that managed care organizations must become "culturally competent" and that the concept of "cultural competence" generates measures for high-quality care. For example, many Latinos, especially children, are at special risk for asthma and its negative sequelae (e.g., Corn et al., 1995; Pachter, et al., 1995; Olopade et al., 1997). Special outreach and treatment are required. Given the bottom line on costs, we must, for example, use cost data showing that untended asthma reduces work days, increases the use of health-care services, as well as generating discomfort.

Similar suggestions are made for other health problems. It is known, for example, that many low-income pregnant women do not seek early and consistent medical care. Strategies focused on this issue are important. Ethnic-sensitive strategies to help African American women especially vulnerable to diabetes (Zaldivar & Smolowitz, 1994) control their diet and other lifestyle matters are additional examples.

Health care continues to be provided in a variety of organizations. There is a thrust toward greater community care, with a decline in the centrality of the acute care hospital. There is more emphasis on care in the home, in assisted living facilities, in nursing homes, and in a variety of group living situations for people with pronounced physical disabilities and those with serious mental health difficulties.

A major need exists for expansion of home-based health services. Many people, especially many of the elderly, can manage on their own if someone can shop, help to clean, and help with some difficult self-care tasks.

Health care is provided in a variety of organizations and contexts. However, any reader of the daily papers knows that the merger movement has affected health care. Groups of physicians are merging with each other, with hospitals, and in other ways, joining together in larger and larger units.

Over the years, efforts have been made to create health-care structures that would be especially responsive to the needs of vulnerable persons. Among these were neighborhood health centers, primarily designed to serve the poor. Hospitals vary in complexity, function, and auspice. They range from the large university-affiliated research centers to community hospitals.

There is no question that the poor and many members of minority groups suffer from comparatively limited availability of and accessibility to services.

### Mrs. Owens

*Mrs. Owens, an African American childless widow in her early 70s, lives with a widowed sister. She and her husband had been accustomed to a comfortable working-class lifestyle. She has a small pension and, although eligible for health services under Medicare because of her age, her income does not make her eligible for services available to Medicaid recipients.*

*Mrs. Owens has hypertension, arteriosclerotic heart disease, and mild diabetes. Although able to perform minor chores, she tires easily and can no longer shop for herself. Her sister, somewhat younger than Mrs. Owens, is also frail but con-*

*tinues to do domestic work several times a week. Some nieces and nephews who used to live nearby helped out by taking the women shopping and to church. Now, they have moved.*

*Mrs. Owens's medical condition is not considered acute. She has not been hospitalized. This disqualifies her from receiving regular homemaker services under the Medicare program.*

*On her regular visits to the hospital outpatient clinic, she shares with the social worker her concern about needing some help at home. Unable to locate a source of funding for ongoing home health services, the social worker asks whether Mrs. Owens would consider going to live in a home for the aged. Mrs. Owens vigorously rejects this suggestion.*

*These families suffer because of the organization of the health-care system, in addition to the health problems that beset them.*

Several possible public and community planning efforts come to mind. The African American churches often provide services to their congregants. Perhaps an outreach effort would help Mrs. Owens and others like her. In some states, medical waiver programs have made home-care programs available.

Medical specialization is extensive. There are more than twenty-two approved medical specialties (Mechanic, 1978). In addition, there are also nurses, physiotherapists, social workers, technicians, physicians' assistants, and many others working within these specialties. The availability of folk healers has already been noted.

Negotiation of this complex, fragmented system, in which the availability and quality of care is in no small measure related to residence, social class, and ethnicity, can be highly problematic. The high technology treatments for cancer, heart disease, and AIDS are very costly and often beyond the means of poor and middle-class people.

The ramifications of the dramatic changes being felt throughout the health-care system are beyond the purview of this book. They are, however, of concern to ethnic-sensitive social workers who watch these developments with an eye toward protecting the care of frail, vulnerable children, minority persons, those with AIDS, and others with health problems.

## Health and Illness Behavior

With few exceptions, all groups and societies view illness as a negative phenomenon. Whether illness is perceived in purely physical terms (as pain and injury) or at an emotional level (as in the case of extreme anxiety, depression, or disorientation), illness involves discomfort and disruption. When people are sick, they are usually totally or partially unable to go about their daily business.

Illness behavior has been defined as the "varying perceptions, thoughts, feelings and acts affecting the personal and social meaning of symptoms, illness, disabilities and their consequences" (Mechanic, 1977, p.79). The relevance of these conceptions for social work practice in health care are illustrated by the cases presented earlier.

*Marie St. Claire does the thing that comes naturally when she is uncomfortable. She engages in behavior that is considered quite appropriate where she comes from. That is, she uncovers her sore wound. In the United States this behavior, which involves uncovering the breast, is considered prurient.*

*Jean Sankowitchia is extremely distressed. All of her instincts tell her that you take care of your own at home and you let them die at home, not in an institution. Circumstances have forced her to depart from accustomed ways of doing things, and she needs counseling, another thing that is alien to the way of coping that her people have developed.*

### Ethnicity and Health and Illness Behavior

It has been suggested that "culture exerts its most fundamental and far-reaching influence through the categories we employ to understand and respond to sickness" (Kleinman, 1978). Considerable evidence exists to support this assertion. Differences between Western and traditional precepts may be profound.

In some groups people are expected to be stoic when experiencing pain (Zborowski, 1952). In others, distress is vigorously expressed. A set of symptoms—which may consist of tearing one's clothing off in public, screaming, and falling into a semiconscious state while twitching—is considered a culturally recognized cry for help when people are experiencing a lot of strain. This set of symptoms, described as an *ataque*, is not uncommon among Puerto Ricans on the mainland (Garrison, 1977; Guarnaccia, 1993; Oquendo, Horvath, & Martinez, 1992). Mechanic (1978) suggested that "illness, illness behavior and reaction to the ill are aspects of an adaptive social process in which participants are often actively striving to meet their social roles and responsibilities, to control their environment, and to make their everyday circumstances less uncertain and, therefore, more tolerable and predictable."

Italians are said to be particularly concerned with the immediate relief of discomfort (Zborowski, 1952). Many American Indians attribute disease to a variety of extrahuman forces that must be dealt with if the causes of the illness are to be removed (Attneave, 1982; Coulehan, 1980). Analogous beliefs are held by many Hispanics (Garrison, 1977; Samora, 1978; Stenger-Castro, 1978; Mayers, 1993).

The problems of all of the people just described can be diagnosed and understood in varying terms. *Ataques* are variously diagnosed as schizophrenia, as the function of being possessed, and as hysteria (Garrison, 1977). The examples cited suggest that they must be viewed within the cultural context of people's lives. An understanding of the interplay between ethnically derived attitudes toward health and illness and biopsychosocial factors are critical to accurate assessment and intervention. Social workers who view folk ministrations as "mumbo jumbo" or, even worse, who fail to inform themselves of their existence, will not gain the trust required for work with people who hold strong adherence to such belief systems.

The discussion to this point has stressed that many health beliefs and behaviors—both those that are congruent with Western medicine and other systems—have ethnic, class, and cultural roots.

The U.S. health-care system is in large measure an outgrowth of our reverence for science and technology and our conviction that nature can be mastered. It is secular, rational, and future oriented. The belief systems of many middle-class people representing various ethnic groups are reasonably congruent with this view (Greenblum, 1974; Zborowski, 1952). This is particularly true of Jews, who have a long history of extensive concern with matters of health, a concern attributed to "the sense of precariousness" and fear concerning survival related to centuries of dispersal and persecution (Howe, 1975). Zborowski (1952) and others (e.g., Greenblum, 1974) have suggested that these cultural themes manifest themselves in a volatile, emotional response to pain accompanied by a concern about how the illness will affect the future. Medical specialists of all sorts are highly valued and their advice sought extensively. A new set of health issues now confront many in the Jewish communities. Holocaust survivors, many of them now aged, may experience special stress as they develop life-threatening diseases such as cancer.

There are other views of illness. Illness is variously viewed as a punishment for sin (Stenger-Castro, 1978), as a function of supernatural forces, as "disharmony" (Coulehan, 1980), as a force to be mastered, or as a fact that is passively accepted. Many tribal cultures make no distinction between religion and medicine. Healing experiences are an integral part of community life. Harmony of people—with nature, with one another, and with gods—is the desired state. Symptoms or disease states as conceived by the Western mind are viewed as reflections of underlying disharmony. This disharmony may be caused by witchcraft, spirits, storms, or animal contamination (Coulehan, 1980).

Analogous beliefs and related health practices are found among Puerto Ricans and Chicanos and many Vietnamese, Cambodians, Laotians, and Chinese. These groups also use non-Western healers. In fact, among many members of these groups, there is a marked tendency to use both folk and Western healers simultaneously (Garrison, 1977; Lazarow, 1979; Schultz, 1982; Mayers, 1993; Pearl, Leo, & Tsang, 1995).

Puerto Ricans use healers known as *espiritistas,* who have supernatural inspiration that they bring to bear on health and illness. Spiritist treatment procedures focus on exorcising harmful spiritual influences and strengthening benign spiritual influences.

Many Mexican American health beliefs relate to the view that God, the creator of the universe, is omnipotent. Personal destiny is subject to God's judgment, and suffering is a consequence of having sinned and is a punishment *(castigo)* for disobeying God's law (Stenger-Castro, 1978). Witchcraft also plays a part in this belief system.

The practice of *curanderismo* invokes the belief that the natural folk illnesses that commonly afflict people within the Mexican American culture can be cured by a *curandero* (folk healer), who has been chosen for this mission by God.

There remains a marked tendency for Latino families to rely on folk beliefs, folk healers, and home remedies instead of health professionals. A number in one study (11 percent) used substances containing lead for treating stomach problems in their children (Mikhail, 1994). Similar findings were obtained in a recent study of Chicano women with diabetes (Zaldivar & Smolowitz, 1994).

The Hmong mountain people, many of whom now live in the midwestern United States, have their Shamans actively involved in traditional healing practices. Sudden nocturnal deaths have been found in disproportionate numbers among Hmong men (e.g., Petzold, 1991). A report by Adler (1994) suggests that supranormal encounters act as triggers for these sudden nocturnal deaths. Korean immigrants describe *hwa-byung,* a folk illness label used to describe a number of physiological and psychological complaints. It has been suggested that this is a culturally patterned way of expression for Koreans experiencing major depression and related conditions (Lin et al., 1992).

Schultz (1982) reviewed the medical systems of the Vietnamese, Laotians, and Cambodians. Each embodies three categories of healers, including traditional and Western. Magic as a source of illness and cure is a common theme. Ancestral spirits are thought to play a protective as well as a malevolent role.

As Vietnamese, Laotian, and Cambodian refugees have settled in this country, they experience conflict and misunderstanding. Some seek links to traditional healers, even if they are at some distance from their homes. Others, although using Western systems, experience conflict and fear, especially in respect to some procedure. For example, laboratory tests and "taking blood," so common in Western medicine, are feared. In the view of some members of this culture, blood is thought to be replenished slowly, and doctors are expected to be competent without the benefit of laboratory work.

The extent to which these types of belief systems intertwine with Western health-care systems and the social worker's role is of major concern here.

Interviews with Anglo social workers in Colorado suggest how closely related these two types of systems are. The following is a typical situation:

> *A Chicano woman who uses the services of a neighborhood health center for routine care for herself and her children one day voiced the opinion that a lizard had entered her stomach. The social worker, though attentive, did not assume that extensive pathology was present, although she did not rule this out. On subsequent visits, she talked some more with the woman. She seemed well and no further mention was made of the lizard. (J. Collins, personal communication, 1978)*

In explaining this situation to one of us, the social worker noted her awareness of Chicano health belief systems and the fact that many clinic patients used *curanderos* to rid themselves of the visits of the spirits. She also knew that, by and large, whites were not privy to the information she obtained, and so she "stayed out of that area." Mexican American patients fear ridicule when they express such beliefs. Furthermore, in some areas *curanderos* are subject to prosecution for practicing medicine illegally, despite the fact that in many places folk healers have been invited to join the health-care team of the official health-care delivery system.

The ethnic-sensitive social worker has many options when working with such populations. Our informant respected the client's belief system and did not impose a definition of pathology. This discussion can only touch on the range of health beliefs and behaviors found among the diverse peoples of the United States.

## The Ethnic Reality

To this point in the discussion we have presented the situation of a number of people experiencing health problems. Each one is illustrative of the interaction between people's ethnic reality and how the health problems are being experienced, as well as the type of individual and systemic response required.

*Marie St. Claire's situation can hardly be understood without reference to her ethnic reality. An illegal immigrant, a woman abandoned by her lover, she is seriously ill and speaks no English.*

*Accustomed ways of responding to stress are being denigrated. Marie continually shifts her position in bed. The nurses become annoyed, not understanding that she is searching for a position that is familiar and comfortable. Finally finding the position that reminds her of home, Marie removes the bed covers as her tradition requires. The nurses respond by insisting that she cover her body, thereby imposing standards for illness behavior that meet the norms of the ward and the larger society.*

*Attending to her ethnic reality involves setting priorities. The nurses must be helped to understand that she is not being prurient but using standards of decorum that are customary in her country.*

*It is important that her boyfriend or another person from her country be located. She needs help in interpreting, in trying to disentangle the components of her illegal status, and in providing for some help in the posthospital period.*

*Jean and Norman Sankowitchia are Czechoslovakian people accustomed to solving problems in their own way, on their own. Counseling is alien, as is the idea of sending someone off to a hospice or a hospital to die. Self-reliance is a highly valued approach to life. Similarly, Slavic people do not readily express their emotions or share them with others, especially strangers (Stein, 1976).*

*The customary ways in which some members of this group deal with their women are not acceptable. Jean was born in this country. She knows that she does not have to be physically and verbally abused, even by a dying man. Therefore, she must resort to unaccustomed approaches to dealing with the present crisis and letting her husband go to a hospice in the hospital.*

*Jose Montero's situation is causing him a great deal of tension. He is the first in his family of Mexican Americans to have graduated from college and to have achieved an important position in a technical field.*

*If he continues to drink and take drugs he will lose his job. He is already in danger of a permanent separation from his wife and his adored daughter. He is a modern man. But he is still a Mexican American man. And men in this society must take care of their families.*

*Mrs. Owens's rejection of placement in a home for the aged was quite appropriate, given her physical and mental state, her age, the availability of caring relatives, and her participation in the church. As an African American woman she has every right to expect that these elements of her ethnic reality—elements that have served her people well—will continue to serve her in her old age. Those not familiar with this important element of African American life can only have a negative impact on Mrs. Owens.*

*Mrs. Green, the African American woman with hypertension, knows that she must solve her problems not only for herself but for her people. The African American community cannot allow so many of its members to die prematurely from strokes. She will work on her eating.*

*Mrs. Green and Mrs. Owens carry with them the burden of race in addition to their illnesses. Early in their lives the health care they received was minimal due to their race and social class position. Now, in later life, this history confounds them. The high incidence of hypertension in the African American community is real and a cause for community concern. However, these women are resilient and able to make decisions about their health care within the context of their ethnic reality.*

In situations involving health and illness, the ethnic reality forms an integral part of people's responses to their health problems and also becomes an integral component of resolution.

## The Route to the Social Worker

When the concept "route to the social worker" was introduced in an earlier chapter, it was pointed out that the route to health-care social workers is usually somewhat coercive. When people go to hospitals, as did Marie St. Claire, they go because of a significant physical or mental health problem. Marie did not ask to see the social worker. In the hectic setting of most contemporary hospitals the social worker is one other person who appears at the patient's bedside to ask questions or make suggestions.

*In Marie St. Claire's case the fact that the social worker is French speaking is welcome. Finally, there is someone with whom Marie can communicate. But it will take considerable skill on the worker's part to help Marie to use her services beyond those of translating.*

*She needs to let her know that she has a choice. But perhaps the worker can help her to figure out the next steps in her life. Where will she go? Who will take care of her? The worker can begin to introduce her to services, to other Haitians in the community.*

*Mrs. Sankowitchia is a voluntary client. She did not need to agree to see the social worker. She found the worker helpful when the worker introduced herself as some-*

*one who can help people deal with some of the stresses that surround such difficult times as the pending death of a spouse.*

*Jose Montero really has no choice at all. His employers have told him that unless he sees someone through the Employee Assistance Program at the company he is finished. This is a hard dose to swallow for a proud Chicano man.*

Health-care social workers are usually sensitive to the fact that their clients have not come seeking them. Some of the skills of rapid engagement, learned when working with people who need help quickly because they are about to be discharged, are helpful in engaging those health-care clients who are not voluntary clients.

## Intervention

The principles of practice presented in this book call attention to the need to pursue simultaneously or sequentially individual and institutional tasks as they are identified by the client, by professional assessment, and by the client's ethnic reality. In many instances the social worker assigned to a particular case is in a position to "follow the demands of the client task" (e.g., Wood & Middleman, 1989), that is, to identify need and act on the need in any of the four quadrants identified in the Wood and Middleman model. At other times, workers are not in a position to act directly but can do so via their departments, their agencies, or their professional association.

*Marie St. Claire's situation calls for action in a number of areas. She requires casework assistance to help her deal with the traumas of her present situation. She has been told she has cancer; at age 25 she has had a mastectomy. Her boyfriend seems to have deserted her.*

*The plight of Mrs. Owens is to some extent shared by many Asian Americans, Chicanos, and other groups. Many elderly Chinese and Japanese live in poverty and alone (Chen, 1970; Kitano, 1976; Takeuchi & Young, 1994), as do more recently arrived Asian immigrants. The old Asian benevolent societies are losing ground as the young move away and become assimilated. However, there is an upsurge of ethnic consciousness. Social workers would do well to take up the challenge of repairing old social networks, as proposed by Mechanic. We saw earlier in this chapter that the ethnic networks still provide extensive support. Ongoing efforts are needed via professional associations and by efforts to effect legislation to bring health-care policy in line with the real needs of population groups such as the elderly and the chronically ill.*

The emergent needs of people with AIDS are major. In Chapter 6 we considered the situation of the Joneses, who were struggling to take care of an infant with AIDS. Respite services would be important for this couple, as was the help offered by the caseworker to help Mrs. Jones deal emotionally with some of the issues raised.

Eligibility for home health care has long been tied to recent hospitalization for an acute condition. Mrs. Owens could use ongoing help with chores. If appropriately revised, new policies would not tie eligibility for home health care to "acute" medical conditions but to social need. Following the demands of the client task (see Chapter 5) is an ongoing obligation. That is, it is necessary to work for environmental change as well as to help in problem solving.

> *Jose Montero's situation requires various levels of intervention. The most critical is to help him to stop drinking and taking drugs. Individual counseling together with groups such as Alcoholics Anonymous are most important. Such self-help groups are often most helpful when they consist of people who are alike in such matters as ethnicity. His social worker should take this into account, check out the literature, and help him to use diverse services.*
>
> *There are other indirect ways to address the problems of Jose Montero and others like him. Mexican American people have high rates of alcoholism. Community outreach and prevention programs that go beyond this individual are an obligation of the profession of social work.*
>
> *Ultimately, to the degree that alcohol and drug abuse are related to oppression, only reduction in oppression will reduce the risks of alcohol abuse for this population.*

### The Role of Social and Community Networks

Our ongoing review of the literature has shown a persistent theme. Over and over again, the importance of family and community as a source of caring and healing was stressed. This source of help takes many forms. The role of the non-Western healers derives legitimacy and success from their understanding of and immersion in community networks, culture, and ritual. Extended family- and community-based ethnic networks play a caring role, help to facilitate the use of health-care resources, and sometimes serve to buffer against stress related to minority status (Dressler, 1985; Gary, 1985; Mirowsky & Ross, 1984). Cento (1977) describes the use of small group approaches to help Hispanic women enhance care during labor and delivery. Starret, Mindel, and Wright (1983) show that informal support systems among the Hispanic elderly positively affect their use of social services by serving as information-processing structures. Formal and informal networks need to dovetail their services. Similarly, immersion in informal social support groups can positively affect the depression symptoms of African American men (Gary, 1985). Dressler (1985) has observed similar effects for men in Southern African American communities. Mirowsky and Ross (1984) noted that among Mexican Americans immersion in culturally based networks reduces anxiety. Schilling et al. (1989) suggested using ethnic networks as sources for work on AIDS prevention. Alcoholics Anonymous and analogous drug rehabilitation programs are a form of social network. Cohen (1985) and others point to the crisis in American Indian communities related to the high incidence of alcoholism. The crisis of drug addiction, especially in the minority communities, is linked to every conceivable ill of modern society, especially AIDS.

Our review of a diverse body of literature (e.g., Cohen, 1985; Schilling, et al., 1989) suggests that drawing on indigenous community strengths and values is one way to attempt to reduce addiction, as well as AIDS, one of its more serious sequela. Collaboration between natural support networks and healers is crucial and requires much thought by ethnic-sensitive social workers.

Culturally appropriate services that are based in the community and that avoid the term *mental health services* when possible are consistent with an understanding of ethnic-based support systems and ethnic-sensitive practice (Murase, Egawa, & Tashini, 1985).

### Folk Medicine

The clients of *espiritistas* receive advice about interpersonal relations, support, encouragement, and physical contact such as stroking or massage; treatment typically takes place at public meetings of spiritist groups. The patient's family is often required to be present in the healing process (Harwood, 1977; Lazarow, 1979).

The Navajo sing is a public event that draws in the entire community on behalf of the afflicted person. Sings are group ceremonials that involve the patient, the singer, his assistants, the immediate and extended family of the patients, and many friends. Family members contribute both money and other resources, such as sheep. When the time comes, all drop their ordinary duties and gather together for the event. The patient becomes the center of interest. The support of the whole community is lavished freely as folk healers perform their ministrations. The community recognizes that by restoring harmony to one person the ceremony improves the harmony of the people as a whole. It relates person to environment, past to present, and natural to supernatural. The sings involve "an interplay between patient, healer, group and the supernatural, which serves to raise the patient's expectancy of cure, helps him to harmonize his inner conflicts, reintegrates him with the group and spirit world…and, in the process, combats his anxiety and strengthens his sense of self-worth" (Coulehan, 1980).

The effectiveness of the sing gives powerful credence to the notion that family and community support systems can and do play an integral part in the healing process. This is especially important among peoples who find that to be designated as having mental health problems is extremely painful.

Giordano and Giordano (1977) and Fandetti and Gelfand (1978) pointed to the fact that "extended family is seen as the frontline resource for intensive advice on emotional problems" for many white ethnic groups. This is not to say that these resources always provide cohesion and caring. The rejection of old practices by the young is frequently noted. There is a risk that folk healers will deal with matters in which they are not expert or that the sing will delay emergency treatment.

Some recent examples are troubling. McVea (1997) recounts a practice of injecting vitamins and antibiotics by Latino immigrant farm workers in the United States. The practice, with strong roots in Latin American cultures, is of concern because of the high HIV prevalence in this population.

People who are enmeshed in community networks need to and do use a range of prevailing mental and physical health services. There is considerable evidence that these facilities, particularly mental health services, are underused. This is particularly true for Asians (Kitano, 1976; Murase, Egawa, & Tashini, 1985; Yamashiro & Matsuoka, 1997), for Mexican Americans (Martinez, 1978), and for many Eastern Europeans. This pattern of underuse is attributed to many factors. Included among these is the system's failure to provide services congruent with the values, belief systems, and support networks available within these communities. Language differences also often pose a major barrier.

In addition to the other roles played by social work in health care, crucial to this connection is the function of interpreting and serving as a source of cohesion and support. Most importantly, skills must be used to marshal and organize ethnic- and class-based sources of support. Effective medical care cannot be rendered—particularly to people who mistrust or who do not understand the system—without such interventions.

### The Population at Risk and Ethnic-Sensitive Practice

The concept of the population at risk, and related epidemiological perspectives basic to public health concerns provide a useful frame of reference for the practice principles proposed here, particularly as they pertain to the incorporation of ethnic-based networks. The emphasis is on identifying those aspects of group life that generate health and those that generate illness.

Public health principles serve to specify and clarify the objectives and concerns of ethnic-sensitive practice in health care. Some of these were long ago supported by the Task Panel on Special Populations, which submitted reports to the President's Commission on Mental Health (1978). The reports focused on Asian Americans, American Indians, and Alaska Natives. Without exception, the various reports stressed the need (1) to train personnel who clearly understand and are sensitive to the needs, values, beliefs, and attitudes of many different population groups, and (2) to increase the number of mental health professionals who themselves are members of these groups. The recommendations continue to be relevant more than ever, as immigration and diversity accelerates.

The preventive components are stressed throughout the reports. These emphasize the provision of day care and recreational facilities. Providing services in the context of the group's own definition of its community, with funding made directly available to service settings that are part of the community's natural support system, is stressed by the report on Americans of European origins. The report on American Indians points to the need for developing family resource centers on the reservations. All of the reports emphasize the need for mechanisms designed to assure the preservation of the cultural heritage and the protection it offers. However, the ethnic-sensitive social worker cannot wait for enactment of legislation designed to enhance ethnic diversity and minimize the effects of oppression. There is much that workers can do from the vantage point of their assignments to a home health agency, the medical health center, and many others.

The underutilization of mental health services by the Asian American community is frequently noted. Among the reasons are Asians' "notion that one's capability to control expression of personal problems or troubled feelings is a measure of maturity" (President's Commission on Mental Health, 1978). Given this, mental health services that emphasize self-revelation are anathema to some members of this population group, although this is not universally true (e.g., Mokuau & Matsuoka, 1986). Generational differences and degree of immersion in the host culture are important factors determining the receptivity to various types of health services.

Culturally relevant mental health services are essential. These may involve the inclusion of folk healers and services based in and organized by the community (see, e.g., Murase, Egawa, & Tashini, 1985.) The Asian community is highly protective of its own; many Asians do not come to the attention of public agencies until mental health problems have reached the stage of psychosis (President's Commission on Mental Health, 1978; Sue, 1994). Benevolent societies and the church might well be drawn in; young Asian students who have a renewed sense of ethnic identity could be called on to help develop culturally relevant mental health programs. Since the evidence suggests that psychopathology among Asian Pacific Americans has been underestimated (Sue, 1994), it is essential that ethnic-based, community-based resources be draw on.

Many of the case examples we have cited involved the need to move from micro to macro tasks and to consider how community networks could be drawn in. The social worker helped Mrs. Green to control her diet by calling on the family to cooperate in a common concern about hypertension. None of these people, or for that matter almost no others who have contact with the health-care social worker, are voluntary clients.

Throughout this chapter, reference has been made to the fact that oppressed ethnic groups are at particular risk for many health problems; that the very nature of our health system makes for fragmentation and pays too little attention to ethnically derived health beliefs; and that supporting, caring networks are an essential component of health-care practice. For all these reasons, simultaneous attention to micro and macro issues is critical. There is a crisis in the situation facing poor young mothers and their infants. People who face the prospect of nursing home placement may be experiencing the major crisis in their lives. Those who are diagnosed as having cancer or severe heart disease must make major changes in the way they live and love. Diabetes and hypertension are insidious diseases. Constant care is required, often in the absence of symptoms. People with these and similar problems often do not quite know whether to view themselves as ill or well. They fear that others will withdraw their love or that they will lose their jobs.

Those who by cultural disposition are prone to reject the sick role will experience such illness as a particular threat to their integrity. Those who have always worried about illness may have their worst, perhaps nonconscious, fears realized.

The illustrations given so far are all focused on chronic illness. Although there are many other health problems, chronic illness is on the increase. Medical treatment can provide some relief from distress, but there are few cures. Social work involvement is essential if the caring, linkage function is to be expanded.

With few exceptions, people do not choose to be ill, physically or emotionally; to go to the doctor; or to be hospitalized. When they do require health services, they usually do not choose to see the social worker. They come because of injury or pain; to deliver babies; or to obtain relief from depression, frightening hallucinations, or overwhelming anxiety. Although social workers are increasingly perceived as professionals who have the skill to intervene and be helpful, involvement with the social worker is often somewhat coercive.

Coercion is illustrated by the highly progressive practice known as high-risk screening, or open access. On the assumption that early social work intervention can forestall some of the psychosocial problems related to illness, when people are hospitalized, social workers assess patient records and see those patients and families who, in their view, might benefit from social services. This practice permits social workers to use their own expert judgment about who might need service, rather than waiting for physician or self-referral. Although patients are free to reject social work services thus offered, it is important to remember that the hospitalized patient is in a vulnerable and dependent state (Wolock & Schlesinger, 1986). Many such patients are members of populations at risk for psychosocial crisis; for example, the young underclass married and unmarried mothers who are at the beginning of a critical life cycle stage. All of these groups require extensive social care. Such care consists of the availability of counseling services, adequate nutrition, home health services, and humane administrative practices. The same is true for those people with alcohol problems who face the loss of a job if they do not enter a treatment center.

In characterizing these services as falling on the coercive end of the route to the social worker, we do not imply that negative factors are involved. Rather, this highlights the fact that problem definition is constrained and affected by the context. Elderly, chronically ill people may prefer to stay in the hospital rather than be transferred to nursing homes or to their own homes if they have no one to care for them. The hospital, constrained by high costs, the need for the bed, and the view that it is set up to care for the acutely ill, views the problem differently.

Given this, social workers have a particular obligation to help patients frame the problems in terms that they understand and in the way they perceive them. The patient who does not want to leave the hospital and is simply put in an ambulance is somewhat like the mother whose child is being taken from her because of her abusive behavior. The social worker who participates in such actions is carrying out a social control function. How much better to anticipate and attempt to forestall such a tragedy! Although this example is extreme, there are many poor, chronically ill, minority people who face these kinds of dilemmas. They fear the fate that would await them in nursing homes, but they do not want to go home. If they are alone, with insufficient resources, their eligibility for publicly financed home health services will vary with their age, whether or not they are eligible for Medicaid and/or Medicare, and the states in which they live. Teenage mothers about to take their newborn babies home from the hospital may not define their problems in psychosocial terms. Outreach is needed to help them anticipate and plan for the day-to-day vicissitudes of caring for the demanding newborn.

These are but a few examples to illustrate the importance of outreach, using our skills in helping people to articulate their concerns. At the same time it must be recognized that institutional constraints have an effect on how these problems are articulated.

Managed care, discussed earlier in this chapter, presents both threat and opportunity. The demands for cost cutting can be creatively used to plan in an ethnic-sensitive manner—helping people to use scarce resources in ways that are comfortable for them. However, the emphasis on cost and "bottom line" makes it essential that we retain our perspective on advocacy and simultaneous attention to psychological and structural issues.

In the process of high-risk screening, those population groups at particular risk for the social consequences of illness are seen without their request. They are often the poor, minorities, the elderly, and those bereft of community networks. Ethnic-sensitive social workers would not be carrying out their responsibilities if they defaulted on these tasks.

## SUMMARY

This chapter has considered the health problems before us and the application of the principles of ethnic-sensitive practice to social work practice in health care. New managed care developments are discussed and their implications for ethnic-sensitive social work practice considered.

People who encounter health-care social workers are, for the most part, involuntary clients. Their problems are pressing, usually involving serious illness; the fear of death, disability, or discomfort; and the need to change lifestyles to alleviate their health problems. The social worker serves as a link between troubled people and the complex health-care system that may well seem fragmented.

The response to illness is in large measure governed by cherished ethnic and cultural dispositions. These affect the way people experience pain and the kind of healers to whom they turn when physical or mental illness strikes.

Caring as well as curing functions are essential. Effective care requires simultaneous attention to micro and macro tasks. The ethnic-sensitive social worker must be knowledgeable about the diverse responses to illness and must call on community-based caring networks in the effort to generate a more humane health-care environment. Public health principles specify and clarify the objectives and concerns of ethnic-sensitive practice in health care.

## REFERENCES

Adler, S. R. (1994). Ethnomedical pathogenesis and Hmong immigrants' sudden nocturnal deaths. *Cult. Med Psychiatry, 18*(1), 23–59.

Anderson, S. C. (1986). Alcohol use and addiction. In A. Minahan (Ed.), *Encyclopedia of social work* (18th ed., pp. 132–142). Silver Spring, MD: National Association of Social Workers.

Anderson, S. (1995). Alcohol abuse. *Encyclopedia of social work* (19th ed. pp. 203–215). Washington, DC: National Association of Social Workers.

Appel, Y., & Abramson, A. (1989). AIDS: A social work perspective. Course outline, School of Social Work, Rutgers University, New Brunswick, NJ.

Attneave, C. (1982). American Indians and Alaska native families: Emigrants in their own homeland. In M. McGoldrick, J. K. Pearce, & J. Giordano (Eds.), *Ethnicity and family therapy* (pp. 58–83). New York: The Guilford Press.

Berkman, B. (1996). The emerging health care world. Implications for social work practice and education. *Social Work 41*(4) September, 541–551.

Bracht, N. R. (1978). The scope and historical development of social work: 1900–1975. In N. F. Bracht (Ed.), *Social work in health care* (pp. 3–18). New York: Haworth.

Cabot, R. (1915). *Social service and the art of healing.* New York: Moffat, Yard & Company, NASW Classic Series.

Caetano, R. (1988). Alcohol use among Hispanic groups in the United States. *American Journal of Drug and Alcohol Abuse, 14,* 293–308.

Cento, M. H. (1977). Group and the Hispanic prenatal patient. *American Journal of Orthopsychiatry, 47,* 689–700.

Chen, P. N. (1970). The Chinese community in Los Angeles. *Social Casework, 51,* 591–598.

Children's Defense Fund. (1994). *The State of America's Children Yearbook 1994.* Washington, DC: Children's Defense Fund.

Cohen, S. (1985). Alcohol and the American Indian. In *The substance abuse problems: New issues for the 1980's.* New York: Haworth.

Corn, B., Hamrung, G., Ellis, A., Kalb, T., & Sperber, K. (1995). Patterns of asthma and near-death in an inner-city tertiary care teaching hospital. *Journal of Asthma 32*(6), 405–12.

Coulehan, J. L. (1980). Navajo Indian medicine: Implications for healing. *Family Practice, 10*(1), 3–20.

Crews, D. E. (1994). Obesity and diabetes. In N. W. S. Zane, D. T. Takeuchi, & K. N. J. Young (Eds.), *Confronting critical health issues of Asian and Pacific Islander Americans.* (pp. 174–208). Thousand Oaks, CA. Sage.

Dressler, W. (1985). Extended family relationships, social support and mental health in a southern black community. *Journal of Health and Social Behavior, 26*(1), 39–40.

Fandetti, D. U., & Gelfand, D. E. (1978). Attitudes towards symptoms and services in the ethnic family neighborhood. *American Journal of Orthopsychiatry, 48*(3).

Garrison, V. (1977). The Puerto Rican syndrome in psychiatry and *espiritismo.* In V. Crapanzano & V. Garrison (Eds.), *Case studies in spirit possession.* New York: John Wiley & Sons.

Gary, L. E. (1985). Depressive symptoms and black men. *Social Work Research and Abstracts, 21*(4), 21–29.

Giordano, J. (1973). *Ethnicity and mental health: Research and recommendations.* New York: American Jewish Committee.

Giordano, J., & Giordano, G. P. (1977). *The ethnocultural factor in mental health: A literature review and bibliography.* New York: American Jewish Committee.

Gock, T. S. (1994). Acquired immune deficiency syndrome. In N. W. S. Zane, D. T. Takeuchi, & K. N. J. Young (Eds.), *Confronting critical health issues of Asian and Pacific Islander Americans* (pp. 247–265). Thousand Oaks: Sage.

Gray, M. C. (1995). Drug abuse. *Encyclopedia of social work* (19th ed. pp. 203–215). Washington, DC: National Association of Social Workers.

Greenblum, J. (1974). Medical and health orientations of American Jews: A case of diminishing distinctiveness. *Social Science Medicine, 8*(3), 127–134.

Guarnaccia, P. J. (1993). Ataques de Nervios in Puerto Rico: Culture-bound syndrome or popular illness? *Medial Anthropology 15*(2), 157–170.

Harwood, A. (1977). Puerto Rican spiritism, part 11: An institution with preventive and therapeutic functions in community psychiatry. *Culture, Medicine and Psychiatry, 1*(2).

*Health United States 1996–97 and Injury Chartbook.* Hyattsville, Maryland: Department of Health and Human Services DHHS Publication No. (PHS) 97–1232, July 1997.

*Health–United States.* (1985). DHHS Publication No. (PHS) 86-1232. Washington, DC: U.S. Government Printing Office.

Hooyman, N. R., & Kiyak, N. A. (1988). *Social gerontology.* Boston: Allyn & Bacon.

Howe, I. (1975, October 13). Immigrant Jewish families in New York: The end of the world of our fathers. *New York,* 51–77.

Hughes, D., Johnson, K., Rosenbaum, S., & Liu, J. (1989). *The health of America's children.* Washington, DC: Children's Defense Fund.

Kitano, H. H. L. (1976). *Japanese Americans* (2nd ed.). Englewood Cliffs, NJ: Prentice-Hall.

Kleinman, A. (1978). Clinical relevance of anthropological and cross-cultural research: Concepts and strategies. *American Journal of Psychiatry, 135*(4).

Lavizzo-Mourey, R., & Mackenzie, E. R. (1996, May). Cultural competence: Essential measurements of quality for managed care organizations. *Annals of Internal Medicine, 124*(10), 919–920.

Lazarow, C. (1979). *Puerto Rican spiritism: Implications for health care professionals.* Unpublished paper, Rutgers University School of Social Work, New Brunswick, NJ.

Lin, K. M., Lau, J. K., Yamamoto, J., Zheng, Y. P., et al. (1992). Hwa-byung: A community study of Korean Americans. *Journal of Nervous and Mental Disorders, 180*(5), 386–391.

Markides, K. S., & Mindel, C. H. (1987). *Aging and ethnicity.* Newbury Park, CA: Sage.

Martinez, R. A. (1978). *Hispanic culture and health care.* St. Louis: C. V. Mosby.

Mayers, R. S., ed. (1993). *Hispanic culture and health care.* Springfield, IL: Charles C Thomas.

McVea, K. L. (1997). Lay injection practices among migrant farmworkers in the age of AIDS: Evolution of a biomedical folk practice. *Social Science and Medicine 45*(1), 91–98.

Mechanic, D. (1977). Illness behavior, social adaptation and the management of illness. *Journal of Nervous and Mental Disease, 165*(2).

Mechanic, D. (1978). *Medical sociology* (2nd ed.). New York: The Free Press.

Mikhail, B. I. (1994). Hispanic mothers' beliefs and practices regarding selected children's health problems. *Western Journal of Nursing Resources 16*(6), 623–638.

Mirowsky, J., & Ross, C. E. (1984). Mexican culture and its emotional contradictions. *Journal of Health and Social Behavior, 25*(1), 2–13.

Mokuau, N., & Matsuoka, J. (1986, March). *The appropriateness of practice theories for working with Asian and Pacific Islanders.* Presented at the Annual Program Meeting, Council on Social Work Education, Miami, FL.

Murase, K., Egawa, J., & Tashini, N. (1985). Alternative mental health service models in Asian/Pacific communities. In T. C. Owan (Ed.), *Southeast Asian mental health: Treatment, pre-vention, services, training and research.* Washington, DC: National Institute of Mental Health. New York: The Free Press.

National Center for Health Statistics. Health United States 1992. Hyattsville, Maryland. Public Health Service 1993.

National Center for Health Statistics Health People 2000 Review. Health United States 1992. Hyattsville, MD. Public Health Service 1993.

Olopade, C. O., Alikakos, Z., Abubaker, J., & Rubenstein, I. R. (1997). Characteristics of predominantly nonwhite patients with frequent hospitalizations for acute asthma in Chicago. *Journal of Asthma 34*(3), 243–8.

Oquendo, M, Horwath, E., & Martinez, A. (1992). Ataques de Nervios: Proposed diagnostic criteria for a culture specific syndrome. *Cultural Medicine Psychiatry 16*(3), 367–376.

Pachter, L. M., Cloutier, M. M., & Bernstein, B. A. (1995). Ethnomedical (folk) remedies for childhood asthma in a mainland Puerto Rican community. *Archives of Pediatric Adolescent Medicine 149*(9), 982–988.

Pearl, W. S., Leo, P., & Tsang, W. O. (1995). Use of Chinese therapies among Chinese patients seeking emergency department care. *Annals of Emergency Medicine 26*(6), 735–738.

Petzold S. (1991). Southeast Asian Refugees and Sudden Unexplained Death Syndrome. *Social Work, 36*(5) 387–39.

President's Commission on Mental Health. (1978). *Task Panel Report* (Vol. 3, Appendix).

Roffman, R. A. (1986). Drug use and abuse. In A. Minahan (Ed.), *Encyclopedia of social work* (18th ed., pp. 477–484). Silver Spring, MD: National Association of Social Workers.

Rosen, G. (1974). *Medical police to social medicine.* New York: Science History Publications.

Samora, J. (1978). Conceptions of health and disease among Spanish Americans. In R. A. Martinez (Ed.), *Hispanic culture and health care.* St. Louis: C. V. Mosby.

Schilling, R. E., Schinke, S. P., Nichols, S. E., Zayas, L. H., Miller, S. O., Orlandi, M. A., & Botvin, G. J. (1989). Developing strategies for AIDS prevention: Research with black and Hispanic drug users. *Public Health Reports, 104*(1), 2–9.

Schultz, S. S. (1982). How Southeast Asian refugees in California adapt to unfamiliar health care practices. *Health and Social Work, 7*(2), 148–156.

Selik, R. M., Castro, K. G., & Pappaioanou, M. (1988). Racial/ethnic differences in the risk of AIDS in the United States. *American Journal of Public Health, 78,* 1539–1545.

Sue, S. (1994). Mental health. In *Confronting critical health issues of Asian and Pacific Islander Americans.* Zane, N. W. S., Takeuchi, D. T., and Young, K. N. J. (Eds.), Thousand Oaks: Sage Publications, pp. 266–288.

Starfield, B. (1989). Child health care and social factors: Poverty, class, race. *Bulletin of the New York Academy of Medicine, 65*(3).

Starrett, R. A., Mindel, C. H., & Wright, R. (1983). Influence of support systems on the use of social services by the Hispanic elderly. *Social Work Research and Abstracts, 19*(4), 35–40.

Stein, H. R. (1976). A dialectical model of health and illness: Attitudes and behavior among Slovac Americans. *International Journal of Mental Health, 5*(2).

Stenger-Castro, E. M. (1978). The Mexican American: How his culture affects his mental health. In R. A. Martinez (Ed.), *Hispanic culture and health care.* St. Louis: C. V. Mosby.

Takeuchi, D. T., & Young, K. N. J. (1994). *An overview of Asian and Pacific Islander Americans in confronting critical health issues of Asian and Pacific Islander Americans* (pp. 3–21). Thousand Oaks: CA: Sage Publications.

Taylor-Brown, S. (1995). HIV/AIDS: Direct practice. In R. Edwards (Ed.), *Encyclopedia of Social Work* (19th ed., pp. 1291–1303). Washington, DC: National Association of Social Workers.

U.S. Department of Health, Education and Welfare, Public Health Service, Health Resources Administration, National Center for Health Statistics and Health Services Research. (1985). *The Changing Face of American Health Care.* Health–United States. Publication No. (HRA) 771232. Washington, DC: U.S. Government Printing Office. U.S. Department of Health and Human Services.

U.S. Department of Health and Human Services, Public Health Service, Office of Minority Health. (No date). *Closing the gap: Health and minorities in the US.* Washington, DC: Department of Health and Human Services.

Wolock, I., & Schlesinger, E. G. (1986). Social work screening in New Jersey hospitals. *Health and Social Work. 11*(1), 15–25.

Wood, G., & Middleman, R. (1989). *The structural approach to direct practice in social work.* New York: Columbia University Press.

Yamashiro, G., & Matsuoka, J. K. (1997). Help-seeking among Asian and Pacific Americans: A multiperspective analysis. *Social Work 42*(2), 176–186.

Zaldivar, A., & Smolowitz, J. (1994). Perceptions of the importance placed on religion and folk medicine by non-Mexican-American Hispanic adults with diabetes. *Diabetes Education 20*(4), 303–306.

Zane, N. W. S., & Kim, J. H. (1994). "Substance Use and Abuse." In *Confronting Critical Health Issues of Asian and Pacific Islander Americans.* N. W. Zane, D. T. Takeuchi and Young, K. N. J., (Eds.). London: Sage Publications.

Zane, N. W., Takeuchi, D. T., & Young, K. N. S. (Eds.), (1994). *Confronting critical health issues of Asian and Pacific Islander Americans.* London: Sage Publications.

Zborowski, M. (1952). Cultural components in response to pain. *Journal of Social Issues, 8* (Fall), 16–30.

# APPENDIX 1

## Community Profile

This outline for a community profile is intended to help the individual worker or agency to develop a detailed picture of the community within which services are located. The profile should serve to highlight the basic population distribution of the community and the relationship between its location and access to major transportation routes; these in turn may affect access to places of employment, health and welfare services, and recreational facilities.

Also important is a picture of existing health and welfare resources, as well as gaps in these resources. Resources are defined to include the formally organized helping institutions, such as those developed by the public sector, trade unions, and churches, as well as those more informal resources, such as identifiable helping networks, folk healers, and the like.

Of importance is the political structure, the representation of ethnic minority groups on the staffs of community institutions such as the schools and social agencies, and the attention to the special language, cultural disposition, and needs of groups represented in the community.

Such a profile can be developed by use of census data, publications developed by local organizations (e.g., League of Women Voters, County Planning Boards, Health and Welfare Councils), interviews with community leaders, and data available in the agency's files.

### Identification

1. Name of community (e.g., "The North Ward," "Watts")
2. City (or township, borough, etc.)
3. County
4. State
5. Traditions and values

### Local History

1. When settled
2. Changes in population
3. Major historical incidents leading to present-day development
4. Principal events in the life of the community
5. Traditions and values

*Geography and Transportation*

1. Location—is it located near any of the following?

   a. Principal highways
   b. Bus routes
   c. Truck routes
   d. Railroad routes
   e. Airports/air routes
   f. Rivers, oceans, lakes

2. Do any of the above facilitate/hamper residents' ability to get to work, major recreational centers, community services?

*Population Characteristics*

1. Total size of population
2. Breakdown by

   a. Age
   b. Sex
   c. Minority groups
   d. Other ethnic groups
   e. Religious affiliations

3. Educational level

   a. Median educational level for total adult population
   b. Median educational level for women
   c. Median educational level for each of the major ethnic and minority groups

4. Have there been major shifts in the population composition over the past five to ten years (e.g., in migration of minority groups, departure of sizable numbers of people in any one population group)?

   a. Are any major urban renewal or other redevelopment efforts being made?

*Employment and Income Characteristics*

1. Employment status

   a. Major sources and types of employment for total adult population
   b. Major sources of employment for women
   c. Major sources of employment for each of the major ethnic and minority groups

2. Median income
3. Income characteristics below poverty level
4. Type of public welfare system (e.g., state, county jurisdictions; state involved in Medicaid program?)

## *Housing Characteristics*

1. Prevailing housing type (apartments, private homes, mix)
2. Percentage of population owning, renting homes
3. Housing conditions (e.g., percentage characterized as "dilapidated" by the census)

## *Educational Facilities and Level*

1. Type of schools available
2. Do the schools have bilingual programs?
3. Are minority and ethnic group members found in the members of staffs, school boards?
4. Are the schools aware of the particular problems and strengths of minority and ethnic group members?
5. Do the schools promote culture awareness and sensitivity programs?

## *Health and Welfare Resources*

1. Important resources available

   a. Health and medical (hospital, clinics, public health facilities, "folk healers")
   b. Recreational and leisure time facilities
   c. Social agencies

2. Are staff members bilingual where appropriate?
3. Is there adequate representation of minority/ethnic group members on the staffs of hospitals and social agencies?
4. Do these facilities develop cultural awareness and sensitivity programs?
5. What are the prevailing formal and informal community networks?

   a. Swapping networks
   b. Church-sponsored health and welfare groups
   c. Ethnic-based lodges, fraternities, benevolent societies
   d. Union-sponsored health and welfare facilities
   e. Self-help groups for people with special problems (e.g., alcoholics, the physically handicapped)

## *Special Problems and Strengths*

1. What are the major social problems (e.g., prevalent health problems, housing, schools)?
2. Is there a particular concern with crime, delinquency, underemployment?
3. Are there particular intergroup tensions, efforts at intergroup coalition?

## *Evaluation*

1. What do you consider as some of the major problems of this community?
2. Does this community have a positive identity, loyalty? Describe.

3. What are the major strengths and weaknesses of the health and welfare community?
4. What are the major gaps in services?

# APPENDIX 2

## Guide for Making an Ethnic Assessment

In keeping with the principles of ethnic-sensitive social work practice, tools are needed to help social workers to develop systematic approaches for assessing key components of the ethnic reality and integrating these understandings into practice.

Fandetti and Goldmeir[1] made an important contribution by identifying three levels of ethnic assessment: the person, the family/client group, and the local and nonlocal community. Using their framework as a point of departure, we have adapted and expanded this tool and suggest that the three levels identified may be viewed as several components of the ethnic reality.

### Level 1—The Person

Assessment of the client ethnic reality at this level involves:

a. Cultural orientation, language(s) spoken, religious identification and practice, and generation of immigration.
b. Ethnic/cultural dispositions to identification of problem source and solution (e.g., is disposition passive as if controlled by external forces, or active mastery; gender/sex role assignment related approaches to problem resolution; affective/introspective or externally oriented; individualistic vs. collectivity oriented).
c. Social class membership/ethclass.

### Level 2—The Family/Client Group

Assessment of the client ethnic reality at this level involves:

a. Cultural orientation; same issues as in level 1a with special focus on whether individualistic or family/collective orientation paramount and/or whether there are clashes between individual family group on these matters; are there intergenerational differences; are there differences within the ethnic group?

---

[1]Fandetti, D. V., & Goldmeir, J. (1988). Social workers as culture mediators in health care settings. *Health and Social Work, 13*, 171–180.

**b.** Ethnic/cultural disposition to identification of problem source and solution, essentially as in level 1b.

**c.** Social class membership/ethclass.

In making assessments at levels 1 and 2, intergenerational differences as well as differences horizontally in family structures must be taken into account.

### Level 3—Macro: The Local and Nonlocal Community

Assessment of the client ethnic reality at this level involves:

**a.** Status of group of which client is a member (e.g., highly valued; held in low esteem, minority status/subject to discrimination).

**b.** Is there a sufficiently sizable population cluster in locality to generate ethnic-based services, support network?

**c.** What are identifiable customs, networks, sources of difficulty, sources of problem amelioration?

### Making an Ethnic Assessment

Sources of Information

1. *Nonclient.* A variety of sources can aid in gaining a basic understanding of any group, its customs, gender role assignments, and typical stances on approaching the kind of problems with which social workers deal:

   **a.** The literature (see possible sources of reference appended).

   **b.** Materials available in agency records, libraries, files, especially as these materials focus on population distribution, changes in populations, problem. See guidelines for developing a community profile in Appendix 1.

2. *Client.* Making an ethnic assessment must become part and parcel of the social worker's interventive repertoire. Just as the social worker learns to ask questions pertaining to sensitive and troubled areas of the client's life, such as the nature of an illness, the status of a troubled marriage, or child rearing conflict, the social worker learns to ask questions about the client's ethnic/cultural background.

A sense of the client's cultural orientation can be obtained by the process of observation and use of a series of open-/closed-ended questions. Guidelines for when these are appropriate are found in major practice texts (e.g., Hepworth & Larsen[2], Schulman[3]).

---

[2]Hepworth, D., & Larsen, J. A. (1993). *Direct social work practice theory and skills* (4th ed.). Pacific Grove, CA: Brooks/Cole Publishing.

[3]Shulman, L. (1992). *The skills of helping individuals, families and groups* (3rd. ed.). Itasca, IL: F. E. Peacock Publishers.

# INDEX